SEMITIC INTERFERENCE
IN MARCAN SYNTAX

SOCIETY
OF BIBLICAL
LITERATURE

DISSERTATION SERIES

edited by
Howard C. Kee

Number 51
SEMITIC INTERFERENCE IN MARCAN SYNTAX
by
Elliott C. Maloney

Elliott C. Maloney

SEMITIC INTERFERENCE IN MARCAN SYNTAX

Scholars Press

Distributed by
Scholars Press
101 Salem Street
Chico, California 95926

SEMITIC INTERFERENCE
IN MARCAN SYNTAX

Elliott C. Maloney

Ph.D., 1979
Fordham University

Adviser:
Joseph A. Fitzmyer

Copyright © 1981
Society of Biblical Literature

Library of Congress Cataloging in Publication Data

Maloney, Elliott C.
  Semitic interference in Marcan syntax.

  (Dissertation series ; no. 51 ISSN 0145-2770)
  Originally presented as the author's thesis, Fordham
University, 1979.
  Bibliography: p.
  1. Greek language, Biblical—Foreign elements—
Hebrew. 2. Greek language, Biblical—Foreign
elements—Aramaic. 3. Bible. N.T. Mark—Language,
Style. I. Title. II. Series: Society of Biblical Literature.
Dissertation series ; no. 51.
PA873.M25   1980   487'.4   80-13016
ISBN 0-89130-406-1

Printed in the United States of America
1 2 3 4 5
Edwards Brothers, Inc.
Ann Arbor, Michigan 48106

To my parents

PREFACE

In December, 1978, I defended *Semitic Interference in
Marcan Syntax* at Fordham University. The form of the disserta-
tion presented here is quite the same as that approved by the
defense committee. A slight modification appears in section
B.2.d.ii of ch. 3 (ἄνθρωπος=τις). It was kindly suggested by
Prof. Richard Dillon, a member of the committee.

I would like to take this moment to express my deepest
appreciation to my thesis adviser, Prof. Joseph A. Fitzmyer,
for his careful and patient reading of my work, and for his
candid suggestions on my presentation of certain difficult
problems in Marcan syntax.

I am also most grateful to Prof. Frank T. Gignac who
introduced me to the problem of bilingual interference by his
own work on Egyptian (Hamitic) interference in the Greek non-
literary papyri, and in his direction of an independent study
course on Semitic interference in the Greek Old Testament.
Thanks, too, to Maurya Horgan, Ph.D., whose careful typing
and reading of the dissertation aided immensely in my preparation for the defense. This is also the place to acknowledge
my own Benedictine community at St. Vincent Archabbey for their
continuing support throughout my whole graduate program, and in
particular for defraying the costs of typing the manuscript in
its original and present forms. To my students at St. Vincent
Seminary I am grateful for their many hours of proofreading and
for the fact that they have taught me so much.

This book represents the beginning of a project I hope to
continue. In future publications I would like to discuss Semitic
interference in the verb, adverb, prepositions, conjunctions,
and other particles in the Gospel of Mark, as well as alleged
Semitisms which occur in other parts of the New Testament.

CONTENTS

ABBREVIATIONS

AP

Cowley, A. *Aramaic Papyri of the Fifth Century B.C.* Oxford: The Clarendon Press, 1923.

Bauer-Arndt-Gingrich

Arndt, William F., and Gingrich, F. Wilber. *A Greek-English Lexicon of the New Testament and Other Early Christian Literature.* A translation and adaptation of Walter Bauer's *Griechisch-Deutsches Wörterbuch zu den Schriften des Neuen Testaments und der übrigen urchristlichen Literatur.* 4th revised and augmented edition, 1952. Chicago: University of Chicago Press, 1957.

Bauer-Leander

Bauer, Hans, and Leander, Pontus. *Grammatik des Biblisch-Aramäischen.* Tübingen: Max Neimeyer Verlag, 1927.

Bib

Biblica

BJRL

Bulletin of the John Rylands University Library of Manchester

Black, *Aramaic Approach*

Black, Matthew. *An Aramaic Approach to the Gospels and Acts.* 3rd ed. Oxford: The Clarendon Press, 1967.

Blass-Debrunner-Funk

Blass, Friedrich, and Debrunner, Albert. *A Greek Grammar of the New Testament and Other Early Christian Literature.* Translated and revised by Robert W. Funk. Chicago: University of Chicago Press, 1961.

BMAP

Kraeling, Emil G. *The Brooklyn Museum Aramaic Papyri.* New Haven: Yale University Press, 1953.

Brown-Driver-Briggs

Brown, F., Driver, S.R., and Briggs, C.A. *A Hebrew and English Lexicon of the Old Testament.* Oxford: The Clarendon Press, 1952.

CBQ

Catholic Biblical Quarterly

ConNT

Coniectanea neotestamentica

Conybeare and Stock,
  Selections

Conybeare, Frederick Cornwallis,
and Stock, St. George. *Selections
from the Septuagint*. Boston:
Ginn & Company, 1905.

DJD

Discoveries in the Judaean Desert

ExpT

Expository Times

Fitzmyer, *Genesis Apo-
  cryphon*

Fitzmyer, Joseph A. *The Genesis
Apocryphon of Qumran Cave I*.
Biblica et Orientalia 18a. 2nd
rev. ed. Rome: Pontifical
Biblical Institute, 1971.

Gesenius-Kautzsch-Cowley

Gesenius' Hebrew Grammar. Edited
and enlarged by E. Kautzsch. 2nd
ed. rev. by A.E. Cowley. Oxford:
The Clarendon Press, 1910.

GGA

Göttingsche Gelehrte Anzeigen

Goodwin-Gulick

Goodwin, William Watson. *Greek
Grammar*. Rev. by Charles Burton
Gulick. Boston: Ginn & Company,
1930.

Howard, "Semitisms"

Howard, Wilbert Francis. "Semi-
tisms in the New Testament."
Accidence and Word-Formation.
Volume 2 of *A Grammar of New
Testament Greek*, by James Hope
Moulton. Edinburgh: T. & T.
Clark, 1929. Pp. 411-85.

IDB

*Interpreter's Dictionary of the
Bible*. Ed. by G.A. Buttrick.
New York: Abingdon Press, 1962.

JBL

Journal of Biblical Literature

Joüon, *Grammaire*

Joüon, Paul. *Grammaire de
l'hébreu biblique*. Rome: Pontifical Biblical Institute, 1923.

JTS

Journal of Theological Studies

Kühner-Gerth

Kühner, Raphael. *Ausführliche
Grammatik der griechischen
Sprache*. 2 vols. 3rd ed. Ed.
by Bernhard Gerth. Hannover and
Leipzig: Hahnsche Buchhandlung,
1898-1904.

Liddell-Scott-Jones	Liddell, Henry George, and Scott, Robert. *A Greek-English Lexicon*. 9th rev. ed. by Stuart Jones and Robert MacKenzie. Oxford: The Clarendon Press, 1925-1940.
Mayser, *Grammatik*	Mayser, Edwin. *Grammatik der griechischen Papyri aus der Ptolemäerzeit: Mit Einschluss der gleichzeitigen Ostraka und der in Ägypten verfassten Inschriften*. 2 vols. 2nd ed. Berlin-Leipzig: W. de Gruyter, 1926-38.
Moulton, *Prolegomena*	Moulton, James Hope. *A Grammar of New Testament Greek*. Vol. I: *Prolegomena*. 3rd rev. ed. Edinburgh: T. & T. Clark, 1908.
Moulton-Milligan	Moulton, James Hope and Milligan, George. *The Vocabulary of the Greek Testament*. 2nd ed. London: Hodder & Stoughton, 1949.
NovT	*Novum Testamentum*
NTS	*New Testament Studies*
OG	*The Old Greek version of the Hebrew Bible*
RB	*Revue biblique*
RevQ	*Revue de Qumran*
SBL	Society of Biblical Literature
Schwyzer, *Greichische Grammatik*	Schwyzer, Eduard. *Griechische Grammatik*. 2 vols. Handbuch der Altertumswissenschaft 2:1. Munich: C.H. Beck'sche Verlagsbuchhandlung, 1953.
Smyth, *Greek Grammar*	Smyth, Herbert Weir. *Greek Grammar*. Rev. by Gordon M. Messing. Cambridge, MA: Harvard University Press, 1956.
TDNT	*Theological Dictionary of the New Testament*. Ed. by G. Kittel and G. Friedrich. Tr. by G.W. Bromiley. 10 vols. Grand Rapids: W.B. Eerdmans Publishing Company, 1964-76.
TLZ	*Theologische Literaturzeitung*

Turner, *Style*

Turner, Nigel. *A Grammar of New Testament Greek by James Hope Moulton*. Vol. IV: *Style*. Edinburgh: T. & T. Clark, 1976.

Turner, *Syntax*

Turner, Nigel. *A Grammar of New Testament Greek by James Hope Moulton*. Vol. III: *Syntax*. Edinburgh: T. & T. Clark, 1963.

TZ

Theologische Zeitschrift

Ungnad, *APE*

Ungnad, Arthur. *Aramäische Papyrus aus Elephantine: Kleine Ausgabe unter Zugrundlegung von Eduard Sachau's Erstausgabe*. Leipzig: J.C. Hinrichs, 1911.

Vergote, "Grec biblique"

Vergote, Joseph. "Grec biblique." *Dictionaire de la Bible. Supplément*. Paris: Librairie Letouzey et Ané, 1938. Vol. 3. Cols. 1320-69.

Vogt, *Lexicon*

Vogt, Ernest, ed. *Lexicon linguae aramaicae Veteris Testamenti documentis antiquis illustratum*. Rome: Pontifical Biblical Institute, 1971.

VT

Vetus Testamentum

VTSup

Vetus Testamentum, Supplements

Winer-Moulton

Winer, Georg Benedikt. *A Treatise on the Grammar of New Testament Greek*. Tr. by W.F. Moulton. Edinburgh: T. & T. Clark, 1882.

Winer-Schmiedel

Schmiedel, Paul Wilhelm. *Georg Benedikt Winer's Grammatik des neutestamentlichen Sprachidioms. I. Theil. Einleitung und Formenlehre*. 8th ed. Göttingen: Vandenhoeck & Ruprecht, 1894.

ZAW

Zeitschrift für die alttestamentliche Wissenschaft

ZNW

Zeitschrift für die neutestamentliche Wissenschaft

Plato, *R*, *PCair.Zen*, *IG* 1^2, etc.

Names of works of ancient Greek writers of papyrological and epigraphical publications. See Liddell-Scott-Jones, pp. xvi-xlii.

1QS, 3Q15, Mur, etc.   Names of Dead Sea Scrolls. See
                                    Joseph A. Fitzmyer, *The Dead Sea
                                    Scrolls: Major Publications and
                                    Tools for Study*. Society of
                                    Biblical Literature Sources for
                                    Biblical Study 8. Missoula, MT:
                                    Society of Biblical Literature
                                    and Scholars Press, 1975, 1977.

b. Ber., *Tg. Onq.*, etc.   Names of targumic, mishnaic and
                                    other rabbinic works. See *JBL*
                                    95 (1976), pp. 336-38.

INTRODUCTION

As early as the fifth century Christian writers have ac-
knowledged that the Greek language of the New Testament is
markedly different from that of the classical Greek authors,
and even from the literary Hellenistic Greek used by Polybius,
Epictetus, and Plutarch.[1] With the renewal of interest in
ancient writing during the Renaissance, scholars studying
biblical languages found that New Testament Greek was full of
problems caused by the influence of a Semitic language they
considered to be Hebrew.[2] At the end of the nineteenth century,
Adolf Deissmann led the way to the reevaluation of New Testament Greek in light of the Greek of the non-literary papyri.
After a thorough study of the Greek language, Albert Thumb
concluded that throughout the entire Eastern Mediterranean
world from 300 B.C. to A.D. 500 there was a common Greek language (the Koine or Hellenistic Greek) which was used by the
common man as well as by the finest literary authors. A few
years after their work, Gustaf Dalman, and then Julius Wellhausen,
made popular the idea that the Semitic language behind many of
the difficulties of New Testament Greek was Aramaic. Through
nearly eight decades, from Deissmann through Wellhausen to the
present, the controversy has raged whether and to what extent
the Greek of the New Testament has been influenced by Aramaic,
Hebrew, and the Semitizing Greek of the so-called Septuagint,
the Old Greek translation of the Hebrew Bible.

Recently, J.A. Fitzmyer has sought to distinguish various
aspects of the problem of the Aramaic substratum of the New
Testament:[3]

(1) Aramaic as a language of first-centure Palestine;
(2) Aramaic words, names, and phrases preserved as such
    in the New Testament;
(3) Aramaisms in New Testament Greek, usually of a lexical
    or syntactic nature;
(4) Mistranslations from an alleged Aramaic substratum;
(5) Aramaic literary forms in prose and poetry;
(6) Aramaic and variant readings in the New Testament
    textual tradition;

1

(7) Jewish literary traditions found in the New Testament
    and in known Aramaic literature;

(8) Aramaic epistolography and New Testament letters.

As we shall see in Chapter II of this study, it is quite possible that Hebrew was spoken in first-century Palestine. Hence,
one might delineate the entire problem of Semitic interference
in the New Testament by adding "and Hebrew" to "Aramaic" in all
of Fitzmyer's categories. One must also realize that in addition
to the possibility of direct influence, the indirect interference of Hebrew through the language of the Greek Old Testament (the OG) is also probable, since that was the Christians'
Bible.

The purpose of this study is to explore one part of the
question of the Semitic substrata of the New Testament, namely,
that of Semitic interference in New Testament syntax. Various
prior studies have all contributed to the present discussion,[4]
but all of them have been found lacking with regard to clarity
of presentation and specification of the Greek and Semitic data
involved. There are two main reasons for this difficulty:
(1) a comprehensive grammar of Hellenistic Greek does not yet
exist; (2) there has been much confusion as to the nature of the
Semitic evidence which can and should be admitted to the study
of New Testament syntax. Since the Gospel of Mark is widely
recognized as the most primitive gospel with regard to its
language, we have chosen to scrutinize more than half of the
alleged Semitisms in it in order to have a body of material upon which to apply a more exact methodology for the exploration
of Semitic interference in New Testament syntax.

In Chapter I a survey of the study of syntactical Semitisms
in New Testament Greek from Deissmann to the present sets the
stage for the development of a new methodology.

Chapter II delineates that methodology, paying particular
attention to the preliminary questions of the text of Mark to
be used, to the Greek, and to the Semitic documents to be employed as control literature for the study.

In Chapter III, the body of the study, the following syntactical phenomena (using and building on Howard's basic list
of alleged Semitisms referred to above) are examined in detail
according to the methodology outlined in Chapter II: the

questions of the general style and structure of the sentence in
the Gospel of Mark, as well as the use of the definite article,
pronouns, numerals and distributives, nouns, and adjectives.
A conclusion on whether or not the specific syntagmeme is the
result of Semitic interference and what kind or kinds of interference might be responsible is written at the end of the
section on each alleged Semitism.

INTRODUCTION

1For example: Ἑλλήνων παῖδες . . . ἐξευτελίζουσι γὰρ
τὴν θείαν Γραφήν, ὡς βαρβαρόφωνον, καὶ ὀνοματοποιίαις ξέναις
συντεταγμένην, συνδέσμων δὲ ἀναγκαίων ἐλλείπουσαν καὶ
περιττῶν παρενθήκῃ τὸν νοῦν τῶν λεγομένων ἐκταράττουσαν,
"The Greeks . . . despise the divine Scripture as barbarous
language, and composed of foreign-sounding words, abandoning
necessary conjunctions, and confusing the mind with the addition
of extraordinary words" (Isidore of Pelusium, *Epist.* 4.28,
in Migne, *Patrologia greca* 78:1080-81); cf. Vergote, "Grec
biblique," cols. 1321-22; E.C. Colwell, "Greek Language," *IDB*
2:486.

2*Sciendum est ita Novum Foedus graece scriptum esse, ut
hebraica sit dictio . . . erant Apostoli natu hebraei, et
peregrina, hoc est graeca lingua scribentes hebraizant,* "One
should know that the New Testament was written in such a way
that its diction be Hebraic . . . [for] the Apostles were
Hebrews by birth, and they hebraized when writing a foreign,
that is, the Greek language" (S. Castellion, in the preface
to *Biblia Sacra* [Basil, 1551]); *Tamen etsi cum Graece scribunt
Apostoli, multum referunt ex proprietate suae linguae,* "Although
the Apostles write in Greek, nevertheless they convey much from
the peculiarity of their own language [Hebrew]" (Eramus,
Paraphrases in Novum Testamentum [Basle, 1516] on Acts 10:33);
see also Theodore Beza, "Digressio de dono linguarum et
apostolico sermone," *Annotationes maiores in Novum Testamentum*
(Geneva, 1556) on Acts 10:46. Cf. Vergote, "Grec biblique,"
col. 1323; Winer-Moulton, p. 13; A. Springhetti, *Introductio
historica-grammatica in graecitatem Novi Testamenti* (Rome:
Gregorian University, 1966), pp. 30-33.

3"The Contribution of Qumran Aramaic to the Study of the
New Testament," *NTS* 20 (1974), p. 383; and "The Study of the
Aramaic Background of the New Testament," *A Wandering Aramean:
Collected Aramaic Essays* (Missoula: Scholars Press, 1979),
pp. 1-27.

4W.F. Howard, "Semitisms"; M. Black, *Aramaic Approach*;
K. Beyer, *Semitische Syntax im Neuen Testament. I. Satzlehre
Teil 1* (Studien zur Umwelt des Neuen Testaments 1; 2nd rev.
ed.; Göttingen: Vandenhoeck & Ruprecht, 1968); N. Turner,
Style, as well as the various New Testament grammars.

CHAPTER I

A SURVEY OF THE STUDY OF SEMITIC INTERFERENCE
IN NEW TESTAMENT GREEK SINCE DEISSMANN

We shall begin this survey of the study of the Semitic
element in New Testament Greek with the discoveries of A.
Deissmann in the 1890's, which launched the modern period of
New Testament grammar. Prior to his study of the papyri, there
were basically two schools of New Testament grammarians, often
called the "Purists" and the "Hebraists," although an occasional
precursor of Deissmann's insights can be found.[1] In general,
the "Purist" school tried to explain all of New Testament
Greek as good Attic usage, while the "Hebraists" maintained
that all the peculiarities of the language of the New Testament
were due to Hebrew.[2]

Since the work of Deissmann, his followers, and his critics
in the early 1900's has been discussed often and at length, we
will simply follow there the outline of the study by J. Vergote,[3]
presenting the period 1890-1938 in less detailed form, but
adding facts of particular interest to the study of Semitic
interference in Marcan syntax.

In 1890, while glancing through an edition of some newly
found Egyptian non-literary papyri, Deissmann found that its
Greek was remarkably similar to that of the New Testament.
In many subsequent publications he sought to establish that the
New Testament is composed in the vernacular Greek Koine, the
same language basically as that of those papyri, and that this
language has a place directly in the development of the main-
stream of the Greek language from Homer to the vernacular spoken
in Greece today. His detailed analyses mainly concerned
lexicography, wherein he produced parallels for Greek words in
the New Testament from the papyri found in Egypt where their
meaning and usage were similar. In his *Bibelstudien* and *Neue
Bibelstudien*[4] Deissmann polemicized against the theory that
there existed a special "Bible-Greek" or a "Jewish-Greek"
dialect, by showing that, in the main, New Testament Greek belonged to the Koine language of the era whose chief representative was Polybius. Other Hellenistic authors artifically

7

referred constantly to Attic standards for their literary
productions, but Deissmann recognized this ("Atticism") as
artificial Greek style. Although he never denied that some
influence of the Semitic languages existed in New Testament
Greek,[5] he did not emphasize the extent to which it was present
there, but always accented his insight that the language of the
New Testament as such as good Hellenistic Greek. "That Aramaisms
exist, I have never denied,"[6] he says, but disagrees with
previous scholarship on their number, basing his statement on
his comparison of the New Testament usage with that of the
papyri.

A. Thumb took up Deissmann's theory and published a long
study on the Greek language of the Hellenistic period.[7] He
found that a common Greek was spoken and written universally
in the Eastern Mediterranean world from 300 B.C. to A.D. 500.
Like Deissmann, his main concern was to show that "biblical"
Greek cannot be isolated from the study of the common Hellenistic
language,[8] and that a special "Jewish-Greek" dialect never
existed.[9] He goes a step further than his predecessor and says
that since the modern Greek vernacular is a direct descendent
of the Koine, this also must be studied before any phenomenon
can be claimed as a Semitism. If a supposed Semitism in the
Bible "es sich als eine natürliche Entwicklungsform der
neugriechischen Volkssprache offenbart . . . wird [es] als
griechisch gelten müssen,"[10] Thumb does not deny that some
Semitic syntax exists in the New Testament, but, he says,
while the New Testament in general goes back to Aramaic sources,
it does so more in style and manner of thought than in its
language in the strict sense.[11] In this manner, Thumb considers
the work of J. Viteau, where the latter finds many constructions
"hebraïsantes ou purement hebraïques,"[12] as unsupported by
comparison with other Greek materials.

Thumb recognized the possibility of the influence of the
Egyptian languages in the papyri, although he dismissed the
problem because only one example of it had been found up to
that time.[13] Nevertheless, in his 1913 revision of Brugmann's
grammar he did point out that there were many levels of Koine
between the literary and the vulgar language of the marketplace.[14]

The reaction to the Deissmann-Thumb theory among Greek
grammarians was almost universal acceptance. F. Blass, whose
immediate response to Deissmann's *Bibelstudien* was denial of the
conformity of New Testament Greek with that of the papyri,[15]
changed his point of view completely the following year in the
introduction to his grammar.[16] H.B. Swete seems to have been
uninfluenced by the new theory in his *Introduction to the Old
Testament in Greek*, where he claims that the OG represents
a spoken Jewish-Greek of Alexandria.[17] By 1907, however, he
too was agreeing that even the language of the Book of
Revelation belonged to the common commercial life. Indeed, he
even defends Deissmann and Thumb when he "deprecates the in-
duction" which was "being somewhat hastily based upon them
[Deissmann and Thumb], that the Greek of the N.T. has been but
slightly influenced by the familiarity of the writers with
Hebrew and Aramaic."[18]

In the study of the Greek Old Testament, J. Psichari,
H. St. J. Thackeray, R. Helbing, and H. Pernot agreed with the
basic thrust of the Deissmann-Thumb opinion,[19] while R.R. Ottley
considered the vernacular theory as immoderate. He argued for
the possibility of widespread Semitic interference in the
papyri themselves.[20] In the works cited, Psichari and Pernot
took up Thumb's idea of the importance of the modern Greek
vernacular for the study of Koine, although the former still
maintained that there were many translation Hebraisms, and
criticized Deissmann, Moulton, and Helbing for their exaggera-
tion on the point.[21] H. Pernot, A. Pallis and S. Antoniadis
have studied the supposed Semitisms in the Gospels with reference to modern Greek, claiming that only a few geniune
Hebraisms remain.[22] In the same type of study, A. Meillet has
gone so far as to say that the modern Greek dialects "sont une
source indispensable pour l'étude de la *koinē*."[23]

The overwhelming acceptance of the Deissmann-Thumb theory
of biblical Greek brought forth a raft of new New Testament
grammars and language studies of the individual authors of
the New Testament.

It was J.H. Moulton who first championed these ideas in
Anglo-Saxon scholarship. In 1901 he began a series of articles
in which he provided additional lexical and syntactical parallels

from the papyri for suspected Semitisms in the New Testament.[24]
Then, in 1904, an article appeared in which he enthusiastically
took up Deissmann's theory, proclaiming "Biblical Greek is no
more."[25] Overuse of certain Greek constructions, in his
opinion, "probably is the furthest extent to which Semitisms
went in the ordinary Greek speech or writing of men whose native
language was Semitic."[26] The only Semitisms for Moulton were
due to translation from the Hebrew Old Testament and from Aramaic sources, while Luke may well have assimilated his style to
that of the OG.

There followed the first part of Moulton's grammar in which
his central position was "that the NT was written in the normal
Koine of the Empire, except for certain parts where over-literal
translation from Semitic originals affected its quality."[27] In
this volume of *Prolegomena*, Moulton discussed many supposed
Semitisms with reference to the papyri and other Hellenistic
(literary) prose compositions, claiming that most of them are
possible in the Greek vernacular. He was "unconvinced that
Egyptian Greek differs materially from that current in the
Empire as a whole," and supported, but did not press, Thumb's
idea that a usage common in modern Greek was "*ipso facto*
no Semitism."[28]

By 1911, however, with the publication in German of his
Introduction to the Study of New Testament Greek in revised
form, he began to relax his hard stand on the purity of New
Testament Greek.[29] Here he even lists some "true Aramaisms"
in Luke. In part 2 of his grammar (edited after his death by
W.F. Howard) he gives his definition of a Semitism in the New
Testament: "a deviation from genuine Greek idiom due to too
literal rendering of the language of a Semitic original."[30]
He reaffirms his general agreement with Deissmann, but admits
that "some applications of the principle" are "too rigorous."[31]

Other New Testament grammars and language studies followed
the vernacular theory of Deissmann, Thumb, and Moulton, allowing
translation Hebraisms and "Septuagintisms" (or "biblicisms"--
conscious or unconscious stylistic imitation by New Testament
authors of the Greek of the Old Testament), but defending the
true Greek character of many New Testament syntactic phenomena
by reference to the papyri.[32]

In spite of the success of the Deissmann-Thumb-Moulton
theory among New Testament grammarians, a revised version of
the "Hebraist" position arose because of advances made in
Semitic studies and an entirely different point of departure
for their study.[33] Vergote has rightly pointed out that the
stimulus for much of the work on the New Testament at the turn
of the century was the unanswered questions about the relationship of the various New Testament authors to each other and to
their sources.[34] The Deissmann school used as its point of
departure the fact that the New Testament was written in Greek
and thus that it was Greek that must be studied to solve the
mysteries of its literary relationships and exegetical problems.
The second school, the "Aramaic School" (as it has been called),
was firmly convinced that the language of first century Palestine was Aramaic. These scholars took as their point of departure the idea that since the New Testament writers were Jews,
or at least dealt with the sayings and stories of Jesus and
the disciples, all of whom were Palestians, a priori they must
have left some trace of Aramaic in their writing.

Thus it was that J. Wellhausen seemed to ignore the
revelations of the papyri, and sought to unravel the mystery
of the gospel sources by tracing the supposed Aramaic sources
through the anomalies of the Greek of the Gospels and Acts.[35]
According to his theory, any non-Greek expression could be a
Hebraism or an Aramaism, but whenever possible it should be considered an Aramaism.[36] In a second edition of his *Einleitung*,
he apparently did make a concession to contemporary Koine
scholarship by omitting his affirmation of a Jewish-Greek dialect and by admitting that many seeming Semitisms are in reality
"biblicisms" because of the influence of the "LXX."[37] In commentaries on Matthew, Mark and Luke he examined the Gospels verse
by verse, pointing out Semitisms and using almost any Semitic
parallel he could find as proof.

By 1898 G. Dalman had claimed that the language of first
century Palestine was Aramaic,[38] an opinion with which many
scholars agree to the present day. In 1894 he had written that
there were two dialects of Aramaic current in Palestine at
this time: a Judean and a Galilean.[39] Since Jesus and his
disciples must have used Aramaic as their spoken language

according to his theory, the method for the proper understanding
of Jesus' words in the Synoptic Gospels was to examine a peculiar syntegmeme first as a possible Aramaism; then only should
Hebrew be consulted for its explanation.[40] As regards the dialect of Aramaic to be used as a control for the supposed Aramaism, Dalman claimed that concurrently with the spoken dialects there was a uniform literary Aramaic throughout Palestine
and that this literary Aramaic is best represented by the Targum
Onqelos.[41] For the spoken language of the first century the
best control would be the anecdotes in the Galilean dialect
known "almost exclusively through the short stories interspersed
in the Palestinian Talmud and Midrash."[42] He was aware that
some of the pecularities supposed by previous scholars as Aramaisms were in reality "Septuagintisms." With these theories
in mind he devoted *The Words of Jesus* and a later work
Jesus-Jeshua[43] to the study of words and concepts in the Gospels with regard to their possible Aramaic background.

C.C. Torrey, C.F. Burney, J.A. Montgomery, R.B.Y. Scott,
and M. Burrows took up the idea that Aramaic was the language
of Jesus and his disciples, and began a search for written
Aramaic originals underlying all four Gospels and the first
part of Acts. That they were not successful in establishing
this theory need not detain us here. The fact, however, that
as part of their argumentation they did explore further the
evidence for syntactic Semitisms in the Gospels in important
for this study, as is the reaction they drew from other New
Testament scholars.

C.C. Torrey denied Dalman's attempt to reconstruct the
Judean Aramaic dialect, saying that Biblical Aramaic, the
language of Targum Onqelos and that of the Megillat Ta⁽anit
("geniune Judean speech of the first or second century"[44])
should be used as a control for Semitisms. In actual fact,
however, he used almost any Hebrew or Aramaic source to prove
Aramaisms, even including Syriac. He denied that biblicisms
exist in the Gospels, claiming that all (except καὶ ἐγένετο
in Luke) are possible in Aramaic and more probably due to
the influence of that language.[45]

For C.F. Burney the main sources for the Aramaic behind
the Gospels were Biblical Aramaic, the Targums, especially

Onqelos and Jonathan, the Palestinian Talmud, the haggadic
Misrashim, the "Palestinian Syriac Lectionary," and even the
Peshitta, because "the exact dialectal form of the original
which we presuppose is a matter of minor importance."[46]
Similarly, J.A. Montgomery used Hebrew, Aramaic, and Syriac
equivalents to point up a Semitism, but omitted discussion of
the Greek evidence in any detail, and did not even give specific parallels for the supposed Semitic equivalents.[47] M. Burrows, another proponent of written Aramaic Gospel originals,
contended that "literary composition in Greek on the basis of
an oral Aramaic tradition would be . . . free from Semitisms."[48]
Since he could not "distinguish [Mark's] own writing from his
sources by the criterion of Aramaic coloring,"[49] he considered
that all of Mark was translation Greek.

A more realistic approach was taken by M.-J. Lagrange.
He ignored the question of Aramaic originals for the Gospels
in his commentaries, and pointed out and discussed supposed
Semitisms first with reference to classical and Hellenistic
Greek grammar. His method then was to examine any non-Greek
turn of phrase for Hebrew influence because of the great influence he saw of the OG in the New Testament. If he could not
trace it to Hebrew, he turned to the Aramaic material for a
parallel. He pointed out with Dalman that caution should be
used with the targums because of their nature as a translation,
but argued that the rabbinic material which Dalman had used
was really not a "source très pure" for the Aramaic of the
first century.[50]

P. Joüon also held that the Greek evidence must be examined first of all, but that the Greek used should be limited
to that of the first century. He claimed that without knowledge and consultation of Aramaic, the tendency would be to
search any period of Greek literature to come up with a
parallel passage. When Aramaic is found, he claimed, it does
not prove translation, but only the influence of the maternal
language of the writer.[51] For parallels in Semitic, however,
almost any of the ancient Aramaic documents would suffice
because "dans tous ces dialectes, en effet, le système
grammaticale est le même."[52]

The reaction to Torrey's articles and books was very
great. In addition to the pursuance of his ideas by some of
the writers mentioned above, many critics emerged to take Torrey
and the "Aramaic School" to task. This criticism has clarified
the approach to New Testament Greek and given many helpful
insights for the methodology of the study of Semitic interference. The critics, in the main, rejected the onesided
approach of the "Aramaic School" (namely their discussion of
the Semitic evidence only), and especially their lack of
scientific method and disregard of other areas of New Testament
study, such as textual criticism, literary problems, the history of the Semitic languages, and the influence of the OG in
New Testament writings.

J. de Zwaan was in full agreement with Radermacher's
opinion[53] that the syntax of the vernacular Greek of the first
century allowed personal caprice and was quite individualistic.
De Zwaan also saw that the "translation Greek of the LXX. was
already in the field as a sort of technical style."[54] Thus to
distinguish between Semitizing Greek and authentic translation
Greek it would be necessary first of all to eliminate "Septuagintisms." When Hebraisms and Aramaisms were found together, it
would not be a case of translation Greek.[55]

E.J. Goodspeed was a harsh critic who denounced the "Aramaic School" constantly for its lack of rigor in argumentation.
He pressed the point of papyrus parallels almost to the extreme
of Deissmann and the early Moulton, claiming that Aramaic
originals would be a priori impossible since no Aramaic literary
tradition had been found to date.[56]

H.J. Cadbury allowed that some expressions in Luke occur
too frequently to deny Semitic influence completely, but noted
that Semitisms could arise in at least five different ways:
(1) from an Aramaic oral tradition, (2) from Greek sources
based on such a tradition, (3) from written Aramaic sources,
(4) from "incomplete bilingualism" which "produces a transfer
of idiom since we are speaking in one language and thinking in
another," and (5) by "imitative Semitism or Biblicism."[57]

A new method of evaluating Semitisms in John was used by
E.C. Colwell. He compared the Greek usage with that of the non-
literary papyri and of the *Discourses* of Epictetus, claiming

that there was no possible influence of the Egyptian language
on Epictetus as there might be in the papyri.[58] Colwell allows
a certain minimum of Semitic elements in New Testament Greek
because of the reverence of early Christians for the OG and because of the Aramaic origin of the teaching of Jesus himself.[59]

Torrey's most effective opponent was D.W. Riddle. In two
articles he pointed out the failure of the proponents of the
translation theory: (1) in their lack of consideration of the
influence of the Old Greek, (2) in their use of a synthetic
language made up of Hebrew, Aramaic, Syriac, and even Arabic
to prove an *Aramaic* source, and (3) in their lack of criteria
for translation Greek as opposed to original Greek composition
by a Semite. Finally, he called for a "full use of control
literature, including the Septuagint, the papyri, and the late
Greek authors."[60]

When F.W. Howard undertook to complete Moulton's project
of a study of all the supposed Semitisms in the New Testament--
Moulton had died suddenly in 1917--he prefaced the work with a
statement that Moulton's own ideas on Semitisms after the first
editions of the *Prolegomena* were "slightly modified." He says
that comparison of Moulton's earlier and later writings "will
reveal a progressive tendency to do full justice to the influence of translation where Semitic originals may be posited
with good reason."[61] The work of R.H. Charles on the language
of Revelation[62] influenced Moulton in his evaluation of the
Semitisms of that New Testament book, but the latter still remained cautious to distinguish "pure Semitisms" from those
"secondary Semitisms" in which the writer betrays his deficient
knowledge of the resources of the Greek language and overuses
locutions "which can be defended as good *Koinē* Greek, but have
their motive clearly in their coincidence with locutions of
the writer's native tongue."[63]

The method Howard chose for his study is "to inspect every
trace of possible Semitic influence in the Greek of the New
Testament in order to determine the degree of probability that
any book has reached us through a Semitic medium, whether near
or remote."[64] In his presentation of the evidence he separated
putative Hebraisms from Aramaisms (following Dalman's lead) and
where possible gives parallels from literary and non-literary

Greek. The result is a fairly comprehensive survey of all
alleged Semitisms in the New Testament, without a definite
decision for or against Semitism, since Howard's intent was
"to assemble the data upon which students will form their own
judgments."[65]

In a general summary of his appendix "Semitisms in the
New Testament," Howard points out that the OG shows Semitisms
even where the Hebrew original lacks the corresponding construction in Hebrew. Thus idioms of the language of the OG can
easily be found in free Greek composition. His conclusion is
that "the presence of numerous Hebraisms will suggest the
influence of the LXX, whereas numerous Aramaisms or idioms
common to Hebrew and Aramaic will point to a background of
Aramaic."[66]

A third result of the work of the "Aramaic School" was
that some of the later grammars and commentaries written from
the Deissmannian point of view (namely those which compared
New Testament Greek with that of the non-literary papyri)
criticized the almost total extinction of Semitisms by Deiss-
mann-Moulton and began to reconsider the effect of the Semitic-
speaking peoples on the Greek language of Egypt and the Koine
in general. [67]

In an effort to resolve the controversy between the two
reactions to the language of the papyri (Deissmann-Thumb-
Moulton: the Greek of the papyri as a common vernacular shows
that few true Semitisms are to be found in the New Testament;
Swete-Ottley-Radermacher: there are Semitisms in the Greek
papyri themselves), as well as to preserve the work done on
syntactic Semitisms by the "Aramaic School," J. Vergote raised
a new issue: He denied that every peculiar idiom in the papyri
is *eo ipso* representative of good vernacular Greek. He maintained that there was no need to posit a general influence of
Semitic upon the Greek vernacular of Egypt to explain the
peculiarities and showed rather that the influence of the
Egyptian language(s) is as evident in the non-literary papyri
as Semitic influence is in the New Testament. By referring
to Coptic grammar, he believes that in every case where a
biblical Semitism has been denied because of a papyrus parallel,
the example in the papyri can just as well be explained by the
interference of Egyptian in its Greek.[68]

This possibility had been overlooked because most students
of the development of Koine accepted Thumb's theory on the
expansion of Hellenistic Greek.[69]   According to his theory, the
Greek language was spread throughout the eastern Mediterranean
world by soldiers and merchants who, as bilinguals, allowed
much of their own native dialect to come through into their
Greek. This gave rise to many vulgarisms in the spoken form
of Koine. Furthermore, Thumb adhereed to an older school of
linguistics according to which possible exchanges between
different languages were limited to phonology and vocabulary
only. Thumb did find evidence, indeed, of phonological confusion because of Egyptian interference (e.g., confusion between
gamma and kappa, voiced and voiceless stops), but also noted
that very few Egyptian words were borrowed into the Greek of
the papyri. Thus, even according to his own linguistic standards, Thumb was incorrect on the amount of exchange possible
between Greek and Egyptian.[70]

Independently, both A. Meillet and E. Mayser theorized
that not vulgar Greek, but the cultured Attic dialect of the
educated was at the base of the universal Hellenistic Greek.[71]
Vergote considers this to be the better opinion, and with it
the development of Hellenistic Greek can be considered as
similar to that of modern languages. More modern linguistic
study shows that interchange of language features in bilinguals
occurs especially in semantics, syntax, and phraseology. Thus
the anomalies of the Greek papyri should first be studied to
see if they are not in reality Egyptianisms and not vulgarisms.[72]
F.T. Gignac has adopted this approach in his grammar of the
non-literary Greek papyri of the Roman and Byzantine periods.[73]

Vergote then develops his own theory of Semitic interference in the New Testament. The Greek of these books is too
well written to have been learned from uneducated Greeks, and
thus most of the peculiarities are more probably Semitisms
than vulgarisms. Since the possibilities of linguistic interference in the languages of a bilingual speaker are almost
limitless, the importance of the question of a special Jewish-
Greek dialect disappears. Since Semitisms sometimes appear
in the OG and in the New Testament where there is no parallel
in the original or where there is no Semitic original at all,

the explanation seems to lie in the fact that an author (or
translator) was bilingual. The language of each book of the
New Testament must be studied individually and compared to that
of the others.[74]

When we look to more recent studies of New Testament Greek,
we find that Vergote's theory of Egyptian interference has
hardly ever been dealt with, although his article on "Grec
biblique" is widely quoted.

In his 1943 revision of Blass's New Testament grammar,
A. Debrunner says that New Testament Greek belongs to the
common Hellenistic Greek, but that such a common language always
undergoes foreign influence.[75] With regard to Semitisms, he
does not go deeply into "dieses vielumstrittene Problem," but
points out that such phenomena may be caused by translation of
an Aramaic source, Semitic thinking by a Jew writing Greek, or
by the influence of the OG.[76]

He discussed Semitisms as they come up in the course of the
grammar, comparing classical and Hellenistic parallels, Mayser's
grammar of the papyri, the OG, and then makes a decision on
whether any syntagmeme is vernacular Greek or a possible Semitism. When he admits a Semitism, he calls it a "Hebraism" or
an "Aramaism" without much discussion of Semitic grammar.
R.W. Funk's 1961 English translation and revision of the grammar does not differ substantially in this area from the German
edition.[77]

The different points of departure which gave rise to the
"Purists" and "Hebraists" of the previous two centures and to
"Deissmannism" and the "Aramaic School" of the first half of
this one, brought about the emergence in the 1940's of two
still further sophisticated, but basically opposed, approaches
to the language of the New Testament: the "Aramaic approach"
of M. Black and a reevaluation of Hellenistic Greek headed by
A. Wifstrand.

The two main influences on Black's work were P. Kahle and
A.J. Wensinck. In 1946 Black published the first edition of his
An Aramaic Approach to the Gospels and Acts, in which he re-
evaluated the Palestinian Aramaic material to be used as a
control for the study of Aramaic interference in New Testament
Greek.[78] Black criticized Dalman, Wellhausen, and the

"Aramaic School" for their use of Targums Onqelos and Jonathan
because of their nature as translation and because of the heavy
influence he saw in them of Babylonian Aramaic.[79] He claimed
that the free Aramaic of Kahle's Cairo Genizah Pentateuch Targum
was a better representative of first-century Aramaic because of
the large number of borrowings from Greek in it and because it
contains halakic material which must pre-date the Mishnah.[80]
Since its language has close affinities to Samaritan Aramaic
and Christian Palestinian Aramaic, these materials are also important for him. Finally Black claims that Syriac was spoken
in Antioch in the first century. Syriac is also important for
New Testament study since "much of the Palestinian Aramaic
Gospel tradition may have passed through the more familiar idiom
of Syriac before it was finally written down in Greek."[81]

In the third edition of his *Aramaic Approach* (1967),
Black allows the foregoing material to remain virtually un-
changed in "The Linguistic Approach" of his second chapter,
adding a new third chapter in which he discusses "Recent Discoveries and Developments in Palestinian Aramaic." He claims
that the discovery of Qumran Aramaic documents (of which he
makes little use in the body of the book) does not necessitate
"any far-reaching modification of the views presented in
Chapter II."[82] He considers the publication of Codex Neofiti I
the most important event in the field of Palestinian Aramaic.
This document is a later (and complete) copy of the Palestinian
Targum contained in fragments in the Cairo Genizah Targum.
Although Black admits here the Palestinian origin of the Targums
Onqelos and Jonathan, he finds the "Palestinian Targum" (by
this he means the Pentateuch Targum of the Genizah and Codex
Neofiti I) much more important for New Testament philology.

Besides helping to persuade Black of the value of the
Genizah targum, the work of A.J. Wensinck[83] influenced his
ideas on the text of the New Testament. Black criticizes the
"Aramaic School" for working only with the so-called neutral
text of the Greek New Testament (represented by codices B and
א) and for not including the variants of Codex Bezae (D).
He claims that the Western text tradition (represented mainly
by D) should equally be subjected to study for Aramaisms, claiming that "the fact that D stands nearer the underlying Aramaic

tradition is of the greatest importance."[84]

In the body of the book Black examines many syntactic "Aramaisms," relying heavily on the work of his predecessors and adducing almost any kind of Semitic parallels to prove his "Aramaic" case.

M. Wilcox, his student, follows the theories of Black's *Aramaic Approach* rather closely in his study of *The Semitisms of Acts*. He makes broad use of Codex Bezae and agrees that the "Palestinian Pentateuch Targum" (which he equates with the Genizah targum) as well as the Fragmentary Targum and Pseudo-Jonathan contain first-century Aramaic, and maintains that the Palestinian Talmud is useful as an original Aramaic compositon (although it dates from the fifth century).[85]

His main idea is to separate out those phenomena of Semitizing Greek that are due to the influence of the OG from those that cannot be. To accomplish this he breaks up possible Semitisms into two categories: Old Testament quotations and non-quotations. Old Testament quotations can be further classified as those which are from the OG and those which do not seem to be such. As regards the non-quotations, he finds similarly that the grammar of some may be paralleled in the OG and that that of others cannot be. He then makes three conclusions about the "Septuagintisms" he has found by this method. (1) Where there is no "identity" between a Hebraism and some passage in the OG there is no objective way of determining whether the phenomenon is a primary (from direct Hebrew interference) or secondary (biblical) Semitism. (2) Similarly, where Septuagintisms are clear he cannot tell whether Luke is consciously using biblical language to set a stage or if there were Septuagintisms present in some of his sources. (3) Since some thirteen Hebraisms of Acts are biblicisms, but are not characteristic of (i.e., not frequent in) the OG, their prominence in Acts may be due to supposed liturgical or apologetical use of the OG texts in which those Hebraisms are found.

For those Semitisms which he finds which are not due to biblicism, he relies primarily on work done by Dalman, Black, Wellhausen, and Torrey.

The English scholar N. Turner has attempted to bring back the nearly extinct concept of Jewish-Greek.[86] He considers

the *Testament of Abraham* "an excellent example of the 'Jewish'
Greek language of the early Christian centuries."[87] More or
less in agreement with this theory are H.S. Gehman and P. Katz,
although Gehman considers the phenomena of Jewish bilinguals'
own type of Greek as only a temporary state of affairs connected
with the time period in which the Old Testament was translated
into Greek.[88] Turner praises the work of Black, saying that he
has successfully modified the extreme position of Torrey (namely
that Semitisms in the Gospels and Acts prove translation Greek)
and left open the possibility that the evangelist (1) wrote
Semitizing Greek, (2) translated, or (3) used Aramaic syntax
but Greek vocabulary. Leaving open the final solution to the
hypothesis of a spoken Jewish-Greek, Turner does suggest that
both Old Testament and New Testament Greek form a unity which
has "a character of its own."[89] Thus he treats "Semitisms,"
many of which he admits are paralleled in the papyri, right
along with the other parts of syntax in his grammar of New
Testament Greek. He clarifies the seeming paradox of parallels
in the papyri to the "strongly Semitic character" of New Testament Greek by claiming (as others before him) Jewish influence
on the "semitisms" of the papyri.[90] In his most recent book,
Turner goes further and claims that the Semitizing idiom found
throughout the entire New Testament "comprised a distinct dialect or branch of the Koine Greek."[91]

C.F.D. Moule, V. Taylor, J. Jeremias and M. Zerwick have
all used Black's *Aramaic Approach* in their work as an authority
for Semitisms.[92]

In a study of the language of Luke, A. Wifstrand demon-
strated that Luke was not influenced by classicism, but wrote
in a kind of literary language best represented by Hellenistic
technical literature.[93] In the same study he showed that the
catch-all category of *Volkssprache* is really unclear. Actually,
he says, much of what has been called "popular usage" belongs
to an ordinary literary Koine of "scholars and scientists and
all who wished to give matter-of-fact accounts without
belletristic aspirings."[94]

His student L. Rydbeck takesup the idea and calls for a
new classification of Koine documents.[95] The older categories
of classicist (Atticist), non-classicist literary and vulgar

speech are obsolete. Taking non-classicist literature (i.e.,
that before the second century A.D., when, according to Rydbeck,
the classicist movement began) he noted that there are different
levels of language in the Greek of Imperial times. He contends
that in various little-known technical texts certain grammatical
phenomena are used commonly. Before his type of study these
had been considered "popular" usage, a designation he considers
far too ambiguous.

In the body of his book Rydbeck considers several of the
syntactic peculiarities of the New Testament in comparison with
this technical language of the Hellenistic period. His conclusion is that around the first century A.D. there was a widespread *Zwischensprache*, a "grammatische Allmende" which was
"der für die vorklassizistischen Verfasser der Zeit gemeinsame
grammatische Bestand."[96] To this "Zwischenschichtsprosa"
belong both the New Testament and the papyri. The search for
"vulgar" or "spoken" Koine should be put to rest, because a
spoken language cannot be retrieved from written documents.[97]
Thus in the study of Semitic interference, the language of the
New Testament must be compared first to the technical writings
of the first century. Only when syntagmemes cannot be found to
exist in this *Zwischensprache*, and that will be seldom, can
they be called Semitisms.[98]

J.C. Doudna has done a study on Marcan Greek with a
slightly different methodology. He attempts to isolate all
unclassical Greek locutions in Mark and compares them to classical constructions and to those of the papyri. The results
are either (1) conformity to some extent to Attic usage,
(2) conformity to the papyri but not to Attic, or (3) non-
conformity to both Attic and the papyri. His conclusion is
that the "Greek of the papyri and that of Mark are phases of the
same development" in the Greek language.[99] The twenty-two
locutions he finds that do not conform to either Attic or
papyrus usage may belong to the following categories:

(1) Hellenistic usage not found in the papyri
(2) usage which is only apparently different from that of
    Attic or the papyri
(3) biblicism

(4) primary Semitism--"awkward Greek due to unfamiliarity
    with Greek or to the necessity of adhering to a
    Semitic original"

(5) secondary Semitism--"permissible Greek usage, but
    overworked due to translation"

(6) tertiary Semitism--"a Semitism of thought not neces-
    sarily due to translation."[100]

Doudna concludes that his study cannot prove whether the
Semitisms of Mark are from translation or are original Greek
composition by Mark or his sources. Only clear mistranslation
could prove the case, and he does not find any Semitisms which
are clearly Marcan editorial work.

K. Beyer's approach to Semitisms is one of skepticism.
Since he thinks that there is hardly any example of common
spoken Aramaic of the first century and since the Greek text
of the New Testament can contain any of a range of possibilities
from literal translation to a rethinking of the source
(Neuformung), Beyer proposes to research the syntax of sentences.[101] He considers this better than examining individual
words because the phrasal structure of a second language is
less known to a writer than its individual words.

For Beyer, Hebrew was not spoken popularly in the first
century, and so true Hebraisms must be biblicisms. The Aramaic
of Jesus, he claims, was a *Volksdialekt* which is best represented by the Jewish Palestinian Aramaic of the stories and
proverbs found in the Palestinian Talmud and the haggadic
Midrashim, where the language is uninfluenced by either Hebrew,
Imperial Aramaic (as is Biblical Aramaic and Qumran Aramaic,
according to Beyer) or Greek. He feels that there would have
been little change in Jewish Palestinian Aramaic from the
first to the fourth centuries A.D., where it is attested. To
use the Christian Palestinian Aramaic and Samaritan material
for control would be dangerous because they have been influenced
by Greek and Hebrew, respectively.[102] The actual area of syntax
which Beyer covers is small: some conditional sentences and
three paratactic connectives.

A statistical approach has been applied to the language
of the New Testament by R.A. Martin in an effort to determine
whether or not it is translation Greek.[103] Although most New

Testament scholars do not feel they can tell if a text is an
original Greek composition or a translation of Hebrew of Aramaic, Martin believes "that there are in fact a number of Greek
syntactical usages which occur with significantly different
frequencies in documents which are or contain translations of
Semitic sources."[104] He adduces seventeen criteria whose
frequencies differ quite a bit in the OG from that of other
Hellenistic prose. He claims that they are not features that
a New Testament writer would use to imitate the style of the
OG, and that they are not the aspects of language someone would
use if he were writing in Greek but thinking in Aramaic or
Hebrew. His results, he claims, can show the difference between
original and translation Greek in any New Testament text
thirty-one to fifty lines in length, in most text units of
sixteen to thirty lines, and even in many of four to fifteen
lines.

        J.A. Fitzmyer has called for a "radical break with some of
the methods of investigation that have been used" and "a more
rigorous critique and sorting out of evidence" in the study of
the Aramaic substratum of the New Testament.[105] He agrees
that Hebrew may well have been spoken in small pockets of popu-
lation in Palestine, but the fact that Aramaic targums which
predate the Christian era have been found at Qumran seems to
favor the general consensus that Aramaic was the most popular
and widely-used language of first-century Palestine.

        For Fitzmyer the illustration of an Aramaism in the New
Testament must be made from contemporary or prior Aramaic. He
claims that the Aramaic of all the non-Qumran targums, of the
Talmud, as well as Syriac, Samaritan, and Christian Palestinian
Aramaic belong to a later place in the development of Aramaic
than that of the first century A.D. The Aramaic of Qumran and
of inscriptions dated to the first century and before by arch-
eological means are the most important monuments of the Middle
phase of the language which Fitzmyer claims was current in Palestine at the time of the writing of the Gospels.[106] Before any
comparison be made to Semitic grammar, however, Fitzmyer insists
that the Greek construction should first be examined according
to the best studies of the Koine language to see if it may not

be good Greek.[107] Finally, Fitzmyer cautions that source-, form-, and redaction-critical data must be reckoned with in any study of Semitic interference in the New Testament.[108]

CHAPTER I

[1]See the discussion of these precursors by J. Vergote, "Grec biblique," cols. 1329-31. Cf. also W.L. Lorimer, "Deissmannism before Deissmann," *ExpT* 32 (1920-21), p. 330, and G. Milligan, *Here and There among the Papyri* (London: Hodder & Stoughton, 1922), pp. 59-62.

[2]For a good survey of the scholars of both schools, see Vergote, "Grec biblique," cols. 1323-27. Cf. also J. Ros, *De Studie van het Bijbelgrieksch van H. Grotius tot A. Deissmann* (Nijmegen: Dekker & van de Vegt, 1940).

[3]"Grec biblique," cols. 1329-44. See also A.T. Robertson, *A Grammar of the Greek New Testament in the Light of Historical Research* (3rd rev. ed.; New York: Hodder & Stoughton, 1919), pp. 5-30, and G. Bonaccorsi, *Primi saggi di filologia neotestamentaria* (Turin: Società Editrice Internazionale, 1933), pp. xxv-1.

[4]A. Deissmann, *Bibelstudien* (Marburg: Elwert, 1895); *Neue Bibelstudien* (Marburg: Elwert, 1897). Both were translated by A. Grieve and bound into a single volume: *Bible Studies* (Edinburgh: T. & T. Clark, 1901).

[5]For example, in his article on "Hellenistisches griechisch" in the *Realencyclopädie für protestantische Theologie* (3rd rev. ed.; ed. J.J. Herzog and A. Hauck; Leipzig: Hinrichs, 1899), Vol. 7, p. 638, he says of Luke and Sirach that "im Prolog schreiben die Verfasser so wie sie sprechen," namely in good Hellenistic Greek, but that "nachher aber sind sie . . . von einer semitischen Vorlage direkt oder indirekt abhängig."

[6]A. Deissmann, *Light from the Ancient East*, trans. by L.R.M. Strachan (London: Hodder & Stoughton, 1927), p. 69, n. 1.

[7]A. Thumb, *Die griechische Sprache im Zeitalter des Hellenismus* (Strassburg: Trübner, 1901).

[8]"In grammatische Beziehung kann überhaupt von einer Eigenart des biblischen Griechisch absolut keine Rede sein." *Ibid.*, p. 182.

[9]While in Palestine the influence of Semitic on Greek could have been strong, the language cannot be considered a dialect because "hier handelt es sich um doppelsprächige Individuen, deren Muttersprache das Aramäische war." *Ibid.*, p. 177.

[10]*Ibid.*, p. 123.

[11]*Ibid.*, p. 121.

[12]J. Viteau, *Etude sur le grec du Nouveau Testament comparé avec celui des Septante. Sujet, complément et attribut* (Paris: Bouillon, 1896), p. 233.

[13]Thumb, *Die griechische Sprache*, p. 124.

[14]K. Brugmann and A. Thumb, *Griechische Grammatik* (4th ed.; Handbuch der klassischen Altertumswissenschaft 2/1; Munich: Beck, 1913), p. 25.

[15]See his review of Deissmann's *Bibelstudien* in *Neue theologische Literaturzeitung* 20 (1895), p. 487.

[16]F. Blass, *Grammatik des neutestamentlichen Griechisch* (Göttingen: Vandenhoeck & Ruprecht, 1896), p. 2.

[17]H.B. Swete, *Introduction to the Old Testament in Greek* (Cambridge: Cambridge University Press, 1900), p. 9.

[18]H.B. Swete, *The Apocalypse of St. John* (London: Macmillan, 1907), p. cxxiv, n. 1.

[19]J. Psichari, "Essai sur le grec de la Septante," *Revue des études juives* 55 (1908), pp. 161-208; also reprinted separately (Paris: Klincksieck, 1908); H. St. J. Thackeray, *A Grammar of the Old Testament in Greek according to the Septuagint* (Cambridge: Cambridge University Press, 1909); R. Helbing, *Die Kasussyntax der Verba bei den Septuaginta* (Göttingen: Vandenhoeck & Ruprecht, 1928); H. Pernot, "Observations sur la langue de la Septante," *Revue des études grecques* 42 (1929), pp. 411-25.

[20]R.R. Ottley, *A Handbook to the Septuagint* (London: Methuen, 1920), p. 166; cf. his revision of Swete's *Introduction to the Old Testament* (Cambridge: Cambridge University Press, 1914), pp. 294-95.

[21]Psichari, "Essai sur le grec," pp. 197 and 193.

[22]A. Pallis, *Notes on St. Mark and St. Matthew* (London: Oxford, 1932); H. Pernot, *Etudes sur la langue des évangiles* (Paris: Belles Lettres, 1927) and *Recherches sur le texte original des évangiles* (Collection de l'Institut Néo-hellénique 4; Paris: Belles Lettres, 1938), pp. 58-63; S. Antoniadis, *L'évangile de Luc: Esquisse de grammaire et de style* (Paris: Belles Lettres, 1930). See the résumé and criticism of their work by J. Munck, "Deux notes sur la langue du Nouveau Testament," *Classica et medievalia* 5 (1943), pp. 187-203.

[23]A. Meillet, *Aperçu d'une histoire de la langue grecque* (4th ed.; Paris: Hachette, 1935), p. 166.

[24]J.H. Moulton, "Grammatical Notes from the Papyri," *Classical Review* 15 (1901), pp. 31-37, 434-42; 18 (1904), pp. 106-12, 151-55; these appear in summarized form in "Characteristics of New Testament Greek," *Expositor* 6/9 (1904), pp. 67-75, 215-25, 310-20, 359-68; 10 (1904), pp. 124-34, 168-74, 276-83, 353-64, 440-50.

[25]Moulton, "Characteristics," p. 68.

[26]*Ibid.*, p. 72.

[27]Moulton, *Prolegomena*, p. xvi.

[28]*Ibid.*, p. xviii.

[29]J.H. Moulton, *Einleitung in die Sprache des Neuen Testaments* (Indogermanische Bibliothek 1/9; Heidelberg: Winter, 1911), p. 15: "Es brachte Redensarten in den Vordergrund, die zwar ziemlich korrekt griechisch waren, die aber verhältnis-mässig selten im Gebrauche geblieben waren, ausser für den Fall, dass sie hebräischen oder aramäischen Phrasen entsprachen."

[30]J.H. Moulton and W.F. Howard, *Grammar of New Testament Greek. II. Accidence and Word Formation* (Edinburgh: T. & T. Clark, 1929), p. 14.

[31]*Ibid.*, p. 14.

[32]In addition to Blass's *Grammatik*, the most important of these are: Winer-Schmiedel; J. Wackernagel, *Die griechische und lateinische Literatur und Sprache* (Berlin: Teubner, 1905), pp. 286-318; S. Angus, "The *koinē*, the Language of the New Testament," *Princeton Theological Review* 8 (1910), pp. 44-92; G. Milligan, *Selections from the Papyri* (Cambridge: Cambridge University Press, 1912); Robertson, *Grammar*; H.G. Meecham, *Light from Ancient Letters* (London: Allen & Unwin, 1923); L. Radermacher, *Neutestamentliche Grammatik* (2nd rev. ed.; Tübingen: J.C.B. Mohr, 1925); F.M. Abel, *Grammaire du grec biblique suivie d'un choix de papyrus* (Etudes bibliques; Paris: Gabalda, 1927); Bonaccorsi, *Primi saggi*.

[33]Already in 1910 A. Boatti noticed that there were two completely different approaches to the description of Semitic interference in the New Testament *(Grammatica del greco del Nuovo Testamento* [Venice: Libreria Emiliana, 1910], p. 16).

[34]"C'est grâce à ce problème, appelé le problème synop-tique, que la langue du Nouveau Testament a pris un si grand développement" (Vergote, "Grec biblique," col. 1342).

[35]J. Wellhausen, *Einleitung in die drei ersten Evangelien* (Berlin: Reimer, 1905), p. 15. For a résumé of Wellhausen's work, see C.C. Torrey, "Julius Wellhausen's Approach to the Aramaic Gospels," *Zeitschrift der deutschen morgenländischen Gesellschaft* 101 (1951), pp. 125-37.

[36]Wellhausen, *Einleitung*, p. 34.

[37]Wellhausen, *Einleitung* (2nd ed.; 1911), p. 7.

[38]G. Dalman, *Die Worte Jesu, mit Berücksichtigung des nachkanonischen jüdischen Schrifttums und der aramäischen Sprache erörtert* (Leipzig: Hinrichs, 1898).

[39]G. Dalman, *Grammatik des jüdisch-palästinischen Aramäisch* (Leipzig: Hinrichs, 1894), p. 5.

[40]G. Dalman, *The Words of Jesus*, trans. by D.M. Kay (Edinburgh: T. & T. Clark, 1902), p. 18.

[41]*Ibid.*, pp. 84-85.

[42]*Ibid.*, p. 84.   Dalman considered Christian Palestinian Aramaic (which J. Schulthess [*Das Problem der Sprache Jesu* (Zürich: Schulthess, 1917)] claimed was the best representative of the language of Jesus) and Samaritan to be later phases of a Middle Palestinian dialect spoken in the first century A.D. (*Ibid.*, p. 81).

[43]G. Dalman, *Jesus-Jeshua. Studies in the Gospels*, trans. by P.P. Levertoff (London: S. P. C. K., 1929).

[44]C.C. Torrey, *The Composition and Date of Acts* (Harvard Theological Studies 1; Cambridge, MA: Harvard University Press, 1916), p. 9.

[45]C.C. Torrey, *Our Translated Gospels. Some of the Evidence* (New York: Harper, 1936), p. lvii.

[46]C.F. Burney, *The Aramaic Origin of the Fourth Gospel* (Oxford: Clarendon Press, 1922), p. 27.

[47]J.A. Montgomery, *The Origin of the Gospel According to St. John* (Philadelphia: Winston, 1923).

[48]M. Burrows, "Mark's Transitions and the Translation Hypothesis," *JBL* 48 (1929), p. 118.

[49]*Ibid.*, p. 123.

[50]M.-J. Lagrange, *Evangile selon Saint Marc* (Etudes bibliques; Paris: Gabalda, 1929), p. lxxxv.

[51]P. Joüon, "Quelques aramaïsmes sous-jacents au grec des Evangiles," *Recherches de science religieuse* 17 (1927), p. 210.

[52]*Ibid.*, p. 212.   For a fuller discussion of the work of the "Aramaic School" and the Gospel of John, see S. Brown, "From Burney to Black: The Fourth Gospel and the Aramaic Question," *CBQ* 26 (1964) 323-39.

[53]L. Radermacher, "Besonderheiten der Koine Syntax," *Wiener Studien* 31 (1909), pp. 1-2.

[54]J. de Zwaan, "The Use of the Greek Language in Acts," *The Beginnings of Christianity*, ed. by F.J. Foakes-Jackson and K. Lake (London: Macmillan, 1922), Vol. 2, p. 33.

[55]*Ibid.*, Vol. 2, p. 47.

[56]E.J. Goodspeed, "The Origin of Acts," *JBL* 39 (1920), p. 96; "The Original Language of the New Testament," *New Chapters in New Testament Study* (New York: Macmillan, 1937), pp. 155, 165-66.

[57]H.J. Cadbury, *The Making of Luke--Acts* (New York: Macmillan, 1927), p. 74.

[58]E.C. Colwell, *The Greek of the Fourth Gospel* (Chicago: Chicago University Press, 1931), pp. 10-95.

[59]E.C. Colwell, "The Greek Language," *IDB*, Vol. 2, p. 484.

[60]D.W. Riddle, "The Logic of the Theory of Translation Greek," *JBL* 51 (1932), p.30.

[61]F.W. Howard, "Semitisms," p. 413.

[62]R.H. Charles, *Studies in the Apocalypse* (Edinburgh: T. & T. Clark, 1913), pp. 79-102.

[63]*Ibid.*, p. 414, quoting Moulton in "New Testament Greek in the Light of Modern Discovery," *Essays on Some Biblical Questions of the Day*, ed. by H.B. Swete (Cambridge Biblical Essays; London: Macmillan, 1909), p. 474.

[64]Howard, "Semitisms," p. 416.

[65]*Ibid.*, p. 416.

[66]*Ibid.*, p. 480.

[67]E.g., Swete, *The Apocalypse*, p. cxxv; G.C. Richards in his review of Moulton's *Prolegomena* in *JTS* 10 (1909), p. 289; Radermacher, *Grammatik*, p. 29; Bonaccorsi, *Primi saggi*, p. lxxxv. Even Howard admits the possibility of "Semitism as a widespread characteristic of popular Hellenistic" in "Semitisms," p. 416.

[68]Vergote, "Grec biblique," cols. 1354-60.

[69]An exploration of this possibility occurred in a review of Abel, *Grammaire*, by L.T. Lefort, "Pour une grammaire des LXX," *Le Muséon* 41 (1928), pp. 152-60, but did not gain much attention.

[70]Vergote's full discussion of Thumb's ideas will be found in "Grec biblique," cols. 1361-65. M.J. Higgins ("The Renaissance of the First Century and the Origin of Standard Late Greek," *Traditio* 3 [1945], p. 95) holds to Thumb's theory that dialectual influence accounts for "vulgarisms" in Hellenistic Greek.

[71]Meillet, *Aperçu*, pp. 249-54; E. Mayser, *Grammatik der griechischen Papyri aus der Ptolemäerzeit* (2 vols.; Berlin/ Leipzig: W. de Gruyter, 1906-34), Vol. 1, pp. 3-4.

[72]Vergote, "Grec biblique," col. 1365.

[73]*A Grammar of the Greek Papyri of the Roman and Byzantine Periods I. Phonology* (Testi e documenti per lo studio dell'- antichità 55; Milan: Istituto editoriale Cisalpino-La Goliardica, 1977), pp. 46-48.

[74]Vergote, "Grec biblique," cols. 1366-67.

[75]F. Blass and A. Debrunner, *Grammatik des neutestament- lichen Griechisch* (Göttinger Theologische Lehrbücher; Göttingen: Vandenhoeck & Ruprecht, 1943), p. 4.

[76]*Ibid.*, pp. 4-5.

[77]Blass-Debrunner-Funk.

[78]M. Black, *Aramaic Approach*, pp. 15-28.

[79]M. Black, "The Recovery of the Language of Jesus," *NTS* 3 (1956-57), p. 306; *Aramaic Approach*, p. 20.

[80]*Ibid.*, pp. 22-23; cf. P. Kahle, *Cairo Geniza* (2nd ed.; Oxford: Blackwell, 1959), pp. 200-203.

[81]*Ibid.*, p. 17.

[82]*Ibid.*, p. 35.

[83]A.J. Wensinck, "The Semitisms of Codex Bezae and their Relation to the Non-Western Text of the Gospel of Saint Luke," *Bulletin of the Bezan Club* 12 (1937), pp. 11-48; Black, "The Unpublished Work of the Late A.J. Wensinck of Leiden," *Aramaic Approach*, pp. 296-304 (first published in *JTS* 49 [1948] 157-65).

[84]*Aramaic Approach*, p. 31.

[85]M. Wilcox, *The Semitisms of Acts* (Oxford: The Clarendon Press, 1965), pp. 14-15.

[86]N. Turner, *Syntax*, p. 9. Cf. "The Relation of Luke i and ii to the Hebraic Sources and to the Rest of Luke-Acts," *NTS* 2 (1955-56), p. 109.

[87]N. Turner, "The 'Testament of Abraham': Problems in Biblical Greek," *NTS* 1 (1954-55), p. 220.

[88]N. Turner, "The Language of the New Testament," *Peake's Commentary on the Bible*, ed. by M. Black and H.H. Rowley (London: Nelson, 1962), p. 660, quoting H.S. Gehman, "The Hebraic Charac- ter of Septuagint Greek," *VT* 1 (1951), p. 90, and P. Katz, "Zur Übersetzungstechnik der Septuaginta," *Welt des Orients* 4 (1954-56), p. 272.

[89]Turner, *Syntax*, p.4.

[90]N. Turner, "Second Thoughts VII. Papyrus Finds," *ExpT* 76 (1964-65), p. 47.

[91]Turner, *Style*, p. 7.

[92]C.F.D. Moule, *An Idiom Book of New Testament Greek* (2nd rev. ed.; Cambridge: Cambridge University Press, 1959); V. Taylor, *The Gospel According to St. Mark* (2nd rev. ed.; London: Macmillan, 1966); J. Jeremias, *The Eucharistic Words of Jesus*, trans. by N. Perrin (New York: Scribner, 1966); M. Zerwick, *Graecitas biblica* (Scripta Pontificii Instituti Biblici 92; 5th ed.; Rome: Pontifical Biblical Institute, 1966).

[93]A. Wifstrand, "Lukas och griekiska klassicismen," *Svensk exegetisk årsbok* 5 (1940), p. 146.

[94]A. Wifstrand, in a review of V. Buchheit, *Studien zu Methodios von Olympus* in *JTS* 10 (1959), p. 387. L. Radermacher expresses much the same idea, but uses the older concept of *Volkssprache* in *Koine* (Sitzungsberichte der Wiener Akademie, Philologisch-historische Klasse 224/5; Vienna: Rohrer, 1947), p. 62.

[95]L. Rydbeck, *Fachprosa, vermeintliche Volkssprache und Neues Testament* (Acta Universitatis Upsaliensis, Studia Graeca Upsal. 5; Stockholm: Almqvist & Wiksell, 1967).

[96]*Ibid.*, p. 195.

[97]*Ibid.*, p. 194. For a similar view see J. Munck, "Deux notes sur la langue du Nouveau Testament. 2) Les Semitismes dans le Nouveau Testament. Reflexions methodologiques," *Classica et medievalia* 6 (1944), p. 127.

[98]Rydbeck, *Fachprosa*, p. 197.

[99]J.C. Doudna, *The Greek of the Gospel of Mark* (SBL Monograph Series 12; Philadelphia: Society of Biblical Literature, 1961), p. 129.

[100]*Ibid.*, pp. 129-30.

[101]K. Beyer, *Semitische Syntax*, pp. 8-9.

[102]*Ibid.*, pp. 14-15.

[103]R.A. Martin, *Syntactical Evidence of Semitic Sources in Greek Documents* (Society of Biblical Literature Septuagint and Cognate Studies 3; Cambridge, MA: Society of Biblical Literature, 1974). This book includes the results of two previous articles by Martin, "Some Syntactical Criteria of Translation Greek," *VT* 10 (1960), pp. 295-310; and "Syntactical Evidence of Aramaic Sources in Acts i-xv," *NTS* 11 (1964-65), pp. 38-59.

[104]Martin, *Syntactical Evidence*, p. 1.

[105]J.A. Fitzmyer, "Methodology in the Study of the Aramaic Substratum of Jesus' Sayings in the New Testament," *Jésus aux origines de la christologie*, ed. by J. Dupont (Bibliotheca ephemeridum theologicarum lovaniensium 40; Gembloux: Duculot, 1975), p. 75.

[106]For his description of the phases of the Aramaic language see J.A. Fitzmyer, *Genesis Apocryphon*, p. 22, n. 60.

[107]J.A. Fitzmyer, review of Black, *Aramaic Approach* (3rd ed.; 1966) in *CBQ* 30 (1968), p. 428.

[108]J.A. Fitzmyer, "The Contribution of Qumran Aramaic to the Study of the New Testament," *NTS* 20 (1974), p. 3.

CHAPTER II

METHODOLOGY

Preliminary Questions

Before outlining the exact methodology to be employed in
this study, we must confront three basic issues on which
scholars disagree: (a) the problem of the text of Mark, (b) the
problem of the Greek documents with which we should compare
Mark's Greek, and (c) the problem of which Semitic languages
and of which documents of those languages we may use as parallels
to test Semitic usage in Mark.

A. THE TEXT OF MARK

In general, the Greek text of the Gospel of Mark printed
in the Nestle-Aland *Novum Testamentum Graece* (revised twenty-
sixth edition) will be used. This text is based primarily on
the nineteenth-century editions of Tischendorf and Westcott and
Hort, which follow the so-called Neutral or Alexandrine text
tradition and rely especially on the Codices Vaticanus and
Sinaiticus. The Nestle-Aland revision utilizes further new
manuscript evidence, especially from papyri, that have more
recently come to light.

However, when there is great disagreement among the manuscripts for a certain text of Mark, we shall weigh the evidence and choose the most likely reading, respecting the
antiquity of the manuscripts and the standard canons of textual
criticism. In short, we shall be following the reasoned eclectic
method of textual criticism used by virtually all twentieth-
century New Testament scholars.

However, the text-critical problem is complicated, because
a scholar such as G.D. Kilpatrick has proposed that a more
Semitizing text is usually the more original. According to him,
most of the deliberate changes have been introduced into the
text before A.D. 200 by scribes who (a) eliminated Semitisms,
(b) corrected non-literary Koine to a more literary style,
and (c) even made corrections to meet the Attic standards.[1]
An example of this is the text in Codices B and א at Mk 9:12,
10:20, 29 and 12:24, which has ἔφη, whereas ἀποκριθεὶς εἶπεν

occurs at all four places in Codices A, W, and D as well as in
the entire Constantinople or "Koine" textual family. Kilpatrick
regards ἔφη as the correction of a more original Semitic ἀποκριθεὶς εἶπεν. Moreover, neither Matthew (17:11; 19:20, 28;
22:29) nor Luke (18:21, 29; 20:34), who use ἔφη freely themselves, takes over such a reading from Mark.

Kilpatrick's thesis cannot, however, be adopted without
some qualifications. In the first place, the authority of the
manuscript in which a "Semitizing" text occurs has to be
weighed much more carefully than Kilpatrick has done. He seems
to accept certain readings even though they have the most mea-
ger textual support.[2] Secondly, when a "Semitizing" text occurs
only in the Western textual family, notably in Codex D, one
cannot accept it as more original without further examination.
This manuscript (and possibly the whole text family) has been
accused of having undergone an Aramaizing (or even a Syriacizing)
process of "correction."[3] Curiously enough, Codex D, which
has been considered as a true carrier of the original Semitic
substratum of the New Testament by Wensinck, Black, and Wilcox,
sometimes corrects a Semitism which is firmly preserved in
most of the other manuscripts.[4]

Since the purpose of this study is to gain some insight
into Marcan style and his sources, neither the Longer nor the
Shorter Endings of the gospel will be considered for Semitisms.

B.   THE GREEK DOCUMENTS TO BE USED FOR COMPARISON

The text of the Gospel of Mark which we possess was written in Greek in the first century A.D. In order to assess its
Greek and to uncover possible Semitic interference in its syntax, we must, first of all, compare it with the kind of Greek
which was used in the first century for similar purposes.

It is well known that Hellenistic Greek was widely used
and rather uniform in the eastern Mediterranean world. But
there are some differences in documents from that time period.
In the first place, Greek grammarians of the first and second
centuries A.D. have made it clear that there was a widespread
movement in the literature of the period to get back to the
more "classical" language of the great dramatists and rhetoricians of ancient Athens. This is the phenomenon of "Atticism."

Secondly, many of the private letters found among the Egyptian
papyri manifest a rather unlearned Greek. Some of these letters exhibit grammatical phenomena which can only be called
mistakes. These were due either to the interference in Greek
of the writer's native Egyptian language or else to simple ig-
norance of proper Greek grammar and style.

It would be fruitless to compare Mark's Greek with that of
classical Athens or with that of the Atticists. That has been
done many times, and the conclusion has always been that Mark
has not written classical Greek. In addition, such a comparison
would run the risk of turning up sporadic parallels to Marcan
constructions from classical texts, the language of which, it
is generally agreed, Mark did not know. The obvious answer to a
Marcan usage which does not conform to the more contemporary
Hellenistic Greek is interference from the Semitic languages of
the milieu about which he wrote, namely, first-century Palestine.
To use classical Attic Greek to explain Mark's non-Hellenistic
syntax would be like explaining a mistake made by a present-day
Italian writing in French by adducing a similar construction
from sixteenth-century French, when, in fact, it occurs regularly in the writer's native Italian.[5]

Similarly, we do not consider the study of modern vernacular Greek to be important for our study. Although it is
agreed that the present-day dialects of Greece are descended
from the Koine, it is very possible that the Greek New Testament
itself has influenced the development of modern Greek, starting
already in the Middle Ages.[6] Furthermore, if modern usage
contains constructions that parallel certain non-Hellenistic
ones in the New Testament, they may very well be due simply
to parallel, but wholly coincidental developments in the syntax
of Greek in its long and continuous development from the first
century up to the present day.

The question remains, however, of just what Greek texts
represent the Hellenistic language which Mark was using. There
are two problems in this question. First, as E.C. Colwell has
pointed out, a Koine grammar can only indicate the direction
of the development of the language, since there were no great
literary works nor imperial (Greek) power to stabilize the
Koine.[7] It is for this reason that grammarians have stressed

that first-century Koine allowed for personal caprice and was
quite individualistic.[8] The second problem is that there is
nothing quite like a gospel in first-century literature with
which we may compare the language of Mark, outside of similar
Christian writings which may share the same phenomenon of
bilingual interference.[9]

Certain Scandinavian scholars have dismissed the term
Volkssprache because of the fact that no one writes exactly as
one speaks except when one uses quotation marks. For example,
as J. Munck has pointed out, the frequent use of participles
in Mark's narrative sections shows up the non-spoken character
of his writing.[10] In our discussion, we will pay special attention to the technical texts whose language L. Rydbeck has
termed *Zwischenprosa*, that is, Greek which lies somewhere between the language of the Hellenistic literary texts and the
simple, often educated, writing in the non-literary papyri.
But we cannot rule out the data from the so-called literary
texts around the turn of the era, except, of course, when they
are demonstrably Atticizing.[11] Furthermore, astrological and
magical documents are also important since they, like the gospels, were written for wide popular consumption.[12]

The Egyptian non-literary papyri are important sources for
comparison. Since the bulk of them are either chancery or
business documents, we may expect to find the same technical
level of language *(Zwischenprosa)* as Rydbeck claims for the
authors he lists on pages 20-24 of his important publication,
Fachprosa.

There is a problem, however, in the evidence of such papyrus texts. As we have seen, Vergote and Gignac have demon-
strated that the Greek in such papyri suffers from Egyptian
interference at times. Therefore, when a construction parallel
to one of Mark's turns up only in the non-literary papyri, and
not in the other Hellenistic literature, its relation to Coptic
grammar has to be examined. The similarity of the papyrus to
the Marcan usage may be due to the similarity of the Hamitic
(Egyptian) and Semitic languages in a given grammatical phenomenon which has respectively influenced the Greek texts in
question.

With regard to the translation of the OG, we will not consider it as a test document of normal Hellenistic Greek for
comparison to Marcan syntax, since it is a translation document
and contains Semitisms even where there seems to be no justifi-
cation for them in the Hebrew or Aramaic of the *Vorlage*.[13]
The importance of the OG will be discussed in the following
section.

C. THE SEMITIC EVIDENCE

The third preliminary problem in this study is the specification of the Semitic languages that might have a bearing on
the Greek of Mark. We know that both Hebrew and Aramaic were
important languages in ancient Palestine, and that the least
we can say about Mark's Gospel is that it was written about
certain inhabitants of that country and purports to preserve
traditions and sayings of persons who would have used such
languages. Therefore, a discussion of the history and use of
both Hebrew and Aramaic in the first century is in order.

a. Hebrew

Although Aramaic was undoubtedly the predominant spoken
language in post-exilic Palestine, the fact remains that most
of the literature (including the Old Testament books) composed
there after 450 B.C. was written in the Hebrew language. The
books of Esther, Qohelet, Chronicles, Canticles, and Lamenta-
taions, however, often use a post-classical type of Hebrew
which developed into post-biblical Hebrew and that used in the
Mishnah.[14] This type of Hebrew is no haphazard amalgam of
biblical Hebrew and Aramaic, but demonstrates in many cases
a consistent inner development of the Hebrew language.[15] We
also know that the Qumran Essenes composed their sectarian
documents in the second/first centuries B.C. and first century
A.D. in a neo-classical post-biblical Hebrew, that is, in
Hebrew that attempted--without perfect success--to imitate
that of the Old Testament. J.T. Milik claims that several additional Hebrew documents of the first two centuries A.D. show
the missing stage in the development of "post-biblical" Hebrew
used in the Old Testament and the language of the Mishnah.[16]

We have indisputable evidence, then, that a type of Proto-
Mishnaic Hebrew was at least being *written* in the time period
with which our study is concerned.

Recently, several Semitists have reopened the question,
posed by M. Segal at the beginning of this century,[17] whether
this type of Hebrew was *spoken* in some parts of Palestine down
to about the third century A.D.[18] These scholars have advanced
arguments that make it impossible to deny flatly that it might
have been spoken in some places,[19] although they have not
given incontrovertible proof of *Mishnaic* Hebrew as a
Volkssprache in the full sense of the word.[20]

The debate as to whether or not Mishnaic Hebrew was ever
spoken is not crucial to our study, but it does bring up the
important possibility that Jesus and the disciples may have
used Hebrew on solemn, religious occasions (such as the Last
Supper),[21] even if not in normal conversation and preaching.
Perhaps too it is remotely possible that some early source of
Mark's Gospel came from a Jewish-Christian community whose oral
or written tradition was in Proto-Mishnaic Hebrew.

Since the Mishnah itself was compiled at the end of the
second century A.D., its language is likely to be more Aramaized
and more Grecized than that of the first century. Another factor that weakens its importance for our study is that medieval
scribes are said to have heavily "biblicized" its language,
that is, they have often changed its original Mishnaic constructions to the more classical usage of the Old Testament. Kutscher
has said that this process of biblicization was so strong that
basic characteristics of Mishnaic Hebrew have completely disap-
peared in the Mishnah.[22]

Since the bulk of Mishnaic Hebrew that we do have, on the
one hand, represents a form of Hebrew that is more developed
than that of the first century, while, on the other hand, the
texts of the Mishnah itself seem to have been largely archaized,
grammars based on the printed editions of the Mishnah, such as
Segal's *Mishnaic Hebrew Grammar* have to be used with considerable
caution. With regard to post-biblical Hebrew parallels to
Marcan Greek constructions, we find ourselves in much the same
position as the "Aramaic School" of the first part of this
century with respect to Aramaic parallels, namely that we do

not have very much first-century material with which to compare
Mark's usage to the Hebrew of that period. Unfortunately, we
must content ourselves with the small amount of post-classical
Hebrew material found in the Old Testament, the post-biblical
Qumran sectarian documents, and Proto-Mishnaic writings and
inscriptions of the Roman period until more can be said about
the original language of the Mishnah.[23]

On the other hand, the importance of classical, biblical
Hebrew for our study is great in an indirect way, for the early
Christians made extensive use of the Greek Old Testament, and,
as we have seen above, its Hebraized Greek became a sort of
sacred language, just as the English of the King James Version
of the Bible is often used to add solemnity to an occasion
today. The language of the OG was well known to Mark, since he
uses that translation *verbatim* very often when he quotes the
Old Testament. Because of this, parallels to Marcan syntax
from classical Hebrew, especially those that turn up in the
Hebraized Greek of our modern editions of the Greek Old
Testament might explain some of the "un-Greek" syntax as indirect
Hebraisms which we have called biblicisms.

b. Aramaic

In the survey in Chapter I we have seen the various
Aramaic documents studied in the past for comparison with
alleged Aramaisms in the New Testament. The discovery of the
Aramaic material at Qumran and elsewhere, however, has neces-
sitated a revision of opinion concerning the development of
Aramaic. It has also raised the question about the proper
documents which should serve as control for first-century Aramaic, the language of Jesus and the earliest Palestinian
Christian community.

J.A. Fitzmyer has made a revision of the phases of the
Aramaic language as follows:[24]

> Old Aramaic (925-700 B.C.)
> Official (Imperial) Aramaic (700-200 B.C.)
> Middle Aramaic (200 B.C.-A.D. 200)
> Late Aramaic (A.D. 200-700 [or later])
> Modern Aramaic (today)

The main cause for Fitzmyer's new division of the phases
of Aramaic is the Aramaic material clearly datable from the
second century B.C. to the second century A.D., found in
Palestime (Qumran, Murabba^cat, and the Khabra and Seiyal areas)
in the last three decades, as well as recent studies on the
early Syriac inscriptions (first-third centuries A.D.) from
Edessa, Dura Europos and their environs. These Syriac texts
exhibit peculiarities "which relate them clearly to the Middle
Phase of Aramaic and set them off from that of the Late Phase."[25]

Fitzmyer establishes a Middle Phase of Aramaic from 200 B.C.
to A.D. 200 because when one examines the Palestinian material
of this period, the early Syriac inscriptions, and the Aramaic
of Nabatea, Palmyrene, and Hatra, they can hardly be called
part of Official Aramaic. These forms of Aramaic have developed
from Official Aramaic and are related to it, but now we have
"the emergence of 'real local dialects.'"[26] At the end of the
Middle Phase (ca. A.D. 200) we have the definite separation of
the eastern and western dialects, but the Palestinian Aramaic
of the Late Phase (namely, that of the non-Qumran targums,
rabbinic, and Tannaitic literature) is far more developed by
comparison to that of Qumran, Murabba^cat and the Seiyal area.

The importance of this division of Aramaic for our study
is that it relegates almost all of the Aramaic texts previously
used to establish first-century Aramaic to a later stage (Late
Aramaic) of the language's development. Thus, because they belong to Late Aramaic, the non-Qumran targums, Christian Palestinian Aramaic, Samaritan, and "so-called Palestinian Jewish
Aramaic in general" are considered as far less important for
comparison in the study of the Aramaic substratum of the New
Testament.[27]

Fitzmyer's description of the development of Aramaic and
especially of its ramifications for New Testament study have
not gone without objection. He is criticized mainly for presenting a diachronic schema (where one phase of the language
follows chronologically upon the text) in which he does not allow
for the development of a spoken Aramaic while, at the same time,
the literary language conservatively (and artificially) imitated
the earlier Official Aramaic.[28]

In particular, P. Kahle's students M. Black and A. Diez Macho hold that the targumic tradition (which they call "the Palestinian Pentateuch Targum") represented especially by the Cairo Genizah targum fragments and Codex Neofiti I, goes back at least to the first century. In their opinion this tradition, minus some later additions, best represents the Aramaic that Jesus and the disciples would have spoken.

The arguments of Black and Diez Macho for a spoken Aramaic contemporary to, but different from, the supposed literary Aramaic used at Qumran have been heavily criticized, and it would be beyond the scope of this study to present and discuss them all.[29] On the other hand, Fitzmyer presents several strong arguments against a first-century spoken dialect that would differ from Qumran Aramaic.[30] First, Palestinian Aramaic datable to the Roman period exists not only in Qumran literary texts, but also in inscriptions, ossuaries, letters (the Bar Cocheba correspondence), IOU's, contracts, and other business documents which are very close in their language to that of Qumran, but not to the Aramaic of Neofiti I. Secondly, it is very difficult to establish what the spoken language of any ancient period was like. As the Scandinavian scholars have pointed out with respect to the problem of the Greek *Volks-sprache*, written documents reflect the spoken language of any period, but can never reproduce exactly the more informal style of actual speech without direct quotation. To claim that the targums which were intended to explain the Hebrew Scriptures in the synagogues must have been written in a *spoken* form of the language is begging the question. "Moreover, we must not forget that the targumim are a form of literature, an Aramaic creation."[31] Thirdly, it is well known that there are many Grecisms in the Cairo Genizah and Neofiti targums. This does not prove their antiquity, but rather the opposite, because the closest parallels to such Greek influence which abounds in the non-Qumran targums are found in inscriptions from synagogues and tombs from the Byzantine period in Palestine (*ca.* from the fourth to the sixth centuries A.D.).[32]

We must agree with R. Le Déaut that the lack of consensus on the dating of the targums "shows that methods of research and the dating criteria have not yet been properly worked out."[33]

Therefore, our study of the Aramaic substratum of Marcan syntax
will not dwell heavily on the Aramaic of the non-Qumran targums.
Their evidence can be used only as confirmatory and secondary.

We can find no proof for a second century A.D. dating for
the Peshitta as we have it, *pace* Black, who would use its
Syriac as a control at least for Lucan Semitisms.[34] On the
contrary, Syriac inscriptions from Edessa dated to the first
and second centuries A.D. show a form of Syriac far less developed than that of the Peshitta.[35] Thus the language of the
Peshitta, like that of the Palestinian Christian Aramaic Lectionary and Samaritan, seems to belong to the Late Phase of
Aramaic, and is not of the first importance to this study.

In the previous discussion we have seen why, in general,
the text of the Gospel of Mark printed in the Nestle-Aland
Novum Testamentum Graece will be used, but how exceptions to
this rule may be made. Since the Koine Greek of the first century A.D. is best represented by contemporaneous Egyptian non-
literary Greek papyri and certain technical texts (Rydbeck's
Zwischenprosa), with the addition of the non-Atticist literary
authors of that period, neither classical Attic nor the modern
Greek dialects are important here. Indirect parallels to Marcan syntax may be taken from biblical Hebrew or Aramaic grammar
because of the influence of the Old Greek translation of the
Bible on first-century Christianity, as well as from the post-
biblical Hebrew of Qumran literature, and the relatively small
amount of Proto-Mishnaic Hebrew literature of the Roman period.
Since the Gospel of Mark was written in the last half of the
first century A.D., the Aramaic used for comparison with its
Greek should be from the same period, namely, the fairly clear-
cut Middle Phase of Aramaic (*ca.* 200 B.D. to A.D. 200).

With these points in mind, and in light of the evolution
of the study of Semitisms surveyed in Chapter I, we propose
the following methodology for the study of Semitic interference
in Marcan syntax.

Methodology

In our examination of the language of the Gospel of Mark
in Chapter III we shall consider in a separate section each
point of syntax in which Semitic interference has been alleged.
Howard's "Semitisms of the New Testament" (discussed above) will
be a guide for the exposition of the various syntagmemes in
question, but the study will include additional grammatical
features suspected of Semitic interference by more recent
authors.

In Chapter III each alleged Semitic construction will be
discussed first in light of the available Hellenistic Greek
evidence. This will include the non-Atticist literary authors,
the texts of Rydbeck's *Zwischenprosa*, especially where it
differs from the Greek of the more literary authors, and the
Greek of the Egyptian non-literary papyri. In this paragraph
on the Greek evidence for and against each alleged Semitism we
shall pay special attention to the frequency of the syntagmeme
in normal Koine writing. We shall also check to see whether
Mark uses a different, more common Greek construction elsewhere.
Using the Two-Source Theory of Synoptic relationships as a
working hypothesis, we shall note the use of the Marcan construction by Matthew and Luke or whatever changes it undergoes.
The discussion will continue with a paragraph on the Hebrew
grammar which is parallel to that of the Greek syntagmeme in
question. It will include the classical and post-classical
Hebrew of the Old Testament, as well as the post-biblical Hebrew of the Qumran documents and Proto-Mishnaic Hebrew materials.
A third subsection on each syntagmeme will discuss the bearing
of the contemporaneous Palestinian Aramaic evidence on the Marcan usage, as well as that of biblical Aramaic. A further paragraph will consider the influence of Hebrew and Aramaic on the
syntactical construction in question as it is found in the OG
(and the Theodotionic version of Daniel). When the evidence
has been set forth and discussed, an attempt will be made to
conclude whether or not the syntagmeme represents a Semitism.

The Conclusion to the study will be a summary of the detailed discussions of Chapter III. This part will answer two
questions about Semitic interference in Marcan syntax: "To what
extent is it present?" and "What kinds of Semitic interference
are present?"

CHAPTER II

[1]"Atticism and the Text of the Greek New Testament,"
Neutestamentliche Aufsätze (Festschrift J. Schmid; ed. by J.
Blinzler *et al.*; Regensburg: Pustet, 1963), pp. 126-27.

[2]For a list of such examples in Kilpatrick's publications,
see B.M. Metzger, *The Text of the New Testament* (2nd ed.; Oxford: Oxford University Press, 1968), p. 178.

[3]For example, by F.H. Chase, *The Old Syriac Element in
the Text of Codex Bezae* (London: Macmillan, 1893), pp. 137-38;
G. Dalman, *Words of Jesus* (1st ed.), p. 55; C.C. Torrey, "The
Aramaic of the Gospels," *JBL* 61 (1942), p. 83; Beyer, *Semitische
Syntax*, p. 10; E. Haenchen in a review of Wilcox's *The Semitisms
of Acts*, *TLZ* 91 (1966), p. 356; J.A. Fitzmyer in a review of
Black's *Aramaic Approach*, *CBQ* 30 (1968), p. 424; S. Brock in a
review of J.D. Yoder's *Concordance to the Distinctive Greek
Text of Codex Bezae*, *TLZ* 88 (1963), col. 353.

[4]For example, at Mk 6:7 Codex Bezae and some of the Old
Latin manuscripts read ἀνὰ δύο *(binos)*, while the rest of the
manuscripts have the Semitizing distributive form δύο δύο.

[5]P. Joüon made this comparison in his *L'Evangile de Nôtre-
Seigneur Jésus-Christ. Traduction et Commentaire* (Verbum
salutis 5; Paris: Beauchesne, 1930), p. xiv.

[6]Cf. E. Schwyzer, *Grammatik*, Vol. 1, p. 126, and N. Turner,
"Second Thoughts," p. 44.

[7]"The Greek Language," p. 480. It was only in the second
century A.D. that grammarians sought to return to classical
Attic prose as a model of style for literary composition. Cf.
Rydbeck, *Fachprosa*, p. 13 and Kilpatrick, "Atticism," p. 127.

[8]Cf. Radermacher, "Besonderheiten," p. 1-2, and de Zwaan,
"The Uses of the Greek Language in Acts," p. 30.

[9]There has been much discussion about the relationship
of the Hellenistic literary form aretalogy (a collection of
stories of the extraordinary deeds of a specially endowed hero)
to the gospels. What has emerged from this study is that
aretalogies were created and used for a variety of purposes.
While some of Mark's sources may reflect the influence of these
Hellenistic forms, "for the overall pattern of a gospel, Mark
had no literary precedent" (H.C. Kee, "Aretalogy and Gospel,"
JBL 92 [1973], p. 422). See also M. Smith, "Prolegomena to
a Discussion of Aretalogies, Divine Men, The Gospels and
Jesus," *JBL* 90 (1971), pp. 195-96; and D.L. Tiede, *The Charis-
matic Figure as Miracle Worker* (SBL Dissertation Series 1;
Missoula: Society of Biblical Literature, 1972), p. 289.

[10]"Deux notes II," p. 205.

[11]W. Bauer lists the most important of these "authors who
were more or less able to avoid the spell of antiquarianism
which we know as "Atticism'"in his introduction to Bauer-Arndt-
Gingrich (p. x).

[12]Cf. Radermacher, *Koine*, p. 65.

[13]Cf. Howard, "Semitisms," p. 478.

[14]Cf. R. Meyer, *Hebräische Grammatik* (3rd rev. ed.; Sammlung Göschen 763; Berlin: W. de Gruyter, 1966), Vol. 1, pp.
31-32; W. Chomsky, "What Was the Jewish Vernacular during the
Second Commonwealth?" *Jewish Quarterly Review* 42 (1951-52),
p. 198; Fitzmyer, "Methodology," p. 81.

[15]Cf. C. Rabin, "The Historical Background of Qumran
Hebrew," *Aspects of the Dead Sea Scrolls*, ed. by C. Rabin and
Y. Yadin (Scripta hierosolymitana 4; Jerusalem: Magnes Press,
1958), p. 145.

[16]"Le rouleau de cuivre provenant de la grotte 3Q (3Q15).
Commentaire et texte," DJD III, p. 222. These Proto-Mishnaic
Hebrew texts include:
  (a) literary texts from Qumran Cave Four (unpublished and
      provisionally labeled by Milik 4QMišm[arot] C[a-d], D,
      E[a,b], and 4QMišn[ique][a-f]. See his preliminary pub-
      lication of them in "Le travail d'édition des manu-
      scrits du désert de Juda," *Volume du Congrès* (VTSup
      4; Leiden: Brill, 1957), pp. 24-26.
  (b) Jewish graffiti and epitaphs from the Roman period,
      published by B. Bagatti and Milik, *Gli scavi del
      "Dominus flevit." La necropoli del periodo romano*
      (Pubblicazione dello Studium Biblicum Franciscanum
      13; Jerusalem: Tipografia dei PP. Francescani, 1958),
      Vol. 1.
  (c) the semi-literary catalogue of treasures called the
      Copper Scroll (3Q15) published in DJD III, pp. 211-302.
  (d) letters and contracts from Murabbaʿat, published in
      DJD II.

[17]"Hebrew in the Period of the Second Temple," *International
Journal of Apocrypha* 6/23 (1910) 79-82 and *A Grammar of Mishnaic Hebrew* (Oxford: Oxford University Press, 1927), pp. 1-20.

[18]The list of these scholars is so long that we will de-
vote a special section of our bibliography to the question.
For a survey of the argument, see J.A. Emerton, "Did Jesus
Speak Hebrew?" *JTS* 12 (1961), pp. 189-202; and J. Barr, "Which
Language Did Jesus Speak--Some Remarks of a Semitist," *BJRL*
53 (1970), pp. 9-29.

[19]For resumées of these arguments, see Rabin, "The His-
torical Background," and A. Díez Macho, "Le targum palestinien,"
Exégèse biblique et judaïsme, ed. by J.E. Ménard; Strasbourg:
Faculté de théologie catholique, 1973), pp. 23-24.

[20]Cf. Meyer, *Hebräische Grammatik*, p. 32, and "Der gegenwärtige Stand der Erforschung der in Palästina neugefundenen
hebräischen Handschriften: 47. Die vier Höhlen von Murabbaʿat,"
TLZ 88 (1963), col. 25.

[21]Cf. J. Jeremias, *The Eucharistic Words of Jesus* (3rd rev.
ed.; trans. by N. Perrin; New York: Scribner, 1966), pp. 196-
201; M. Black, *"EPHPHATHA* (Mk. 7.34)," *Mélanges bibliques en
hommage au R.P. Béda Rigaux*, ed. by A. Descamps and A. de
Halleux; Gembloux: Duculot, 1970), pp. 58, 60.

[22]"Im Laufe der Zeit wurde dieser Einfluss immer stärker
bis es dem BH gelang, sogar grundlegende Charakteristiken des
MH vollkommen zu verwischen" ("Mišnisches Hebräisch," *Rocznik
Orientalistyczny* 28 (1964), p. 37; cf. Díez Macho, "Le targum
palestinien," p. 24.

[23]Perhaps Kutscher's technique of examining individual
manuscripts of the Mishnah for authenticity is a start in this
much-needed area of study ("Mišnisches Hebräisch," pp. 33-48).

[24]*The Genesis Apocryphon of Qumran Cave I*, p. 22, n. 60,
and "Methodology," p. 84, n. 38. This dating has been accepted
by E.Y. Kutscher in "Aramaic," *Current Trends in Linguistics:
6. Linguistics in South West Asia and North Africa* (The Hague:
Mouton, 1971), p. 347; E. Vogt, *Lexicon*, pp. 6*-8*; H.L. Ginsberg in a review of Fitzmyer's *Genesis Apocryphon*, *TZ* 28 (1967),
p. 574; and T. Muraoka, "The Aramaic of the Old Targum of Job
from Qumran Cave XI," *Journal of Jewish Studies* 25 (1974),
p. 426, n. 7.

[25]"The Phases of the Aramaic Language," *A Wandering
Aramean: Collected Aramaic Essays* (Society of Biblical Litera-
ture Monograph Series; Missoula, MT: Scholars Press, 1979),
p. 71. Cf. H.J.W. Drijvers, *Old-Syriac (Edessean) Inscriptions*
(Semitic Study Series 3; Leiden: Brill, 1972), pp. xii-xiii.
"The language of the inscriptions stands midway between Official
Aramaic and the later literary Syriac, which was an East-
Aramaic dialect, and so does the script" (*Ibid.*, p. xiii).

[26]"The Phases of the Aramaic Language," p. 61.

[27]Fitzmyer, "Methodology," p. 87.

[28]Cf. Díez Macho, "Le targum palestinien," p. 26. Other
recent authors who hold that there existed a more developed
spoken language in the first century are Beyer (*Semitische
Syntax*, pp. 14-15); P. Grelot (review of Fitzmyer's *Genesis
Apocryphon* in *RB* 74 [1967], pp. 102-105); S.A. Kaufman ("The
Job Targum from Qumran," *Journal of the American Oriental
Society* 93 [1973], p. 325).

[29]For a collection of the arguments for Díez Macho's
position see Díez Macho, "Le targum palestinien," pp. 26-43.
The arguments of Kahle, Black, and Díez Macho have been discussed and criticized by the following: M. Delcor ("Le Targum
de Job et l'araméen du temps de Jésus," *Revue des sciences
religieuses* 47 [1973], pp. 254-61); Fitzmyer ("The Languages

of Palestine," pp. 521-27, and "Methodology," pp. 85-87);
Kaufman, ("The Job Targum," pp. 326-27); Kutscher ("Das zur
Zeit Jesu gesprochene Aramäisch," *ZNW* 51 [1960], pp. 53-54);
R. Le Déaut ("The Current State of Targumic Studies," *Biblical
Theology Bulletin* 4 [1974], pp. 3-32); H. Ott ("Um die Mutter-
sprache Jesu Forschungen seit Gustaf Dalman," *NovT* 9 [1967],
pp. 8-19); D. Rieder ("On Targum Yerushalmi Neofiti I," [in
Hebrew] *Tarbiz* 38 [1968], pp. 81-86); A.D. York ("The Dating
of Targumic Literature," *Journal for the Study of Judaism in
the Persian, Hellenistic and Roman Period* 5 [1974], pp. 49-62).

[30]"The Phases of the Aramaic Language," pp. 72-74.

[31]*Ibid.*, p. 74.

[32]"The Languages of Palestine," p. 526.

[33]"The Current State of Targumic Studies," p. 23. See
S.A. Kaufman's important review of G.J. Kuiper, *The Pseudo-
Jonathan Targum and its Relation to Targum Onqelos, Journal of
Near Eastern Studies* 35 (1976), pp. 61-62.

[34]*Aramaic Approach*, p. 17. In his book *Peschitta und
Targum des Pentateuchs* (Papers of the Estonian Theological
Society in Exile 9; Stockholm: ETSE, 1958), A. Vööbus has
established that the Peshitta is a kind of Syriac targum and
that it depends on the traditions of the classical Jewish targums. These, as we have pointed out, belong to a later stage
of Aramaic than that which we consider relevant for the study
of New Testament Greek. Vööbus also maintains that there was
a revision of the Peshitta's "textual pattern . . . already
before the end of the fourth century" (*Early Versions of the
New Testament* [Papers of the Estonian Theological Society in
Exile 6; Stockholm: ETSE, 1954], p. 96). Thus the present
text of the Peshitta is even later than the original which
may have been based on traditions earlier than the writing of
the classical targums. S.R. Isenberg points out that although
a few Western Aramaic elements have been isolated in the
Peshitta, "these are rare and theoretically might have crept
in at a late stage" ("On the Jewish-Palestinian Origins of the
Peshitta to the Pentateuch," *JBL* 90 [1971], p. 71).

[35]Cf. Drijvers, *Old-Syriac Inscriptions*, p. xiii.

CHAPTER III

ALLEGED SEMITISMS IN MARCAN SYNTAX

A. THE GENERAL STYLE AND STRUCTURE OF THE SENTENCE

    1. Word Order

(a) The Position of the Verb in the Sentence

    The normal word order in an independent clause in Helleni-
stic Greek is the subject--verb.[1] Hellenistic Greek word
order, however, is much freer than that of modern languages,
and thus the verb, or any other word, may be brought forward
in the sentence for the sake of emphasis.[2] A. Thumb has
pointed out that the modern Greek usage of the initial position
of the verb in subordinate clauses began to assert itself already in the Koine,[3] and this has been confirmed by H. Frisk.
The latter's extensive study of word order shows remarkable
percentage increases of verb--subject word order in the subordinate clauses of Herodotus, Xenophon, Demosthenes, Polybius,
and the papyri over that in their main clauses. For example,
in Polybius, while in main clauses the word order is verb--sub-
ject only 16% of the time, in relative clauses (where the subject
must come first if, as is very frequently the case, it is the
relative pronoun) it is 42%, in temporal clauses 33%, and in
conditional clauses 46%.[4] Since these figures for subordinate
clauses so closely approximate those in Mark,[5] we will confine
this study to the word order of verb and subject in independent
clauses only. In an extensive study of the order of subject
and verb in the Gospel of Mark, M. Zerwick has shown that because of emphasis upon the subject of the sentence in much of
the non-narrative material of the gospel (the *Redeteil*: the
various sayings and discourses), significant deviation from the
normal Hellenistic Greek word order subject--verb occurs only
in the narrative part of the gospel.[6] Since because of emphasis
the subject may be first in the sentence in both Hebrew and
Aramaic, as well as in Greek, this study must be restricted to
the narrative material of Mark.

    Within this narrative material, in sentences which are
introduced by the post-positive conjunction δέ, in only one

instance (Mk 14:44) does the verb precede the subject, whereas
the word order subject--verb is the case almost 90 times.
Whatever the reasons for this (emphasis, stylistic preference,
etc.[7]), this is normal Greek word order. Hence these sentences
of Mark are omitted from this study. The bulk of the rest of
the independent clauses in the narrative part of Mark which
have an expressed subject are introduced by the conjunction
καί.[8] Here, in independent clauses introduced by καί within
the narrative part of the gospel, Mark's preference for placing
the verb before the subject is striking in comparison to the
more normal Greek word order subject--verb.[9]

     In addition to emphatic usage, the verb may precede the
subject in Hellenistic Greek independent clauses for any of
the following reasons:[10]

  (i) the imperative usually comes first in the sentence;
  (ii) in the apodosis after a subordinate clause the verb
usually comes first: e.g., ἐπεὶ δ' εἰσῆλθεν, ἐκάλει ὁ Δερκυλίδας
τοὺς ταμίας, "And when he entered, Dercylidas called the
stewards" (Xenophon, *Historia Graeca* 3.1.27);[11]
(iii) the verb may come first when it acts as a connector in
a narrative (but, according to Blass-Debrunner-Funk, this is
common only with verbs "to say"[12]);
  (iv) the verb "to be" when it means "to exist" usually stands
first in a clause;
  (v) the order is usually verb--subject when the verb is
singular and has a double subject.[13]

     In biblical Hebrew the normal word order in a verbal clause
is verb--subject. As in Greek, however, it may be changed for
emphasis.[14] The O.G., as a rule, follows the Hebrew word order.

     Qumran Hebrew is quite like biblical Hebrew in the matter
of word order in that the normal order is subject--verb. Unfortunately, there is not enough material in Proto-Mishnaic
Hebrew to make a judgment on its preference for word order of
subject and verb.

     In Middle Aramaic the order verb--subject seems to be the
rule (as opposed to biblical Aramaic, where the subject precedes
the verb more often than not[15]). For example, in the Genesis
Apocryphon (1QapGn) 19:7--20:34, in the thirty-five verbal
clauses which have a noun as subject, only five have the order

subject--verb (19:15; 20:6, 8, 12, 34), and the emphatic nature
of this word order is clear in nearly every one of these exceptions.

Hence, in independent clauses where the subject is expressed
and the word order in Mark is verb--subject and the verb is not
emphatic or placed first because of one of the reasons listed
above, there is a good chance of Semitic interference from
Aramaic or from imitation of the OG, while less likely from
contemporaneous Hebrew. It is impossible to be definite in
every case, but the preponderance of the order verb--subject in
Mark forces the conclusion of M. Black that "no native Greek
writer, uninfluenced by Semitic sources or a Semitic language,
would have written [in such a manner]."[16]

(b) The Position of the Attributive Adjective

In Hellenestic Greek, a noun determined by the definite
article may take an attributive adjective in either of two
positions: (i) between the article and the noun (ὁ ἀγαθὸς
ἀνήρ) or (ii) after the noun with repetition of the article
(ὁ ἀνὴρ ὁ ἀγαθός). The original emphatic nature of the second
position diminished in Hellenistic Greek so that sometimes the
same writer uses both positions inadvertently with no difference
in meaning, e.g., οἱ παῖδες οἱ ἀποδράντες (1. 3) is used along
with τοὺς ἀποδράντας παῖδας (1. 58) in Cairo Zenon Papyrus
59015.[17] As early as the second century B.C., however, the use
of the second position (namely, ὁ ἀνὴρ ὁ ἀγαθός) diminished
greatly in many writers. In his study of the Tebtunis papyri
(nos. 5-124, second-first century B.C.) E. Mayser found only
four or five examples out of over 150 attributive adjectives
(and participles) modifying articular substantives where the
second position of the attributive adjective is used.[18] According to R.A. Martin, Polybius uses the first position 6.1
times as often as the second, Josephus 5.6 times, and Epictetus
3.4 times, while Plutarch uses the first position only 1.3
times as often as the second (Atticism?).[19]

With regard to the anarthrous noun, an attributuve adjective may be placed before it (ἀγαθὸς ἀνήρ) or after it (ἀνὴρ
ἀγαθός, or, with the addition of the article to the adjective,
ἀνὴρ ὁ ἀγαθός[20]). Thus in Polybius 1.13.11, in a string of

anarthrous nouns modified by adjectives, the position of the
adjectives can be either pre- or post-positive: οὔτε παρασκευὰς
ὁλοσχερεστέρας οὔτε συνεχεστέρας πράξεις οὔτε πλείους ἀγῶνας
οὔτε περιπετείας μείζους, "neither more complete preparations,
nor more continuous activities, nor more battles, nor greater
changes of fortune." Another random example of the same apparent indifferences as to the position of the simple attributive
adjective occurs in l. 5 of Papyrus Elephantinus 1--γυναικὶ
ἐλευθέρα, "for a free woman," together with κοινῇ βουλῇ, "in
common consultation," in the same sentence.

In biblical Hebrew, however, the adjective normally stands
after its substantive whether the article is used or not, although it may be placed before it "for the sake of emphasis."[21]
The OG generally keeps the Hebrew word order.

Qumran Hebrew follows this norm, e.g., špṭym gdwlym,
"great judgments" (1QS 5:12-13), as does Proto-Mishnaic, e.g.,
bbwr hgdwl, "in the large cistern" (3Q15 i 6).

In the Genesis Apocryphon "the attributive adjective follows the noun in the same state as the noun,"[22] and this is the
rule also in the other published Middle Aramaic texts, as well
as in biblical Aramaic.[23]

Now in the Gospel of Mark the attributive adjective (excluding πᾶς and the numerals whose Semitic counterparts may
both precede or follow their substantive, as well as the interrogative adjectives ποῖος, πόσος, and ποταπός whose Semitic equivalents would also precede their substantives) follows its
substantive about three times as often as it precedes it,
whether the substantive is articular or not.[24]

Although the frequency of postpositive attributive adjectives is very high in Mark, no individual example of such word
order may be singled out as a Semitism. In fact, the reverse
is true: an unemphatic attributive adjective placed before its
noun is a "Grecism" and would eliminate the possibility of
literal translation or of the author's thinking in Semitic in
such a phrase. However, in a pericope where all unemphatic
attributive adjectives follow their substantives, that fact
lends to its Semitic flavor, although Semitic interference as
such would have to be proved by additional means.

(c) The Position of the Dependent Genitive

The classical position of a genitive which was dependent
on an arthrous substantive was the attributive position, i.e.,
either between the article and the substantive (τὸ τοῦ πατρὸς
βίβλιον) or after the substantive with repetition of the article
(τὸ βίβλιον τὸ τοῦ πατρός). In Hellenistic Greek the second
form of the phrase was generally replaced by the postpositive
genitive without repetition of the article (τὸ βίβλιον τοῦ
πατρός).[25] In the papyri of the second and first centuries
B.C. the genitive is postpositive about twice as often as prepositive.[26]

When the substantive upon which the genitive is dependent
is anarthrous, however, the postpositive position of the genitive, whether the latter has the article (βίβλιον τοῦ πατρός)
or not (βίβλιον πατρός) is almost always the case.[27]

In biblical Hebrew, Qumran Hebrew, and Proto-Mishnaic
Hebrew, as well as in Aramaic, the "genitive" is always placed
after the substantive on which it depends, either as the
nomen rectum after a substantive which is in the construct
state, or subordinated by means of a preposition, the particle
dy (in Aramaic), or the particle *šĕl* (in Proto-Mishnaic Hebrew).

Hence little can be said about the Semitic character of any
single example in Mark where a genitive follows the substantive
it modifies. Since in Hebrew and Aramaic the "genitive" always
follows its substantive, a dependent genitive placed *before* its
substantive cannot reflect a literal translation. On the other
hand, the fact that no genitive precedes its substantive in an
entire pericope may lend to its Semitic flavor, although Semitic
interference as such in the pericope would have to be proved
by other means.

(d) A Phrase Made Up of an Adjective, a Substantive, and a Genitive

The normal Greek word order for this phrase would be
(article)--adjective--substantive--genitive (τὴν δεξιὰν χεῖρα
αὐτοῦ), or genitive--(article)--adjective--substantive (αὐτοῦ
τὴν δεξιὰν χεῖρα),[28] or even (article)--adjective--gentive--sub-
stantive (e.g., τὴν δὲ πρώτην ᾿Αντιγόνου τοῦ μονοφθάλμου
κατάληψιν, "the first occupation of Antigonus Monophthalmus"
[Polybius, *Histories* 5.67.6]). But at Mk 5:11 we read

ἀγέλη χοίρων μεγάλη. The postpositive position of the adjective might seem to give it a predicative meaning ("a heard of swine, which was large"), whereas it is clear that the phrase simply means "a large herd of swine."[29] In Mk 1:11 and 9:27, ὁ υἱός μου ὁ ἀγαπητός may be another example of this word order (with a genitive possessive pronoun occurring between a noun [υἱός] and its attributive adjective [ἀγαπητός]). However, since ἀγαπητός is articular, it may be a substantivized adjective in apposition to υἱός, to be rendered: "my son, the beloved (one)."[30]

In biblical Hebrew the usual word order of a phrase consisting (as does Mk 5:11) of a noun, an adjective, and a dependent "genitive" which is also a noun is: *nomen regens--nomen rectum* (the "genitive")--adjective, e.g., *mê hannāhār hāʿăṣûmîm wĕharabbîm*, "the great and many waters of the river" (Isa 8:7). Qumran and Proto-Mishnaic Hebrew also have this usage, e.g., *bkwl mʿśy plʾkh hgdwlym*, "in all the great works of your wondrous-power" (1QH 10:11); *pnt hʾstʾn hdrwmt*, "the southern corner of the portico" (3Q15 xi 2). A second word order for the phrase in question turns up in Proto-Mishnaic Hebrew, namely, noun--adjective--"genitive" (the particle *šl* and a noun): *bbybʾ hgdwl šl hbrk*, "the great sewer of hab-Baruk" (3Q15 xii 8).

In biblical Aramaic the word order of the phrase in question is the same as in biblical Hebrew, namely, noun--"genitive" (either [i] a *nomen rectum* or [ii] the particle *dî* and a noun) --adjective. Examples: *bêt ʾĕlāhāʾ dĕnâ*, "this house of God" (Ezra 6:16, 17; 7:24); *nidbakîn dî ʾeben gĕlāl tĕlātāʾ wĕnidbāk dî ʾāʿ ḥădat*, "three layers of large stones and one layer of timber" (Ezra 6:4).

In the three instances of the phrase in question which occur in Middle Aramaic, the word order is similar to the alternative word order in Proto-Mishnaic Hebrew, namely, noun-- adjective--"genitive" (the particle *dy* and a noun): *qnyʾ ṭbyʾ dy bśmʾ*, (literally) "good reeds of spice" (4QEn[c] 1 xii 24); *lbwš śgy dy bwṣ wʾrgwʾn*, "many garments of linen and purple" (1QapGn 20:31); *ymʾ rbʾ dn dy mlḥʾ*, "this great sea of salt" (1QapGn 21:16).

The OG generally translates the phrase in question with the same order as in Hebrew, e.g., τὸ ὕδωρ τοῦ ποταμοῦ τὸ

ἰσχυρὸν καὶ τὸ πολύ, "the powerful and plentiful water of the
river" (Isa 8:7). The translator of the book of Ezra, however,
has consistently avoided the difficult Greek word order either
by changing the "genitive" to an adjective: δόμοι λίθινοι
κραταιοὶ τρεῖς καὶ δόμος ξύλινος εἷς, "three mighty stone layers
and one wooden layer" (2 Esdr 6:4), or by dropping the (demonstrative) adjective: τοῦ οἴκου τοῦ θεοῦ, "of the house of God"
(2 Esdr 6:16, 17); οἴκου θεοῦ (2 Esdr 7:24).

When the phrase consists of a noun, an adjective, and a
"possessive pronoun" (a pronominal suffix in Semitic) as in
Mk 1:11 and 9:27 (if ἀγαπητός is not a substantive), the word
order of the phrase in both Hebrew and Aramaic is: noun plus
suffix--adjective. Examples: biblical Hebrew: wᵉšiḥattā
dᵉbārêkā hanneʿîmîm, "and you will waste your good words"
(Prv 23:8); Qumran Hebrew: kmᶜśykh hgdwlym, "according to
your great deeds" (1QM 10:8); in Proto-Mishnaic Hebrew there is
no example of the phrase in question; biblical Aramaic:
lᵉrabrᵉbānôhî ʾālap,(for his thousand nobles" (Dan 5:1);
Middle Aramaic: wnpq glglh ryqn mn kl nhwr, "there emerges its
disc, empty of all light" (4QEnastrᵇ 6:9).

The OG usually translates this type of phrase literally,
e.g., καὶ λυμανεῖται τοὺς λόγους σου τοὺς καλούς, "and he will
waste your good words" (Prv 23:8). The difficult word order
even occurs where the text differs from the Masoretic Text:
ὁ υἱός σου ὁ κάλλιστος, "your best son" (Isa 3:25; see also 2:20).

Hence, since the word order of Mk 5:11 and possibly 1:11
and 9:27 (if ἀγαπητός in those texts is merely an attributive
adjective) is not attested in non-biblical Greek, it is most
probably due to Semitic interference, whether from Hebrew or
Aramaic, or from imitation of the OG.

(e) The Phrase τὸ αἷμά μου τῆς διαθήκης τὸ ἐκχυννόμενον ὑπὲρ
    πολλῶν (Mk 14:24)

Several grammatical points may be raised with regard to
the Semitic provenience of this phrase: (i) the use of the
pronoun πολλοί where normal Greek would use πάντες; (ii) the
position of the prepositional phrase ὑπὲρ πολλῶν after the
participle; (iii) the fact that the genitive τῆς διαθήκης
follows the genitive of the personal pronoun, μου, with both

genitives dependent on τὸ αἷμα; (iv) the participle in the
attributive position is separated from its substantive τὸ αἷμα
by the two genitives.

(i) We shall speak of the use of πολλοί, "many" for πάντες,
"all" below in the section on pronouns (B.2.e).

(ii) J. Jeremias has stated that in Mk 14:24 "the placing
of the participle [ἐκχυννόμενον] before the prepositional
phrase [ὑπὲρ πολλῶν] corresponds to the Semitic word order,"
and that both Matthew and Luke inverted that word order "pre-
sumably. . . to avoid the hiatus."[31] While it is true that in
Semitic the prepositional phrase usually does come after the
participle, the same word order is also quite common in Hellenistic Greek,[32] e.g., τὰ ἀναλώματα τὰ γενόμενα εἰς τὴν γῆν,
"the expenses which went for the land" (PMagd. 28.5); τῶν
σκαφείων τῶν ὑπολιφθέντων ὑπὸ Τιμοκλέους, "of the hoes left
behind by Timocleos" (Preisigke, Sammelb. 7203.4). Hence the
Marcan position of ὑπὲρ πολλῶν does not constitute a serious
problem in its Greek formulation, and is not necessarily to be
ascribed to a Semitic background.

(iii) There has been much discussion about the possibility
fo a Semitic Vorlage for the words τὸ αἷμά μου τῆς διαθήκης,[33]
since in Hebrew and Aramaic the construct chain construction is
inadmissible when a noun to be modified by a "genitive" also
has a suffix (= μου in the Marcan verse).[34]

The real question, however, is whether such a construction
would be possible in Greek with the same word order as in the
Marcan text, namely, where the genitive of a possessive pronoun follows immediately after a substantive, but comes before
another genitive dependent on the same substantive. In the
Greek papyri, whenever an arthrous noun which has another
attribute takes the genitive of a personal pronoun, the personal
pronoun always follows the other attribute.[35] Moreover, in
every example of such a phrase given by Mayser, the two attributes always come between the article and its substantive:
article--possessive genitive pronoun--substantive, e.g., τοῦ
ἀπὸ ἀπηλιώτου αὐτοῦ παραδείσου, "of his enclosed park away
from the east wind" (PLond. 401.12); Ἀπολλώνιον τὸν νεότερόν

μου ἀδελφόν, "Apollonius, my younger brother" (*PLond*. 23.9).
In Epictetus as well, a possessive genitive pronoun always
follows the other attribute when an arthrous substantive takes
both a possessive genitive pronoun and another attribute (e.g.,
τὰ δυστηνά μου σαρκίδια, "my wretched bits of flesh" [1.3.5]),
even when the article is not separated from its substantive in
such a phrase, e.g., ὅλην σου τὴν οἰκίαν, "your whole household" (1.9.3). Hence, the word order of the phrase τὸ αἷμά μου
τῆς διαθήκης is extraordinary in Hellenistic Greek.[36] Furthermore, when such a phrase occurs in biblical Hebrew and Aramaic,
the OG translator changes the difficult phrase (compare the
Semitic texts cited below): οὐ δώσεις κοίτην σπέρματός σου,
"you shall not give the copulation of your seed" (Lev 18:20);
ἐπὶ τοὺς πόδας τοὺς σιδηροῦς καὶ ὀστρακίνους, "on (its) iron
and clay feet" (Dan 2:34, in both the Old Greek and Theodotion).

Although a noun with a suffix is never followed by a
dependent noun-modifier in the construct chain construction in
either Hebrew or Aramaic, there are other ways of expressing a
"genitive" in both languages. In biblical Hebrew a genitive
relationship may be expressed by a noun with the preposition *l*
after the noun on which it depends, in various instances. One
of these instances is the case in which the first noun is
modified by a suffix,[37] e.g., *wĕʾel ʾēšet ʿămîtĕkā lōʾ tittēn
šĕkābtĕkā lĕzāraʿ lĕtomʾâ bâ*, "and to your neighbor's wife you
shall not give your copulation of seed so that you become unclean
because of her" (Lev 18:20). The construction also occurs in
Qumran Hebrew: *btkwnm lzkrwn*, "in their fixed place of memor-
ial" (1QS 10:5), and possibly also in Proto-Mishnaic Hebrew:
bbyʾtk lymwmyt, "in your entering of the small basin" (3Q15
xi 13).[38]

In Aramaic a genitive relationship may be expressed by
the particle *dy* as well as by the use of the construct state.
The former construction is commonly used when the noun which
is modified by a "genitive" has a prospective suffix,[39] e.g.,
šĕmēh dî ʾĕlāhāʾ, "the name of God" (literally,"his name, of
God" in Dan 2:20); *lwṭ br ʾhwy dy ʾbrm*, "Lot, the son of Abram's
brother" (literally "the son of his brother, of Abram" in
1QapGn 21:34--22:1; see also 11QtgJb 38:2).

In biblical Aramaic, however, there is one verse in which
a noun with a suffix takes a "genitive" where the suffix is not
prospective of the "genitive," but where, as in Mk 14:24, the
"genitive" adds a different attribute to the noun:[40] *ûmĕḥāt*
lĕṣalmā᾿ ῾al raglôhî dî parzĕlā᾿ wĕḥaspā᾿, "and it struck the
image on its feet of iron and clay" (Dan 2:34). This same
construction does not occur in Middle Aramaic, but turns up
several times in Late Aramaic: *byt mqdšk tqyp᾿ dyśr᾿l*, "the
house of your mighty temple of Israel" (Tg. Ps. 68:36); *῾mk dbyt
yśr᾿l*, "your people of the house of Israel" (Tg. Ps. 110:3);
gwbt᾿y dkwḥl᾿, "my tube of eye-paint" (*b. Ber.* 18b).[41] Hence
we must consider that the double genitival expression as in
the Greek of Mk 14:24 is at least possible in Middle Aramaic
as well.

(iv) The fourth problem with the Greek of Mk 14:24 is
similar to that of Mk 5:11, treated in section (d) above, namely,
the word order: noun--genitive--attributive adjective (in Mk
14:24 the participle ἐκχυννόμενον is in the attributive position). As we have seen above in that discussion, in non-
biblical Greek a dependent genitive noun (τῆς διαθήκης in Mk
14:24) never occurs between the noun on which it depends
(αἷμα) and the latter's attributive adjective (the participle
ἐκχυννόμενον), as it indeed does in Mk 14:24--τὸ αἷμά μου τῆς
διαθήκης τὸ ἐκχυννόμενον.[42]

Precisely this word order (noun--"genitive"--attributive
participle) is attested in Hebrew. Examples: biblical Hebrew:
mibbĕkôr par῾oh hayyōšēb ῾al kis᾿ô, "from the firstborn of
Pharoah who sits (= "will sit") on his throne" (Exod 11:5);
Qumran Hebrew: *whrwkbym ῾lyhm ᾿nšy ḥyl lmlḥmh mlwmdy rkb*,
"and the riders of them (the horses) (shall be) men of strength
in (or "of") battle trained to ride" (1QM 6:13);[43] Proto-Mishnaic Hebrew: *bšlp šl hšw᾿ hswp᾿ m῾rb bdrwm bśryḥ ḥswp᾿ ṣpwn*,
"in the fallow land of haš-Šo᾿ looking (to) the west: in the
southern part, in the cellar looking (to) the north" (3Q15
8:10-12; see also 6:2, 8).[44]

While in Middle Aramaic there is no text in which a dependent "genitive" noun (corresponding to διαθήκης in Mk 14:24)
intervenes between a noun and its attributive participle, there
are several texts in which a noun is followed by a first

attribute other than a dependent "genitive" noun, and then by
an attributive participle: [wḥz]w dm sgy šp[yk ⁽l ⁾r⁽]⁾,
"[and] they [saw] much blood sp[illed upon] the [earth]"
(4QEn^a 1 iv 7; cf. another copy of the same text [= *1 Enoch*
9:1]: [wḥzw dm sgy špy]k [⁽]l ⁾r⁽⁾, "[and they saw much blood
spi]lled [up]on the earth" (4QEn^b 1 iii 8].[45] In this text both
the noun and its attributive participle are indefinite and lack
the article, but the first attribute (the adjective *sgy*) comes
between the two as does the genitive διαθήκης in Mk 14:24.
Wnpq glglh ryqn mn kl nhwr mṭmr ⁽m š[mš⁾], "and there emerges
its disc, empty of all light, hidden by the s[un]" (4QEnastr^b
6:9). In this text two attributes come between the noun *glgl*
(determined by the suffix *h*) and its attributive participle *mṭmr*
(note the absolute state). The two attributes are: the suffix
h, "its" (which corresponds in position to the possessive pronoun σου in Mk 14:24), and the adjective *ryqn* (in the absolute
state). *W⁾škḥ kwl sg⁾hwn mt[smyn]*, "and he found all the majority of them [blind]ed" (4QEn^c 4:5 = *1 Enoch* 89:33). In this
text the suffix *kwn* also corresponds in position to μου in
Mk 14:24. *Wk⁽n šrw⁾ ⁾swrkwn mḥ[bl]*, "and now, loosen your
chain bi[nding . . .]" (4QEnGiants^a 8:14); [wtr⁽] l[qbl tr]⁽
ptyḥ lgw⁾ przyt⁾ kmšḥt tr⁽⁾ bry⁾, "[And a door] in [front of a
do]or opened onto the middle of the block (is) according to
the dimensions of the exterior door" (5Q*15* 1 ii 1-2). In this
text, if the restoration is correct, an attributive prepositional phrase *(lqbl tr⁽)* comes between a noun *(tr⁽*, the first door)
and its attributive participle *(ptyḥ)*.

There are no examples of the usage in question in biblical
Aramaic.

Hence, while the phrase τὸ αἷμά μου τῆς διαθήκης τὸ
ἐκχυννόμενον ὑπὲρ πολλῶν is difficult in Greek both in its use
of a genitive after a genitive of the possessive pronoun where
both genitives are dependent on the same substantive, and in
its placement of an attributive participle after a genitive
which is dependent on the same noun, such a phrase is possible
in first-century Hebrew, namely, *dmy lbryt hnšpk ⁽l rbym*, "my
blood of the covenant (which is) poured out on behalf of many."

As many commentators have pointed out,[46] the text of Mk
14:24 alludes in obvious fashion to at least two Old Testament

texts: *hinnēh dam habbĕrît*, (Old Greek: ἰδοὺ τὸ αἷμα τῆς
διαθήκης) "behold the blood of the covenant (which the Lord has
made with you)" (Exod 24:8), and *bĕdam bĕrîtēk*, (Old Greek: ἐν
αἵματι διαθήκης, "and as for you also) because of the blood of
your covenant (I will set your captives free)" (Zech 9:11).
Nevertheless, imitation of the OG for the exact wording of
Mk 14:24 must be ruled out because a phrase like τὸ αἷμά μου
τῆς διαθήκης (noun--genitive possessive pronoun--attributive
genitive) is never found the OG, even though such a phrase
occurs in the Hebrew of Lev 18:20 and the Aramaic of Dan 2:34.

The phrase would also be possible in Middle Aramaic:
dĕmî dî qĕyāmā᾿ sĕpîkā᾿(or *mistapkā᾿*) *῾al saggî᾿în* (or *saggî᾿-
în*).[47] Hence, Semitic interference (whether from comtempora-
neous Hebrew or Aramaic) is almost certain in Mk 14:24, both in
the position of the genitive τῆς διαθήκης after the genitive
possessive pronoun μου, and in the position of the participle
ἐκχυννόμενον.

(f) Separation of the Substantive from its Article

As we have seen in (b), the most common position of the
attributive adjective in Hellenistic Greek was between the
article and its noun. We have also seen in (c) that a dependent
genitive could come between the article and the noun. Furthermore, any postpositive particle (e.g., γάρ, δέ, μέν, οὖν, γε,
τε) would normally come after the article and before the noun
if the article was the first word in the sentence. Prepositional phrases, too, often separate article and noun. Finally, the
normal position of an attributive adverb is between the article
and noun.[48]

Since there are so many possibilities of separation of the
substantive from its article, some studies have been made to see
just how often this phenomenon occurs in various Greek writers.
J.M. Rife saw that in the translation Greek of the Old Testament only 4% of the substantives were separated from their
articles, while in a selection of classical, Koine, and modern
Greek writers 25% was the figure; even the New Testament
epistles have 18% separation.[49] Martin's figures are: Plutarch
24%, Polybius 43%, Epictetus 18%, Josephus 30%, and for the
papyri he selected, 22%.[50]

Now in the Gospel of Mark the article occurs some 1470 times. In 59 cases it represents a pronoun, e.g., Mk 1:45--ὁ δὲ ἐξελθὼν ἤρξατο, "But he, having come out, began . . . ."[51] Of the remaining 1411 cases, where ὁ, ἡ, τὸ represent the definite article, it is separated from its substantive only 91 times,[52] or less than 6.5%.

Since in both Hebrew and Aramaic the article is attached to the substantive itself (i.e., the prefixed h in Hebrew and the emphatic ending in Aramaic), the overwhelming percentage of the placement of the substantive immediately after its article in Mark is due to Semitic interference. Of course, no individual case of the noun and article together may be called a Semitism on this ground alone, but the lack of the separation of article and noun throughout the gospel adds strongly to its Semitic flavor.

(g) The Position of Unemphatic Personal Pronouns as Direct or Indirect Objects[53]

Although the more literary Hellenistic authors use personal pronouns as unemphatic direct or indirect objects very infrequently, the popular style of the non-literary papyri employs them often. For example, in Milligan's collection of papyri, numbers 1-49 (third century B.C. to third A.D.)[54] there are some 145 personal pronouns which express a direct or indirect object. Of these, 96 follow immediately the verb on which they depend, while 49 either come before the verb or are separated from it by some other word, a ratio of about two to one.

The Gospel of Mark contains 556 personal pronouns used in this way, but only 62 of them either precede the verb or are separated from it by another word, a ratio of about 7 immediately postpositive pronouns to one which is not.

In biblical Hebrew the non-emphatic pronominal direct object is either attached to the verb as a suffix, or expressed as a suffix on the particle ʾet, or occasionally as a suffix on the preposition l.[55] Except in emphatic usage these forms with ʾet and l come after the verb. All three forms are normally translated by the pronoun in the accusative case and follow the verb in the OG.

Qumran Hebrew is the same as biblical in this aspect: e.g.,
ybrknw, "he shall bless him" (1QS 9:26); *lhwšyʿ ʾtkmh*, "to save
you" (1QM 10:4-5), with the particle *ʾet*; *kʾšr ḥqq lhm*, "as he
ordered them" (1QpHab 7:13-14), using the preposition *l*. In the
Proto-Mishnaic Hebrew texts we have been studying there are no
examples of pronominal direct objects.

In Middle Aramaic an unemphatic pronominal direct object
may be expressed by the independent pronoun,[56] by a suffix
added to the verb, or by the suffixal form added to the preposition *l*. In all cases it comes after the verb: e.g., *wʾškḥ
ʾnwn*, "and he found them" (1QapGn 22:7); *lʿwrʿh*, "to meet him"
(1QapGn 22:13); *rdp lhwn*, "he pursued them" (1QapGn 22:9).

In biblical Aramaic the pronominal direct object is expressed by the verbal suffix or, less frequently, by a suffix
on the preposition *l*, or even by the independent personal pronoun (only in the third person plural, e.g., *ʾaḥēt himmô*, "put
them" [Ezra 5:15]) placed immediately after the verb. The
form with the preposition *l* may follow immediately after the
verb (Ezra 5:2; Dan 6:17, 21), but may also be placed first in
the clause for emphasis or contrast (Dan 4:22 [*bis*]), 29 [*bis*]
33; 7:14, 27). The OG (and Theodotionic Daniel) generally
keep the same word order as the Aramaic, translating by the
simple accusative of the pronoun for all three forms of the
Aramaic accusative. However, at times, when the Aramaic form
with *l* precedes the verb, the Greek places the pronoun immediately after the verb (OG Dan 4:32 [= Masoretic Text 4:29];
Theodotionic Dan 4:25, 32, 36 [= Masoretic Text 4:22, 29, 33]).

With regard to the unemphatic pronominal indirect object,
biblical Hebrew generally uses the preposition *l* with a suffix
following the verb, and sometimes even the verbal suffix.[57]
The OG usually translates with the simple dative, placed after
the verb: e.g., δώσω ὑμῖν, "I shall give you" (for Hebrew--
ʾettĕnāh lākem in Gen 45:18) and νενηστεύκατέ μοι, "Have you
fasted for me?" (for Hebrew--*ṣamtûnî* in Zech 7:5). Qumran
Hebrew generally uses the prepositional phrase with *l* after
the verb, e.g., *tglh lhm*, "it will be revealed to them" (1QpHab
11:1), as does Proto-Mishnaic Hebrew, e.g., *ttqn lhn*, "you
will prepare for them" (Mur *44* 4).

Middle Aramaic uses the preposition l with a suffix, normally placed after the verb, for the pronominal indirect object,
as well as the verbal suffix: e.g., $ymy^{\flat}$ $^{\flat}nh$ lk, "I swear to
you" (1QapGn 2:14)[58] and $t\dot{h}wynny$, "you must tell me" (1QapGn
2:6).[59]

In biblical Aramaic the pronominal indirect object is
usually expressed by a suffix on the preposition l, but the
verbal suffix may also be used. The indirect object expressed
with the preposition l usually follows immediately after the
verb (Jer 10:11; Ezra 4:14, 16; 5:3 [bis], 4, 9 [bis], 10, 15;
6:9; 7:19, 20; Dan 2:9, 16, 23, 25, 30, 46; 3:4, 14; 4:4, 6, 13,
32; 5:23; 6:3, 7, 11, 17, 23; 7:4 [bis], 5, 6, 7 [bis], 16, 20).
However, like the direct object, it is placed before the verb
for emphasis or contrast in Dan 2:23; 4:22, 23, 28, 33; 5:17;
7:6, 14, 27. The OG and Theodotion usually translate keeping
the same word order as the Aramaic, but sometimes place the
indirect pronominal object after the verb when it precedes it
in the Aramaic (OG Dan 4:25 [= Masoretic Text 4:22]; 7:6, 14;
Theodotionic Dan 5:17).

Since the postpositive position of pronominal direct and
indirect objects is notably higher in the Gospel of Mark than
even in the non-literary papyri, we conclude that this fact is
due to Semitic interference, either of Hebrew or Aramaic or
both. Although we may not claim that any single example of
such word order is a Semitism, such word order throughout a
given pericope may help to establish its Semitic provenience,
with consideration of all other factors.

(h) The Position of Demonstrative Adjectives

In Greek the position of the demonstrative adjectives is
either before the article and substantive or after the substantive (that is, the predicative position). By the first
century A.D., however, the position where the demonstrative
follows the substantive came to be preferred three to one in
the non-literary papyri.[60]

In biblical Hebrew the demonstrative adjectives are nor-
mally postpositive. Very rarely, as in Exod 32:1--zeh $m\bar{o}\check{s}eh$,
"this Moses," the demonstrative zeh can be prepositive.[61]
Qumran and Proto-Mishnaic Hebrew follow this general rule,

and no instance of prepositive adjectival *zeh* has yet turned
up.

In Aramaic, however, although the demonstrative adjectives
are usually postpositive, they may be placed before the substantive they modify since "sie ursprünglich Deutewörter allge-
meinster Art waren, denen das Substantiv dann als Apposition
folgte."[62] as in Ezra 5:4--*dĕnāh binyānāʾ*, "this building" and
Dan 2:32--*hûʾ ṣalmāʾ*, "this image." However, no such example
has yet come to light in Middle Aramaic.

Hence, there is nothing to be said for or against Semitic
interference in any individual text where a demonstrative follows its substantive in Mark. Such word order, however, remains
a factor in determining the general quality of a given pericope,
since its opposite (demonstrative adjective first) may help to
preclude direct translation or "thinking in Semitic" in that
particular instance.

2. Parataxis

(a) Coordination of Independent Clauses with Καί

A running style where independent clauses are strung together by the simple copula "and" (parataxis) and not subordinated to one another by means of participles, subordinating
conjunctions, and other particles (hypotaxis), is possible in
many Indo-European languages. It is generally agreed that
although the periodic (hypotactic) style is normal in Hellenistic literature, parataxis is quite possible in the Greek of
a writer whose literary education was minimal.[63] There are
many examples of paratactic καί in non-literary papyri,[64] and
even sporadic instances of it in Hellenistic historians and
other writers.[65] But no non-biblical (or non-biblically-related)
writing of any length even approaches Mark in his use of paratactic καί.[66] For example, Mark's preference for it over the
post-positive conjunction δέ is remarkable. Καί is used in
Mark 591 times to coordinate independent clauses (i.e., not
counting when it joins nouns, adjectives, adverbs, phrases,
infinitives, participles), while δέ occurs in the same usage
only 113 times.[67] Thus we can say that καί occurs roughly
5.2 times as often as δέ in this function. Now in Martin's
study of these two words used in this function, in passages

selected at random from Plutarch, Polybius, Epictetus, Josephus, and some 104 papyri, καί occurs only .24, .06, .44, .36, and .39 times, respectively, as often as δέ.[68] Even the Pauline epistles use καί only about half as often as δέ.[69]

In classical Hebrew, on the other hand, parataxis with *waw* is the rule in syntax, and the OG frequently translates this *waw* with the word καί. The statistics vary depending on the literalness of the translation of the various Old Testament books. Thus in Genesis (usually considered a fairly good Koine translation) chapters 1-4, 6, and 39, the ratio of καί to δέ is 6 to 1, while in the more literal translations of the Books of Kings we find the following ratios: 1Kgdms 17--58 to 1, and 2Kgdms 13--61 to 1.[70]

The Qumran Hebrew sectarian writings are in accord with biblical Hebrew in their use of parataxis using *waw*. Unfortunately, none of the Proto-Mishnaic material that we have been using contains narrative material which we can compare with biblical Hebrew with regard to parataxis.

The Middle Aramaic texts 1QapGn and the Enochic materials from Qumran Cave 4 all show that *waw* was used extensively to coordinate clauses. Biblical Aramaic also uses coordinating *waw* very frequently in narrative, and the OG and Theodotion translate literally with καί.

We conclude, then, that paratactic καί is found in Mark with such a high frequency (paralleled only by a minority of short, rudimentary papyri) that the likelihood of the influence of Hebrew and/or Aramaic in this matter of Mark's style is very high. Since in both Hebrew and Aramaic *waw* not only joins coordinate clauses, but also introduces what in more literary Greek would be subordinate clauses,[71] we must discuss further some types of paratactic clauses with καί as the connecting word which may not be possible even in the most elementary of the papyri.

(b) Καί Beginning a New Paragraph

Even in the highly paratactic non-biblical Greek texts mentioned above (nn. 64-65, p. 202), καί never begins a new paragraph, that is, a new story or line of thought. The Greek manner of introducing a new tract in a narrative is with

(μεν . . .) δέ, some other connecting particle(s), or no
particle at all.

In Mark 80 out of 88 or 89 paragraphs begins with καί.[72]
For the explanation we must turn to Hebrew. In biblical Hebrew
an independent narrative, or a new section of a narrative, may
be loosely connected to the foregoing by *waw* and the imperfect
of the verb. This *waw* is often translated by καί in the OG,
more often, of course, in the more literally translated books.
In the Qumran sectarian literature this use of *waw* is also the
rule in the introduction of new narrative sections, e.g., 1QS
1:16, 18, 21, 24; 2:1, 4, 11, and so on. As we have mentioned,
there is no narrative material in the published Proto-Mishnaic
Hebrew texts.

Middle Aramaic may use *waw* to begin a new section of a
narrative (e.g., 4QEn^c 1 xii 25, 4QEn^e 1 xxvi 18, 1QapGn 2:12,
23; 19:14, 17, 23, and so on), but, like biblical Aramaic, it
often uses an adverb, an adverbial expression, or a prepositional phrase without *waw* for the purpose: e.g., *b'dn* (1QapGn 2:3,
8, 19; 20:21, etc.; 4QLevi^b 2:11, 15); *h' b'dn* (1QapGn 2:1);
ywm' dn (1QapGn 21:5); *blyly'* (QapGn 20:12, 16).

Because Mark consistently uses καί to introduce a new paragraph, and because he does use the normal Greek particle δέ
in six of the remaining eight or nine paragraphs where he does
not use καί, his use of introductory καί is most likely a
Hebraism, probably taken over from the style of the OG, although
at some places it may represent Aramaic thinking or translation.

(c) Paratactic Καί to Introduce Logically Subordinate Clauses

Among the many examples of paratactic καί in the Gospel
of Mark, some of the clauses which are coordinated by that
particle seem to be logically subordinate to the previous
clause. But because subordinating conjunctions are not used
in these cases, it is difficult at times to determine the precise nuance of the relationship between the two clauses. For
this reason scholars differ in their interpretation of this
nuance. Moreover, there is always the danger of a subjective
reading into the Greek what seems to be better *in translation*.
Καί seems to introduce the following types of clauses:

(i) temporal or circumstantial (καί = "when; while"): καί
γίνεται κατακεῖσθαι αὐτὸν ἐν τῇ οἰκίᾳ αὐτοῦ, καὶ πολλοὶ τελῶναι
καὶ ἁμαρτωλοὶ συνανέκειντο τῷ Ἰησοῦ, "And it happened that he
was reclining in his [Levi's] house *while* many tax collectors
and sinners were reclining (at table) with Jesus" (2:15);
καὶ καθεύδῃ καὶ ἐγείρηται νύκτα καὶ ἡμέραν, καὶ ὁ σπόρος βλαστᾷ,
"he goes to sleep and rises night and day *while* the seed
sprouts" (4:27); ἦν δὲ ὥρα τρίτη καὶ ἐσταύρωσαν αὐτόν, "it was
the third hour *when* they crucified him" (15:25);

(ii) containing the result of or a sequence to the action
of the first clause (καί = "and then; and so"): οἵτινες
ἀκούουσιν τὸν λόγον καὶ παραδέχονται καὶ καρποφοροῦσιν, "who
hear the word and accept it *and then* bear fruit" (4:20);[73]
θεωροῦσιν τὸν δαιμονιζόμενον καθήμενον ἱματισμένον καὶ σωφρο-
νοῦντα, τὸν ἐσχηκότα τὸν λεγιῶνα, καὶ ἐφοβήθησαν, "they saw the
demoniac sitting there, clothed and in his right mind, the man
who had the legion, *and so* they were afraid" (5:15); καὶ διέβλε-
ψεν καὶ ἀπεκατέστη, καὶ ἐνέβλεπεν τηλαυγῶς ἅπαντα, "and he
looked intently and was restored, *and so* saw everything clearly"
(8:25); καὶ ἀράτω τὸν σταυρὸν αὐτοῦ, καὶ ἀκολουθείτω μοι, "and
let him take up his cross *and then* follow me" (8:34);[74] οὐδεὶς
γάρ ἐστιν ὃς ποιήσει δύναμιν ἐπὶ τῷ ὀνόματί μου καὶ δυνήσεται
ταχὺ κακολογῆσαί με, "For there is no one who will do a mighty
work in my name *and then* be able immediately afterward to
speak evil of me" (9:39). To this group must be added those
cases where an initial imperative is followed by καί and a
future indicative (Mk 1:17; 6:22; 10:21; 11:2, 24, 29; 14:13,
14-15);

(iii) relative (καί = "who"): ἦσαν γὰρ πολλοί, καὶ ἠκολού-
θουν αὐτῷ, "For there were many *who* were following him" (2:15);

(iv) adversative (καί = "but; and yet; nevertheless"):
καὶ πολλὰ παθοῦσα ὑπὸ πολλῶν ἰατρῶν καὶ δαπανήσασα τὰ παρ᾿
αὐτῆς πάντα, καὶ μηδὲν ὠφεληθεῖσα, "and who had suffered much
under many physicians and had spent all that she had, *and yet*
was no better" (5:26); βλέπεις τὸν ὄχλον συνθλίβοντά σε καὶ
λέγεις· τίς μου ἥψατο, "You see the crowd pressing you, *and yet*
you say 'Who touched me?'" (5:31); καὶ ἐζήτουν αὐτὸν κρατῆσαι,
καὶ ἐφοβήθησαν τὸν ὄχλον, "And they sought to arrest him, *but*
they feared the crowd" (12:12); ἐάν τινος ἀδελφὸς ἀποθάνῃ καὶ

καταλίπη γυναῖκα καὶ μὴ ἀφῇ τέκνον, "if someone's brother dies
and leaves a wife, *but* leaves no child" (12:19); καθ᾽ ἡμέραν
ἤμην πρὸς ὑμᾶς ἐν τῷ ἱερῷ διδάσκων, καὶ οὐκ ἐκρατήσατέ με,
"Every day I was with you in the temple teaching, *but* you did
not seize me" (14:49); πολλοὶ γὰρ ἐψευδομαρτύρουν κατ᾽ αὐτοῦ,
καὶ ἴσαι αἱ μαρτυρίαι οὐκ ἦσαν, "For many bore false witness
against him, *but* their witness did not agree" (14:56).

In non-literary Hellenistic Greek, especially that of the
non-official papyri, there are many examples of parataxis with
καί for what we may consider logically subordinate clauses,[75]
although the more literary Greek writers, like those of most
Indo-European languages, prefer hypotaxis with a variety of
particles, participles, and infinitive constructions.

In biblical Hebrew, too, the copula *waw* is used to join a
variety of logically subordinate clauses. A finite verb with
waw consecutive "is frequently employed with a certain emphasis
to introduce the apodosis after sentences which contain a condition, a reason, or a statement of time."[76] An example of the
temporal use of *waw* consecutive: *hinnēh yāmîm ba᾽îm nĕ᾽um yhwh
wĕkārattî ᾽et bêt yiśrā᾽ēl wĕ᾽et bêt yehûdā bĕrît ḥadāšā,*
"Behold, the days are coming, says YHWH, and [= "when"] I will
make a new covenant with the house of Israel and with the house
of Judah" (Jer 31:31). *Waw* consecutive may introduce a result:
wĕhinnēh miṣrayim nōsēāʿ ᾽aḥărêhem wayyîr᾽û, "And behold, the
Egyptians were marching after them, and [= "so"] they were
afraid" (Exod 14:10). Although relative clauses are usually
introduced by the relative particle *᾽ăšer,* "very frequently
the attributive relation is expressed by simple coordination"
with *waw* copulative,[77] e.g., *qārā᾽ yhwh lārāʿāb wĕgam bā᾽ ᾽el
hā᾽āreṣ,* "YHWH has called for a famine and [= "which"] will
come indeed upon the earth" (2 Kgs 8:1). *Waw* copulative may
also be used as an adversative particle,[78] e.g., *wĕteben lō᾽
yinnātēn lākem wĕtōken lĕbēnîm tittēhû,* "for no straw shall be
given to you, and [= "but"] you shall deliver the fixed number
of bricks" (Exod 5:18).

Qumran Hebrew also demonstrates these uses of the copula
waw, e.g., temporal: *ky᾽ hy᾽h ʿt ṣrh . . . wgwrl ᾽l bpdwt
ʿwlmym,* "For it will be a time of distress . . . and [= "when"]
the lot of God [will be set] in eternal redemption" (1QM 15:1);

consecutive: *kyᵓ bm bḥr ᵓl lbryt ʿwlmym . . . wᵓyn ʿwlh,*
"for God has chosen them for an eternal covenant . . . and
[= "and then"] evil will exist no more" (1QS 4:22-23); relative:
ᵓz yrṣh bkpwry nyḥwḥ lpny ᵓl whyth lw lbryt, "Then he will be
acceptable with agreeable expiation before God and [= "which"]
will be a covenant for him" (1QS 3:11); adversative: *wrwb*
ᵓnš⟨y⟩ šḥt lwᵓ ᵓtpwś ʿd ywm nqm wᵓpyᵓ lwᵓ ᵓšyb mᵓnšy ʿwlh,
"I will not seize the multitude of the men of the Pit until the
Day of Vengeance, and [= "but"] I will not remove my anger from
the men of wickedness" (1QS 10:19-20).

There are no clear examples of these uses of *waw* in the
scanty amount of published Proto-Mishnaic Hebrew material.

Examples of these types of coordination where one might
expect subordination abound in the Middle Aramaic of the Genesis
Apocryphon. Examples: temporal: *mᵓ ʿbdth ly bdyl [šr]y*
wtᵓmr ly, "What did you do to me for [Sar]ai's sake, and
[= "when"] you were telling me" (20:26); consequential: *ʿd kʿn*
lᵓ dbqth ltwrᵓ qdyšᵓ wngdt, "Up until now I had not reached
the holy mountain, and [= "so"] I set out" (19:8); relative:
blylyᵓ dn šlḥ lh ᵓl ʿlywn rwḥ mkdš lmktšh wlkwl ᵓnš byth rwḥ
bᵓyšᵓ whwᵓt ktšᵓ lh, "That night God Most High sent him a
pestilential spirit to afflict him and all the men of his
household, an evil spirit and it [= "that"] kept afflicting
him" (20:16-17); adversative: *whwᵓ kpnᵓ bᵓrʿᵓ dᵓ kwlᵓ wšmʿt*
dy ʿ[bw]rᵓ h[wᵓ] bmṣrym, "And there was a famine in all this
land, and [= "but"] I hear that [there was] gr[ai]n in Egypt"
(19:10).

Examples in biblical Aramaic: temporal: *ûmannî ʿal*
ʿăbîdtāᵓ dî mĕdînat bābel lĕšadrak mêšak waʿăbēd nĕgô wĕdānîyeᵓl
bitraʿ malkāᵓ, "and he (the king) set Shadrach, Meshach, and
Abed-nego over the affairs of the province of Babylon and
[= "while"] Daniel (remained) at the king's court" (Dan 2:49);[79]
consequential: *wĕlēh yĕhîb šolṭān wîqār ûmalkû wĕkol ʿammayyāᵓ*
ᵓumayyāᵓ wĕliššānayyāᵓ lēh yiplĕḥûn, "And to him was given
dominion and glory and kingdom and [= "so that"] all peoples,
nations, and languages should serve him" (Dan 7:14); relative:
wĕqarnāᵓ dikkēn wĕ ʿaynîn lah ûpum mĕmallil rabrĕbān wĕhezwah
rab min ḥabrātah, "and that horn and [= "which"] had eyes and
[= "whose"] mouth spoke great things and [= "whose"] appearance

was greater than its companions" (Dan 7:20); adversative:
malkû pĕlîgâ tehĕwēh ûmin niṣbĕtā' dî parzēlā' lehĕwēh bah,
"it shall be a divided kingdom, and [= "but"] some of the firm-
ness of iron shall be in it" (Dan 2:41).

The OG (and Theodotion) generally translates *waw* in both
Hebrew and Aramaic by καί, as it does in every example cited
above.

Since parataxis for these types of logically subordinate
clauses is possible in Greek, even though more common in Hebrew
and Aramaic, none of the Marcan examples given above can be
definitely labelled a Semitism. Moreover, Matthew rarely
changes the Marcan text when he takes over these sentences
with paratactic καί, while Luke uses more literary conjunctions
somewhat more frequently when reproducing such Marcan verses.
However, there always remains the possibility that the abundant
use of καί in the Marcan text is derived from a Semitic *Vorlage*
where this parataxis is even more at home.

(d) Καί Introducing the Apodosis of a Conditional Sentence

In Greek no conjunction is normally used at the beginning
of the apodosis of a conditional sentence.[80] Yet in the Gospel
of Mark we find this role assigned to the conjunction καί
twice, perhaps three times: ὅς γὰρ ἐὰν ἐπαισχυνθῇ με καὶ τοὺς
ἐμοὺς λόγους ἐν τῇ γενεᾷ ταύτῃ τῇ μοιχαλίδι καὶ ἁμαρτωλῷ, καὶ
ὁ υἱὸς τοῦ ἀνθρώπου ἐπαισχυνθήσεται αὐτόν, "For whoever is
ashamed of me and my words in this adulterous and sinful generation, *and* the son of man will be ashamed of him" (8:38);
ὅπου ἐὰν κηρυχθῇ τὸ εὐαγγέλιον εἰς ὅλον τὸν κόσμον, καὶ ὃ
ἐποίησεν αὕτη λαληθήσεται, "Whenever the gospel is preached in
the whole world, *and* what she has done will be told" (14:9);
ἐὰν εἴπῃ ἄνθρωπος τῷ πατρὶ ἤ τῇ μητρί· κορβᾶν . . . , καὶ οὐκέτι
ἀφίετε, "If a man say to his father or mother 'Korban' . . . ,
and you no longer permit" (7:11-12 p[45]𝔎 A W). When Matthew
and Luke use these verses in their gospels, they omit the καί
of the apodosis in every case.

We must turn to the Semitic languages for the explanation
of this phenomonon. In biblical Hebrew "the perfect consecutive is frequently employed with a certain emphasis to introduce
the apodosis after sentences which contain a condition.[81]

For example, ʾim lōʾ yittĕnû lak wĕhāyîtā nāqî mēʾālātî, "if they
do not give to you *and* you will be free from my oath" (Gen 24:41).
The OG renders this sentence literally--ἐάν μή σοι δῶσιν καὶ ἔσῃ
ἀθῷος ἀπὸ τοῦ ὁρκισμοῦ μου. But the Greek translators omit the
superfluous καί at Gen 18:26; 24:8; 32:9 and very often.

Waw of the apodosis is also used in Qumran Hebrew, for example, at 1QS 7:1--ʾm qll . . . whbdylhw, "if he has blasphemed
. . . *and* let them separate him." The same use of *waw* turns up
in the Proto-Mishnaic Hebrew of the contract Mur 24 B 11-12--
bšlʾ ᶜwsh . . . whwrd, "if he does not cultivate . . . *and* he
will be sent back." Cf. C 10 and D 12 in the same papyrus.

This use of *waw* exists also in Middle Aramaic in the marriage contract Mur 21 1-3 vss. 10-11--whn b[nn yhyn lk mny] /
knmsʾ wh[nn y]hyh ytbn byty, "and if [you have] dau[ghters by me]
according to law *and* t[hey shall] reside in my house." Waw of
the apodosis after the conditional hēn never occurs in biblical
Aramaic.

Hence καί of the apodosis in Mk 8:28; 14:9 and 7:11-12
(P⁴⁵ ℵ A W may have the correct text here as the *lectio difficilior*) is the result of either Hebrew or Aramaic[82] interference
in the sources or the thinking of the author of the gospel.

(e) Καί Introducing an Incredulous Question

In the Gospel of Mark there are five examples where the conjunction καί introduces an independent clause which contains a
question expressing surprise or irony to what has gone before:

οὐκ οἴδατε τὴν παραβολὴν ταύτην, καὶ πῶς πάσας τὰς παραβολὰς
γνώσεσθε; "You do not understand this parable, *and* how will
you know all the parables?" (4:13);

Ἠλίας μὲν ἐλθὼν πρῶτον ἀποκαθιστάνει πάντα καὶ πῶς γέγραπται
ἐπὶ τὸν υἱὸν τοῦ ἀνθρώπου ἵνα πολλὰ πάθῃ; "Elijah, coming
first, restores all things, *and* how is it written of the son
of man that he should suffer all things?" (9:12);

οἱ δὲ περισσῶς ἐξεπλήσσοντο λέγοντες πρὸς ἑαυτούς· καὶ τίς
δύναται σωθῆναι; "And they were extremely astonished, saying
to him '*And* who can be saved?'" (10:26);

ἐν ποίᾳ ἐξουσίᾳ ταῦτα ποιεῖς; καὶ τίς σοι ἔδωκεν τὴν
ἐξουσίαν ταύτην; "By what authority are you doing these
things? *And* who gave you this authority?" (11:28 ℵ A W T

Γ Φ λ φ lat syr^{sp} bo^{pt});

αὐτὸς Δαυὶδ λέγει αὐτὸν κύριον, καὶ πόθεν αὐτοῦ ἐστιν υἱός;
"David himself calls him lord, *and* how is he his son?"
(12:37).[83]

The use of καί to introduce an ironic question is quite
possible in Greek and can be traced in that language from Homer
to the later papyri.[84]

In biblical Hebrew a question is usually introduced by the
interrogative particle *h*, but it may also be expressed without
it, interrogative pronouns, or adverbs "especially when the
interrogative clause is connected with a preceding sentency by
wě,"[85] e.g., Judg 11:23--*wě ʾattāh tîrāšennû*, "and will you take
possession of him?" after "the Lord dispossessed the Amorite"
(Judg 11:23). The OG does not always translate as an ironic
question introduced by καί (cf. Jon 4:11; Exod 8:22; Isa 37:11;
44:11 and often) but does so in Judg 11:23--καὶ σὺ κληρονομήσεις
αὐτόν;.

An example of an ironic question introduced by *waw* in Qumran Hebrew is 1QH 1:25--*wmh yspr ʾnwš ḥṭʾtw*, "and how can a man
count up his sins?" after the description of the omniscience
of God in lines 21-25.

Unfortunately, there are no interrogative sentences in the
Proto-Mishnaic Hebrew material.

The conjunction *waw* introduces two questions of surprise
in the Middle Aramaic of 1QapGn 22:32-33--*wlmʾ ly kwl [ʾ]ln* and
wḥd mn bny byty yrtnny, "*and* why do I have all these things?"
"*and* shall one of my household servants inherit me?" after
line 32, "My wealth and flocks are vast." An example in biblical Aramaic: "You shall immediately be thrown into a fiery
furnace, *and* who is the god *(ûman hûʾ ʾĕlāh)* who will deliver
you out of my hands?" (Dan 3:15). Both the OG and Theodotion
use καί.

Thus καί introducing the ironic question in Mk 4:13; 9:12;
10:26; 11:28 (possibly the original reading) and 12:37 is
idiomatic Hellenistic Greek. This does not mean, however, that
it could not reflect imitation of the OG or literal translation
or thinking in Aramaic or post-biblical Hebrew.

(f) Coordinate Use of the Subjunctive after (i) an Imperative,
    (ii) θέλειν

(i) after an imperative

     In Mark 1:44, ὅρα μηδενὶ μηδὲν εἴπῃς has been considered
to be a coordinate use of the subjunctive εἴπῃς after the imperative ὅρα.[86] Μηδενὶ μηδὲν εἴπῃς, however, is not coordinated
with ὅρα, but is an object clause dependent on the verb of
caution ὅρα. In both classical and Hellenistic Greek such a
verb may take either μή or ὅπως μή with the subjunctive to express what is cautioned: e.g., ὁρᾶτε μὴ πάθωμεν, "take care
lest we suffer" (Xenophon, Cyr. 4.1.15); ὅρα οὖν μὴ αὐτὸν
κατάσχῃς, "see then that you do not detain him" (BGU 1.37.5).[87]
Μηδενὶ in Mk 1:44 is the equivalent of μή in pronominal form.
     There is no exact equivalent of this type of clause in
either Aramaic or Hebrew. The imperative of ὁράω followed by
μή and an object clause occurs twice in the OG, but in both
cases the subordinate verb is in the indicative: ὅρα μὴ ἐν
ἐμοὶ κατοικεῖς, "see that you do not settle near me" (Josh 9:7);
ὁρᾶτε μὴ πληγὴν ἄλλην ἐπάξω ἐγώ, "see that I do not lay on
another blow" (Exod 33:5). In both cases there is no Hebrew
equivalent in the Masoretic Text.
     Hence Mk 1:44--ὅρα μηδενὶ μηδὲν εἴπῃς is perfectly good
Greek and is not a literal translation of either Aramaic or
Hebrew.

(ii) after θέλειν

     Τί θέλετέ με ποιήσω (Mk 10:36),[88] τί σοι θέλεις ποιήσω
(10:51), and ποῦ θέλεις . . . ἑτοιμάσωμεν (14:12) have been
considered to be constructions in which a subjunctive is coordinated with indicative forms of θέλειν.[89] This is not so;
rather, the second verb in each example is a deliberative subjunctive dependent on the verb θέλειν. This construction was
already common in classical Greek, where both βούλεσθαι and
θέλειν could take such a subjunctive either with or without
the subordinating conjunction ἵνα.[90] Commentators usually explain Mk 10:36 as "mixing two [Greek] constructions, τί θέλετέ
με ποιῆσαι and τί θέλετε ποιήσω.[91]
     Biblical Hebrew almost always uses an infinitive after
the verbs of wishing ʾbh, ḥpṣ, mʾn, ṣʾl, e.g., ʾābîtem laʿalot,

"you want to go up" (Deut 1:26); ḥāpēṣ laʿăśot, "he wanted to
do" (1 Kgs 9:1); wayĕmāʾēn . . . nĕton, "and he wanted . . . to
give" (Num 20:21); wayyišʾal . . . lamût, "and he wanted . . .
to die" (1 Kgs 19:4). The OG translates literally in these
four cases as it normally does, namely, with an infinitive.
This, of course, is also good Greek.

Qumran Hebrew uses the words ḥpṣ and mʾn to mean "to
wish" (šʾl always means "to ask"). Ḥpṣ takes a complementary
clause both times it is used, using the particles ʾšr and ky
to introduce imperfect forms of the verb: my gwy ḥpṣ ʾšr yʿws-
qnw, "What people desires that they oppress it?" (1Q27 1 i 10)
and my yḥpṣ ky ygzl, "Who will wish that he steal?" (1 i 10-11).
Mʾn takes an infinitive construction as in the Old Testament:
lwʾ ymʾnw lšwb, "they do not wish to turn away" (4QpPsᵃ 2:2).
There are no examples of this in the Proto-Mishnaic Hebrew
material.

In the Genesis Apocryphon the verb bʿ is used four times
in the sense "to want to do something": wbʿwn lmqṣ, "they
wanted to cut down" (19:15); ybʿwn lmqṭlny, "they will seek to
kill me" (19:19); wbʿ lmqṭlny, "he sought to kill me" (20:9);
wbʿ mny dy ʾth, "and he wanted me to come" (20:21). In the
first three cases an infinitive expresses what is wanted to be
done, while in the last it is expressed by the particle dy
and a finite verb.[92] With the exception of Dan 2:49, biblical
Aramaic uses the verb bʿ in the same manner as Middle Aramaic,
namely, it is followed by l and an infinitive (Dan 2:13; 6:5) or
by dî and a finite verb (Dan 2:16). In Dan 2:49, we have seen
above (in section c) that bʿ is coordinated with a finite verb
by the conjunction waw , although the latter clause is logically
an object clause. This waw has been translated logically by
ἵνα in the OG. Biblical Aramaic also uses the word ṣbʾ for "to
wish, to want" in Dan 4:14, 22, 29, 32; 5:19 (quater), 21, but
here the verb never governs a subsequent clause.

We conclude that Mk 10:36--τί θέλετέ με ποιήσω, 10:51--
τί σοι θέλεις ποιήσω, and 14:12--ποῦ θέλεις . . . ἑτοιμάσωμεν
are examples of idiomatic Greek and that there is no literal
parallel for the phrase in contemporary Semitic writing or in
the OG.

(g) Asyndeton

M. Black has argued for Aramaic interference in the frequent use of asyndeton in Mark, claiming that "asyndeton is, on
the whole, contrary to the spirit of the Greek language."[93]
In order to discuss the question properly we must point out that
there are four types of asyndetic coordination in Mark:

(1) where direct discourse is set down after a verb of
saying without an introductory particle, e.g., Mk 2:8, 9, 17,
25; 3:34; 4:24; 5:39; 6:38; 8:2, 15, 29; 9:24, 38; 10:14, 24,
27, 28; 11:28; 12:36; 14:6, 19, 61, 63; 16:6;[94]

(2) where two sentences are joined without conjunction
or other linking word(s), e.g., 1:8, 27; 2:7, 21; 3:35; 4:24,
28; 5:35; *8:19, 29;* 9:24, *38;* 10:25, *27, 28, 29;* 11:30; 12:9,
20, 23, *24,* 27, *29,* 31, 32, 36, *36, 37;* 13:5, 6, 7, 8 (*ter*),
9, 15, 23, 34; 14:*3,* 6, 8 (*bis*), *19,* 41, 44, 64 (*bis*); 16:6
(*bis*);[95]

(3) where two imperatives are set down side by side, asyndetically, e.g., 2:11--ἔγειρε ἆρον; 4:39--σιώπα πεφίμωσο;
6:38--ὑπάγετε ἴδετε; 8:15--ὁρᾶτε βλέπετε; 10:14--ἄφετε . . . μὴ
κωλύετε; 14:42--ἐγείρεσθε ἄγωμεν (a hortatory subjunctive);

(4) the unusual case of Mk 2:7--τί οὗτος οὕτως λαλεῖ
βλασφημεῖ where two indicatives are set down side by side without connecting particle.
The Greek evidence with regard to asyndeton is the following:

(1) Direct discourse without an introductory particle, of
course, has never been claimed as a Semitism. It is good Greek
and has been in use from Homer to the present day.

(2) While the placing of sentences together asyndetically
"is repugnant by and large to the spirit of the [classical!]
Greek language,"[96] there are certain instances where it was normal, especially in rhetoric, as well as with verbs of saying
which introduce direct discourse.[97] In Hellenistic Greek, however, asyndeton (which is, after all, a common feature of language in general) becomes very frequent in a variety of writers.[98]

(3) Asyndetic imperatives are not unknown in classical
Greek, although there the normal usage would be a subordinating
aorist participle with an imperative or even the conjunction καί
connecting the two imperatives. In Hellenistic Greek, however,
the construction is common.[99]

(4) As it stands, Mk 2:7 is perfectly intelligible Greek:
"What is this man thus saying? He blasphemes!" i.e., the second
verb is a short sentence joined asyndetically to the previous
one.

Biblical Hebrew generally subjoins direct discourse without
any introductory particle. Asyndeton between sentences is
found mainly in "poetic and otherwise elevated style."[100] "Assez
souvent un developpement explicatif est ajouté asyndétiquement,"[101]
e.g., *dābēq lō' sār mimmennâ*, "he clung [to the sin of Jeroboam],
he did not depart from it" (2 Kgs 3:3). This is translated
literally in the Greek--ἐκολλήθη οὐκ ἀπέστη ἀπ' αὐτῆς, (4 Kgdms
3:3). In asyndeton "the imperatives *qûm* and *lēk* [from *hālak*]
are exceedingly common with the sense of interjections, before
verbs which express a movement or other action."[102] For example,
qûm rîb, "rise, judge" (Mic 6:1); *lek rēd*, "go, get down"
(Exod 19:24); with a following cohortative (cf. Mk 14:42) *lěkāh
nikrětāh*, "come, let us make [a covenant]" (Gen 31:44). The
Greek translates some of these verses literally: ἀνάστηθι
κρίθητι (Mic 6:1); βάδιζε κατάβηθι (Exod 19:24); but very often
it puts the first Hebrew imperative in the aorist participle
(e.g., Gen 13:17; 19:15; 27:43; Josh 1:2; Judg 8:20) or adds
the conjunction καί before the second imperative (e.g., Gen 19:14;
3 Kgdms [= Hebrew 1 Kgs] 19:5; Ezek 3:22; 1 Kgdms [= Hebrew
1 Sam] 9:10 with a cohortative). With regard to the fourth type
of asyndeton we are discussing (cf. Mk 2:7), two indicatives
are placed side by side without a conjunction in biblical Hebrew, usually in elevated style and where the first verb is one
of movement,[103] e.g., (in a poetic discourse of Jacob) *kāra'
rābaṣ*, "he stooped, he couched" (Gen 49:9); (in the oracle of
Balaam) *kāra' šākab*, "he stooped, he lay down" (Num 24:9);
(in the Song of Deborah) *kāra' nāpal šākāb*, "he stooped, he fell,
he lay down" (Judg 5:27). The OG prefers to translate the first
verb as a participle in all these instances (many textual witnesses of Judges use the indicative, but join the last two
verbs in this text with καί).

In Qumran Hebrew direct discourse may also lack an introductory particle, e.g., *w'wmrym ybrkkh*, "and saying: 'May he
bless you'" (1QS 2:2). Asyndeton in narrative prose is much
more common in Qumran Hebrew than in biblical, e.g., 1QS 2:7,

8, 9, 15 (*bis*), 17, 19 and so on; 1QM 1:1, 2, [8], 10, 11 and
so on. A good example of asyndeton with imperatives is the
long invocation in 1QM 12:10-14, although some of these are
joined syndetically--*qwmh* . . . *šbh* . . . *wšwl* . . . *tn* . . .
mhṣ . . . *ml⁾* . . . *šmhy* . . . *whwpyᶜy* . . . *whglnh* . . . *pthy*,
"arise . . . lead away . . . *and* plunder . . . set . . . strike
. . . fill . . . rejoice . . . *and* appear . . . *and* show . . .
open." Related finite verbs are strung together in 1QS 1:24-25
--*nᶜwynw* [*pšᶜnw ḥṭ*]*⁾nw hršᶜnw*, "we have been sinful, [we have
rebelled,] we have s[inned,] we have been wicked."

    In Proto-Mishnaic Hebrew it is possible to introduce direct
discourse without an introductory particle, e.g., Mur *24* B 5-6.
Sentences are often set down asyndetically in the Proto-Mishnaic
Hebrew contracts and letters from Murabbaᶜat: Mur *24* C 8, [10],
11, [13], 18; D 8, 10; *30* ii 10, 16, 17; *42* 2, 7; *43* 3, 4; *44*
6, 8; *45* 2, 8. There are examples of asyndeton imperatives in
the letter of Simon bar Kokebah: *yhw* (a jussive) . . . *hzw*
"let them be . . . see to it" (Mur *44* 5); *whthzq whzq* . . . *hw⁾*,
"*and* be courageous *and* be strong . . . be" (7-8). Finally,
there is nothing in the Proto-Mishnaic Hebrew material comparable
to the asyndeton in Mk 2:7.

    In Middle Aramaic direct discourse may be set down with-
out any introductory particle, as it is throughout 4QᶜAmramᵇ.
Asyndeton as a means of coordinating sentences, however, is a
different matter. In all the published Middle Aramaic material
(apart from the Aramaic translation of the Book of Job in
11QtgJob) there is only one example of such asyndeton: *zbnt lk*,
"I have sold you" (papHevB ar 5). All other sentences (except
for the beginning of contracts) start with the coordinating
conjunction *waw*, some other particle such as *b⁾dyn* (e.g., 4QLevi
ii 11), *⁾dyn* (e.g., 1QapGn 2:8), *⁾ry* (e.g., 4QEnAstrᵃ 6), or
some time designation such as in 4QEnAstrᵇ 1, *blyl⁾ dn*, "during
that night." Asyndetic imperatives, *⁾zl ⁾mr*, "go, tell" and
qwm hlk, "rise, walk," turn up in 1QapGn 20:23 and 21:13. In
addition to verbs of motion (as in biblical Hebrew), other
finite verbs in Aramaic may be followed immediately and asyndetically be verbs "die einheitliche oder einmittelbar aneinander
anschliessende Handlungen bezeichnen."[104] Examples from Middle
Aramaic: *šlḥ lᶜwbᶜ dbrh⁾*, "he sent off in haste, he had her

brought" (1QapGn 20:8-9); *šlḥ qr³*, "he sent, he called" (20:18-
19); *³zl ³mr*, "he went, he said" (20:24); *qm [³w]d⁶*, "he rose,
he [made] known" (20:29); *šlḥt qryt*, "I sent, I called" (21:21).

In biblical Aramaic direct discourse may occur without
an introductory particle, e.g., *wa³āmar lēh ³ēlleh ma³nayyā
šē³*, "and he said to him: 'Take these vessels'" (Ezra 5:15),
translated literally in the OG. Although sentences are usually
coordinated by *waw* or introduced by a temporal adverb or some
other adverbial expression, asyndeton between sentences is not
infrequent in biblical Aramaic, e.g., Ezra 4:16, 17; Dan 3:1;
5:2. The OG avoids asyndeton by adding καί at the beginning of
Ezra 4:17; Dan 3:1; 5:2, as does Theodotion in Dan 3:1 and 5:2.
Imperatives are coordinated asyndetically after the imperatives
³ēzel and *qûm*, e.g., *³ēzel ³āḥēt himmô*, "go, put them" (Ezra
5:15); *qûmî ³ăkulî*, "rise, eat" (Dan 7:5). The OG translates
the second imperative by an aorist participle in 2 Esdr 5:15:
πορεύου θὲς αὐτά, while both the OG and Theodotion translate
Dan 7:5 literally: ἀνάστα κατάφαγε (OG) and ἀνάστηθι φάγε
(Theodotion). As in Middle Aramaic, verbs whose actions are
closely related may be placed together without conjunction,[105]
e.g., *³ēdayin šešbassar dek ³ātā³ yěhab ³uššayyā³*, "Then this
Sheshbazzar came, he laid the foundations" (Ezra 5:16). The
OG avoids asyndeton by adding καί here: τότε Σασαβασαρ ἐκεῖνος
ἦλθεν καὶ ἔδωκεν. Hence there may be a definite prejudice against
asyndeton in the Greek translations of the Old Testament,
probably due to the influence of the Hebrew parts of the Old
Testament.

We conclude (1) that direct discourse in Mark, which is
set down after a verb of saying and without an introductory
particle, is obviously good Greek, but that there is no evidence
to deny that it could be literal translation from a Semitic
source or imitation of the OG. (2) Asyndeton between sentences
was common in Hellenistic Greek. In this usage Mark is showing
his preference for "le style plus rapide, et par suite plus
expressif,"[106] over against Matthew and Luke who usually add
καί, δὲ οὖν, γάρ, or some other particle. This stylistic feature of Mark is hardly an Aramaism, in view of the evidence
presented above (*pace* Black *et al.*), and does not reflect
imitation of the OG. However, it is interesting to note that

this same feature of style is quite common in the post-biblical
Hebrew of Qumran and of the later Proto-Mishnaic Hebrew documents from Murabbaᶜat.

(3) With regard to asyndetic imperatives, we conclude with
Colwell that "the Greek readers of John's gospel [and Mark's]
found nothing unusual in his employment of an occasional asyndeton imperative."[107] We point out, however, that the vocabulary
of Mk 2:11--ἔγειρε ἆρον, and 14:42--ἐγείρεσθε ἄγωμεν may be considered a lexical Semitism since the Hebrew and Aramaic equivalent of ἔγειρε, namely *qwm/qm*, is often used in precisely this
fashion (see Mic 6:1; 1QM 12:10; 1QapGn 21:13 cited above),
while this pleonastic imperative (ἔγειρε) is not used in
Greek.[108]

(4) From what we have seen above, we conclude that τί
οὗτος οὕτως λαλεῖ βλασφημεῖ (Mk 2:7) is not necessarily the result of Semitic interference. This saying, however, could be
a literal translation of an Aramaic or post-biblical Hebrew
source.

3. Constructions with καὶ ἐγένετο

In the Gospel of Mark there are four verses in which the
phrase καὶ ἐγένετο, "and it happened (that)" (or, in one case,
the equivalent form with the historical present καὶ γίνεται,
"and it happened that") serves to introduce a past event:

καὶ ἐγένετο ἐν ἐκείναις ταῖς ἡμέραις ἦλθεν Ἰησοῦς ἀπὸ
Ναζαρέθ, "And it happened in those days (that) Jesus came
from Nazareth" (1:9);[109]

καὶ γίνεται κατακεῖσθαι αὐτὸν ἐν τῇ οἰκίᾳ αὐτοῦ καὶ πολλοὶ
τελῶναι καὶ ἁμαρτωλοὶ συνανέκειντο τῷ Ἰησοῦ, "And it
happened (that) he was reclining (at table) in his
[Levi's] house and many tax collectors and sinners were
sitting with Jesus" (2:15);

καὶ ἐγένετο αὐτὸν ἐν τοῖς σάββασιν παραπορεύεσθαι διὰ τῶν
σπορίμων καὶ οἱ μαθηταὶ αὐτοῦ ἤρξαντο ὁδὸν ποιεῖν, "And it
happened (that) he was going through the grainfields on
the Sabbath and his disciples began to make their way"
(2:23);

καὶ ἐγένετο ἐν τῷ σπείρειν ὃ μὲν ἔπεσεν παρὰ τὴν ὁδόν, "And
it happened when he sowed (that) some fell on the path" (4:4).

The normal Greek construction which expresses the occurrence of a past event, "it happened that . . . , it came to
pass that . . ." was, from classical times, some form of the
verb συμβαίνειν followed by an infinitive,[110] e.g., συνέβη τῆς
αὐτῆς ἡμέρης ἔν τε τῇ Σικελίῃ Γέλωνα καὶ Θήρωνα νικᾶν Ἀμίλκαν,
"It happened on the same day that Gelon and Theron defeated
Amilcas in Sicily" (Herodotus 7.166; cf. 3.50; 6.103); καὶ
ξυνέβη ἐν τῇ μάχῃ ταύτῃ τοὺς Ἴωνας ἀμφοτέρων τῶν Δωριῶν
κρατῆσαι, "And it happened in this battle that the Ionians were
victorious over both (sides) of the Dorians" (Thucydides 8.25.5).
This construction was widely used in Hellenistic Greek, too,
e.g., συνέβη τεθῆναι αὐτήν, "It happened that she was appointed"
(PMagd. 12.5); συνέβη καὶ πόλιν καὶ ἄκραν καθ᾽ ἡμᾶς γενέσθαι,
"It happened that both the city and the hilltop came into our
power" (PPetr. 2.45.11). Similarly, in the books of the OG
which were originally composed in Greek: καὶ μετὰ πᾶσαν τὴν
πρᾶξιν ταύτην Ιωσιου συνέβη Φαραω βασιλέα Αἰγύπτου ἐλθόντα
πόλεμον ἐγεῖραι ἐν Χαρκαμυς, "And after all this activity of
Josiah it happened that Pharoah, king of Egypt, having arrived,
stirred up war in Carchemish" (1 Esdr 1:23); καὶ ἐν τῷ ἔτει τῷ
δευτέρῳ τῆς βασιλείας Ναβουχοδονοσορ συνέβη εἰς ὁράματα καὶ
ἐνύπνια ἐμπεσεῖν τὸν βασιλέα, "And in the second year of the
reign of Nebuchadnezzar it happened that the king fell into
visions and dreams" (Dan 2:1--lacking in the Hebrew text of
Daniel); and frequently in 2 and 3 Maccabees (2 Macc 3:2; 4:30;
5:2, 18; 9:7; 10:5; 12:34; 13:7; 3 Macc 1:3, 5, 8; 4:19).
Cf. συνέβη βαστάζεσθαι αὐτὸν ὑπὸ τῶν στρατιωτῶν, "It happened
that he was carried by the soldiers" (Acts 21:35).[111] In this
Hellenistic phase of Greek the verb γίνεσθαι was also used
impersonally to mean "it is possible that; it happens/may
happen that," e.g., γίνεται γὰρ ἐντραπῆναι, "For it happens
that one is ashamed" (PPar. 49.29). It, too, was frequently
followed by a dative or an accusative with infinitive, e.g.,
σοὶ δὲ γίνοιτο εὐημερεῖν, "May it happen that you succeed"
(PLond. 1.21.29); ἐὰν γένηται ἡμᾶς μὴ ὑπογύως ἀναπλεῖν, "If it
should happen that we do not sail up suddenly" (PAmh. 2.135.10).[112]
However, in texts of the classical and Hellenistic periods of
the Greek language neither the aorist indicative nor the historical present of γίνεσθαι is ever used with a finite verb

(with or without καί) or with an infinitive to introduce a past
event: "It happened that X (occurred)."[113]

   In biblical Hebrew, on the other hand, the narration of
an event was often introduced by the verb "to be" used impersonally with *waw* conversive: (a) The imperfect form *wayĕhî*,
generally followed by some temporal expression,[114] serves to
introduce "eine einmalige Handlung in der Vergangenheit."[115]
This past action is most frequently expressed (about 75% of the
time) in Hebrew by a following imperfect form of the verb with
waw conversive,[116] e.g., *wayĕhî bĕšahēt ᵓĕlōhîm ᵓet ᶜārē
hakkikār wayyizkor ᵓelōhîm ᵓet ᵓabrāhām*, "And it happened as
God destroyed the cities of the valley that (literally, "and")
God remembered Abraham" (Gen 19:29). At times the past action
may have a durative or iterative nuance by way of exception
to the rule where a simple past action would be expected,[117]
e.g., *wayĕhî bĕredet mōšeh mēhar sînai ûšĕnē luhōt hāᶜēdut bĕyad
mōšeh bĕridtô min hāhār ûmōšeh lōᵓ yādaᶜ*, "And it happened
when Moses descended from Mount Sinai (and the two tables of
the testimony [were] in the hand of Moses in his descent from
the mountain) that (literally, "and") Moses did not know (that
the skin of his face shone)" (Exod 34:29); *wayĕhî kĕdabbĕrāh
ᵓel yôsēp yôm yôm wĕlōᵓ šāmaᶜ ᵓēle(y)hā*, "And it happened that
when she spoke to Moses day after day that (literally, "and")
he did not hear her" (Gen 39:10). Beyer claims that the few
examples of the construction with the durative or iterative
nuance have come about through the conflation of source texts
in the compilation of the canonical books or through the mis-
reading of the perfect form *wĕhāyāh* as the imperfect form
wayĕhî.[118]

   (b) The perfect form *wĕhāyāh* is also used to introduce
events of the past, but these are always actions which are
frequently repeated (iterative),[119] e.g., *wĕhāyāh ᵓim zāraᶜ
yiśrāᵓēl wĕᶜālāh midyān*, "And it happened whenever Israel
sowed seed that (literally, "and") Midian came up (and attacked
him)" (Judg 6:3; cf. Exod 17:11; 1 Sam 16:23).

   The impersonal construction where *wayĕhî* introduces a past
event is usually translated in the OG by καί ἐγένετο.[120] The
past event itself (expressed in Hebrew by an imperfect with
waw conversive) is generally rendered in the Greek by καί and

the aorist, e.g., καὶ ἐγένετο ἐν τῷ εἶναι αὐτους ἐν τῷ πεδίῳ
καὶ ἀνέστη Καιν ἐπὶ Αβελ, "And it happened when they were in the
plain that (literally, "and") Cain rose up against Abel" (Gen
4:8). The Greek translators sometimes omitted the second "and"
in the Hebrew (especially in the books of Genesis and Exodus),
e.g., καὶ ἐγένετο ἐν τῷ ἐκτρῖψαι κύριον πάσας τὰς πόλεις τῆς
περιοίκου ἐμνήσθη ὁ θεὸς τοῦ Αβρααμ, "And it happened, when the
Lord destroyed the cities of the vicinity, (that) God remembered
Abraham" (Gen 19:29).[121] Καὶ ἐγένετο is also the normal translation for the Hebrew construction where the perfect of the
verb "to be" with *waw* (*wĕhāyāh*) introduces an iterative action
in the past,[122] e.g., καὶ ἐγένετο ὅταν ἔσπειρεν ἀνὴρ Ισραηλ καὶ
ἀνέβαινεν Μαδιαμ, "And it happened when an Israelite sowed that
(literally, "and") Midian used to come up" (Judg 6:3; Manuscript
B has καὶ ἐγένετο ἐὰν ἔσπειραν, etc.). The construction where
καὶ ἐγένετο introduces a past event which, in turn, is expressed by an infinitive, never occurs in the OG.[123]

In the Qumran sectarian documents the verb "to be" is
never used impersonally to introduce a past event. In fact,
the verb "to be" is used impersonally only twice in all this
literature, and both times it has a future nuance: *whyh bšwmᶜw
ʾt dbry hbryt hzwt ytbrk*, "and it will be when he hears the
words of this covenant (that) he will bless himself" (1QS 2:12-
13); *whyh kyʾ yᶜrwkw hšwlḥn lʾkwl ʾw htyrwš lštwt hkwhn yšlḥ
ydw*, "and it will be when they set the table to eat or the
wine to drink (that) the priest will stretch out his hand"
(1QS 6:4-5). These uses of the perfect with *waw* consecutive
(whyh) correspond to a biblical use of that form to introduce
a command or wish, e.g., *wĕhāyāh batĕbûʾōt ûnĕtatten ḥămîšît*,
"And it shall be in the harvests that you give one fifth"
(Gen 47:24).[124] This form is usually translated καὶ ἔσται
in the Greek, as here: καὶ ἔσται τὰ γενήματα αὐτῆς δώσετε τὸ
πέμπτον. Thus even in the many narrative sections of Qumran
Hebrew there is no example of the construction which would be
translated καὶ ἐγένετο (καί) plus a simple, past event. There
are no examples of this impersonal use of the verb "to be"
in Proto-Mishnaic Hebrew, where *waw* consecutive seems to have
dropped out of use.

The construction does not occur in biblical Aramaic. In
one Middle Aramaic text the verb "to be" with *waw* introduces
a past event: *whwy³ kd[y . . .]* (4QEn^b 1 i 2). Unfortunately,
the Aramaic text is fragmentary, but we do have the Greek text
for this passage (= *l Enoch* 6:1): καὶ ἐγένετο ὅταν (or ὅτε)
ἐπληθύνθησαν οἱ υἱοὶ τῶν ἀνθρώπων ἐν ἐκείναις ταῖς ἡμέραις
ἐγεννήθησαν αὐτοῖς θυγατέρες, "And it happened when (whenever)
the sons of men multiplied in those days (that) daughters were
born to them." Thus we may restore the Aramaic text (with
Milik[125]): *whwy³ kd[y śgy³ w bny ³nš³ bywmy³ ³lyn ³tyldh lhwn
bnt]*. Although this usage may be an imitation of the Hebrew
construction discussed above, there is a text in Imperial
Aramaic not related to the Old Testament in which the verb
"to be" is also used impersonally to introduce a past event
(with ³p instead of *waw*): *³p hwh tr^cn zy ³bn 5 bnyn psylh zy
³bn zy hww b³gwr³ zk ndšw*, "Also it happened (that) they destroyed five gateways of stone, built of hewn blocks of stone,
which were in that temple" (Cowley, *AP* 30:9-10). Hence we must
allow that in Middle Aramaic the construction with *waw* and the
verb "to be" used impersonally, followed by a temporal expression (the clause with *kdy*), is used to introduce a past event
(expressed by a finite verb, but without *waw* as in biblical
Hebrew).

Mk 1:9 and 4:4 have exactly the same formula (καὶ ἐγένετο,
a temporal expression, and a finite verb [without a second καί]
narrating a past event). Such a construction never occurs in
non-biblical Greek. Therefore, its existence in Mk 1:9 and
4:4 is due to Semitic interference, whether from first-century
Aramaic or from imitation of the OG.[126] Literal translation
from Hebrew may be ruled out because the biblical Hebrew
construction always has the conjunction *waw* before the verb
which narrates the past event. As we have seen, the OG sometimes omits this second *waw* in its translation.

Mk 2:15 and 23 are more difficult. Mk 2:23 is made up of
καὶ ἐγένετο, a temporal expression (ἐν τοῖς σάββασιν), and an
accusative with infinitive clause (αὐτὸν παραπορεύεσθαι διὰ τῶν
σπορίμων), followed by καί with a finite verb indicating a past
event (οἱ μαθηταὶ αὐτοῦ ἤρξαντο ὁδὸν ποιεῖν). Such a construction, in its entirety, is correct in neither Greek, nor Hebrew,

nor Aramaic. Καὶ ἐγένετο, as we have seen, is never used in
non-biblical Greek to introduce a past event, although some
form of γίνεσθαι with an accusative plus infinitive construction may be used to indicate a present/future possibility or a
usual occurrence. On the other hand, in Hebrew wayĕhî
wĕhāyāh (= καὶ ἐγένετο in the OG) and Aramaic whwh never introduce a past event which is expressed by an infinitive (αὐτὸν
παραπορεύεσθαι in the Marcan verse). But if the past event
introduced by καὶ ἐγένετο is not the infinitive but rather
καὶ οἱ μαθηταὶ αὐτοῦ ἤρξαντο ὁδὸν ποιεῖν, then the temporal
expression would include the infinitive (παραπορεύεσθαι). But
this could not be a literal translation from a Hebrew or Aramaic Vorlage.[127] Furthermore, in the Semitic construction the
subject of the past event (οἱ μαθηταὶ in the Marcan verse)
cannot come first in the clause.[128] With these things in mind,
we conclude that Mark or his source considered καὶ ἐγένετο in
the OG or whwh in Aramaic (which he translated with καὶ ἐγένετο)
as an expression used to introduce a past event. Instead of
the usual expression of the past event which καὶ ἐγένετο introduces, namely (καὶ plus) a finite verb, he used an accusative
with infinitive construction, since γίνομαι may take such a
construction in another context in Hellenistic Greek. Hence
Mk 2:23 reflects, although inexactly, a Hebraism common to the
OG, namely that of καὶ ἐγένετο introducing a past event,[129]
or the similar Aramaic construction with whwh.

Much the same is true of Mk 2:15: καὶ γίνεται (an historical present which equals καὶ ἐγένετο in meaning[130]) is followed
by a past event expressed by an accusative with infinitive
construction (κατακεῖσθαι αὐτὸν ἐν τῇ οἰκίᾳ αὐτοῦ). Therefore
it too is an imperfect imitation of the OG Hebraism or contemporaneous Aramaic idiom in which καὶ ἐγένετο introduces a
past event.[131]

4. *Casus Pendens* Followed by a Resumptive Pronoun

There are thirteen examples in the Gospel of Mark in which
either a substantive, a relative clause, or a participle precedes and stands grammatically separate from the sentence
(*casus pendens*) and is joined to it only by a pronoun which
resumes it in the proper case ending:

ὃς ἂν ποιήσῃ τὸ θέλημα τοῦ Θεοῦ, οὗτος ἀδελφός μου καὶ
ἀδελφὴ καὶ μήτηρ ἐστίν, "Whoever does the will of God,
this one is my brother and sister and mother" (Mk 3:35);
ὃς γὰρ ἔχει, δοθήσεται αὐτῷ, "For as for him who has, it
will be given to him" (4:25a);
καὶ ὃς οὐκ ἔχει, καὶ ὃ ἔχει ἀρθήσεται ἀπ'·αὐτοῦ, "and as
for him who does not have, even what he has will be taken
away from him" (4:25b);
ὃν ἐγὼ ἀπεκεφάλισα 'Ιωάννην, οὗτος ἠγέρθη, "As for John
whom I beheaded, this man has been raised" (6:16);
τὸ ἐκ τοῦ ἀνθρώπου ἐκπορευόμενον, ἐκεῖνο κοινοῖ τὸν
ἄνθρωπον, "Whatever comes out of a man, that defiles the
man" (7:20);
ὃς γὰρ ἐὰν ἐπαισχυνθῇ με . . . , καὶ ὁ υἱὸς τοῦ ἀνθρώπου
ἐπαισχυνθήσεται αὐτόν, "For whoever is ashamed of me . . . ,
the son of man will be ashamed of him" (8:38);
καὶ ὃς ἂν σκανδαλίσῃ ἕνα τῶν μικρῶν τούτων τῶν πιστευόντων,
καλόν ἐστιν αὐτῷ μᾶλλον . . . , "and whoever scandalizes one
of these little ones who believe, it would be better for
him . . ." (9:42);
ὃς ἂν εἴπῃ· τῷ ὄρει τούτῳ ἄρθητι καὶ βλήθητι εἰς τὴν
θάλασσαν, καὶ μὴ διακριθῇ ἐν τῇ καρδίᾳ αὐτοῦ ἀλλὰ πιστεύῃ
ὅτι ὃ λαλεῖ γίνεται ἔσται αὐτῷ, "Whoever says to this
mountain 'Be taken up and cast into the sea,' and does not
doubt in his heart, but believes that what he says will
happen, it will be done for him" (11:23);
λίθον ὃν ἀπεδοκίμασαν οἱ οἰκοδομοῦντες, οὗτος ἐγενήθη εἰς
κεφαλὴν γωνίας, "The stone which the builders rejected,
this has been raised to the head of the corner" (12:10 =
Ps 117:22 in the OG);
οἱ κατέσθοντες τὰς οἰκίας τῶν χηρῶν καὶ προφάσει μακρὰ
προσευχόμενοι, οὗτοι λήμψονται περισσότερον κρίμα, "Those
who devour the houses of widows and, in pretense, make
long prayers, these will receive the greater judgment"
(12:40);
ὃ ἐὰν δοθῇ ὑμῖν ἐν ἐκείνῃ τῇ ὥρᾳ, τοῦτο λαλεῖτε, "Whatever
is given you in that hour, say this" (13:11);
ὁ δὲ ὑπομείνας εἰς τέλος, οὗτος σωθήσεται, "Whoever endures
to the end, this one will be saved" (13:13);

ὃν ἂν φιλήσω, αὐτός ἐστιν, "Whomever I kiss, he it is"
(14:44).

Casus pendens is a type of anacolouthon and is rather common in Greek. *Casus pendens* may be a substantive, or a relative
clause, or a participle used as a substantive, and, although it
is psychologically the subject of the sentence, it is separated
from it grammatically, being set down in this fashion to add
emphasis.[132] The words ᾿Ιωάννην in Mk 6:16 and λίθον in 12:10
are the logical subjects although they are in the accusative
case because of inverse attraction to the relative clause.
This phenomenon too occurs elsewhere in Greek.[133]

When the pronoun which resumes the *casus pendens* in the
sentence is a demonstrative and lends further emphasis to it,
the construction is normal in Hellenistic Greek. Examples
abound in Epictetus and Xenophon:[134]   (a) with a substantive
as *casus pendens*: τὰ δ᾿ ἀναγκαῖα θεωρήματα, ἀφ᾿ ὧν ἐστιν
ὁρμώμενον ἄλυπον γενέσθαι, ἄφοβον, ἀπαθῆ, ἀκώλυτον, ἐλεύθερον,
ταῦτα δ᾿ οὐ γυμνάζω, "However, the necessary principles by reason of which one begins to become untroubled, fearless, free
from emotion, unhindered, free, these things I do not exercise"
(Epictetus 4.6.16; cf. Mk 6:16 and 12:10 above); (b) with a
relative clause as *casus pendens*: ἃ γὰρ οὗτος ἐθαύμαζεν τούτων
οὐδενὸς εἶχεν ἐκεῖνος ἐξουσίαν, "For the things which he ad-
mired, over none of these things did he have power" (Epictetus
2.13.14; cf. Mk 3:35 and 13:11 above); (c) with an articular
participle as *casus pendens*: ὁ γὰρ λόγχην ἀκονῶν, ἐκεῖνος
καὶ τὴν ψυχήν τι παρακονᾷ, "for he who sharpens his spear, this
one whets also his spirit in a way" (Xenophon, *Cyr.* 6.2.33; cf.
Mk 7:20; 12:40; 13:13 above).[135]

When, however, the resumptive is a personal pronoun and
lacks emphasis (as in Mk 4:25a, b; 9:42; 11:23), such a construction is not normal in Hellenistic Greek. Excluding the
Egyptian papyri, the examples where *casus pendens* is resumed by
a personal pronoun are very few,[136] and a certain emphasis on
the pronoun is clear in every case. It is true that *casus
pendens* is resumed by an unemphatic pronoun in the Greek of a
fair number of the Egyptian papyri, e.g., τὰς οὖν δράχμας
ἐξήκοντα δὸς αὐτὰ ῞Ηλιτι τῷ ἐμῷ, "Therefore, as for the sixty
drachmas, give them to my man Elis" (*BGU* 2.523.21-22).[137]

Such usage occurs only here, and one may have to suspect that
interference from the Egyptian language is at work. The parallel
construction does exist in Coptic; as Vergote has shown, it may
explain the occurence of the construction in the Greek papyri.[138]

In biblical Hebrew a noun, pronoun, participle, or relative clause *(casus pendens)* may be joined to an independent
nominal or verbal clause which "refers to the principle subject [the *casus pendens*] by means of a pronoun,"[139] e.g., *ʾet
kol hāʾāreṣ ʾăšer ʾattāh rōʾeh lĕkā ʾettĕnennāh*, "All the land
which you see, I will give it to you" (Gen 13:15). The resumptive pronoun is most often a suffixal form of the personal pronoun, but sometimes the independent personal pronoun *hûʾ* is used,
e.g., *wĕhāyāh ʾăšer ʾōmar ʾēlêkā zeh yēlēk ʾittāk*, "And it
shall be that of whomever I shall say to you 'This man shall go
with you' he shall go with you" (Judg 7:4). The resumptive
pronoun is always a personal pronoun; it is never a demonstrative, as it sometimes is in Greek.

Examples from Qumran Hebrew where a personal pronoun resumes the *casus pendens*: *whʾyš ʾšr ylk rkyl brᶜhw whbdylhw šnh
ʾḥt mṭhrt hrbym*, "And as for the man who goes about as a slander-
er against his fellow, they shall separate him (suffix) from
the Purification of the Many for one year" (1QS 7:15-16); *wʾyš
brbym ylk rkyl lšlh hwʾh mʾtm*, ". . . and as for the man who
goes about slandering the Many, send him (independent *hwʾh*)
away from them" (1QS 7:16). In Proto-Mishnaic Hebrew we have
a similar example: *šydᶜ yhy lk šhprh šlqḥ yhwsp bn ʾrsṭwn mn
yᶜqb bn yhwdh šywšb ʾbyt mškw šhy šlw mzbnwt*, "that it be
known to you that as for the cow which Joseph son of Ariston
acquired from Jacob son of Yehudah, who resides at Bet Mashiko,
that it is his by purchase" (Mur *42* 2-4).

No examples of this construction are attested in Middle
Aramaic, but it does occur in biblical Aramaic: *wĕkol dî lāʾ
lehĕwēʾ ᶜābēd dātāʾ dî ʾĕlāhāk wĕdātāʾ dî malkāʾ ʾosparnāʾ
dînāh lehĕwēh mitᶜăbēd minnēh*, "And whoever shall not do the
law of your God and the law of the king, let judgment be strictly executed upon him" (Ezra 7:26).

The OG generally translates the resumptive pronoun with a
form of αὐτός, e.g., from Hebrew: πᾶσαν τὴν γῆν ἣν σὺ ὁρᾷς
σοὶ δώσω αὐτήν, "All the land which you see, I shall give it

to you" (Gen 13:15; Masoretic Text cited above); πᾶς ὃς ἂν μὴ
ᾖ ποιῶν νόμον τοῦ θεοῦ καὶ νόμον τοῦ βασιλέως, ἑτοίμως τὸ
κρίμα ἔσται γιγνόμενον ἐξ αὐτοῦ, "Whoever does not do the law
of God and the law of the king, the judgment shall happen to
him immediately" (2 Esdr 7:26; Masoretic Text cited above).
The demonstrative pronoun in OG Ps 117[118]:22 (quoted in Mk
12:10) has been added in translating the Hebrew original:
ʾeben māʾasû habbōnîm hāyĕtā lĕrōʾš pinnâ, "The stone the
builders rejected has become the head of the corner."

     Casus pendens followed by a resumptive demonstrative pro-
noun (Mk 3:35; 6:16; 7:20; 12:10, 40; 13:11, 13) is normal in
Greek, but unattested in Hebrew or Aramaic. When the resumptive
pronoun is a personal pronoun which adds emphasis (Mk 8:38;
14:44), such usage is attested (though rarely) in Hellenistic
Greek. When, however, *casus pendens* is resumed by an unemphatic
personal pronoun (Mk 4:25a, b; 9:42; 11:23), it is probably
the result of Semitic interference, whether from Hebrew, imitation of the OG, or (possibly) from Aramaic, since the construction does occur in biblical Aramaic.

     5. The Conditional Sentence

     In his study of Semitic syntax in New Testament Greek,
K. Beyer claims that the influence of Semitic languages extends
to some types of conditional sentences.[140] Having already
discussed the grammatical phenomenon of an apodosis of a conditional sentence introduced by the conjunction καί,[141] we shall
treat here those other conditional constructions in the Gospel
of Mark for which Beyer claims Semitic interference.

(a) The Shortening of Parallel Conditional Sentences

     Ἐὰν εἴπωμεν· ἐξ οὐρανοῦ, ἐρεῖ· διὰ τί οὖν οὐκ ἐπιστεύσατε
αὐτῷ; ἀλλὰ εἴπωμεν· ἐξ ἀνθρώπων--ἐφοβοῦντο τὸν ὄχλον, "If we
say, 'From heaven' he will say 'Why then did you not believe
him?' But (if) we say 'From men'--they feared the crowd"
(Mk 11:31-32). Beyer claims that in verse 32 the conjunction
ἐάν, which he considers necessary in Greek, was omitted from
before the verb εἴπωμεν because of the Semitic practice of
shortening parallel conditional sentences.[142]

In biblical Hebrew, when two conditional sentences with short apodoses are coordinated by *waw* copulative, the force of the conditional particle may extend beyond the apodosis of the first sentence to the second one. The result is that the conditional particle (*ʾim* or *kî*) may be omitted in the protasis of the second sentence,[143] e.g., *ʾim ʾessaq šāmayim šām ʾattāh wĕʾaṣṣîʿāh šĕʾōl hinnekā*, "If I ascend to the heavens, you are there, and (if) I make my bed in Sheol, there you are" (Ps 139:8).

In Qumran Hebrew there is only one example of parallel conditional sentences, but here the conditional particle is always expressed: *wʾny ʾm ʾmwṭ ḥsdy ʾl yšwʿty lʿd wʾm ʾkšwl bʿwwn bśr mšpṭy bṣdqt ʾl tʿmwd lnḥym wʾm ypth ṣrty wmšḥt yḥlṣ npšy*, "And I, if I stagger, the mercies of God are my salvation forever, and if I stumble because of the sin of the flesh, my judgment stands in the uprightness of God forever. And if he looses my distress, He will draw my soul back from the pit" (1QS 11:11-13). There are no parallel conditional sentences in Proto-Mishnaic Hebrew. However, Beyer cites several examples of such sentences in Mishnaic Hebrew, in which the conditional particle is omitted from the second sentence.[144]

There are no examples of parallel conditional sentences in Middle Aramaic. We note, however, that in a fragmentary text the Qumran Targum of Job changes the construction in question when it occurs in Hebrew. Whereas the Hebrew text reads: "If (*ʾim*) you have sinned, what do you accomplish against him, and ("if" not expressed) your transgressions are multiplied, what do you do to him?" (Job 35:6), the targum has *wbśgy ʿwytk mʾ t[ʿbd lh]*, "and *in* the multitude of your sins what do you [do to him]?" (11QtgJb 26:1).

Wherever parallel conditional sentences occur in biblical Aramaic, the conditional particle *hēn* is always used in the protasis of each conditional sentence (Dan 2:5; 3:15, 17-18).

However, Beyer has found an example of such an omission in parallel conditional sentences in Imperial Aramaic (*BMAP* 3.22a) and several examples of it in Late Aramaic (*Gen. Rab.* 45.10; 74.3; *y.Qidd.* 64c; *y. B. Meṣ.* 8c; *b. Yebam.* 63a).[145]

The OG always inserts the conditional conjunction in the
protasis of the second conditional sentence when it is omitted
in Hebrew, or understands the second sentence differently.[146]

The problem with Beyer's conclusion that the omission of
the particle ἐάν from Mk 11:32 must be due to Semitic interference arises from the fact that he has not fully analyzed the
Greek grammar of the verse. Vs. 31 is a vivid future conditional sentence with ἐάν and the subjunctive (εἴπωμεν) in the protasis and a future tense in the apodosis. Vs. 32 is really the
same thing. The anacolouthon in vs. 32 (--ἐφοβοῦντο τὸν ὄχλον,
"--they feared the crowd") shows the elliptical nature of the
verse. Moreover, both Matthew and Luke seem to take the verb
εἴπωμεν in the Marcan verse to be conditional in meaning and
add the conditional particle ἐάν. Thus ἐάν is omitted by ellipsis from before the verb of the protasis in Mk 11:32 (the identical form as that of the protasis of the parallel sentence
in vs. 31, εἴπωμεν), and the anacolouthon forms the apodosis.
Ellipsis of a conditional conjunction may also occur in non-
biblical Greek, e.g., τί γάρ, εἰ ἐκεῖνοι μὲν γενναῖοι ἦσαν, σὺ
δ' ἀγεννής; ἐκεῖνοι μὲν ἄφοβοι, σὺ δὲ δειλός; ἐκεῖνοι μὲν
ἐγκρατεῖς, σὺ δ' ἀκόλαστος; "For what (does it prove) if they
were noble, and you are mean-spirited? (If) they were fearless,
and you a coward? (If) they were self-controlled, and you
unrestrained?" (Epictetus 4.1.10); τί, ἂν οἰνωμένος ᾖ; τί ἂν
μελαγχολῶν; τί ἐν ὕπνοις; "What if he be drunk? What if he (be)
melancholy? What (if) asleep?" (Epictetus 1.18.23).

Ellipsis is possible in most languages and is usually
found in common phrases or expressions of popular speech.
Hence it is not necessary to assert that Semitic interference
was the cause of the ellipsis of ἐάν in Mk 11:32, because this
figure of speech is equally at home in Greek.

(b) Abridged Exceptive Clauses

Exceptive clauses are usually introduced in Greek by the
conjunctions εἰ/ἐάν (with the negative particle μή), ἀλλά (or
the more colloquial ἀλλ' ἤ), or by the preposition πλήν (used
as a conjunction).[147] In such an exceptive clause the verb is
usually omitted when it would be the same as that of the main
clause of the sentence,[148] e.g., οὐδεὶς δὲ πένης τραγῳδίαν

συμπληροῖ εἰ μὴ ὡς χορευτής, "No poor man fills a tragic role
except (he fill it) as a member of the chorus" (Epictetus
1.24.15). However, the conjunctions εἰ/ἐάν (μή), ἀλλά and
ἀλλ' ἤ may take on a mere prepositional force ("only; except"),
simply introducing an exception to the previous statement,[149]
e.g., χαλεποὶ οὖν καὶ ξυγγενέσθαι εἰσίν, οὐδὲν ἐλθόντες ἐπαινεῖν ἀλλ' ἤ τὸν πλοῦτον, "Thus they are hard to communicate
with since they wish to praise nothing except wealth" (= "to
praise only wealth," Plato, *Rep.* 330c). In this example the
conjunction ἀλλ' ἤ has almost the force of a preposition,
"except wealth." In a similar fashion the preposition πλήν
may be used as a preposition governing the genitive, "except,
save," e.g., ἀφειστήκεσαν . . . πᾶσαι πλὴν Μιλήτου, "All
(the Ionic cities) had revolted except Miletus" (Xenophon, *An.*
1.1.6). A noun may follow πλήν, not in the genitive, but in
the case required by the verb of the sentence,[150] e.g.,
συνῆλθον πάντες πλὴν οἱ Νέωνος, "All assembled except Neon's
men" (Xenophon, *An.* 7.3.2).

In the Gospel of Mark abridged exceptive clauses and
phrases, in which there is no verb, occur frequently: Mk 2:7,
26; 5:37; 6:4, 5, 8; 8:14; 9:8, 9, 29; 10:18; 11:13; 13:32
(with εἰ μή); 12:32 (with πλήν); 4:22a (with ἐάν μή); 4:22b
(with ἀλλά). Beyer attributes the frequency of the exceptives
with εἰ μή, nine times that of the OG, to Semitic interference,
specifically that of the Late Aramaic and Mishnaic Hebrew exceptive particle *'ellā'*.[151]

In biblical Hebrew several exceptive constructions are
possible:

(i) verbal and nominal clauses introduced by the conjunctions *'epes kî* (the substantive *'epes*, "cessation" and the conjunction *kî*, "that"), *kî 'im* (*kî* with the conditional particle
'im, "if"), *biltî 'im* (the old genitive form of the substantive
blh, "non-existence" and *'im*), meaning "unless," e.g., Num 13:28;
Gen 32:27; Amos 3:4;

(ii) nominal clauses introduced by the substantive *biltî*
which acts as a conjunction, meaning "unless, except," e.g.,
Gen 43:3;

(iii) abridged exceptive clauses introduced by the conjunction *kî 'im* in which the verb is omitted since it would be the

same as that of the main clause. The result is that *kî ᵓim*
acts almost as a preposition introducing a substantive which is
the single exception to the foregoing statement (the main
clause), e.g., 2 Kgs 9:35; 1 Sam 21:7;

(iv) noun phrases in which the substantive *biltî* and
zûlātî (the old genitive form of the substantive *zûlāh*,
"removal") are used as prepositions, meaning "except," e.g.,
Num 32:12; Deut 1:36;

(v) noun phrases in which the noun phrase *millĕbad* (the
prepositions *min* and *l* and the substantive *bad*, "part, portion")
is used itself as a preposition meaning "except," e.g., 2 Chr
31:16;

(vi) noun phrases with the composite preposition *mibbalᶜădê*
(*min* and the preposition *balᶜădê*, "besides") meaning "except,
besides," e.g., Num 5:20.

In Qumran Hebrew exceptive clauses of types (i) and (iii)
with *kî ᵓim* occur: (i) 1QS 5:14; 1QSa 1:10; CD 10:23; 11:3;
12:13; (iii) 1QH 4:31; CD 9:5; 10:22; 11:5, 18; 12:8; 13:15.
Exceptive phrases with *mlbd* and *zwlt* as prepositions turn up
in CD 5:5; 11:18 and 1QS 11:18; 1QH 7:32.

In Proto-Mishnaic Hebrew exceptive clauses occur twice:
[ᵓyn] *ṣryk lw ᵓḥt ᵓlh šlw*, "[Not] one (other thing) is needed
by him except what is his" (Mur 46:6); [. . .] *lhn ᵓlh ᵓḥy*
ᶜ[. . .], ". . . among them except my brother . . ."
(Mur 45:8). The conjunction *ᵓlh* is the same as Mishnaic
Hebrew *ᵓellāᵓ* (a contraction of the conditional particle *ᵓm/ᵓn*
and the negative *lᵓ*), meaning "unless, except."[152] In both
texts *ᵓlh* introduces an abridged exceptive clause similar to
type (iii) of the biblical Hebrew examples above.

In exceptive clauses biblical Aramaic uses the conjunction
lāhēn (the negative particle *lāᵓ* and the conditional conjunction *hēn*, "if") to introduce a complete exceptive clause in
Dan 6:6, as well as abridged exceptive clauses (in which there
is no verb) in Dan 2:11; 3:28; 6:8, 13.

The exceptive conjunction *lhn* turns up only three times
in Middle Aramaic, and in all cases it is used in an adversative
sense, "but" (see below). The Late Aramaic exceptive *ᵓellāᵓ*
(= *ᵓen* + *lāᵓ*) is not used in Middle Aramaic.

The OG uses various conjunctions and prepositions to
translate the Hebrew exceptive conjunctions and prepositions
outlined above. It is significant that εἰ μή is used only three
times (out of a possible 60 exceptive clauses and phrases[153])
to translate an exceptive in the Hebrew: Judg 7:14; 2 Esdr
12:2, 12 (= Neh 2:2, 12).[154] The explanation for this is that
εἰ μή is not a literal translation for any of the exceptive
conjunctions or "prepositions" in Hebrew outlined above, but
rather was chosen to translate into Greek the sense of these
texts. For the Aramaic exceptive *lāhēn* (which could be translated almost literally by εἰ μή) both the OG and Theodotion
usually render it with the colloquial ἀλλ' ἥ, except in Dan 2:11
(OG: εἰ μήτι), 6:6 (Theodotion: εἰ μή), and 6:13 (OG: ἀλλά).

Εἰ/ἐάν μή used as an exceptive particle in the Gospel of
Mark could possibly be a translation of Middle Aramaic *lhn* or
Proto-Mishnaic Hebrew *ʾlh*. From the rarity of the use of εἰ
μή to introduce exceptive clauses in the OG, we may conclude
that Semitic interference from imitation of the OG is unlikely
in the Marcan use of εἰ μή. Furthermore, the influence of the
type of Hebrew used at Qumran is also unlikely since there
the exceptive conjunction *kî ʾim* and the "prepositions" *mlbd*
and *zwlt* are not likely *Vorlagen* for εἰ μή. Although it is
possible that Middle Aramaic *lhn* or Proto-Mishnaic Hebrew *ʾlh*
could stand behind certain instances of εἰ μή in Mark, the
frequency of εἰ μή = "except" in Mark cannot be attributed to
the interference of either of these contemporary Semitic
languages, since these particles occur so infrequently in the
texts of Middle Aramaic and Proto-Mishnaic Hebrew published
to date. This, of course, may be coincidental, but it should
at least be noted and considered.

Beyer admits that most of the time Mark uses the exceptive
particles in a manner common to Greek (namely, in Mk 2:7; 5:37;
6:5, 8; 9:8, 29; 10:18; 11:13; 12:32), but he claims that the
use of exceptive particles in certain abridged clauses in the
Godpel of Mark is either very rare in Greek, or completely
foreign to that language:

(i) καὶ εἰ μὴ ἕνα ἄρτον οὐκ εἶχον μεθ' ἑαυτῶν ἐν τῷ πλοίῳ,
"and they did not have (anything) with them in the boat except
one loaf" (Mk 8:14). Beyer claims that in this verse the

main clause taken by itself is incomplete and senseless because the direct object of the verb, ἕνα ἄρτον (which, as he
says, would appear in Semitic as the subject of the verb "to
be"[155]), comes only after the exceptive particle εἰ μή.[156]
He is surprised to find two examples of such a sentence in
Hellenistic Greek,[157] and considers the usage a Semitism, "im
Griechischen nur sehr selten."[158]

(ii) τοὺς ἄρτους . . . οὓς οὐκ ἔξεστιν φαγεῖν εἰ μὴ
τοὺς ἱερεῖς, "the bread . . . which it is unlawful that (anyone)
except the priests eat" (Mk 2:26); διεστείλατο αὐτοῖς ἵνα
μηδενὶ ἃ εἶδον διηγήσωνται εἰ μὴ ὅταν ὁ υἱὸς τοῦ ἀνθρώπου ἐκ
νεκρῶν ἀναστῇ, "He ordered them to tell no one what they saw
except when the son of man should rise from the dead" (Mk 9:9).
Beyer claims that although the main clauses are complete in
Mk 2:26 and 9:9, an exception is stated which is not alluded
to in the main clause. This, he claims, is due to Semitic
interference because the usage is found much more frequently
in Semitic than in Greek.[159]

(iii) οὐ γὰρ ἐστίν τι .κρυπτὸν ἐὰν μὴ ἵνα φανερωθῇ, "For
there is nothing hidden except that it might be made known"
(Mk 4:22a); οὐδε ἐγένετο ἀπόκρυφον ἀλλ' ἵνα ἔλθῃ εἰς φανερόν,
"nor did anything become secret except that it might come to
light" (Mk 4:22b); οὐκ ἔστιν προφήτης ἄτιμος εἰ μὴ ἐν τῇ
πατρίδι αὐτοῦ, "a prophet is not without honor except in his
own country" (Mk 6:4). Beyer maintains that in these verses
an exceptive particle merely emphasizes something, but does
not thereby exclude something else in an unconditional way.[160]
He claims that such usage is never found in Greek, and that it
is unquestionably a Semitism.[161]

(iv) περὶ δὲ τῆς ἡμέρας ἐκείνης ἢ τῆς ὥρας οὐδεὶς οἶδεν,
οὐδὲ οἱ ἄγγελοι ἐν οὐρανῷ οὐδὲ ὁ υἱός, εἰ μὴ ὁ πατήρ, "Concerning that day or the hour no one knows, not even the angels in
heaven nor even the son, except the Father" (Mk 13:32). In
this verse Beyer claims that εἰ μή, the exceptive particle, is
used as an adversative, "but (sondern)," and is thus most
probably a Semitism.[162]

Concerning these instances mentioned by Beyer, we may
note the following:

(i) A correct analysis of Mk 8:14 shows that in it the exceptive particle εἰ μή introduces an abridged exceptive clause (in which the verb has been omitted). The direct object of the main verb, τι, has been omitted (by ellipsis). The result of this is that εἰ μή is used adverbially, almost as a preposition, simply to introduce an exception to the statement of the main clause, "except one loaf." This, as we have seen, is quite normal in Greek. While it is true that this adverbial use of a conditional particle frequently follows the pronouns τι or οὐδείς (ἄλλος),[163] these pronouns are not absolutely necessary to the expression of the sentence; they could be understood. In the following Greek texts the exceptive particles εἰ μή and ἀλλ' ἤ are used as prepositions to introduce an exception to the foregoing statement in which the direct object τι or οὐδέν has been omitted, exactly as in Mk 8:14: οὐ γὰρ δὴ ἐκ τοῦ ἐναντίου ὁρῶμεν εἰ μὴ ὀλίγους τούτους ἀνθρώπους, "for at this point we do not see (anyone) on the other side except these few men" (Xenophon, An. 4.7.5); φάσκειν μὴ καθήκειν αὐτὸν ἀλλ' ἤ τὸ τρίτον μέρος, "to allege that he receives (nothing) except a third portion" (Preisigke, Sammelb. 7267.7; also PSI 4.422.5; UPZ 54.6, 7, 8, 26; 52.15; 53.17; PHamb. 1.27.16, 18; PCair.Zen. 59186.7).

Thus, although such an exceptive construction is possible in Middle Aramaic (with the particle lhn) and in Proto-Mishnaic Hebrew (with ᵓlh), there is no need to posit Semitic interference for its use in Mk 8:14 since the usage is quite at home in non-biblical Greek.

(ii) In Mk 2:26 the subject accusative (τινα) of the infinitive φαγεῖν has been omitted and εἰ μή acting adverbially introduces the exception, "except the priests," As we have pointed out, such adverbial use of εἰ μή is not infrequent in Greek, e.g., οὐκ ἐπιτρέπομεν παιδεύεσθαι εἰ μὴ τοῖς ἐλευθέροις; "Do we allow education (literally "to be educated") (to no one) except to the free?" (Epictetus 2.1.25). In this text the indirect object of the verb (τινι) has been omitted, and εἰ μή is used adverbially, as in Mk 2:26, to introduce an exception, "except to the free."

Similarly, in Mk 9:9 εἰ μή is used adverbially to introduce an exception to the foregoing statement. The exception

is expressed by the temporal clause, ὅταν ὁ υἱός . . . ἀναστῇ,
"when the son . . . should rise," and is not alluded to in the
main clause.[164] But here again the foregoing pronoun (in this
case pronominal adverb οὐδέποτε) has been omitted. Εἰ μή, used
adverbially, may also introduce an exception which is expressed
by a subordinate clause in non-biblical Greek, e.g., καὶ γὰρ
ἀγωνίζεται εἰ μὴ ὅπου μὴ κρείσσων ἐστίν, "for he does not contest (anywhere) except where he is superior" (Epictetus 3.6.5);
ἐγὼ μέν μιν οὐκ εἶδον εἰ μὴ ὅσον γραφῇ, "I myself have never
seen (any) except what has been drawn" (Herodotus 2.73; cf.
1.45).

     Thus, although the use of the exceptive particle in Mk
9:9 is likely in Middle Aramaic and Proto-Mishnaic Hebrew, it
is equally possible in Hellenistic Greek.

     (iii) Beyer claims that εἰ μή in Mk 4:22a and 6:4, and
ἀλλά in Mk 4:22b introduce abridged exceptive clauses which
simply emphasize a point but are not true Greek exceptives
since they do not present the only exception to the absolute
statement of the main clause. As we have seen, both εἰ μή and
ἀλλά in Greek may introduce abridged exceptive clauses, and that
is what they do in Mk 4:22a, b, and 6:4. The case in which a
grammatically exceptive clause is not *psychologically* totally
exclusive, that is, when it does not present the only exception
to an otherwise absolute statement, is also quite normal in
both classical and Hellenistic Greek. The following examples
are good parallels to the Marcan use of exceptives in question
and suffice to show that this usage is quite at home in both
classical and Hellenistic Greek: χαλεποὶ οὖν καὶ ξυγγενέσθαι
εἰσίν, οὐδὲν ἐθέλοντες ἐπαινεῖν ἀλλ᾿ ἢ τὸν πλοῦτον, "Thus they
are hard to communicate with since they wish to praise nothing
except wealth" (Plato, *Rep.* 330c); διεφθάρμεθα . . . ὑπ᾿
ἀνθρώπων οὐδὲν ἀλλ᾿ ἢ φενακίζειν δυνάμενον, "we have been
ruined . . . by men who are able (to do) nothing except
deceive" (Isocrates 8.36); τί γὰρ ἄλλο δύναμαι γέρων χωλὸς εἰ
μὴ ὑμνεῖν τὸν θεόν; "For what else can I, a lame old man, do
except sing of God?" (Epictetus 1.16.20); ἡμῖν οὐδὲν ἐστιν
ἀγαθὸν ἄλλο εἰ μὴ ὅπλα καὶ ἀρετή, "We have no other possession
except arms and courage" (Xenophon, *An.* 2.1.12).

Hence there is no reason to claim Semitic interference in
the use of εἰ μή and ἀλλά in Mk 4:22a, b, and 6:4.[165]

(iv) A correct analysis of Mk 13:32 shows that εἰ μή
is used adverbially to introduce an exception to the foregoing
statement, "except the Father." As we have seen, this is normal
in Hellenistic Greek, especially after the pronoun οὐδείς, as in
Mk 13:32, οὐδεὶς οἶδεν, "no one knows." The words οὐδὲ οἱ
ἄγγελοι ἐν οὐρανῷ οὐδὲ ὁ υἱός, "not even the angels in heaven
nor even the son" are in apposition to οὐδείς, the subject of
the sentence. In Beyer's analysis of Mk 13:32 εἰ μή would be
used as an adversative, "but" after an abridged clause οὐδὲ οἱ
ἄγγελοι ἐν οὐρανῷ οὐδὲ ὁ υἱός, "not even the angels in heaven
nor even the son (know), but the Father (knows)." This is
simply incorrect. Εἰ μή may be used as an adversative particle
in Gal 1:7, but never in the Gospel of Mark. In Mk 13:32 εἰ
μή is used normally as an exceptive particle introducing an
exception to the foregoing statement.

6. General Relative Clauses

In his study of Semitic syntax in the New Testament, K.
Beyer has claimed that the frequency of general relative
clauses and conditional participles over against that of indefinite conditional clauses (εἰ/ἐάν τις) is remarkably high.[166]
This, he says, is almost certainly due to the influence of
Semitic because in Semitic there is no indefinite pronoun
corresponding to τις in Greek.[167] Furthermore, he claims that
a general relative clause standing absolutely at the head of a
sentence (as *casus pendens*) is very infrequent in Hellenistic
Greek.[168] When such a clause does occur in Greek, he maintains,
it is usually resumed in the following main clause by some form
of the demonstrative pronoun οὗτος or ἐκεῖνος and only very
infrequently by the personal pronoun αὐτός.[169] Because of this
he concludes that five verses in the Gospel of Mark in which a
general relative clause stands as *casus pendens* and is resumed
by some form of αὐτός are due to Semitic interference "so gut
wie sicher."[170] The verses in question are:

ὃς γὰρ ἔχει, δοθήσεται αὐτῷ, "as for him who has, it will
be given to him" (4:25a);

καὶ ὃς οὐκ ἔχει, καὶ ὃ ἔχει ἀρθήσεται ἀπ᾽ αὐτοῦ, "and as

for him who does not have, even what he has will be taken
away from him" (4:25b);

ὃς γὰρ ἐὰν ἐπαισχυνθῇ με καὶ τοὺς ἐμοὺς λόγους ἐν τῇ
γενεᾷ ταύτῃ τῇ μοιχαλίδι καὶ ἁμαρτωλῷ, καὶ ὁ υἱὸς τοῦ
ἀνθρώπου ἐπαισχυνθήσεται αὐτόν, "As for him who is ashamed
of me and my words in this adulterous and sinful generation, the son of man will be ashamed of him" (8:38);

καὶ ὃς ἂν σκανδαλίσῃ ἕνα τῶν μικρῶν τούτων τῶν πιστευόντων,
καλόν ἐστιν αὐτῷ μᾶλλον εἰ περίκειται μύλος ὀνικὸς περὶ
τὸν τράχηλον αὐτοῦ, "And as for whoever scandalizes one of
these little ones who believe, it is better for him if a
great millstone were hung around his neck . . . " (9:42);

ὃς ἂν εἴπῃ τῷ ὄρει τούτῳ . . . , ἔσται αὐτῷ, "As for whoever shall say to this mountain ' . . . ,' it will come
to pass for him" (11:23).

The general relative clause, that is, a relative clause
whose antecedent is generic or indefinite, occurs frequently
in Hellenistic Greek. It is usually introduced by the relative
pronouns ὅς or ὅστις (which are hardly differentiated in the
Greek language by the first century A.D.),[171] or the pronoun
ὅσος, usually followed by the modal particle ἄν, or, starting
already in the third century B.C., by ἐάν,[172] with the verb in
the subjunctive. However, the verb may also be in the indicative (without ἄν) since, because of previous statements, it may
express as definite the supposition that such a state of affairs
exists.[173] Furthermore, in the New Testament as well as "in the
papyri which concern official decrees and statutes, the distinction [between the indicative and subjunctive in general relative clauses] is often effaced and in fact the two moods can be
used quite promiscuously."[174] Because of this fact a relative
clause with ὅς or ὅστις and an indicative verb can be determined as definite or indefinite (general) only by the context.[175]
Examples: περὶ ὧν ἂν αἱρῆσθε γραφέτε, "Concerning whatever you
take, write" (PLips. 1.104.13); ὃ ἐὰν περισσὸν γένηται, μέτρησον
αὐτοῖς, "Measure out to them whatever is superfluous" (PTebt.
459.4); ὅντινα οὖν ἐπ' ἄλλῳ κωλῦσαι ἐστι καὶ ἀναγκάσαι, θαρρῶν
λέγε μὴ εἶναι ἐλεύθερον, "Therefore, say confidently that whomever it is in another's power to hinder and constrain is not
free" (Epictetus 4.1.56).

ᏊᏗᎥᎦᎩ

With regard to frequency, in the first two books of the
Discourses of Epictetus there are at least 26 general relative
clauses with the pronouns ὅς, ὅστις, and ὅσος as over against
only ten indefinite conditional clauses with εἰ/ἐάν τις.[176]
Of the 26 general relative clauses 8 of them stand absolutely
as *casus pendentes* (1.4.4; 11.19; 25.24; 27.2; 2.1.24; 10.23;
21.4; 22.3) with a resumptive pronoun in the following main
clause. Apart from one instance (1.4.4--αὐτό) the resumptive
pronoun in these instances is always the demonstrative οὗτος
or ἐκεῖνος. In the Egyptian non-literary papyri there is a
decided preference against using the general relative clause
as a *casus pendens:* out of over 120 general relative clauses
with the pronouns ὅς or ὅστις cited by Mayser,[177] in no case
does the relative clause stand absolutely as *casus pendens*
in the sentence.

In biblical Hebrew the general relative clause occurs rather
frequently with either the relative particle ᵓǎšer, the interrogative pronoun mî with ᵓǎšer, or mî/mãh alone. Wide generali-
zations are made by the addition of kol to the relative particle.
When the general relative clause stands independently in a
sentence (as a *casus pendens*), it may be resumed by the personal
pronoun expressed as a suffix on a noun, verb, or preposition.[178]
Examples: ᵓǎšer yakkeh ᵓet qiryat sēper ûlĕkādāh wĕnātattî lô
ᵓet ᶜaksâ bittî lĕᵓiššâ, "Whoever smites Kiriath-sepher and
takes it, to him I will give Achsah my daughter as wife"
(Jos 15:16); mî ᵓǎšer ḥāṭāᵓ lî ᵓemḥennû missiprî, "Whoever has
sinned against me, him I will blot out of my book" (Exod 32:33);
mî yāṣar ᵓel ûpesel nāsāk lĕbiltî hôᶜîl, hēn kôl ḥǎbērāy(w)
yēbōšû, "Whoever fashions a god or casts an image without profit,
behold all his companions shall be put to shame" (Isa 44:10-11);
kol ᵓǎšer yālōq bilšônô min hammayim kaᵓǎšer yālōq hakkeleb
taṣṣîg ᵓōtô lĕbād, "anyone who laps up water with his tongue
as a dog laps you shall set him by himself" (Judg 7:5).

General relative clauses occur in Qumran Hebrew only with
ᵓšr and kl ᵓšr. They too may stand independently of the sentence as *casus pendentes* to be resumed in the following clause
by a suffixal form of the personal pronoun, e.g., wᵓšr yšyb ᵓt
rᶜhw bqšy ᶜwrp . . . [hw]šyᶜh ydw lwᵓ [= lw], "And whoever
answers his fellow stubbornly . . . his own hand has helped

him" (1QS 6:25-27); *kl ᵓšr [yqy]m ᵓyš ᶜl npšw lswr m[n htw]rh ᶜd mḥyr mwt ᵓl yqymhw*, "Everything which a man has raised up before his soul to depart from the law, he shall not carry it out even at the price of death" (CD 16:8-9).

In Proto-Mishnaic Hebrew the general relative clause is expressed by the interrogative pronoun *my* with the relative particle *š*: *wpqdty t my šytn lk thṭyn šlh ᵓḥr hšbt yṭlwn*, "And I have ordered whoever shall give you his wheat to take (it) back after the Sabbath" (literally, "that they take . . .") (Mur 44:8-10). There are several examples with *kl* and the relative particle *š*: *lᶜšwt bw kl šthpṣ*, "to do with it whatever you wish" (Mur 30:23a; cf. 30:19, 23b); with *kl* and a substantive and *š*: *mᶜyd ᵓny ᶜly t šmym yps[d] mn hgll ᵓym šhglkm kl ᵓdm šᵓny ntn t kblym brglkm*, "I take the heavens as witness against me that, if any man of the Galileans who are with you is mistreated, I shall put chains on your feet" (Mur 43:3-5). In none of these texts is the general relative clause a *casus pendens* followed by a resumptive pronoun.

In Middle Aramaic a general relative clause begins with several expressions: with *dy* alone: *wryq wbṭln dy ytnk [ᶜ]l [ᵓtr ᵓ dk]*, "and whatever (else) they might offer you [con]cerning [this land] is invalid and without legal effect" (Mur 25:7; cf. 26:5); with a substantive and *dy*: *wbzmn [dy t]mryn ly [ᵓ]ḥlp lky štrh*, "and at whatever time [you] ask (it) of me, [I] shall give over the document to you" (Mur 19:23-24; cf. 21:19; 27:5; 20:14 and 26:7 contain the same formula but are fragmentary); with the interrogative pronoun (probably): *wmn hwᵓ [. . .]*, "And whoever . . ." (1Q20 1 i 1); with *kl dy*: *ᵓn ᵓsb mn kwl dy yty lk*, "that I shall not take anything which is yours" (1QapGn 22:22; cf. 4Q Testuz 4; 11QtgJb 38:4); with *kl*, a substantive, and *dy*: *bkwl [ᵓtr] dy [nhwh bh ᵓmry] ᶜly*, "in whatever [place we shall be, say] about me . . ." (1QapGn 19:20).[179] In none of these examples is the general relative clause a *casus pendens*.

In biblical Aramaic general relative clauses are introduced by (a) the interrogative pronoun *man* and the relative particle *dî* (e.g., Dan 3:6), (b) *kol dî*, and (c) *kol*, a substantive, and *dî*. The general relative clause is a *casus pendens* followed by a resumptive personal pronoun in two

instances representing types (b) and (c): wĕkol dî lā᾽ lehĕwē᾽
ᶜābēd dātā᾽ dî ᾽elāhāk wĕdātā᾽ dî malkā᾽ ᾽āsparnā᾽ dînāh lehĕwē᾽
mit ᶜăbēd minnēh, "And anyone who will not do the law of your
God and the law of the king, let judgment be strictly executed
on him" (Ezra 7:26); kol ᾽ĕnāš dî yĕhašnē᾽ pitgāmā᾽ dĕnāh
yitnĕsāḥ ᾽āᶜ min bayĕtēh, "Any man who alters this edict, a beam
shall be pulled out of his house" (Ezra 6:11).

The OG usually translates a general relative clause with
᾽ăšer, mî ᾽ăšer, mî, or māh in Hebrew by ὅς/ὅστις (ἐ)άν with
kol ᾽ăšer by πᾶς ὅς ἐάν. When the clause is a *casus pendens*
followed by a resumptive personal pronoun, the OG usual translates the pronoun by some form of αὐτός, e.g., ὅς ἐάν λάβῃ καὶ
ἐκκόψῃ τὴν πόλιν τῶν γραμμάτων καὶ κυριεύσῃ αὐτῆς, δώσω αὐτῷ
τὴν Αχσαν θυγατέρα μου εἰς γυναῖκα, "Whoever takes and strikes
the city of the scribes and rules it, I will give him Achsah
my daughter as wife" (Jos 15:16); πᾶς ὅς ἄν λάψῃ τῇ γλώσσῃ αὐτοῦ
ἐκ τοῦ ὕδατος, ὡς ἐάν λάψῃ ὁ κύων, στήσεις αὐτὸν κατὰ μόνας,
"Anyone who laps up water with his tongue as a dog laps, you
shall set him by himself" (Judg 7:5). Similarly, the OG translates general relative clauses in Aramaic with man dî or
kol, (a substantive), dî by ὅς ἄν and πᾶς ὅς respectively.
When the general relative clause acts as *casus pendens* the
following resumptive pronoun is translated by αὐτός: πᾶς
ἄνθρωπος ὅς ἀλλάξει τὸ ῥῆμα τοῦτο, καθαιρεθήσεται ξύλον ἐκ τῆς
οἰκίας αὐτοῦ, "Any man who alters this edict, a beam shall be
pulled out of his house" (2 Esdr 6:11); πᾶς ὅς ἄν μὴ ᾖ ποιῶν
νόμον τοῦ θεοῦ καὶ νόμον τοῦ βασιλέως ἑτοίμως, τὸ κρίμα ἔσται
γιγνόμενον ἐξ αὐτοῦ, "Anyone who is not readily a doer of the
law of God and the law of the king, the judgment will be made
on him" (2 Esdr 7:26).

By way of conclusion to this examination of general relative clauses it must be stated, first of all, that the frequency
of general relative clauses over against that of indefinite
conditional clauses (εἰ/ἐάν τις) in the Gospel of Mark is not
remarkably high. While there are 28 general relative clauses
of various sorts in Mark,[180] there are ten indefinite conditional clauses with εἰ/ἐάν τις.[181] These figures are almost the
same as those for the first two books of the Discourses of
Epictetus: 26 general relative clauses with ὅς, ὅστις, or

ὅσος to 10 indefinite conditional clauses with εἰ/ἐάν τις. [182]

Secondly, most of the general relative clauses in Mark are used in the same manner as those in non-biblical Greek.

Finally, seven Marcan general relative clauses stand absolutely at the head of the sentence as *casus pendentes* and are followed by a resumptive pronoun. This, too, is acceptable in Greek. In Mk 3:35 the resumptive pronoun is οὗτος, the normal resumptive pronoun for this type of construction in Greek. In Mk 6:11 the general relative clause is used adverbially, resumed in the following clause by the pronominal adverb ἐκεῖθεν, also correct in Greek. However, in the five remaining texts, namely, Mk 4:25a, b; 8:38; 9:42; 11:23, the resumptive pronoun is some form of the personal pronoun αὐτός. As we have seen above in section A. 4, "*Casus Pendens* Followed by a Resumptive Pronoun," *casus pendens* is followed by a resumptive personal pronoun (αὐτός) in non-biblical Greek only very infrequently, and then only with a certain emphasis. Hence, as we concluded in the section on *Casus Pendens*, Mk 4:25a, b; 8:38; 9:42; 11:23 most probably contain Semitic interference.

B. SEVERAL PARTS OF SPEECH

    1. The Definite Article

(a) Unusual Insertion of the Article

J. Wellhausen has claimed that the article is used in Semitic more frequently than in Indo-European languages before substantives which represent a favorite example of a class or type of thing, or where the substantive is general. [183] Hence, for him, the article is used in certain New Testament texts where it would not normally occur in Greek.

M. Black also claims that the article is used improperly in the New Testament, but for a different reason. He recognizes the Hebrew idiom by which a noun which is specially present to the mind of the writer takes the article although it is indefinite in the context. However, such usage is doubtful in Aramaic because "there certainly was no form by which it [the definite article] could be recognized, for the *status emphaticus*, by which the definite article was originally expressed, had lost its significance in first-century Aramaic

and was used for definite and indefinite nouns alike."[184]
Hence, for Black, an unusual insertion of the definite article
in New Testament Greek could be due to a writer's literal translation into Greek of a noun which was in the emphatic state
in Aramaic, even though in that context it was undetermined.[185]
N. Turner seens to concur with this opinion.[186]

J. Jeremias also claims that certain uses of the definite
article in New Testament Greek are incorrect and due to Aramaic
interference.[187] He has expressed caution at Black's view that
the emphatic state no longer maintained its determining character in the first century A.D.[188] He points out, rather, that
the practice of using the emphatic state of nouns in Aramaic
with an indefinite meaning already occurs frequently in the Old
Testament in parables and pictorial narratives. "This usage,"
he says, "is characteristic of Semitic imagery."[189]

These authors have claimed Semitic interference for the
allegedly improper use of the definite article in the following
texts of the Gospel of Mark:

Wellhausen:[190] τῆς τρυμαλιᾶς τῆς ῥαφίδος (10:25); τοὺς
πτωχούς (14:7);

Black:[191] ὑπὸ τὸν μόδιον, ἐπὶ τὴν λυχνίαν (4:21); τὰ
δαιμόνια (1:39, used in similar fashion in Mt 12:24);
πρὸς τῷ ὄρει (Mk 5:11, as in Mt 15:29); ἐπὶ τοῖς κραβάτοις
(Mk 6:55);

Jeremias:[192] ὁ σπείρων (4:3); τὴν ὁδόν, τὰ πετεινά (4:4);
τὸ πετρῶδες (4:5); τὰς ἀκάνθας (4:7, 18); τὴν γῆν τὴν
καλήν (4:8, 20); τὴν ὁδόν (4:15); τὰ πετρώδη (4:16); ὁ
λύχνος, τὸν μόδιον, τὴν κλίνην, τὴν λυχνίαν (4:21); τὸν
σπόρον (4:26). Further instances of substantives which
have the article, but which we might translate as indefinite are: εἰς τὸ ὄρος (3:13; 6:46); τὸ προσκεφάλαιον
(4:38); τῶν μνημείων (5:2); τοὺς ἄρτους (7:2); τὴν οἰκίαν
(10:10); τοῦ δώματος (13:15); τὸν ἀγρόν (13:16).

In classical and Hellenistic Greek the article may denote
a particular person or thing, whether "already mentioned or in
the mind of the speaker or writer (the anaphoric article)" or
"objects specially present to the senses or mind (the deictic
article)."[193] Thus the definite article may be used when an

object has not been mentioned explicitly, but is specific from
the picture being drawn by the writer. For example, in the
context of a description of the activity of the Boeotians'
army, a certain Pagondas calls up his soldiers βουλόμενος
τὴν μάχην ποιῆσαι, "wishing to bring on *the* battle" (Thucydides
4.91.1); in the context of teaching Roman soldiers how to row,
the instructors made the men sit ἐπὶ τῶν εἰρεσιῶν ἐν τῇ χέρσῳ,
"on *the* rowers' benches on *the* dry land" (Polybius 1.21.2); to a
man who sees that if he does otherwise he will be punished,
Epictetus says that: εὔλογον τὸ ἀμίδαν παρακρατεῖν, "it seems
reasonable to hold *the* chamber pot" (Epictetus 1.2.8); seeing
to the personal needs of a student, a certain Hierocles asks
someone to hasten to send the student a bathing apron, a tunic,
a cloak, καὶ τὸ στρωμάτιον καὶ περίστρωμα, "and *the* mattress
and coverlet" (*PCair.Zen.* 59060.9); in a description of agri-
cultural practices, the Egyptians "unload *the* pigs (τὰς ὗς)
which by trampling and rooting quickly turn over *the* soil
(τὴν γῆν) deeply and cover over *the* seed (τὸν σπόρον)"
(Plutarch, *Mor.* 670B).

The Greek also uses the article in a generic sense. When the
generic article is used with a plural substantive, it "denotes
an entire class as distinguished from other classes,"[194] e.g.,
οὐκ ἄν τις εἴποι ὡς τοὺς κακούργους καὶ ἀδίκους εἴα καταγελᾶν,
"No one could say that he permitted *malefactors and wrongdoers*
to deride him" (Xenophon, *An.* 1.9.13); ἐν τοῖς πλουσίοις καὶ
βασιλεῦσι καὶ τυράννοις αἱ τραγῳδίαι τόπον ἔχουσιν, "*tragedies*
have a place among *rich people* and kings and tyrants" (Epictetus
1.24.15).

The Greek article modifying substantives may take the
place of a possessive pronoun "when there is no doubt as to
their possessor,"[195] e.g., Κῦρός τε καταπηδήσας ἀπὸ τοῦ ἅρματος
τὸν θώρακα ἐνεδύετο, "Having leapt down from *his* chariot, Cyrus
put on *his* breastplate" (Xenophon, *An.* 1.8.3); συμβαλλέσθω τὸ
μέρος ἕκαστος, "Let each man receive *his* share" (*PHal.* 1.108).

In biblical Hebrew the article may be used "to denote a
single person or thing as being present to the mind under
given circumstances,"[196] e.g., "as if a man fled from *the* lion
(hā ʾărî) and *the* bear (haddōb) met him" (Amos 5:19).

This use of the article does not occur in Qumran Hebrew.
Nor is the article so used in Proto-Mishnaic Hebrew. However,
in Mishnaic Hebrew the article is used with nouns that are
definite in the mind of the speaker even more commonly than in
biblical Hebrew.[197] Hence, the fact that such usage does not
occur in the Proto-Mishnaic Hebrew material may simply be
coincidental, since this use of the article normally occurs in
narrative writing, a type of writing totally lacking in these
documents.

   In Middle Aramaic, "the emphatic state usually expressed
the definite or determined quality of the noun,"[198] e.g.,
ᶜwlym⁾ dn⁾, "this child" (1QapGn 2:2); w⁾tply mnh mktš⁾, "And
the plague (mentioned before in 20:19) was removed from him"
(1QapGn 20:29). There are two types of usage, however, in
which the use of the emphatic state does not appear to be
consistent with this rule: (i) abstract nouns, and (ii) certain
nouns which may be definite in the mind of the writer but not
in the context of the writing.

   (i) Abstract nouns are used with apparent inconsistency
now in the emphatic, now in the absolute, state already in
Official Aramaic, e.g., ⁾rk⁾, "length" (AP 26.18, 19, 20) together with ⁾rk, "length" (AP 15.8, 9, 11); ḥkmt⁾, "wisdom"
(Aḥiqar 146) and ḥkmh, "wisdom" (Aḥiqar 92).[199] This is also
true in biblical Aramaic,[200] e.g., mandĕᶜā⁾ lĕyādĕᶜê bînāh,
"(he gives) understanding (emphatic state) to those who know
discernment (absolute state)" (Dan 2:21). In Middle Aramaic,
too, abstract nouns appear in both the emphatic and the absolute
states, sometimes within the same document, e.g., ᶜd kwl⁾ bqwšṭ
tḥwynny, "that you make everything known to me in truth"
(1QapGn 2:5); lmndᶜ mnh kwl⁾ bqwšṭ⁾, "to learn everything from
him in truth" (2:22); ᶜd bqwšṭ ᶜmy tmllyn wl⁾ bkdbyn, "that you
are speaking to me in truth and not in lies" (2:7); ⁾nh bqwšṭ
kwl [⁾ ⁾ḥwynk], "I [shall tell you] everything in truth" (2:10);
[⁾nh] bqwšṭ mmll⁾ ᶜmk, "[I] am speaking to you in truth" (2:18);
in 2:5 and 22 the emphatic form qwšṭ⁾ on the preposition b
means "in truth," while the absolute form means the same thing
in 2:7, 10, and 18.[201] Another example is the word for "wisdom"
which is used once in the emphatic and once in the absolute
state with no apparent difference in the same document:

[. . .] *ṭbt> whkmt> wqwšt >*, "[. . .] kindness and wisdom
and truth" (19:25); *w<m kwl špr> dn ḥkm> šgy> <mh>*, "and with
all this beauty there is much wisdom in her" (20:7). The same
inconsistency occurs with different abstract words within a
single document, e.g., *wznwt> dh>*, "and avoid fornication"
(4QLevi^b i 13), while in the next line three abstract words
occur in the absolute state: [. . . *ḥ*]*kmh wmnd< wgbwrh*,
" . . . wisdom and understanding and force" (i 14).

     (ii) In Middle Aramaic singular nouns which are not abstract
are sometimes used in the emphatic where we should expect the
absolute state, since they are undetermined in their context.
Examples: *whw> kpn> b>r<> d> kwl>*, "And there was *the* famine
in all this land" (1QapGn 19:10); *w>thzy ly >lh> bḥzw> dy lyly>*,
"And God appeared to me in *the* vision of the night" (1QapGn
21:8); *>thzy >lh> l>brm bḥzw>*, "God appeared to Abram in *the*
vision" (1QapGn 22:27; but cf. *>dyn ḥzywn >ḥzyt*, "Then I was
shown *a* vision" [4QLevi^b ii 15]); [*kdy hwy ktyš*] *bšḥn> b>yš>*,
"[when he was afflicted] with *the* bad boil" (4QṣNab 1-2);
wql> [slq qwdm š]*my>*, "and· the cry [was going up to] the
[h]eavens" (4QEn^b 1 iii 6). All of these examples occur in
narrative text and are similar to the biblical and Mishnaic
Hebrew practice of using the article when a noun, although
undetermined in the context, is specially present to the mind
of the author.

     E. Kautzsch has pointed out that this usage is also to
be found in biblical Aramaic,[202] e.g., *wĕdātā> nepqat wĕhakkî-
mayyā> mitqaṭṭĕlîn*, "And *the* decree went out that the wise men
were to be slain" (Dan 2:13); *lĕgōb >aryāwātā>*, "(whoever makes
petition to any god or man, except to you, O King, shall be
cast) into the den of *the* lions" (Dan 6:8).

     Hence, in Middle and biblical Aramaic the emphatic state
is used inconsistently, although in only two contexts: (i)
abstract nouns, and (ii) concrete nouns in certain narrative
texts. The latter usage is far from universal in narrative
texts, and is the exception to the rule that nouns which are
undetermined in their context normally occur in the absolute
state.

     The OG (and Theodotion) usually translates the above ex-
amples literally, i.e., with the article in Greek when the noun

is determined in either Hebrew or Aramaic, e.g., "whenever a
man flees from the face of *the* lion (τοῦ λέοντος)and *the* bear
(ἡ ἄρκος) meets him" (Amos 5:19); εἰς τὸν λάκκον τῶν λεόντων,
"into the den of *the* lions" (Dan 6:8 Old Greek and Theodotion).

Although Hebrew and Aramaic usage of the article generally
coincides with that of the Gospel of Mark, nevertheless, Marcan
usage of it is quite normal in Hellenistic Greek in all cases.
Moreover, both Matthew and Luke use the article in almost all
cases when they take over the Marcan texts in question. Thus,
the normal Hellenistic usage of the deictic article occurs in
Mk 3:13; 4:3, 4 *(bis)*, 5, 7, 8, 21 *(quater;* both Matthew and
Luke omit the article from before λύχνος, and Luke alone omits
it before κλίνην and λυχνίαν), 26, 38; 5:2, 11; 6:46; 10:10,
25 (here both Matthew and Luke omit the article); 13:15, 16.
In Mk 4:15, 16, 18, 20 the article is simply anaphoric, referring back to the nouns in question in the parable in 4:3-8.
In 1:39 τὰ δαιμόνια and 14:7 τοὺς πτωχούς the article is generic,
while in 6:55 (ἐπὶ τοῖς κραβάτοις, "on *their* beds"), and 7:2
(ἐσθίουσιν τοὺς ἄρτους, "they eat *their* food") the article
takes the place of a possessive pronoun.[203]

(b) Unusual Omission of the Article

J. Wellhausen has suspected that the omission of the article
before a determined noun which is followed by a dependent genitive is due to Semitic interference, namely, to imitation or
literal translation of a Hebrew or Aramaic construct chain in
which the *nomen regens* never takes the article.[204] Blass-
Debrunner-Funk point out that Semitic interference may be at
work when an anarthrous noun is followed by the genitive of a
personal pronoun. In Hebrew and Aramaic the usual form of a
possessive personal pronoun is suffixal, and nouns with suffixes
always lack the article.[205]

The Marcan texts in question are: πρὸ προσώπου σου,
"before your face" (1:2); εἰς οἶκον αὐτῶν, "into their house"
(8:3); εἰς οἶκον αὐτοῦ, "into his house" (8:26); ἐν ὀφθαλμοῖς
ἡμῶν, "in our eyes" (12:11); εἰς χεῖρας ἀνθρώπων, "into (the)
hands of men" (9:31); εἰς πρόσωπον ἀνθρώπων, "into (the) face
of men" (12:14).

Finally, M. Black claims that the article is lacking before the word σχίσμα in Mk 2:21 (χεῖρον σχίσμα γίνεται, "[the]
tear becomes worse"). To account for this, he claims that since
in first-century Aramaic the formal distinction is lacking between the emphatic and the absolute state of nouns with regard
to their definite or indefinite nature, the noun for σχίσμα
in an Aramaic *Vorlage* may have been in the absolute state, although definite. The Greek translator, then, would have translated literally, i.e., without the definite article.[206]

In Hellenistic Greek when a substantive which is followed
by a dependent genitive is governed by a preposition, the
omission of its article is acceptable, especially when the
whole phrase describes a collective idea *(Gesamtbegriff)*,[207]
e.g., φύγειν ἀπὸ προσώπου Κύρου, "to flee from (the) face of
Cyrus" (Ctesias, *Pers.* 2); εἰς φυτείαν φοινίκων, "for (the)
planting of date palms" (*PAmh.* 31.8).

When a substantive is followed by the genitive of a personal pronoun in Greek, the first word usually takes the definite
article unless (i) no particular object is meant (βιβλίον μου
= "a book of mine"), or (ii) the pronoun belongs to the predicate (e.g., ὄντα δ᾿ αὐτοῦ ὑπὸ σκέπην, "being under the protec-
tion which is his" [*PTebt.* 34.11]).[208] The phrases in question
(in Mk 1:2; 8:3, 26; 12:11), however, do not belong to either
category (i) or (ii), and, furthermore, in other instances of
this type of phrase Mark does use the article, namely, εἰς τὸν
οἶκόν σου, "to your home" (2:11, 5:19); εἰς τον οἶκον αὐτῆς,
"to her home" (7:30); ἐπὶ τοὺς ὀφθαλμοὺς αὐτοῦ, "upon his eyes"
(8:25). Nevertheless, the article is sometimes omitted in
Hellenistic Greek from the type of phrase in question in fixed
propositional phrases,[209] e.g., ἐν ᾿Αθήναις δ᾿ οὐδένα ἑώρας
εἰς οἶκον αὐτοῦ φοιτῶν; "In Athens did you see no one when you
were going to his home?" (Epictetus 3.24.54); πολλὰ ἀσελγήματα
λέγων εἰς πρόσωπόν μου, "using many terms of abuse to my face"
(*BGU* 3.909.12); εἰς πρόσωπόν μου, "to my face" (*PPetr.* 3.1.2.8).

Hence, the omission of the article before χεῖρας in Mk
9:31 and πρόσωπον in 12:14, since these nouns are followed by
a dependent genitive, could be due to literal translation from
either Hebrew or Aramaic. However, such usage is well attested
in Hellenistic Greek, especially when the anarthrous noun

follows a preposition.[210] Similarly, in Mk 1:2; 8:3, 26;
12:11, where the genitive of a personal pronoun follows an
anarthrous noun which, in turn, is governed by a preposition,
Semitic interference cannot be proved. Although such omission
corresponds to both Hebrew and Aramaic usage, and even though
Mark does use the article in other instances of the same
phrases (namely, in Mk 2:11; 5:19; 7:30; 8:25), we may not conclude that the article was omitted in the phrases in question
by Mark or his sources (Mk 1:2 and 12:11 are direct quotations
from the OG: Exod 23:20 and Ps 117:23) because of Semitic,
since such usage is idiomatic in Hellenistic Greek.[211]

     With regard to Mk 2:21--χεῖρων σχίσμα γίνεται, there is
no reason (*pace* Black) to suspect that the definite article was
omitted from before the word σχίσμα because of Aramaic interference. As we have seen above in section (a), apart from
abstract nouns, the absolute state of nouns in Aramaic is used
for undetermined nouns, and the emphatic state, with rare exception is used for determined nouns. There is no evidence
that the absolute state is ever used for a substantive which
is determined in its context. The (anaphoric) article would
be necessary before σχίσμα only if that word appeared earlier
in the pericope. Since, however, σχίσμα is not mentioned before
vs. 21, it is meant to be undetermined. The clause should
therefore be translated "and a worse tear is the result" or
"is made."[212]

     Hence there is no need to consider that the definite
article has been omitted because of Semitic interference in
Mk 1:2; 2:21; 8:3, 26; 9:31; 12:11, 14. The texts are perfectly acceptable without the article, according to Hellenistic
Greek usage.

2. Pronouns

(a) Personal Pronouns

   (i) Unusual Frequency in Oblique Cases

   J. Wellhausen has claimed that the frequency of unemphatic
personal pronouns in the oblique cases is extremely high in the
New Testament in comparison with that of non-biblical Greek.
He noted that the use of these pronouns corresponds more to
Semitic than to Greek usage, especially where a pronominal
direct or indirect object is repeated after every verb in a
compound sentence, and where a possessive genitive of a pronoun is repeated after every substantive, or is unnecessary in
Greek.[213] N. Turner has also attributed the high frequency
of these pronouns to Semitic interference.[214]

   In classical Greek personal pronouns were used only "where
they were necessary for clarity,"[215] and this is true also of
Hellenistic literary Greek,[216] as well as the papyri written
by more literate persons.[217] In the more vulgar papyri, however, the frequent use of umemphatic personal pronouns is "ein
characteristischer Zug der Umgangssprache."[218] Some examples:
ὅτι μεταβέβλ[ηκα] τὴν κοίτην μου, "because I looked after my
parcel of land" (PPar. 51.11); ὃν ἔφη ἀδελφὸν αὐτοῦ εἶναι,
"whom he said was his brother" (PSI 4.384.4); κατατρέχω αὐτὴν
λέγων οὐ μὴ ἀφῶ αὐτὴν φυγῖν. καταλαμβάνω αὐτὴν καὶ ἐμβάλλω
αὐτήν, "I pursued her saying 'I do not allow her to flee'; I
seize her and strike her" (PPar. 50.17). This fact may simply
be due to the theory that "vernacular Greek, like all vulgar
tongues, does not shun redundancy."[219] On the other hand,
since no really consistent use of unemphatic personal pronouns
in Greek has ever been found outside of the corpus of the
Egyptian non-literary papyri, and since the number of these
papyri in which this syntactical feature obtains is not large,
there may be another explanation for this usage. It is quite
possible that Egyptian interference may account for the overuse
of at least genitive pronouns in the papyri since in Coptic "le
suffixe désignant le possesseur accompagne chaque substantif
déterminé."[220]

   In Hebrew and Aramaic unemphatic pronouns abound as suffixal forms on nouns, verbs, and prepositions. For this reason

the unemphatic personal pronoun is a conspicuous feature of
the OG.[221]

Hence, although the extreme frequency of unemphatic personal pronouns in the oblique cases in the Gospel of Mark is
almost surely due to Semitic interference, in regard to any
particular instance of such a pronoun we must quote in full
agreement the conclusion of Blass-Debrunner-Funk on the subject:
"a rule cannot be formulated since usage varies according to
the degree of dependence on the vernacular or possibly on a
Semitic original, and according to the preference of the author
at the moment."[222]

(ii) Prepositive Use of a Personal Pronoun to Emphasize
     a Noun

J. Wellhausen[223] has claimed that a personal pronoun has
been used prepositively, as in Aramaic, to strengthen the
determination of a noun in two Marcan texts: αὐτὸς γὰρ ὁ
'Ηρῴδης (6:17), and εἰσελθούσης τῆς θυγατρὸς αὐτῆς τῆς 'Ηρῳδιάδος
(6:22).[224] M. Black concurs with this opinion and claims two
more instances as Aramaisms: αὐτὸς Δαυίδ (Mk 12:36 and 37).[225]

In classical and Hellenistic Greek the pronoun αὐτός is
used with an arthrous substantive as an intensive pronoun
("-self") in the prepositive predicate position (αὐτὸς ὁ X),[226]
e.g., αὐτὸς γὰρ μ' ὁ θεὸς ἐποίησεν, "For God himself created
me" (Epictetus 2.6.9). In this intensive use of adjectival
αὐτός the article is often, but not always, omitted with a
proper name or a word denoting an individual,[227] e.g., τὸ γὰρ
κλέψαι οὐδ' αὐτὸς 'Επίκουρος ἀποφαίνει κακόν, "For even Epicurus
himself does not consider theft evil" (Epictetus 3.7.12).
Compare, however, οὐ τῷ ὑποκριτῇ ἀλλ' αὐτῷ τῷ Οἰδίποδι,
" . . . not for the actor but for Oedipus himself" (1.24.18).
When adjectival αὐτος appears in the attributive position
(ὁ αὐτὸς X), it means "the same,"[228] e.g., οὗτος τῇ αὐτῇ ὁδῷ
καὶ τοῦ δουλεύειν ἀπήλλακται, "This man has been set free also
from slavery by the same course (of action)" (Epictetus 2.1.24).
However, in the chancery style of the non-literary papyri there
seems to be a weakening of the distinction between αὐτός ὁ
("-self") and ὁ αὐτός ("the same").[229] With the result that
αὐτός ὁ X often means "this same X, the aforesaid X" and

approaches the meaning of the demonstrative οὗτος or ἐκεῖνος.[230]
In the following examples αὐτός ὁ is to be translated as a
quasi-demonstrative: ὑπὲρ ὃν καὶ ἔθου χειρόγραφον [διὰ 'Αρ]τέ-
ματός μοι περὶ τοῦ αὐτὸν τὸν 'Αντᾶν ἀποστήσειν, "for which you
drew me up a bond through Artemas that said Antas would make
repayment" (POxy. 745.2-3); ἵνα μὴ τοῖς ἀδελφοῖς ἑαυτῶν
[. . . λόγ]ους παρέξονται ὑπὲρ αὐτοῦ τοῦ πράγματος, "lest
for their own brothers . . . they produce accounts for this
business" (BGU 1655.41-42). With proper names or a word which
denotes an individual the article is usually omitted:[231]
κοντωτὸν βασιλικὸν ἐφ' οὗ ναύκληρος καὶ κυβερνήτης αὐτὸς ῟Ωρος,
" . . . the state barge of which the master and pilot is the
said Horus" (PHib. 39.5-7); μετὰ κύριου αὐτοῦ Διονυσίου,
"with the master of the said Dionysius" (PRein. 26.11);
[οἱ]κ(ίαν) καὶ χρηστ(ήρια) πρότ(ερον) α[ὐ(τοῦ)] πατρός μου
κοινωνικὸν πρὸς Κλέωνα, "(I register) a house and fixtures
formerly belonging to (literally, "of") my said father in
common with Cleon" (POxy. 480.2-4).[232]

Since the third person pronoun in Semitic (hû') has been
claimed by Wellhausen and Black to underlie αὐτός in Mk 6:17;
12:36 and 37, and since a Semitic proleptic suffixal pronoun
is claimed to underlie αὐτῆς in Mk 6:22, the following syntactical features of Semitic have to be considered:

In biblical Hebrew (1) in rare instances the personal pronoun hû' may precede a noun in order to emphasize it, with the
meaning "this same X,"[233] e.g., hû' ᶜezrā' ᶜālâ mibbābel,
"This same Ezra went up from Bablylonia" (Ezra 7:6); wĕhû'
yĕḥizqîyāhû sātam 'et môṣā', "And this same Hezekiah closed the
exit" (2 Chr 32:30; also Ezek 3:18; 33:8; 1 Chr 26:26; 2 Chr
28:22; 32:12; 33:23). (2) Extremely rare, if indeed possible,
is the use of a proleptic suffix before a "genitive" (a noun
on the preposition l). As examples of this usage in biblical
Hebrew, Joüon cites the following texts: pĕqudĕhem lĕmattēh
rĕ'ûbēn, "their numbered men (literally "mustered men"),
(namely those) of the tribe of Reuben" (Num 1:21); kĕtôᶜăbōtêhem
lakkĕna ᶜănî, "according to their abominations, (namely those)
of the Canaanite" (Ezra 9:1); millĕbad hityaḥĕśām lizĕkārîm,
"except for the (genealogical) enrollment of them, (namely) of
the men" (2 Chr 31:16).[234]

In Qumran Hebrew neither of these two uses of the pronoun
turns up. In Proto-Mishnaic Hebrew a suffix proleptic of a
following "genitive" occurs: *w^ᵓny šlwm ᵓštw šl dwsts zh*, "and
I Salome, his wife, (namely that) of this Dostes" (Mur 30:25-26).

Black maintains that "the employment of a personal pronoun
in the nominative case . . . to anticipate, for the sake of
emphasis, a following noun, is a well-known Aramaic idiom."[235]
While this is true of Syriac,[236] in biblical and Middle Aramaic
the independent form of the third person pronoun (*hû*ᵓ) is never
used prepositively to emphasize a following noun.[237] Bauer-
Leander claim that in Dan 2:32 *(hû*ᵓ *ṣalmā*ᵓ *rē*ᵓ*šēh dî dᵉhab ṭōb)*
the personal pronoun *hû*ᵓ acts as a prolepsis for the psycholog-
ical subject of the sentence, *ṣalmā*ᵓ, "the statue,"[238] but
this is not correct. Since the independent third person pronoun is never used proleptically elsewhere in Aramaic, the
more plausible explanation is that in Dan 2:32 the pronoun *hû*ᵓ
is a demonstrative adjective, placed before the noun it modifies, as demonstratives sometimes are in Aramaic.[239] Thus the
text should be translated: "As for that statue, its head (was)
of fine gold." On the other hand, in Aramaic a genitive relationship of two determined substantives may be expressed by the
third person suffix on the first substantive, followed by the
particle *dî* and the substantive which is the "genitive" in the
emphatic state,[240] e.g., *šᵉmēh dî *ᵓ*ēlāhā*ᵓ, "his name, (namely
that) of God" (Dan 2:20); *ᵓ*ḥwy dy *ᵓ*brm*, "his brother, (namely
that) of Abram" (1QapGn 21:34).

The OG translates emphatic *hû*ᵓ in Hebrew when it precedes
a noun with the Greek pronoun αὐτός four times: αὐτὸς ὁ
ἄνομος, "this same lawless man" (Ezek 33:8); αὐτὸς Εσδρας
(2 Esdr 7:6); αὐτὸς Σαλωμωθ (1 Chr 26:26); αὐτὸς Εζεκιας
(2 Chr 32:30); once by the demonstrative: ὁ ἄνομος ἐκεῖνος,
"that lawless man" (Ezek 3:18); once as if the Hebrew were a
nominal clause: οὗτός ἐστιν Εζεκιας, "this is Hezekiah"
(2 Chr 32:12); once by paraphrase: υἱὸς αὐτοῦ Αμων, "his son,
Amon" (2 Chr 33:23); OG omits 2 Chr 28:22b. The OG does not
translate in literal fashion the three Hebrew texts adduced
above as possible examples of a proleptic suffix in Hebrew:
ἡ ἐπίσκεψις αὐτῶν ἐκ τῆς φυλῆς Ρουβην, "the numbering of them
from the tribe of Reuben" (Num 1:21); ἐν μακρύμμασιν αὐτῶν τῷ

Χανανι, "in their abominations, for Canaan" (2 Esdr 9:1);
ἐκτὸς τῆς ἐπιγονῆς τῶν ἀρσενικῶν, "except for the offspring
of males" (2 Chr 31:16).

When a proleptic suffix occurs on a noun followed by a
"genitive" in Aramaic, both the OG and Theodotion omit it from
their translations, e.g., τὸ ὄνομα τοῦ κυρίου, "the name of the
Lord" (Dan 2:20 OG); τὸ ὄνομα τοῦ θεοῦ, "the name of God"
(Dan 2:20 Theodotion).

In conclusion, therefore, the pronoun αὐτός in Mk 6:17;
12:36 and 37 should be translated normally as in non-biblical
Greek: "himself," or possibly as "the aforesaid."[241] as in
the papyri. Indeed there is no corresponding usage of a third
person pronoun in either Hebrew or Aramaic contemporaneous with
the writing of the Gospel of Mark. The infrequent use of *hû*
for emphasis in the biblical Hebrew construction discussed
above, and the even more infrequent literal translation of it
into Greek rule out imitation of the OG in these texts. In
Mk 6:22 the use of αὐτῆς does correspond to that of non-biblical
Greek documents ("when the daughter of the aforesaid Herodias
came in"), but it is possible that the common Aramaic construction of a proleptic suffix before a "genitive" has influenced
the writer of the text ("when her daughter, [namely that] of
Herodias, came in").

(iii) Redundant Use after a Relative Pronoun

Οὗ οὐκ εἰμὶ ἱκανὸς κύψας λῦσαι τὸν ἱμάντα τῶν ὑποδημάτων
αὐτοῦ, "of whom I am not worthy to stoop down and untie
the straps of his sandals" (Mk 1:7; in the Synoptic parallels to this verse Matthew omits αὐτου while Luke retains
it);
ἧς εἶχεν τὸ θυγάτριον αὐτῆς πνεῦμα ἀκάθαρτον, "of whom her
daughter had an unclean spirit" (Mk 7:25; the verse is
changed to direct discourse in the Matthean parallel and
omitted entirely in Luke);
θλῖψις οἷα οὐ γέγονεν τοιαύτη ἀπ' ἀρχῆς κτίσεως, "tribula-
tion of such kind that such has not been from the beginning
of creation" (Mk 13:19; τοιαύτη is omitted in Matthew while
the verse does not appear in Luke).

In the first two of these texts a relative pronoun is
resumed by a pleonastic personal pronoun within the same clause.[242]

In the third text a relative pronoun (οἵα) is resumed by its
correlative demonstrative (τοιαύτη), also redundant.

In classical Greek there are a few examples in which a
personal pronoun resumes a relative pronoun in the same clause,
but in these cases the personal pronoun may have been added
for emphasis: Νεοκλείδα . . . ὧν ὁ μὲν ὑμῶν πατρίδα δουλοσύνας
ῥύσαθ᾿, "Sons of Neocles . . . of whom one of you saved his
country from slavery" (Greek Anthology 7.72); πίθον . . . εἰς
ὅν τῶν ἱερέων ἐξήκοντα καὶ τριακοσίους καθ᾿ ἑκάστην ἡμέραν
ὕδωρ φέρειν εἰς αὐτὸν ἐκ τοῦ Νείλου, "a jar . . . into which
three hundred sixty priests, one each day, bring water into it
from the Nile" (Diodorus Siculus 1.97.2). Οἷος and its correlative demonstrative τοιοῦτος are never found within the same
clause.

In Hellenistic Greek such a redundant pronoun is never
found in any of the literary writings outside of the OG. Although, as we have seen, the personal pronouns are used very
frequently in the Greek of the non-literary papyri, only two
examples of the usage in question in that vast amount of writing
have been pointed out: ἐξ ὧν δώσεις τοῖς παιδίοις σου ἓν ἐξ
αὐτῶν, "of which things you gave your children one (of them)"
(POxy. 117.14-16); μηδενὸς ὧν ἔχομεν αὐτῶν φειδομένη, "sparing
nothing of the things which we have (them)" (POxy. 1070.25-26).
These two examples are most probably due to Egyptian interference.[243] There is no instance where a form of τοιοῦτος resumes
a relative outside of the OG. In the latter, τοιοῦτος resumes
the relative οἷος in Gen 41:19, and the relative ὅστις in Exod
9:18, 24; 11:6.

In Hebrew and Aramaic the relative particles ᵓăšer and
dî are undeclined and are often specified by the addition of an
adverb or a suffixal pronoun on a noun, verb, or preposition,
e.g., baqqereb ᵓăšer ᵓîš hāᵓĕlōhîm qābûr bô, "(literally) in
the grave which the man of God was buried in it (= in the
grave which the man of God was buried)" (1 Kgs 13:31); Qumran
Hebrew: wkwl ᵓyš ᵓšr yš ᵓtw dbr ldbr lrbym, "(literally) and
anyone which there is a word with him (= and anyone with whom
there is a word) to be addressed to the Many" (1QS 6:12).
There are no examples in the Proto-Mishnaic material, but
such usage occurs in Mishnaic Hebrew.[244] Biblical Aramaic:

lē ᵓlāhāᵓ dî niš̆mĕtāk bîdēh, "(literally) God which your life-
breath (is) in his hand (= God in whose hand [is] your life-
breath)" (Dan 5:23); Middle Aramaic: *lᵓtrᵓ dy bnyt tmn bh
mdbḥᵓ,* "(literally) to the place which I built there an altar
in it (= to the place in which I built [there] an altar)"
(1QapGn 21:1). In this example one also has an adverb specify-
ing the undeclined relative.

The OG frequently translates the redundant pronoun in
question,[245]e.g., τὰς πόλεις ταύτας ἃς ἐκάλεσεν αὐτὰς ἐπ' ὀνόματος,
"these cities which he called (them) by name" (1 Chr 6:50);
ἐν τῷ τάφῳ τούτῳ οὗ ὁ ἄνθρωπος τοῦ θεοῦ τέθαπται ἐν αὐτῷ,
"in this grave where the man of God was buried (in it)"
(3 Kgdms 13:31).[246]

Hence the redundant pronoun in Mk 1:7 and 7:25 is a result
of Semitic interference whether from imitation of the OG, or
from contemporaneous Hebrew or Aramaic. Redundant τοιαύτη in
Mk 13:19 is most probably due to imitation of the OG, since it
is a conflation of two Old Testament texts: θλίψις οἵα οὐ
γέγονεν, (Dan 12:1 Theodotion; OG has ἡμέρα θλίψεως οἵα οὐκ
ἐγενήθη) and χάλαζαν . . . ἥτις τοιαύτη οὐ γέγονεν ἐν Αἰγύπτῳ
ἀφ' ἧς ἡμέρας ἔκτισται, for Hebrew: *bārād . . . ᵓǎšer lōᵓ hāyâ
kāmōhû bĕmiṣrayim lĕmin hayyôm hiwwāsĕdâ,* "hail . . . which there
has not been such in Egypt from the day of its foundation"
(Exod 9:18).

(b) Ψυχή as a Substitute for the Reflexive Pronoun

In three instances in the Gospel of Mark the use of the
word Ψυχή has been interpreted as a possible Semitizing peri-
phrase for the reflexive pronoun (ἑαυτοῦ), which is lacking in
Hebrew and Aramaic:[247]

τί γὰρ ὠφελεῖ ἄνθρωπον κερδῆσαι τὸν κόσμον ὅλον καὶ
ζημιωθῆναι τὴν ψυχὴν αὐτοῦ, "For what does it profit a
man to gain the whole world but suffer the loss of his
life" (Mk 8:36);
δοῦναι τὴν ψυχὴν αὐτοῦ λύτρον ἀντὶ πολλῶν, "to give his
life as a ransom for many" (Mk 10:45; compare ὁ δοὺς
ἑαυτὸν ἀντίλυτρον ὑπὲρ πάντων, "who gave himself as a
ransom for all" [1 Tim 2:6]);

περίλυπός ἐστιν ἡ ψυχή μου ἕως θανάτου, "My soul is sorrowful unto death" (Mk 14:34; ἵνα τί περίλυπος εἶ ψυχή;
"Why are you sorrowful, O soul?" [Ps 41:6 OG for Hebrew
mah tištôḥaḥî napšî Ps 42:6]).[248]

In Greek ψυχή can mean "life," the immaterial and immortal
"soul," the "conscious self" or "personality" as the center of
the emotions, among other meanings not pertinent to the present
discussion.[249]

In Hebrew the word *nepeš* can signify, among other things,
"throat; neck."[250] Its more usual meanings are: (i) "breath"
which makes man and animal living beings, i.e., the strictly
Semitic notion of "soul," (ii) a "soul" = a living being, an
individual, (iii) "breath" as the life of man: therefore "life,"
(iv) "breath, soul, person" which may express the idea of
"self," e.g., *qōneh lēb ᵓōhēb napšô*, "he who acquires a heart
loves himself" (literally "his soul"--Prov 19:8).[251] With regard to meaning (iv) it is important to note that, though there
is no reflexive pronoun in Hebrew, the reflexive idea can also
be conveyed by the use of the separate forms of the personal
pronouns and by the suffixal forms of the pronoun on a preposition, or on the *nota accusativa* (ᵓ*et*).[252] Thus even when it
is used in sense (iv) *nepeš* "is never a merely otiose peri-
phrasis for the personal pronoun, but always involves a reference to the *mental* personality, as affected by the senses,
desires, etc.[253]

Besides the other meanings of *nepeš*, both Qumran and Proto-
Mishnaic Hebrew use *nepeš* with the nuance of "self" as in
sense (v) above, e.g., *wyqm ᶜl npšw bšbwᶜt ᵓšr lšwb ᵓl twrt
mwšh*, "and let him bind upon himself by an oath (of obligation)
to return to the law of Moses (1QS 5:8); *wbywm ᵓšr yqym hᵓyš
ᶜl npšw lšwb ᵓl twrt mšh*, "And on the day on which a man shall
bind upon himself to return to the Law of Moses . . . "
(CD 16:4-5); in a Proto-Mishnaic Hebrew contract: *špyrh bt
yšwᶜ ᶜl npšh h[k]tbyn š[ᵓlh]*, "Šappirah daughter of Yeshuaᶜ
de[manded] the contracts for herself" (Mur 29 verso 3).[254]

The word *nepeš* is not used in biblical Aramaic, but in
Middle Aramaic it reflects the various meanings of Hebrew
nepeš: (i) [*dḥlt y]tyrᵓ bnpšh*, "[she feared ve]ry much in
her soul" (1QapGn 19:23); (ii) *hb ly npšᵓ dy ᵓyty ly*, "give

me the men (literally "soul," a collective singular) who are
mine" (1QapGn 22:19); (iii) *wtplṭ npšy bdylky*, "and my life
will be saved because of you" (1QapGn 19:20; this text reflects
the Hebrew of Gen 12:13); (iv) "self" in various contracts
exactly as in the Proto-Mishnaic Hebrew contracts: *yhwsp br
nq[sn] ᶜl npš[h]*, "Joseph son of Naq[san] for himself" (Mur
19:26; also 18:9; 19:6, 18; papHevB ar 15, 16).

The OG generally translates Hebrew *nepeš* with the Greek
word ψυχή,[255] but sometimes, when *nepeš* has a reflexive nuance,
the reflexive pronoun is used, e.g., ἀγαπᾷ ἑαυτόν, "he loves
himself" (Prov 19:8; even a personal pronoun is used twice to
translate *nepeš*, in Jer 37:9 and Job 18:4).

In Mk 8:36 ψυχή means "life." This is quite acceptable
in Greek,[256] even though Semitic *nepeš* may also have this meaning (sense [iii] above). Mark uses ψυχή with this meaning in
8:35 (*bis*), 37, and 3:4. Matthew takes over ψυχή in his parallels to these verses (except Mk 3:4, which verse he has entirely omitted). In fact, the whole question of Semitism seems to
arise from the fact that Luke changes ψυχήν in Mk 8:36 to the
reflexive ἑαυτόν. However, he does not hesitate to take over
ψυχή from the other Marcan texts where it means "life,"
namely in his parallels to Mk 3:4 and 8:35 (he omits Mk 8:37).
Hence Luke has changed the sense of Mk 8:36 when he changes
ψυχήν to an emphatic ἑαυτόν: "but to lose *himself*" (Lk 9:25).[257]

Similarly, in Mk 10:45 ψυχή has the meaning "life," just
as it does in the sayings about "life" in chapter 8. Again
Matthew has no problem with the word in his parallel to the
verse, while Luke omits the entire verse. It is true that in
1 Tim 2:6 (cited above) there is a similar, but un-Semitic, version of the saying, and in that text the reflexive pronoun
ἑαυτόν is used. But, although the text is obviously a conflation of ideas which occur in the Old Testament,[258] Mk 10:45
is not a direct quotation from the Old Testament, and therefore not necessarily based on a Semitic *Vorlage*. Hence, although it is possible that the Semitic word *nepeš* is behind
the saying in Mk 10:45, the Greek word ψυχήν ("life") is not
to be taken as a simple reflexive (for ἑαυτόν), and the verse
makes perfectly good sense in Greek.

Finally, in Mk 14:34 ψυχή does not have a reflexive meaning. In fact, even if ψυχή did have the meaning "-self" in
this text, it would have an intensive, not reflexive, function.
In Mk 14:34, however, ψυχή means "soul" or "the conscious self
or personality as the center of emotions, desires, and affec-
tions."[259] This is a good Greek meaning for the word even if
it is also a possible meaning for Semitic nepeš. A similar
use of ψυχή occurs in Mk 12:30, where ψυχή is mentioned among
other faculties: ἐξ ὅλης τῆς καρδίας σου καὶ ἐξ ὅλης τῆς
ψυχῆς σου καὶ ἐξ ὅλης τῆς διανοίας σου καὶ ἐξ ὅλης τῆς ἰσχύος
σου, "with your whole heart and with your whole soul and with
your whole mind and with your whole strength." Both Matthew
and Luke take over this quotation from Deut 6:4-5 without
changing the word ψυχῆς, just as Mt 26:38 reproduces ἡ ψυχή
μου from Mk 14:34 (Luke omits the entire verse). In fact, the
whole question of Semitism arises because Mk 14:34 is similar
to an OG verse, namely Ps 41:6 (cited above). Hence, although
it may well translate a Semitic saying in which nepeš was
used, ψυχή in Mk 14:34 is perfectly good Greek.[260]

(c) The Demonstrative Pronoun

    (i) Frequency of ἐκεῖνος

    In classical times the remote demonstrative ἐκεῖνος was
used both as a pronoun and as an adjective. In Hellenistic
Greek, however, the adjectival use was almost completely
abandoned. In the non-literary papyri as early as the third
century B.C., the definite article alone sufficed for the
deictic nuance once given by the demonstrative adjectives.[261]
This is also true in Epictetus where, although ἐκεῖνος is used
as a pronoun almost 350 times, it occurs as an adjective only
32 times,[262] a proportion of almost 11 to 1.

    The Marcan use of ἐκεῖνος as a pronoun (only twice) and
as an adjective (17 times) yields a proportion of 1 to 8.5, the
complete reverse of that of Epictetus and the papyri. Matthew
and Luke-Acts use ἐκεῖνος similarly to Mark (with ratios of about
1 to 12 and 1 to 8 respectively).[263]

    In biblical Hebrew there are two sets of demonstratives:
(1) zeh (feminine zōʾt, plural ʾēlleh), the proximate

demonstrative, which "almost always points out a (new) person
or thing present," and (2) the personal pronoun *hû*ʾ (feminine
hîʾ, plural *hemmâ*) which serves as a remote demonstrative and
"refers to a person or thing already mentioned or known."[264]
These demonstratives may be used either pronominally or adjectivally.

Qumran Hebrew also uses both sets of demonstratives frequently both as pronouns and as adjectives, e.g., (1) proximate:
(a) as pronoun: *wzh hsrk lʾnšy hyḥd*, "And this is the rule for
the men of the community" (1QS 5:1); *wmh ʾdbr ᶜl zwt*, "And what
shall I say about this?" (1QH 12:32); (b) as adjective: *dbry
hbryt hzwt*, "the words of this covenant" (1QS 2:13); *kyʾ mwᶜd
mlḥmh hywm hzh*, "for the appointed time of war (is) this day"
(1QM 15:12); (2) remote: (a) as pronoun: *kyʾ hwʾh ywm yᶜwd lw*,
"for that is the day appointed by him" (1QM 1:10); *hwʾ hdbr
ʾšr ʾmr yrmyhw*, "That is the word which Jeremiah spoke" (CD
8:20); (b) as adjective: *bywm hhwʾh yᶜmwd kwhn hrwʾš*, "on that
day the chief priest will stand" (1QM 18:5); [. . . *b*]*l*[*y*]*lh
hhwʾ lmnwḥ ᶜd hbwqr*, "[. . . on] that nigh[t] for rest until
morning" (1QM 19:9).

Proto-Mishnaic Hebrew uses both demonstratives as well,
although in the only clear examples of them *zeh* is always used
adjectivally, e.g., *mšnʾ hktb hzh*, "a copy of this document"
(3Q15 12:11); *wʾny šlwm ʾštw šl dwsts zh*, "and I, Salome, wife
of this Dostes . . . " (Mur 30:25-26). Demonstrative *hû*ʾ
(spelled *hw*) occurs only once in this material and is used
pronominally in that text: *hw hpth*, "(In the basin of the
Valley of . . . on the west side a rock is joined by two hooks;)
this (is) the entrance" (3Q15 10:10).

Although in Imperial Aramaic there existed both proximate
(*z/dn*, feminine *z/dʾ*, plural *ʾln*) and remote (*z/dk*, feminine
z/dk, plural *ʾlk; z/dkn*) demonstratives which were used both
as pronouns and as adjectives, in biblical Aramaic the distinction between proximate and remote seems to have broken down,[265]
e.g., *ᶜal děnâ qiryětāʾ dāk hoḥorbat*, "because of this this city
(namely Jerusalem, the city presently under discussion) has
been destroyed" (Ezra 4:15). In this and similar texts (cf.
Ezra 4:13, 16, 19, 21) one would have expected the proximate
demonstrative *dāʾ*, but even here a case can be made for the

translation of *dāk* as the remote demonstrative "that." These
demonstratives may also be used both pronominally and adjectivally in biblical Aramaic. In addition to these forms, the personal pronoun *hû*ʾ may be used adjectivally as a demonstrative,
e.g., *hûʾ ṣalmāʾ*, "that statue" (Dan 2:32). Finally, a pronominal suffix may be used proleptically as a kind of demonstrative,[266] e.g., *bah šaʿătāʾ*, "at this (very) hour" (Dan 3:6,
15; 4:30; 5:5).

In Middle Aramaic the following demonstratives occur:
(1) *dn* is used pronominally and adjectivally and may point out
both proximate and remote objects. Examples: (a) proximate:
(i) as pronoun: *lʾ yrtnk dn lhn dy ypwq*, "this one shall not
inherit you but the one who shall go forth . . . " (1QapGn
22:34); (ii) as adjective: *blylyʾ dn*, "in this night"
(4QEnGiants^b ii 6); (b) remote: (i) as pronoun: *wănt šmth dh*,
"(And if I do not pay back up to this time, the money will be
paid to you at five per cent until it is totally paid back)
even if (literally "and") that (be) a Sabbath year" (Mur 18:7);
(ii) as adjective: *qdmt ywmyʾ ʾln ʾth kdrlʿwmr*, "before those
days (in the remote past) there came Chedorlaomer (the event
presently being narrated)" (1QapGn 21:23; also 4QEn^c 4:11).
(2) *Dk* turns up only in second century documents. It is always
used adjectivally and points out a proximate object: *thmʾ bth*
dk [dy ʾnh] ʾlʿzr zbnh, "the limits of this house [which I]
Eleazar am buying" (papḤevB ar 8; also in lines 5, 7, 11, 13);
byt ywsp dk, "the house of this Joseph" (Mur 31 4 recto 1;
also 21 1-3 14; 25 1 4; 28 1-2 8; 31 3 1; 32:2, 3 [*zk* for *dk*]).
(3) *Hwʾ*, the personal pronoun, is used as a demonstrative adjective: *wṣlyt ʿl [. . .]dpʾ hw*, "and I prayed for that
[. . .]" (1QapGn 20:29); *wnwrʾ hwʾ [dy lmʿrb dbrwnh hwʾ rdp*
lkwl mnyrt], "and this fire [whose course is to the west follows all the luminaries]" (4QEn^d 1 xi 5-6).

In the books of the OG which have been translated from
Hebrew, ἐκεῖνος is used much more frequently as an adjective
than as a pronoun, while in the non-translated books 2-4
Maccabees and Wisdom the proportional usage is nearly one to
one.[267] The reason for this is that the OG translators kept
the Greek distinction between proximate and remote demonstratives even though there is no such clear distinction in Hebrew.[268]

Thus the demonstrative *zeh*, since it usually points out a present object, is usually translated by the proximate demonstrative
in Greek (οὗτος) whether it is used independently or as an adjective.[269] When the pronoun *hû*ᵓ is used adjectivally it is
almost always rendered by the remote demonstrative (ἐκεῖνος)
e.g., ἐν τῇ ἡμέρᾳ ἐκείνη, "on that day" for Hebrew *bayyôm hahûᵓ*
(Gen 15:18). Independent *hûᵓ*, on the other hand, is very
rarely rendered by a form of ἐκεῖνος.[270] When it has little or
no demonstrative force (it is, after all, also used as a personal pronoun in Hebrew), the OG generally translates it with
some form of the pronoun αὐτός. When independent *hûᵓ* does have
demonstrative force, the OG usually renders it by the proximate
demonstrative οὗτος, since demonstrative pronoun *hûᵓ* usually
refers to something psychologically proximate, e.g., οὗτος ὁ
κυκλῶν πᾶσαν τὴν γῆν Αἰθιοπίας, "(The name of the second river
is Gihon;) this (is) the one which circles all the land of
Ethiopia," for Hebrew *hûᵓ hassôbēb ᵓet kol ᵓereṣ kûš* (Gen 2:13).

The OG renders the Aramaic demonstratives in similar fashion
to Hebrew with the result that in the translated Aramaic portions
of Ezra and Daniel ἐκεῖνος occurs 25 times as an adjective,
whereas it is never used pronominally.

Hence, since demonstratives abound in Semitic, and since
translators (of the OG immediately previous to the composition
of the Gospel of Mark render them as described above, the high
frequency of adjectival ἐκεῖνος and a correspondingly low frequency of pronominal ἐκεῖνος in Mark must be due to the interference of Hebrew or Aramaic. Imitation of the OG may also be
at work here, especially in the Old Testament eschatological
phrases ἐκείνη ἡ ἡμέρα (ἡ ἡμέρα ἐκείνη) in Mk 2:20 and 14:25,
and ἐκεῖναι αἱ ἡμέραι (αἱ ἡμέραι ἐκεῖναι) in Mk 13:17, 19, 24.[271]

(ii) Pleonastic Use of the Demonstratives

J. Jeremias has claimed that in the following Marcan texts
a demonstrative adjective has been used pleonastically ("entirely unstressed") and "owes its existence most probably to a
pleonastically placed Aramaic or Hebrew demonstrative pronoun":[272]

ὑμῖν τὸ μυστήριον δέδοται τῆς βασιλείας τοῦ θεοῦ·
ἐκείνοις δὲ τοῖς ἔξω ἐν παραβολαῖς τὰ πάντα γίνεται,

"To you has been given the mystery of the kingdom of God;
to those outside, however, everything is in parables"
(4:11);

καὶ ὃς ἂν σκανδαλίσῃ ἕνα τῶν μικρῶν τούτων τῶν πιστευόντων,
"and whoever skandalizes one of these little ones who
believe . . . " (9:42);

ἀλλὰ ἐν ἐκείναις ταῖς ἡμέραις μετὰ τὴν θλῖψιν ἐκείνην ὁ
ἥλιος σκοτισθήσεται, "But in those days, after *that* tribu-
lation, the sun will be darkened" (13:24);

οὐαὶ δὲ τῷ ἀνθρώπῳ ἐκείνῳ δι᾿ οὗ ὁ υἱὸς τοῦ ἀνθρώπου
παραδίδοται, "Woe to that man by whom the son of man is
betrayed" (14:21);

οὐ μὴ πίω ἐκ τοῦ γενήματος τῆς ἀμπέλου ἕως τῆς ἡμέρας
ἐκείνης ὅταν αὐτὸ πίνω καινὸν ἐν τῇ βασιλείᾳ τοῦ θεοῦ,
"I shall not drink of the fruit of the vine until that
day when I drink it anew in the kingdom of God" (14:25).

As we have seen in section (i) above, the demonstrative
adjective ἐκεῖνος was rarely used in Hellenistic Greek. The
same phenomenon occurred, although to a lesser extent, in the
use of the demonstrative οὗτος: its adjectival use has been
usurped to a great extent by the definite article.[273] Nevertheless, both forms are used by Hellenistic literary authors and
by the more educated of the writers of letters among the non-
literary papyri.[274] Some examples from Epictetus will show
the range of usage by that author and provide some good parallels to the Marcan texts in question:

ἐκεῖνοι μὲν οἱ ὀλίγοι, ὅσοι πρὸς πίστιν οἴονται γεγονέναι
. . . οὐδὲν ταπεινὸν οὐδ᾿ ἀγεννὲς ἐνθυμοῦνται περὶ αὑτῶν,
"these few, who think that they have been born for fidelity
. . . conlcude nothing humble or ignoble concerning themselves" (1.3.4; compare Mk 4:11);

ἄφες λυθῆναί ποτε τῶν δεσμῶν τούτων τῶν ἐξηρτημένων καὶ
βαρούντων, "Allow us to be freed at last from these fet-
ters that are fastened to us and weigh us down" (1.9.14;
compare Mk 9:42);

διὰ ταύτην τὴν μαντείαν ἔρχομαι ἐπὶ τὸν θύτην τουτον,
"Because of this prophecy I come to this diviner" (1.17.29;
compare the use of οὗτος in this text to that of ἐκεῖνος
in Mk 13:24);

μόνον ἐκείνης τῆς διαιρέσεως μέμνησο καθ᾿ ἣν διορίζεται
τὰ σὰ καὶ οὐ τὰ σά, "Only remember that distinction according to which what is yours and what is not yours are
separated" (2.6.24; compare Mk 14:21);

μὴ γένοιτο, φησίν, ἐκείνη ἡ ἡμέρα, "May that day, he says,
never come!" (3.17.4; compare the similar phrase in Mk
14:25; see also Epictetus 1.9.2; 1.26.8; 4.1.26).

In Late Aramaic a "completely superfluous" demonstrative
adjective may be used with little more force than a definite
article,[275] e.g., *hdyn spr ᵓwryt*ᵓ, "the lawbook" (literally
"this lawbook," an object not mentioned before in this text,
y. Šabb. 14ᵈ). Such usage, however, does not occur in either
biblical or Middle Aramaic, nor in biblical, Qumran or Proto-
Mishnaic Hebrew.[276]

Hence, although as we have seen in section (i) that the
demonstrative pronoun ἐκεῖνος (and οὗτος) occurs with abnormal
frequency in the Gospel of Mark, it is impossible to state with
certainty in which texts their use is due to Semitic interference.[277] In regard to the use of the demonstratives in Mk 4:11;
9:42; 13:24; 14:21, and 25 three statements are pertinent:
(1) it is by no means certain that the demonstratives in these
texts do not retain some demonstrative force; (2) there is no
use of pleonastic demonstratives in biblical or contemporaneous
Hebrew or Aramaic; (3) there are almost perfect parallels to
Marcan usage of demonstratives in the Hellenistic author
Epictetus.

(d) The Indefinite Pronoun

    (i) The Numeral εἷς Used as an Indefinite Pronoun

M. Black has claimed that the numeral εἷς ("one") has been
used in the Gospel of Mark (1) as an indefinite pronoun ("someone, a certain X"), and (2) as a kind of indefinite article
("a, an"), because of Semitic interference.[278] M. Zerwick,[279]
N. Turner,[280] and Blass-Debrunner-Funk[281] also see a high
probability of the influence of Hebrew or Aramaic in some of the
Marcan texts cited by Black, and add other Marcan examples of
this use of εἷς. The texts in question are:

(1) εἷς as an indefinite pronoun:[282]

καὶ ἔρχεται εἷς τῶν ἀρχισυναγώγων, "and one of the rulers
of the synagogue came" (5:22);

προφήτης ὡς εἷς τῶν προφητῶν, "a prophet like one of the
prophets" (6:15);

εἷς τῶν προφητῶν, "one of the prophets" (8:28);

καὶ ἀπεκρίθη αὐτῷ εἷς ἐκ τοῦ ὄχλου, "and someone from the
crowd answered him" (9:17);

προσδραμὼν εἷς καὶ γονυπετήσας αὐτὸν ἐπηρώτα αὐτόν," and
someone ran up, knelt before him, and asked him (a question)" (10:17);

καὶ προσελθὼν εἷς τῶν γραμματέων . . ἐπηρώτησεν αὐτόν,"
and coming up, one of the scribes. . .asked him" (12:28);

λέγει αὐτῷ εἷς τῶν μαθητῶν αὐτοῦ," One of his disciples
said to him" (13:1);

'Ιούδας 'Ισκαριώθ, ὁ εἷς τῶν δώδεκα," Judas Iscariot, one
of the Twelve" (14:10);

εἷς τῶν δώδεκα, "one of the Twelve" (14:20);

'Ιούδας εἷς τῶν δώδεκα, "Judas, one of the Twelve" (14:43);

ἔρχεται μία τῶν παιδισκῶν τοῦ ἀρχιερέως, "there came one
of the maids of the chief priest" (14:66);

(2) εἷς as an indefinite article:

ἐπερωτήσω ὑμᾶς ἕνα λόγον, "I shall ask you one (or "a")
question" (11:29);

καὶ ἐλθοῦσα μία χήρα πτωχὴ ἔβαλεν λεπτὰ δύο, "And one (or
"a") poor widow came and put in two copper coins" (12:42).

In classical Greek the indefinite pronoun was the unaccented
form of τις. This word could also act as a kind of indefinite
article when used adjectivally,[283] e.g., ἕτερόν τινα. . .
δυνάστην,"another dignitary" (Xenophon, An. 1.2.20). Various
scholars have contended that the numeral εἷς ("one") was used
substantivally in classical Greek as an indefinite pronoun,
and adjectivally as a kind of indefinite article.[284] However,
in no text adduced by them as evidence has εἷς ever lost its
numerical value, whether it is used as a substantive or as an
adjective.[285]

Although Modern Greek has developed a new form for the
indefinite pronoun, κανείς (from κάν and εἷς),[286] in Hellenistic
Greek the indefinite pronoun is still τις, e.g., εἰσελθόντος

τινὸς τῶν ᾿Ρωμαικῶν, "When a certain Roman came in. . ."
(Epictetus 2.14.1); ἐάν τισιν τῶν ναυκλήρων τοιοῦτο τι συμβηι,
"if such a thing should happen to certain of the pilots. . ."
(*PMagd*. 11.8). There is no Hellenistic literary text in which
substantival εἷς has lost its numerical value and means the same
thing as τις.[287] However, among the non-literary papyri of
Egypt there are several clear examples of εἷς used in place of
the indefinite pronoun (= "a certain one, someone"), e.g.,
ἕνα τῶν παρά σοι τεκτόνων, "a certain one of your carpenters"
(*PFlor*. 185.10); ἑνὸς τῶν γεωργῶν μου, "of a certain one of my
farmers" (*Stud. Pal*. 1.1.2; so also *PSI* 571.5; *PCair.Zen.*
59024.1; 59049.2; 59230.1; *PAmh*. 30.28; *PPar*. 15.15; *PTebt*.
230.11; *BGU* 1044.6). Such usage of εἷς is most probably due to
the interference of Egyptian in the Greek of these texts for the
following reasons: such usage is restricted to a few papyri from
Egypt; in the majority of these same papyri τις is still used as
the indefinite pronoun (as in *PMagd*. 11.8 cited above); in Coptic
the numeral "one" (*oua*) serves as the indefinite pronoun;[288]
the Modern Greek indefinite pronoun is not εἷς, but κανείς.
Hence the indefinite pronoun in Hellenistic Greek is τις, and
not εἷς. The use of εἷς as an indefinite pronoun in the papyri
(and in the Old and New Testaments) does not reflect an internal
development of the Greek language in any level from classical to
Modern Greek, and is due to the interference of other languages
than Greek upon that language.[289]

    With regard to the use of adjectival εἷς as a kind of
indefinite article in Hellenistic Greek the conclusion of
grammarians is almost unanimous. Since the Modern Greek indefinite article is ἕνας (from εἷς),[290] and since there are un-
equivocal examples of this use of adjectival εἷς in both literary
and non-literary texts, such usage must be seen as a genuine
internal development of the Greek language, beginning already in
the second century B.C.[291] Some examples: εἰσελθόντος τινὸς
τῶν ᾿Ρωμαικῶν μετὰ υἱοῦ καὶ ἐπακούοντος ἑνὸς ἀναγνώσματος,
"When a certain Roman had come in with his son and was listening
to a reading" (Epictetus 2.14.1);[292] ἐπηγγείλατο ἕνα ἀγῶνα
ἱππικόν, "he announced a horse race" (Strabo 5.3.2); πορφύρα ἐν
προσκεφαλαίωι ἐνί, "purple dye in a cushion" (*PCair.Zen.*
59069.8; also Plutarch, *Crass*. 4.2; Achilles Tatius 1.1.6;

Longus 4.8; Josephus *AJ* 7.344 [14.3]; Dittenberger, *SIG* 1170.16;
PCair.Zen. 59176.41 and 56; *PSI* 98.4; *PPar.* 6.9; *PTor.* 1.1.27;
2.20; *UPZ* 162.1.27).

In biblical Hebrew the numeral "one" (*ʾeḥād*) may be used
substantivally as an indefinite pronoun (always followed by a
"partitive genitive," a plural noun either as *nomen rectum* or
as the object of the preposition *min*), and adjectivally as a kind
of indefinite article. Examples: *bĕʾaḥad habbōrōt*, "into one
of the pits" (Gen 37:20--where "pits" have not been mentioned
before); *qaḥ nāʾ ʾittĕkā ʾet ʾaḥad mēhannĕʿārîm*, "take one of
the servants with you" (1 Sam 9:3); *wayyiqqaḥ šĕmûʾēl ṭĕlēh ḥālāb
ʾeḥād*, "And Samuel took a suckling lamb" (1 Sam 7:9).

Qumran Hebrew uses *ʾeḥād* as an indefinite pronoun even without a following "genitive": *wlʾ hwšbh <t>pʾ rtm bpy ʾḥd*, "and
their glory is not denied by the mouth of anyone" (CD 6:7); with
a following "genitive": *wkwl ʾyš mnwgʿ bʾḥt mkwl ṭmʾwt hʾdm*,
"and every man who is afflicted with any of all the impurities
of man" (1QSa 2:3; also 4Q*161* 8-10 24; CD 11:19; 12:18); and as
a kind of indefinite article: *wʾnh (= whnh) ʾyš ʾrwr ʾḥd blyʿl
ʿwmd*, "and behold an accursed man of Belial rising" (4Q*175* 23).

In Proto-Mishnaic Hebrew *ʾeḥād* functions as an indefinite
pronoun (without a following "genitive"): [*ʾyn*] *ṣryk lw ʾḥt ʾlh
šlw*, "there is not anything lacking to him except what is his"
(Mur 46:6; cf. 48:5), and as the indefinite article: *šm qll bw
spr ʾḥd tḥtw kk 42*, "(there is) a vessel there; in it (is) a
book: under it 42 talents" (3Q*15* vi 4-6).

Both biblical and Middle Aramaic use the numeral "one"
(*ḥad*) as a kind of indefinite article: *waʾălû ṣĕlēm ḥad śaggî*
"and behold, a great image" (Dan 2:31; also 4:16; 6:18; Ezra
4:8; 6:2); [*wh*]*ʾ ʾrz ḥd wtmrʾ ḥdʾ [yʾy]ʾ*, "[and be]hold (there
was) a cedar and a date palm (which was) beautiful" (1QapGn
19:14-15; also 4QLevi[b] 2:18; see also the following Official
Aramaic texts: Cowley, *AP* 27:5; Kraeling, *BMAP* 10:2; Ahiqar 38).
Both biblical and Middle Aramaic also use *ḥd* as an indefinite
pronoun (always followed by a "partitive genitive" composed of
the preposition *min* and a plural noun), e.g., *qirbēt ʿal ḥad min
qāʾămayyāʾ*, "I approached one of those who stood" (Dan 7:16; see
also in Official Aramaic: Ahiqar 33); *ḥd mn bny byty*, "one of my
household servants (literally "the sons of my house")"

(1QapGn 22:33; also 10:12; 19:11; 22:1; 4Q ⁶Amramᵇ 1:13 [re-
stored]). In neither biblical nor Middle Aramaic, however, is
ḥad used as an indefinite pronoun without a plural "genitive"
following. In this literature the words ᵓn(w)š, "a man" or
br ᵓn(w)š, "a son of man" are used to express the indefinite
"someone," apart from the idiom ḥad min X, "one of the X" explained above, e.g., lāᵓ ᵓîtay ᵓĕnāš ⁶al yabbeštāᵓ dî millat
malkāᵓ yûkal lĕhaḥăwāyâ, "There is no one (literally "no man")
on earth who can explain the matter of the king" (Dan 2:10);
dy lᵓ yškḥ kwl br ᵓnwš lmmnyh, "(descendents) which no one
(literally "no son of man") can number" (1QapGn 21:13). Yet
since ḥad turns up in earlier Aramaic as a kind of indefinite
pronoun without a following "genitive,"²⁹³ we must at least admit
the possibility of such usage in Middle Aramaic.

     When the Hebrew numeral ᵓeḥād acts as an indefinite pronoun
and is followed by a "genitive," the OG usually translates with
the Greek numeral εἷς and a partitive genitive, as in the examples cited above: εἰς ἕνα τῶν λάκκων, "into one of the pits"
(Gen 37:20); ἓν τῶν παιδαρίων, "one of the servants" (1 Kgdms
9:3). When adjectival ᵓeḥād represents the indefinite article,
the OG usually translates literally, with the proper form of
εἷς, e.g., ἄρνα γαλαθηνὸν ἕνα, "a suckling lamb" (1 Kgdms 7:9);
ἀνὴρ εἷς, "a man" (Judg 13:2 B; text A simply has ἀνήρ). The
same is true when the OG and Theodotion translate Aramaic ḥad
in the biblical examples used above: εἰκὼν μία, "an image"
(Dan 2:31); προσῆλθον πρὸς ἕνα τῶν ἑστώτων, "I approached one
of those who stood" (Dan 7:16 OG); προσῆλθον ἑνὶ τῶν ἑστηκότων,
(Dan 7:16 Theodotion).

     With regard to the Marcan texts in question: εἷς in Mk
6:15; 8:28 ("one of the [ancient] prophets"); 14:10, 20, 43
("one of the Twelve") has a numerical force and thus is correct
Greek.²⁹⁴ In 5:22; 12:28; 13:1; 14:66, where εἷς is used as an
indefinite pronoun and is followed by a plural partitive genitive, such usage is incorrect in Hellenistic Greek, and due to
Semitic interference (whether from Hebrew, Aramaic, or imitation
of the OG).²⁹⁵ Εἷς is also used as an indefinite pronoun in
Mk 9:17 and 10:17, and is also incorrect in Greek.²⁹⁶ This use
of the numeral "one" as an indefinite pronoun without a following plural "genitive" is found in Qumran and Proto-Mishnaic

Hebrew, as well as in Official Aramaic. Hence εἷς in Mk 9:17
and 10:17 is a Semitism due to the influence of contemporaneous
Hebrew or (at least possibly) Aramaic.

Finally, it seems that adjectival εἷς in Mk 11:29 and 12:42
has numerical force: "I shall ask you a *single* question"
(11:29);[297] "*one* poor widow" as opposed to the πολλοὶ πλούσιοι,
("many rich people") in Mk 12:41.[298] If in these texts, however,
εἷς has no numerical force, but merely represents the indefinite
article ("a question"; "a poor widow"), such usage is to be
found, if rarely, in contemporaneous non-biblical Greek. It is
much more common, of course, in Hebrew and Aramaic.

Hence Semitic interference has been at work in the use of
the Greek numeral εἷς in place of the indefinite pronoun τις
in Mk 5:22; 9:17; 10:17; 12:28; 13:1; 14:66. Whether adjectival
εἷς is used as a kind of indefinite article or retains its
numerical force in Mk 11:29 and/or 12:42, the usage is quite
correct in Hellenistic Greek.

(ii) Ἄνθρωπος = τις

M. Black has claimed that in certain New Testament texts
the Greek noun ἄνθρωπος has lost its normal meaning ("man, a
human being") and is used as a kind of indefinite pronoun
(= τις, "someone, anyone").[299] Such usage, he claims, is due to
Semitic interference in the following Marcan texts:

ἦν ἐν τῇ συναγωγῇ αὐτῶν ἄνθρωπος ἐν πνεύματι ἀκαθάρτῳ,
"there was in their synagogue a man with an unclean spirit
(1:23);

καὶ ἦν ἐκεῖ ἄνθρωπος ἐξηραμμένην ἔχων τὴν χεῖρα, "and
there was a man there who had (literally "having") a
withered hand" (3:1);

ὡς ἄνθρωπος βάλῃ τὸν σπόρον "as if a man should scatter
seed" (4:26);

ὑπήντησεν αὐτῷ ἐκ τῶν μνημείων ἄνθρωπος ἐν πνεύματι
ἀκαθάρτῳ, "a man from the tombs with an unclean spirit met
him" (5:2);

ἐὰν εἴπῃ ἄνθρωπος τῷ πατρὶ ἢ τῇ μητρὶ κορβᾶν, "If a man
should say to his father or to his mother 'Corban'. . ."
(7:11);

οὐδέν ἐστιν ἔξωθεν τοῦ ἀνθρώπου εἰσπορευόμενον εἰς αὐτὸν
ὃ δύναται κοινῶσαι αὐτόν· ἀλλὰ τὰ ἐκ τοῦ ἀνθρώπου
ἐκπορευόμενά ἐστιν τὰ κοινοῦντα τὸν ἄνθρωπον, "There is
nothing outside of a man which (by) going into him can
defile him; but the things which come out of a man are
what defile the man" (7:15);

πᾶν τὸ ἔξωθεν εἰσπορευόμενον εἰς τὸν ἄνθρωπον οὐ δύναται
αὐτὸν κοινῶσαι, "whatever goes into a man from outside
cannot defile him" (7:18);

τὸ ἐκ τοῦ ἀνθρώπου ἐκπορευόμενον, ἐκεῖνο κοινοῖ τὸν
ἄνθρωπον, "whatever comes out of a man, this defiles the
man" (7:20);

πάντα ταῦτα τὰ πονηρὰ ἔσωθεν ἐκπορεύεται καὶ κοιμοῖ τὸν
ἄνθρωπον, "All these evil things come from within and defile a man" (7:23);

τί γὰρ ὠφελεῖ ἄνθρωπον κερδῆσαι τὸν κόσμον ὅλον, "For what
does it profit a man to gain the whole world?" (8:36);

τί γὰρ δοῖ ἄνθρωπος ἀντάλλαγμα τῆς ψυχῆς αὐτοῦ, "For what
should a man give in exchange for his life?" (8:37);

ἕνεκεν τούτου καταλείψει ἄνθρωπος τὸν πατέρα αὐτοῦ, "For
this a man leaves his father" (10:7 = Gen 2:24 OG);

ὃ οὖν ὁ θεὸς συνέζευξεν ἄνθρωπος μὴ χωριζέτω, "Therefore
what God has joined together let not man separate" (10:9);

πῶλον δεδεμένον ἐφ᾿ ὃν οὐδεὶς οὔπω ἀνθρώπων ἐκάθισεν,
"a bound colt upon which no human being (literally "no one
of men") has ever sat" (11:2);

ἀμπελῶνα ἄνθρωπος ἐφύτευσεν, "a man planted a vineyard"
(12:1);

ὡς ἄνθρωπος ἀπόδημος, "(It is) like a man going on a
journey" (13:34).[300]

In classical Greek there is only one idiom in which the noun
ἄνθρωπος ("a human being, man") does not retain its full meaning
and approximates the meaning of the indefinite pronoun τις.[301]
In this construction anarthrous ἄνθρωπος (and even more frequently, ἀνήρ, "man, a male") is placed in apposition to another
anarthrous noun in order to express the occupation, condition,
or age of someone,[302] e.g., λόγος σπουδαῖος ἀνθρώπου φίλου,
"the earnest counsel of some friend (literally "of a man, a
friend")" (Menander, *frag.* 630). Frequently, the noun in

apposition to ἄνθρωπος or ἀνήρ was originally a participle,[303]
e.g., γέρων ἀνήρ, "some old man" (Plato, *Ly.* 223B). In Hellenistic Greek this usage was extended with the result that
anarthrous ἄνθρωπος (ἀνήρ), when modified by a real participle
or even an adjective denoting action or condition, means no more
than τις: "someone who, an X person," e.g., δεικνύω πῶς ἄνθρωπος
ἀναστρέφεται πεπαιδευμένος, "I show how someone who is educated
(literally "an educated human being") behaves" (Epictetus
1.29.44); ἄνθρωπος συνειδὼς ἑαυτῷ μηθὲν ἀγαθὸν μήτε πεποιηκότι
μήτ' ἐνθυμουμένῳ, "someone conscious in himself that he has never
done or thought a good thing" (Epictetus 3.23.15; also 1.29.54;
2.13.1; 3.20.13; 4.13.14); ἐκδὸς [= ἐκτὸς] ἀνθρώποις ἀσφα[λέσ]ι,
"except for sick people" (*BGU* 1031.13). Apart from this idiom,
that is to say, where ἄνθρωπος is not modified by a participle
or an adjective, or where ἄνθρωπος stands in apposition to
another noun which describes occupation, condition, age, etc.,
in non-biblical Hellenistic Greek ἄνθρωπος means "man, a human
being."[304]

In biblical and Qumran Hebrew the substantive ᵓyš, "man"
can be used in an indefinite sense, e.g., ᵓim yûkal ᵓîš limnôt
ᵓet ⁶ᵃpar hāᵓāreṣ, "If a man (= "anyone") can count the dust of
the earth. . ." (Gen 13:16); ᵓm ymṣᵓ bm ᵓyš ᵓšr yšqr, "If a
man (= "anyone") is found among them who lies. . ." (1QS 6:24).

Similarly, in biblical and Middle Aramaic the substantive
ᵓnš/ᵓnwš, "man, a human being" is used for the indefinite idea
"someone, anyone,"[305] e.g., lāᵓ ᵓîtay ᵓěnāš ⁶al yabbeštāᵓ dî
millat malkāᵓ yûkal lěhaḥăwāyâ, "There is no man (= "not anyone") on earth who can explain the matter of the king" (Dan
2:10); wmny ⁶my ᵓnwš dy ynpq[. . .], "and he appointed a man
(= "someone") to escort [me] out" (1QapGn 20:32).[306]

The OG usually translates Hebrew ᵓîš by ἀνήρ, although
sometimes by ἄνθρωπος, e.g., καὶ εὗρεν αὐτὸν ἄνθρωπος, "and a
man (= "someone") found him" (Gen 37:15). Similarly, Aramaic
ᵓěnāš/ ᵓenōš may be translated by ἀνήρ, e.g., πᾶς ἀνὴρ ὃς ἂν
ὑποδείξῃ τὸ σύγκριμα τῆς γραφῆς, "anyone (literally "every man")
who shows the judgment of the writing. . ." (Dan 5:7), or by
ἄνθρωπος e.g., πᾶς ἄνθρωπος ὃς ἀλλάξει τὸ ῥῆμα τοῦτο, "anyone
(literally "every man") who alters this edict . . ." (2 Esdr
6:11).

Mk 7:11; 8:36, 37; 10:7 (= Gen 2:24 OG) are maxims in
which anarthrous ἄνθρωπος means "man in general; any human
being," and this is good Greek usage (cf. ἀνθρώπῳ μέτρον πάσης
πράξεως τὸ φαινόμενον, "The measure of man's every action is the
sense impression (literally "what appears," Epictetus 1.28.10).
But where ἄνθρωπος occurs anarthrously, without an attributive
participle or adjective, without a noun in apposition to it, but
with the indefinite meaning "someone, anyone" (= τις), the usage
is due to Semitic interference. Thus in Mk 1:23; 4:26; 5:2;
12:1 the use of ἄνθρωπος is probably the result of the influence
of contemporaneous Hebrew or Aramaic, or of imitation of the OG.
While ἄνθρωπος also has an indefinite meaning in Mk 3:1; 13:34,
it is modified in these verses by an attributive participle or
adjective. Thus, while ἄνθρωπος could be a translation from
Semitic in these verses, it is also acceptable Hellenistic Greek
usage. In Mk 7:15 (ter), 18, 20 (bis), 23, the matter is quite
different, since ἄνθρωπος is preceded by the definite article.
These verses do not contain examples of the usage in question,
but are instances of the generic (and anaphoric in 7:15c and
7:20b) use of the definite article with the noun ἄνθρωπος, "man,
a human being." In Mk 10:9 ἄνθρωπος retains its full meaning
of "a human being" in contrast to ὁ θεός, "God" in the same
verse. Finally, ἄνθρωπος in Mk 11:2 is no example of the usage
in question. In this verse the negative pronoun οὐδείς is
followed by the partitive genitive ἀνθρώπων, literally, "no one
of men (= no human being)." Hence ἀνθρώπων in Mk 11:2 cannot
be translated by the indefinite pronoun in English and retains
its full meaning of "human being."[308]

(iii) Ἀπό and a Genitive = an Indefinite Plural

N. Turner has claimed that a prepositional phrase made up
of ἀπό and the genitive plural of a noun (ἀπό X, "[some] of X"),
when used as the subject or object of a verb, is due to Semitic
interference (= the Semitic prepositional phrase with partitive
min).[309] The verses in question in the Gospel of Mark are:
    καὶ ἦραν κλάσματα δώδεκα κοφίνων πληρώματα καὶ ἀπὸ τῶν
    ἰχθύων, "And they gathered up fragments filling twelve
    baskets and some fish" (6:43);

TABLE

The Synoptic parallels to the Marcan texts in question in which:

a) ἄνθρωπος retains its normal meaning "human being"

Marcan verse	Matthean parallel	Lucan parallel
7:11 ἄνθπωπος	ὃς ἄν	--
8:36 ἄνθρωπον	same as Mark	same as Mark
8:37 ἄνθρωπος	same as Mark	--
10:7 ἄνθρωπος	same as Mark	--
10:9 ἄνθρωπος	same as Mark	--
11:2 οὐδεὶς ἀνθρώπων	--	same as Mark

b) ἄωθρωπος as a kind of indefinite pronoun without attributive

1:23 ἄνθρωπος	--	ἄνθρωπος ἔχων
4:26 ἄνθρωπος	--	
5:2 ἄνθρωπος	δύο δαιμονιζόμενοι	ἀνήρ τις
12:1 ἄνθρωπος	ὅστις	same as Mark

c) ἄνθρωπος is modified by an attributive adjective or participle

3:1 ἄνθρωπος ἔχων	same as Mark	καὶ and finite verb instead of participle
13:34 ἄνθρωπος ἀπόδημος	similar to Mark (ἄνθρωπος ἀποδήμων)	ἄνθρωπος τις

d) ἄνθρωπος appears with either the generic or the anaphoric
   article

7:15 τοῦ ἀνθρώπου	similar to Mark (τὸν ἄνθρωπον)	--
7:15 ἐκ τοῦ ἀνθρώπου	ἐκ τοῦ στόματος	--
7:15 τὸν ἄνθρωπον	same as Mark	--
7:18 εἰς τὸν ἄνθρωπον	εἰς τὸ στόμα	--
7:20 τοῦ ἀνθρώπου	τοῦ στόματος	--
7:20 τὸν ἄνθρωπον	same as Mark	--
7:23 τὸν ἄνθρωπον	same as Mark	--

ἵνα παρὰ τῶν γεωργῶν λάβῃ ἀπὸ τῶν καρπῶν τοῦ ἀμπελῶνος,
"(he sent a servant to the tenants) in order to get from
the tenants (some) of the fruits of the vineyard" (12:2).
M. Black says that the sources of this construction in the New
Testament are "almost certainly Semitic,"[310] and adds two texts
to Turner's list:
ἔτι αὐτοῦ λαλοῦντος ἔρχονται ἀπὸ τοῦ ἀρχισυναγώγου,
"While he was still speaking there came (some men) from the
leader of the synagogue" (5:35);
καὶ ἀπ' ἀγορᾶς ἐὰν μὴ ῥαντίσωνται οὐκ ἐσθίουσιν,"and unless
they purify themselves they do not eat (anything) from the
market place" (7:4).[311]

In classical Greek a partitive genitive may be used as the
direct object of a verb,[312] e.g., τῶν πώλων λαμβάνει, "he takes
(some) of the colts" (Xenophon, *An.* 4.5.35), and, though more
rarely, even as the subject,[313] e.g., ἐν χώρᾳ ἔπιπτον ἑκατέρων,
"(some) of those on the other side fell in (their) place"
(Xenophon, *Hell.* 4.2.20).

In Hellenistic Greek (but beginning already in classical
times) the prepositional phrase with either ἀπό or ἐκ replaced
the partitive genitive.[314] The former partitive expression
standing alone, like the classical partitive genitive, may act
as the direct object of a verb, e.g., ἐφάνη ὅτι νενόσφισται
ἀπο τῶν ἀμφιτάτων, "It appeared that he had appropriated (some)
of the carpets" (*PSI* 442.4); συνετάξατο ἀποδώσειν ἀπὸ τῶν
γενημάτων, "he agreed to give back (some) of the produce"
(*PMagd.* 25.3). Prepositional phrases with ἀπό or ἐκ may even
act as the subject of a verb, although the instances of this
usage are extremely rare,[315] e.g., τίθεται ἐν τῶι ὑπολόγωι τῶν
ἐν τῶι ν ἔτει καὶ ἀπὸ τῶν ἕως τοῦ μθ (ἔτους) κειμένων ἐν τοῖς
ἐπισκεφθησομένοις, "there is being placed on the list of the
fifty year old (literally "in the fiftieth year") (fallow plots)
even (some) of the (plots of land) submitted up to the forty-
ninth (year) in the revision" (*PTebt.* 61[b]213). However, this
usage of a prepositional phrase with ἀπό (or ἐκ) as the subject
of a verb has never been cited in any Hellenistic literary
work.[316]

On the other hand, in biblical Hebrew a prepositional
phrase with *min* (= "some, something, one of X") may be used,

rather commonly, either as the subject or the direct object of
a verb, [317] e.g., >im yippōl miśśaᶜărat rō>šô >arṣâ, "Not (any)
of the hair of his head shall fall to the ground" (1 Sam 14:45);
wĕlāqaḥtā middam happār, "and you shall take (some) of the blood
of the bullock" (Exod 29:12).

The usage in question does not occur in either Qumran or
Proto-Mishnaic Hebrew, nor in biblical or Middle Aramaic.

The OG may translate the construction in question with a
partitive genitive alone: εἰ πεσεῖται τῆς τριχὸς τῆς κεφαλῆς
αὐτοῦ, "(literally) if there shall fall (some) of the hair of
his head" (1 Kgdms 14:45); with a prepositional phrase with
ἀπό; καὶ λήμψῃ ἀπὸ τοῦ αἵματος τοῦ μόσχου, "and you shall take
(some) of the blood of the calf" (Exod 29:12); or with a prepositional phrase with ἐκ: ἔπεσαν ἐκ τοῦ λαοῦ, "(some) of the
people fell" (2 Kgdms 11:17).

Hence, the use of a prepositional phrase with ἀπό as the
direct object of a verb in Mk 6:43; 7:4 (if ἀπ' ἀγορᾶς is not
a *constructio praegnans*); 12:2 is Hellenistic Greek usage,
although the construction may have been chosen by the writer of
the gospel or by his sources in imitation of the style of the
OG.[318] In Mk 5:35, however, the prepositional phrase ἀπὸ τοῦ
ἀρχισυναγώγου is not the subject of the sentence, but merely
an adverbial phrase (*pace* Black). The subject of the sentence
is "they," or "some people" contained in the verb. This
impersonal or indefinite use of a plural verb has long been
recognized as a stylistic feature of Mark acceptable in both
classical and Hellenistic Greek. Hence there is no need to
posit Semitic interference for this Marcan usage.[319]

(iv) Οὐ . . . πᾶς = οὐδείς

In classical and Hellenistic Greek the negative οὐδείς
can be used either as a pronoun, e.g., οὐδεὶς ἀλλοτρίου
ἡγεμονικοῦ κυριεύει, "No one is master of another's governing
(principle)" (Epictetus 4.5.4), or as an adjective, e.g.,
οὐδεὶς ἀγὼν δίχα θορύβου γίνεται, "No contest takes place without turmoil" (Epictetus 4.4.31). When adjectival πᾶς, "every,
all," is preceded by a negative particle, it usually means
"not every/all (but some) X," e.g., πᾶσαν οὖν τὴν δοθεῖσαν
παραχωρητέον ἢ οὐ πᾶσαν; καὶ εἰ οὐ πᾶσαν, τίνα; "Must one

concede every (hypothesis) which is proposed, or not every one?
And if not every one, which one?" (Epictetus 1.7.23); πάντα
μοι ἔξεστιν, ἀλλ᾿ οὐ πάντα συμφέρει, "All things are lawful for
me, but not all things are helpful" (1 Cor 6:12; also 10:23).
Yet in one Marcan text: οὐκ ἂν ἐσώθη πᾶσα σάρξ, "(and if the
Lord had not shortened the days) no human being would be saved"
(literally "all flesh would not be saved," Mk 13:20), the expression οὐκ. . .πᾶσα σάρξ, "all flesh. . .not" occurs where
one would expect οὐδείς, "no one," or οὐδεὶς ἄνθρωπος, "no
human being."[320]

It has long been known that in Hellenistic Greek adjectival
πᾶς may be used with a noun after a preposition which has a
negative meaning instead of an indefinite adjective,[321] e.g.,
ἄνευ πάσης αἰτίας ἐξάγεις ἡμῖν ἄνθρωπον ἐκ τοῦ ζῆν φίλον, "Without any (literally "every") reason you are taking out of (this)
life a man friendly to us" (Epictetus 2.15.10; also Plutarch,
Mor., Cons. ad Uxor. 1); ἀπ[οκα]ταστήσω σοι ἄνευ πάσης
ὑπε[ρθέ]σεως [καὶ] εὑρησολογ[ία]ς, "I shall restore to you
(600 drachmas) without any (literally "all") delay or equivoca-
tion" (POxy. 1039.9-11).[322] Moreover, H. Ljungvik has shown
that in a few non-literary papyri adjectival πᾶς preceded by a
negative particle means "no X," as in the Marcan verse in
question:[323] μὴ ἔχοντας πᾶν πρᾶγμα πρὸς ἐμέ, "not having any
(literally "every") crime against me (they served me a summons)"
(PRyl. 113.12-13); ἀπεντεῦθεν οὐ μὴ κρύψω αὐτή<ν>[324] πάσας μου
τὰς κλεῖς, "Henceforward, I will not hide any of (literally "all")
my keys from her" (POxy. 903.16; also PLond. 142.12-16 [This is
the only first century A.D. example]; 932.15-16; BGU 196.27-30;
PFay. 94.11; PSI 1081.15-17; POxy. 1901.53-54). Hence the
Marcan use of οὐ. . .πᾶς = "not any, no" is at least possible
in first-century Greek.[325]

In Hebrew and Aramaic there is no single word which serves
the function of adjectival οὐδείς in Greek. Rather, to express
the idea "not any, no X," these languages use the negative
particle and kl/kwl, "all." Examples:

biblical Hebrew: lō᾿ taʿăśeh kol mĕlā᾿kâ ᾿attâ, "You
shall not do any work" (Exod 20:10; also 12:16; Deut 5:14);
Qumran Hebrew: lw᾿ lht᾿hr mkwl mwʿdyhm, "(And they shall
make no single step. . .) to delay them from any of their
feasts" (1QS 1:14-15; also 2:23; 3:5);

Proto-Mishnaic Hebrew: ᵓl tšmᶜ lk[l] dbr, "you shall
not hear any word" (Mur 17 A 2);

biblical Aramaic: wᵉlāᵓ yisgᵉdûn lᵉkol ᵓĕlāh lāhēn lᵉ-
lāhᵃhôn, "and they did not serve any god except their God"
(Dan 3:28; also 4:15; 6:5);

Middle Aramaic: wlᵓ mn kwl zr wlᵓ mn kwl ᶜyryn, "and not
from any stranger nor from any of the Watchers" (1QapGn
2:16; also 19:23; 20:20).

The OG frequently translates Hebrew lōᵓ. . .kōl by οὐ. . .
πας, e.g., οὐ ποιήσεις ἐν αὐτῇ πᾶν ἔργον, "You shall not do any
(literally "all") work on it" (Exod 20:10). The proper Greek
translation with οὐδείς also occurs frequently, e.g., οὐχ
ὑπελείφθη χλωρὸν οὐδέν, "Not a green thing remained" (Exod 10:15).
As for Aramaic lāᵓ. . . kol, the OG usually translates with
οὐδείς, e.g., οὐδεμίαν ἁμαρτίαν, "no sin" (Dan 6:5). Theodotion
uses the literal οὐ. . .πᾶς in the same verse: πᾶσαν πρόφασιν
. . .οὐχ εὗρον, "they did not find any (literally "every")
pretense."

The use of the phrase πᾶσα σάρξ to mean "everyone, every
human being" is foreign to non-biblical Greek, yet kol bāśār,
"all flesh," is a common expression with this meaning in Hebrew,
e.g., kî hišḥît kol bāśār ᵓet darkô ᶜal hāᵓāreṣ, "for all flesh
had corrupted its way on the earth" (Gen 6:12; also in Num 16:22;
27:16; Deut 5:23; Isa 40:5). The corresponding Aramaic word
biśrāᵓ has the meaning "mankind" in biblical Aramaic: mᵉdārᵉhôn
ᶜim biśrāᵓ lāᵓ ᵓîtôhî, "their (the gods') dwelling is not with
flesh" (Dan 2:11). In Middle Aramaic the following text is
restored with certainty: [wywkḥ lkwl b]śrᵓ, "[and he will con-
vict all f]lesh" (4QEnᶜ 1 i 16 = 1 Enoch 1:9; the Greek text
has πᾶσαν σάρκα).

Hence, although the expression οὐ. . .πᾶς = οὐδείς occurs
in a few non-literary Greek papyri, such usage in Mk 13:20 is
probably due to Semitic interference, whether from imitation
of the OG, or directly from contemporaneous Hebrew or Aramaic,
since the expression πᾶσα σάρξ is obviously Semitic.

(e) Πολλοί = πάντες

J. Jeremias has claimed that in two Marcan verses the Greek
word πολλοί has the inclusive meaning "all" as a result of

Semitic interference.[326] The verses in question are:

δοῦναι τὴν ψυχὴν αὐτοῦ λύτρον ἀντὶ πολλῶν, "to give his
life as a ransom for all (literally "many")" (Mk 10:45);
τὸ αἷμά μου τῆς διαθήκης τὸ ἐκχυννόμενον ὑπὲρ πολλῶν,
"my blood of the covenant (which is) poured out for all
(literally "many")" (Mk 14:24).[327]

In Greek the plural of πολύς means "many," and stands in
contrast to the inclusive idea "all" for which the word πάντες
is used. For example, the two ideas may occur in the same
sentence: διὰ τί οὖν. . .οὐ πάντες ἢ πολλοὶ γίνονται τοιοῦτοι;
"Why then, (if we are endowed by nature for such greatness,) do
not all (men), or (at least) many, become so (namely, so great
as Socrates)?" (Epictetus 1.2.34). In both classical and
Hellenistic Greek, however, the plural of πολύς may be used
with the article as a substantive to mean "the multitude, the
majority," usually with a derogatory nuance: "the vulgar, common crowd, e.g., οἶσθα ὅτι τοῖς μὲν πολλοῖς ἡδονὴ δοκεῖ εἶναι
τὸ ἀγαθόν, "You know that to the vulgar crowd (literally "to
the many") pleasure seems to be the good" (Plato, *R.* 505B);
καταγελῶνται ὑπὸ τῶν πολλῶν, "They (the philosophers) are
laughed to scorn by the crowd (literally "the many") (Epictetus
2.14.29). It is important to note that such usage of οἱ πολλοί
= "the multitude, the crowd" always includes the article, for
without the article substantival πολλοί simply means "many
(people)." This fact may be illustrated by the following text:
κἀγὼ συγκατατάττω ἐμαυτὸν σὺν τοῖς πολλοῖς καὶ μετὰ πολλῶν
περιπατῶ, "I too fall in line with the multitude and walk with
many (people)" (Epictetus 1.24.19). This distinction between
substantival πολλοί without the article = "many (people)" and
οἱ πολλοί is maintained consistently throughout all four books
of Epictetus, even when the latter expression follows a preposition.[328]   Hence in view of this Greek evidence the Marcan texts
ἀντὶ πολλῶν and ὑπὲρ πολλῶν would mean "for many (but not for
all)" in non-biblical Greek.

In biblical Hebrew the corresponding plual for the word
"many," *rabbîm,* may be used without the article in the inclusive
sense "all,"[329] e.g., *ûbĕtôk rabbîm ᵓăhallennû,* "I will praise
him in the midst of all (= the whole congregation; literally
"in the midst of many," Ps 109: 30); *wĕhûᵓ ḥēṭᵓ rabbîm nāśāᵓ,*

"and he bore the sin of all (literally "many," Isa 53:12; also
Exod 23:2; Ps 71:7; Neh 7:2).

In Qumran Hebrew *rbym* usually refers to the community of
full members of the religious sect of Qumran,[330] e.g., *mwšb*
hrbym, "the assembly of the many" (1QS 6:8, 11; 7:10, 13).
The word usually has the article, but in a few texts anarthrous
rbym also describes the entire community of the "Many":
wybdylhw mtwk ṭhrt rbym šnh ᵓḥt, "and they shall separate him
from the midst of the Purification of (the) Many for one year"
(1QS 6:25; also 7:3 and 1QH 15:11). In two instances, however,
rbym without the article does not refer specifically to the Qumran community and apparently has the same inclusive meaning as
it does in the Old Testament texts cited above: *wbswd plᵓkh*
hgbrth ᶜmdy whplᵓ lngd rbym bᶜbwr kbwdkh wlhwdyᵓ lkwl hḥyym
gbwrwtykh, "and with your marvelous counsel you have made your-
self great with me, and you have done marvels to *many* for the
sake of your glory and to make known your mighty deeds to *all*
the living" (1QH 4:28-29); *wyšymkh. . .lmᵓwr [gdwl lᵓwr] ltbl*
bdᶜt wlhᵓyr pny rbym, "and may He make you. . .as a great torch
to shine upon the *world* with knowledge and to enlighten the face
of *many*" (1QSb 4:27). Note the parallelism between the words
rbym and *kwl hḥym* in the first example and between *tbl* and
rbym in the second. *Rbym* is never used in this way in Proto-
Mishnaic Hebrew.

In biblical and Middle Aramaic the corresponding plural
word *ś/śgyᵓyn* is always used adjectivally: *mattĕnān rabrĕbān*
śaggîᵓān, "many great gifts" (Dan 2:48; also Ezra 5:11); *bnksyn*
śgyᵓyn, "with many flocks" (1QapGn 20:33; see also 20:34;
4QEn^d 2 iii 28; 4QEn^e 4 i 11).

The OG usually translates anarthrous *rabbîm* in literal
fashion, e.g., καὶ αὐτὸς ἁμαρτίας πολλῶν ἀνήνεγκεν, "and he
bore the sins of many (= "all")" (Isa 53:12; also 52:14; Ps
108[109]:30; 2 Esdr 17:2 [= Neh 7:2]). In a few instances the
OG adds the article, e.g., ὡσεὶ τέρας ἐγενήθην τοῖς πολλοῖς,
"I have become as a portent for the multitude" (Ps 70[71]:7),
or uses the comparative degree of πολύς (without the article),
e.g., οὐκ ἔσῃ μετὰ πλειόνων ἐπὶ κακίᾳ, "You shall not be with
a multitude for wickedness" (Exod 23:2).

Hence the use of πολλοί = πάντες in Mk 10:45 and 14:24 is
due to Semitic interference. There are clear parallels in
biblical and Qumran Hebrew to the expression in question in the
use of anarthrous *rabbîm* in an inclusive sense (= "all, the
multitude"). Since πολλοί is used in the OG where πάντες might
be expected, imitation of the OG is at least theoretically
possible in the Marcan verses.[331] Finally, since the Late
Aramaic Targum on Isa 53:11 and 12 has *saggî²în* for Hebrew
rabbîm, we cannot rule out an Aramaic *Vorlage* for either of the
two Marcan verses, even though such use of *ś/saggî²în* is not
attested in either biblical Aramaic or the Middle Aramaic material published to date.[332]

(f) Interrogative Pronoun Introducing a Question Expressing
     Wonder or Indignation

     M. Black has stated that in several texts of the New Testa-
ment the interrogative pronoun τί is used "to introduce a
rhetorical question expressing wonder or indignation."[333] This,
he claims, is due to the influence of Aramaic in which the
interrogative particle *mâ* commonly introduces such questions.
The Marcan texts in question are:
     τί οὗτος οὕτως λαλεῖ; Βλασφημεῖ, "Why does this man speak
     thus? He blasphemes!" (2:7);
     τί ταῦτα διαλογίζεσθε ἐν ταῖς καρδίαις ὑμῶν, "Why do you
     consider these things in your heart?" (2:8);
     ἴδε τί ποιοῦσιν τοῖς σάββασιν ὃ οὐκ ἔξεστιν, "Look, why are
     they doing what is not permitted on the Sabbath? (2:24);
     τί δειλοί ἐστε οὕτως, "Why are you thus afraid?" (4:40);
     τί ἡ γενεὰ αὕτη ζητεῖ σημεῖον, "Why does this generation
     seek a sign?" (8:12);
     τί με λέγεις ἀγαθόν, "Why do you call me good?" (10:18);
     εἰς τί ἐγκατέλιπές με, "Why have you forsaken me?"
     (15:34).[334]
Instead of "why?", the normal translation of τί in these texts
(which we have given above), Black would translate τί in all
these verses as "can it be that. . .?", expressing surprise or
indignation. Black also thinks that Mk 2:7 and 8:12 may even
be exclamations: "How this man speaks!" and "How doth this

generation seek a sign!"[335] Such use of τί would not be normal
in Greek, but due to the Semitic use of the interrogative *mâ*
in exclamations.

In both classical and Hellenistic Greek the neuter singular
accusative of the interrogative pronoun, τί, is used adverbially
to mean "why?"[336] e.g., ἀλλὰ τί δὴ οὕτω πρῷ ἀφῖξαι, "But why
have you come so early?" (Plato, *Cri.* 43C); καὶ τί σοι λέγω
χεῖρα, "And why do I say to you 'hand'?" (Epictetus 4.1.79).

In biblical Hebrew the interrogative pronoun *mâ* can be used
to introduce a variety of exclamations and rhetorical questions
expressing wonder or indignation,[337] e.g., *mah nikbad hayyôm
melek yiśrā'ēl*, "How the king of Israel honored himself today!"
(2 Sam 6:20); *mah zeh mihartā limṣō'*, "How is it that you have
found it so quickly?" (Gen 27:20); *ûmâ 'etbônēn ᶜal bĕtûlâ*, "(I
have made a covenant with my eyes), how is it that I should look
upon a virgin?" (Job 31:1).

In Qumran Hebrew *mâ* introduces a rhetorical question expressing wonder, e.g., *wmh yspr' nwš ḥṭ'tw*, "But how shall a man
count up his sins?" (1QH 1:25; also 1:26; 7:32; 12:27). Exclamatory *mâ* does not occur in the Proto-Mishnaic Hebrew material.

In biblical Aramaic the interrogative pronoun *mâ* with the
preposition *k* introduces an exclamation, e.g., *'ātôhî kĕmâ
rabrĕbîn*, "How great (are) his signs!" (Dan 3:33a; also 3:33b).
In Middle Aramaic *mā'* alone may introduce an exclamation, e.g.
drᶜyh' m' špyrn, "Her arms, how beautiful!" (1QapGn 20:4);
m' 'rykn wqṭynn kwl 'ṣbᶜt ydyh', "how long and dainty (are)
all the fingers of her hands!" (1QapGn 20:5). Only in Late
Aramaic, however, does the interrogative pronoun introduce a
rhetorical question expressing wonder or indignation, e.g.,
mh ḥṭ' dyn mn kl yrq', "Did this one then sin more than all the
other plants?" (*y. Šeb.* vi 4, folio 37 verso, col. a, line 8).[338]

The OG sometimes translates exclamatory *mâ* with the Greek
interrogative pronoun τί, e.g., τί δεδόξασται σήμερον ὁ βασιλεὺς
Ισραηλ, (literally) "Why has the king of Israel honored himself
today!" (2 Kgdms 6:20; also Gen 27:20). In other texts, however, a more idiomatic Greek translation has been made, e.g.,
καὶ οὐ συνήσω ἐπὶ παρθένον, "and I will not take notice of a
virgin!" (Job 31:1).

The translation of the interrogative pronoun τί as "why?"
in Mk 2:7, 8, 24; 4:40; 8:12; 10:18 makes perfectly good sense
(as in the translations given above) in Greek. Moreover, it is
the translation used by virtually all commentators and grammarians (with the exception of Turner, mentioned above). Hence,
there is no need to claim a Semitic substratum for the use of τί
in these verses as introducing questions in a manner not possible
in Greek. As for Mk 15:34, εἰς τί, "for what (reason)?" is a
literal translation of the Aramaic lᵉmâ (šᵉbaqtannî) which is
cited in Mk 15:34. This, in turn, translates Hebrew Ps 22:2--
lāmâ ᶜᵃzabtannî, "Why have you forsaken me?" Yet even εἰς τί
= "why, for what (reason)?" is possible in Greek,[339] e.g.,
σὺ δ' εἰς τί δή με τοῦτ' ἐρωτήσας ἔχεις, "And you, for what
(reason) have you asked me this?" (Sophocles, *Tr.* 403; also
OC 524).

3. Numerals and Distributives
(a) Use of the Cardinal for the Ordinal

In the Greek language there are both cardinal and ordinal
numerals, which are normally kept distinct. Yet in Mk 16:2 the
cardinal numeral μία, "one," is used where the ordinal πρώτη
"first," would be expected in Greek: καὶ λίαν πρωΐ τῇ μιᾷ τῶν
σαββάτων ἔρχονται ἐπὶ τὸ μνῆμα, "And very early on the first
(literally "one") (day) of the week (literally "Sabbath")[340]
they came to the tomb." In Hebrew and Aramaic both cardinal
and ordinal numerals exist, but in certain instances the ordinal
is used where the cardinal would be expected in Greek. Hence
some scholars have suspected that the cardinal μία has been used
for the ordinal in Mk 16:2 because of Semitic interference.[341]

In classical and Hellenistic Greek the cardinal number is
used, as it is in English, to indicate how many objects are
being discussed, e.g., Ἀθηναῖοι μὲν δυοῖν νεοῖν ἐναντίαιν αἰεὶ
τὴν νῆσον περιπλέοντες, "The Athenians, constantly sailing
around the island with two ships (going) in opposite directions
. . ." (Thucydides 4.23.2); νικῶσιν τοίνυν οἱ δέκα τὸν ἕνα ἐν
τούτῳ ἐν ᾧ κρείσσονές εἰσιν, "Therefore, the ten (men) overcome
the one (man) in the matter in which they are better" (Epictetus
1.29.14). The Greek ordinals, also as in English, indicate

which particular rank or order of several objects is under
discussion, e.g., περὶ πρώτου ξύλου ἀθρόοι καταρρέοντες,
"rushing all at once for the first bench" (Aristophanes, *Ach*.
25-26); γόνυ λαβεῖν τὸ πρῶτον, εἶτα τὸ δεύτερον, εἶτα τὸ τρίτον,
"to receive the first joint, then the second, then the third"
(Epictetus 4.8.40). The one exception to this rule is the use
of the cardinal εἷς, "one," to indicate the first in a list or
series of things, with the ordinals (and sometimes ἄλλος,
"another," for the second item) to enumerate the subsequent
items in the series, e.g., τῶν περιοίκων μίαν μοῖραν ἐποίησε,
ἄλλην δὲ Πελοποννησίων καὶ Κρητῶν, τρίτην δὲ νησιωτέων πάντων,
"He made one part out of free villagers, a second (literally
"another") out of Peloponnesians and Cretans, a third out of
all the islanders" (Herodotus 4.161); ὕδωρ ὄμβριον ἔγχριε μέχρι
μίας καὶ δευτέρας ἡμέρας, "Rainwater poured down for one and a
second day" (Galen, *De compositione medicamentorum* 4 [Kühn ed.
12.746]).[342] It is important to note, however, that the cardinal
εἷς is used to enumerate the first in a series only when the
other items in the series ("a second, a third") are named.[343]

In biblical Hebrew the distinction between the uses of the
cardinals and the ordinals[344] is generally the same as it is
in Greek, e.g., ʾak dābār ʾeḥād ʾānōkî šōʾēl mēʾittĕkā, "but one
thing I demand from you" (2 Sam 3:13); an ordinal: *min hayyôm
hārîʾšôn ʿad hayyôm hāʾaḥărôn*, "from the first day to the last
day" (Neh 8:18). However, the cardinal numeral ʾeḥād, "one,"
may be used instead of the ordinal *riʾšôn*, "first," to enumerate
the first in a series, e.g., *šēm hāʾaḥat ʿādâ wĕšēm haššēnît
ṣillâ*, "the name of the one was Adah and the name of the second
was Zillah" (Gen 4:19; see also Exod 1:15; 25:12; Num 11:26;
Ruth 1:4); *šēm hāʾeḥād pîšôn. . .wĕšēm hannāhār haššēnî gîḥôn
. . .wĕšēm hannāhār haššēlîšî ḥiddeqel*, "The name of the one
is Pishon. . .and the name of the second river is Gihon. . .
and the name of the third river is Tigris" (Gen 2:11-14; see
also 1:5; Job 42:14). But here we see the same phenomenon that
we noted above about Greek: the other items in a series are
enumerated with the ordinal.

In Qumran Hebrew, except in the enumeration of dates (see
below), the cardinal and ordinal numerals are used with the
proper distinction. A possible exception might be at 1QM 7:12.

The context of this text is a discussion of the role of "seven priests": *wyṣᵓw*. . .* šbᶜh kwhnym mbny ᵓhrwn*, "Seven priests of the sons of Aaron. . .shall go out" (7:9-10). Then follows: *hkwhn hᵓḥd yhyh mhlk ᶜl pny kwl ᵓnšy hmᶜrkh*. . .*wbyd hššh yhyw hṣwṣrwt hmqrᵓ*, "The one priest shall walk in front of all the men of the line. . .and in the hand of the six shall be the trumpets of summons" (7:12-13). The cardinals *ᵓḥd* and *ššh* are used with the article for "the one" and "the six." If *hkwhn hᵓḥd* means "the first priest," then we have an example in which the cardinal is used where the ordinal might be expected. This may be the case,[345] but there occur similar phrases with *hāᵓeḥād* in biblical Hebrew in which there is no idea of priority ("the first X"): *wĕlāqaḥ hakkōhēn ᵓet hakkebeś hāᵓeḥād*, "(A leper shall bring two male lambs and one ewe lamb) and the priest shall take the one male lamb" (Lev 14:12; see also Gen 42:32; Deut 25:11; 1 Kgs 18:25; 2 Kgs 6:3; 1 Chr 1:19). In Lev 14:12 there is no mention of a second or another male lamb, and the phrase *hakkebeś hāᵓeḥād* seems to mean simply "one of the lambs." Furthermore, when the ordinal idea of "first" is meant elsewhere in the same Qumran document, the ordinal forms are used: *yktwbw ᶜl hrᵓyšwn my[k]l* . . .*ᶜl hrby ᶜy rpᵓl*,"they shall write on the first 'Mi[chae]l'. . .on the fourth 'Raphael'" (1QM 9:15). Hence, 1QM 7:12 should probably be translated "one of the priests. . .(and) the six (others)."[346]

In Proto-Mishnaic Hebrew a cardinal is never used where one would use an ordinal, except in the enumeration of dates (see below).

In biblical and Middle Aramaic, too, the cardinal numerals are usually used with their proper distinction, except in the system of dating discussed below.

Since the only clear instance in which Hebrew and Aramaic use a cardinal numeral where Greek would use an ordinal is in the enumeration of dates, and since the Marcan usage in question (in Mk 16:2) concerns the enumeration of a day of the week, a discussion of the ancient Greek and Jewish systems of dating follows.

In ancient Greece the month was divided at various times and places into units of ten, five, and nine days.[347] Around the first century A.D. the Egyptian division of the month into

seven day periods began to gain acceptance. In this system,
however, each of the seven days was named after one of the
planets.[348]

Certain periods of feasting and fasting of seven days are
mentioned in the Old Testament, e.g., *šibᶜat yāmîm maṣṣōt
tōʔkēlû ʔak bayyôm hāriʔšôn tašbîtû śeʔōr*, "Seven days you
shall eat unleavened bread, indeed on the first day you shall
put away leaven" (Exod 12:15; see also Lev 6:6, 39, 40; Num
28:17; Deut 16:4), and the numbering of the days in those contexts is always with the ordinals, e.g., Exod 12:15 (cited
above); *ûbayyôm haššēbîᶜî*, "and on the seventh day. . ."
(Exod 12:16; see also Lev 6:7, 35, 39, 40; Num 28:18; Deut 16:4).
However, the days of a seven-day week as a regular time interval
never occur in the Hebrew Old Testament. The regular system of
dating in the Hebrew Old Testament refers to the days of the
month, frequently also with the enumeration of the year. The
days of the month are always expressed by the cardinal number
(with or without the word *yôm*, "day")[349] e.g., *bĕʔeḥād laḥōdeš*,
"on (day) one (= "the first") of the month" (Exod 40:2); *bĕyôm
šĕmōnā laḥōdeš*, "on day eight (= "the eighth") of the month"
(2 Chr 29:17). The number of the month is always expressed by
the ordinal, but the number of the year may be either a cardinal
or an ordinal number, e.g., cardinal: *bišnat ʔarbaᶜ. . .
bĕʔarbāᶜā laḥōdeš hattĕšiᶜî*, "in year four (= "the fourth"). . .
on (day) four (= "the fourth") of the ninth month" (Zech 7:1);
ordinal: *bišnat hattĕšîᶜît*, "in the ninth year" (2 Kgs 25:1).
However, whenever the year enumerated is the "first year," the
cardinal *ʔaḥat* (and never the ordinal) is always used, e.g.,
bišnat ʔaḥat lĕdāryāweš, "in year one (= "the first") of
Darius" (Dan 9:1); *ûbišnat ʔaḥat lĕkōreš*, "in year one (= "the
first") of Cyrus" (2 Chr 36:22).

A day of the week is mentioned only once in Qumran Hebrew,
in a discussion about the Sabbath: *bywm hšyšy*, "on the sixth
day" (CD 10:14-15). The ordinal is used. In this literature
the days of the month are enumerated by the cardinals as in
biblical Hebrew: *hʔḥd l[ḥw]dš*, "(day) one (= "the first") of
the [mon]th" (1Q22 1:22); *[ᶜ]šr lḥwdš*, "(day) four (= "the
fourth") of the month" (1Q22 3:10).

In Proto-Mishnaic Hebrew the number for the day of the
month as well as the number of the year is always the cardinal:
b^cšrym $w^{\jmath}$ḥd ltšry šnt $^{\jmath}$rb^c lg$^{\jmath}$wlt yśr$^{\jmath}$l, "on the twenty-first of
Tishri of the year four (= "the fourth") of the liberation of
Israel" (Mur 30:8); b14 lmrhšwn šnt $^{\jmath}$ḥt lg$^{\jmath}$wlt yśr$^{\jmath}$l, "on the
fourteenth of Marheshwan of the year one (= "the first") of the
liberation of Israel" (Mur 22 1-9:1; also 24 A 1, B 1, C 1,
D 1, E 1; 29 1).

The days of the week are never mentioned in either biblical
or Middle Aramaic. The day of the month is always enumerated
by the cardinal number in both these levels of Aramaic, e.g.,
biblical: ^{c}ad yôm tĕlātâ lîraḥ $^{\jmath}$ădār, "up to day three (= "the
third") of the month Adar" (Ezra 6:15); bywm ḥd lšt$^{\jmath}$ ḥmyšytˀ,
"on day one (= "the first") of the fifth year" (1QapGn 12:15);
b$^{\jmath}$ḥd lmrhšwn šnt št, "on (day) one (= "the first") of Marheshwan
of year six" (Mur 19:1). In biblical Aramaic and in the Middle
Aramaic of Murabba^{c}at and Hever the number of the year is always
expressed by the cardinal, e.g., bišnat ḥădâ lĕkôreš, "in year
one (= "the first") of Cyrus" (Ezra 5:13; see also 4:24); b10
lšbṭ šnt hdh lḥr[wt. . .], "on (day) ten (= "the tenth"), year
one (= "the first") of the liber[ation of Israel]" (Mur 23:1;
the number of the year is also expressed by the cardinal in
Mur 18:1; 19:1 [cited above]; 20:1; 25 1:1); b^{c}sry[n] $l^{\jmath}$[y]r
šnt tlt lhrt yśr$^{\jmath}$l, "on day twenty (= "the twentieth"), year
three (= "the third") of the liberation of Israel (pap?HevB ar 1).
In Qumran Aramaic, however, the number of the year is expressed
by the ordinal in 1QapGn 12:15 (cited above).[350]

The use of cardinals in dates in Aramaic documents may
have been derived from the ancient custom of writing the numbers
as ciphers. Thus dates in Egyptian Aramaic documents (Official
Aramaic) were often expressed by ciphers following the words šnt
and ywm (in the construct state), and acting as a nomen rectum,
e.g., by[w]m 2 l[y]rḥ $^{\jmath}$pp šnt 27 ldrywš mlk$^{\jmath}$, "on day two of
the month Epiphi of year twenty-seven of King Darius" (Cowley,
AP 1:1; also 5:1; 8:1; 9:1 and frequently; Kraeling, BMAP 1:1;
2:[1]; 3:1 etc.; but cf. [with the numeral written out] šnt šb^c
$^{\jmath}$rthšsš mlk$^{\jmath}$, "year seven of King Artaxerxes" [Ungnad, APE
98:4]; Ezra 6:15 [cited above]; Dan 7:1). It is impossible to
say whether the same process could have been at work in Hebrew

dating, because it is not known whether before the second
century B.C. "there existed in Israel, as in other nations,
special signs for figures, or whether numerical notation was
entirely unknown."[351]

In Late Aramaic the days of the week are designated by the
cardinal numeral followed by the word "Sabbath" (šb²/šwb² absolute
form, šbt²/šwbt² emphatic form) with the preposition b, e.g.,
ḥd bšbt² try, tlt² ²rbᶜ t² , ḥmš ² ᶜrwbt², šbt² lyt lh bn zwg,
"The first (day) in the week has the second (as a mate), the
third (has) the fourth, the fifth (has) the preparation day;
the Sabbath has no partner" (Gen. Rab. 11:8); ḥd bšb², "the
first (day) in the week" (Tg. Esth. II 3:7); b²rbᶜ bšbt², "on
the fourth (day) in the week" (Tg. Esth. I 2:9).[352]

The OG usually translates Hebrew ²eḥād when it refers to
the first of a series by the cardinal εἷς (Gen 1:5; 2:11; 4:19;
Exod 1:15; 25:12; Num 11:26; Ruth 1:4; but cf. Job 42:14, where
πρώτην is used). In dates, where the days of the month are
always enumerated by the cardinal in both Hebrew and Aramaic,
the OG almost always translates the first day of the month by
the cardinal (ἡμέρα) μία,[353] e.g., ἐν ἡμέρᾳ μιᾳ τοῦ μηνὸς τοῦ
πρώτου, "on day one (= "the first") of the first month" (Exod
40:2); ἐν ἡμέρᾳ μιᾷ τοῦ μηνὸς τοῦ ἑβδόμου, "on day one (= "the
first") of the seventh month" (2 Esdr 3:6). By contrast, the
OG always renders the other days of the month by the ordinal
number,[354] e.g., τῇ ἡμέρᾳ τῇ ὀγδόῃ τοῦ μηνός, "on the eighth
day of the month" (2 Chr 29:17); ἑβδόμη τοῦ μηνός, "on the
seventh (day) of the month" (Ezek 30:20; see also 1:1; Lev 23:32;
4 Kgdms 25:8; Zech 7:1).

Expressions for the days of the week occur in the titles
of three Psalms in the OG (not in the Hebrew text): τῆς μιᾶς
σαββάτων, "of the one (= "the first day") of the week" (Ps 23
[24]:1); δευτέρᾳ σαββάτου, "on the second (day) of the week"
(Ps 47[48]:1); τετράδι σαββάτων, "on the fourth day of the week"
(Ps 93[94]:1).

In addition to the synoptic parallels to Mk 16:2 (Mt 28:1
and Lk 24:1), the phrase τῇ μιᾷ (τῶν) σαββάτων, "on the first
(day) of the week" also occurs in Acts 20:7; Jn 20:1 and 19.
We note also the phrase κατὰ μίαν σαββάτου, "every (day) one
of the week (= "every Sunday," 1 Cor 16:2).

Since the phrase μία σαββάτων/ου occurs in the OG, in all
four gospels, in Acts, and in 1 Corinthians, it was probably a
fixed formula deriving from a Jewish or Semitic system of dating. Since this system of dating does not conform to that of
later Rabbinism, but is identical in its use of the cardinal
μία and the ordinals for the rest of the days with the OG translation of the days of the month, this use of the cardinal--
unacceptable to Hellenistic Greek usage--is most likely due to
imitation of the OG.[355]

(b) Ἐν and a Cardinal for a Multiplicative Numeral

In the Marcan texts καὶ ἔφερεν ἓν τριάκοντα καὶ ἓν ἐξήκοντα
καὶ ἓν ἑκατόν, "and it bore (fruit) thirtyfold and sixtyfold and
a hundredfold" (Mk 4:8), and καρποφοροῦσιν ἓν τριάκοντα καὶ ἓν
ἐξήκοντα καὶ ἓν ἑκατόν, "and it yields thirtyfold and sixtyfold
and a hundredfold" (Mk 4:20), there are two problems: (i) the
great divergence in the text tradition, and (ii) the use of
and a cardinal numeral to express a multiplicative numeral.

(i) At Mk 4:8 the uncial manuscripts ℵ and C* read ΕΙΣ
three times; ℜ A D Θ have ΕΝ three times; W has ΤΟ ΕΝ three
times; B has ΕΙΣ. . .ΕΝ. . .ΕΝ. At Mk 4:20 all uncials have
ΕΝ (W has ΤΟ ΕΝ) before τριάκοντα, B C* omit ΕΝ before ἐξήκοντα,
and B alone omits ΕΝ before ἑκατόν. In the text of B at Mk 4:8
the change of prepositions or of genders of the numeral from
ΕΙΣ to ΕΝ in the obviously parallel phrases would be meaning-
less and "intolerably harsh."[356] With the text of B thus called
in question, the preferred text of Mk 4:8 is triple ΕΝ.[357]
Whatever the correct text of Mk 4:20 may be, ΕΝ occurs before a
cardinal number (τριάκοντα) at least once, but most probably
three times as in Mk 4:8.

(ii) the question, therefore, is whether ΕΝ in these two
texts represents the preposition ἐν or the neuter of the numeral
ἕν ("one"). Rough and smooth breathing marks (which indicate
whether or not a word beginning with a vowel is pronounced, or
at least was pronounced originally, with or without initial
[h]) were only added to the uncials much later.[358] Hence the
evidence of the uncial manuscripts themselves on this point may
be discarded. The preposition ἐν with the dative is found

with the meaning "amounting to" in a few papyri, e.g., ἔσχες τὴν πρώτην δόσιν ἐν δραχμαῖς τεσσεράκοντα, "you had the first gift in (the form of) forty drachmas" (POxy. 724.7); καὶ ἐπλήρωσα [αὐ]τὸν [το]ὺς μισθοὺς τῆς παρακομιδῆς τοῦ σώματος ὄντας ἐν δραχμαις τριακοσίαις τεσσαράκοντα, "and I paid him (the grave-digger) the costs of the transportation of the body amounting to three hundred forty drachmas" (PGrenf. 2.77.4-6; also BGU 72.11; 970.14; 1050.8; POxy. 56.8; 708.4). However, in all of these texts, a numerical amount of some particular unit or measure (drachmas, artabas, acres) is always specified, unlike the Marcan texts in question. Furthermore, both Matthew and Luke understand Mk 4:8 in a multiplicative sense.[359] On the other hand, the word in question may be the numeral ἕν. As has long been recognized, the Marcan phrase with ἕν and another number to express a multiplicative numeral is unintelligible in Greek. Moreover, Mark himself elsewhere uses the correct form for a multiplicative: ἐὰν μὴ λάβῃ ἑκατονταπλασίονα, "if he should not receive a hundredfold" (Mk 10:30).

In biblical Hebrew the multiplicatives are expressed by the cardinal number, e.g., $šeba^c$, "seven times" (Lev 26:21), by the dual of the numeral, e.g. $šib^catayim$, "sevenfold" (Gen 4:15), or with $pě^cāmîm$ (literally "steps") and the cardinal, e.g., $mē^â$ $pě^cāmîm$, "a hundredfold" (2 Sam 24:3).[360]

In Qumran Hebrew the multiplicative is always expressed with p^cmym, e.g., $šb^c$ p^cmym, "seven times" (1QM 6:1); ^cd $šlwš$ p^cmym, "up to three times" (1QS 7:11). There is no example of the multiplicative in Proto-Mishnaic Hebrew.

In Aramaic, however, a multiplicative may be expressed by the numeral $ḥd$ ("one") followed by a cardinal number, e.g., Official Aramaic: $ḥd$ ^âlp, "a thousandfold" (Cowley, AP 30.3); biblical Aramaic: $ḥad$ $šib^câ$, "sevenfold" (Dan 3:19); Middle Aramaic: $wyhb$ lh $ḥd$ $tryn$ bkl dy $hw^â$ lh, "and he gave him two times (the amount) of all he had (before)" (11QtgJb 38:4, for Hebrew $wayyōsep$ $YHWH$ ^et kol ^ăšer $lě^îyōb$ $lěmišneh$, "And YHWH added to all that Job had a double [amount]" [Job 42:10]). The expression of a multiplicative by the cardinal number alone (as in biblical Hebrew) in the Targum of Job is probably due to literal translation: $wtrtyn$ w^clyhn $l^â$ ^âwsp, "(I spoke once and I will not answer), twice, and I will not add to them"

(11 QtgJb 37:5, for Hebrew ûšětayim wělō᾿ ᾿ōsîp, "twice, and
I will not continue" [Job 40:5]).

The OG and Theodotion translate the Aramaic of Dan 3:19
with the correct Greek multiplicative ἑπταπλασίως, "sevenfold."
As for the Hebrew multiplicative, the OG translates either with
the Greek multiplicative, e.g., ἑκατονταπλασίονα, "a hundredfold" (2 Kgdms 24:3), or by adding a substantive to the cardinal
according to the sense, e.g., ἑπτὰ ἐκδικούμενα, "seven punish-
ments" (Gen 4:15); πληγὰς ἑπτά, "seven plagues" (Lev 26:21).

Hence the phrase ἓν τριάκοντα καὶ ἓν ἑξήκοντα καὶ ἓν
ἑκατόν, "thirtyfold or sixtyfold or a hundredfold" (Mk 4:8 and
20) is the result of Aramaic interference.

(c) Distributives Expressed by Repetition

In two Marcan texts a distributive numeral is expressed by
repetition of the cardinal numeral: ἤρξατο αὐτοὺς ἀποστέλλειν
δύο δύο, "he began to send them out two by two" (Mk 6:7);
ἤρξαντο λυπεῖσθαι καὶ λέγειν αὐτῷ εἷς κατὰ εἷς· μήτι ἐγώ, "They
began to be sorrowful and to say to him one by one, 'It isn't I,
is it?'" (Mk 14:19). In both texts the doubled numerals may be
in the same case as the pronouns with which they are in apposition. Both Matthew and Luke omit the difficult δύο δύο in their
parallels to Mk 6:7. Matthew changes the phrase εἷς κατὰ εἷς
to εἷς ἕκαστος, "each one" in his parallel to Mk 14:19, and
Luke omits the pericope entirely.

The normal expression in both classical and Hellenistic
Greek for the distributive is the preposition κατά (or ἀνά)
with the accusative of the cardinal numeral,[361] e.g., ἐγίνοντο
σποράδες κατὰ μίαν τε καὶ δύο, "and they (the Amazons) were
scattered one by one and two by two" (Herodotus 4.113); ἄν τε
ὁμοῦ ἄν τε καθ᾿ ἕνα ὁμοίως κακόν ἐστιν, "whether (they die)
all together or one by one it is equally an evil" (Epictetus
3.22.33); κατὰ ἑκατὸν καὶ κατὰ πεντήκοντα, "by hundreds and
by fifties" (Mk 6:40). There are two texts in classical Greek
in which the distributive idea is allegedly expressed by repetition of a numeral: ἦ καὶ τὸν Περσᾶν αὐτοῦ τὸν σὸν πιστὸν πάντ᾿
ὀφθαλμὸν μυρία μυρία πεμπαστάν. . .ἔλιπες ἔλιπες, "In truth. . .
did you leave, did you leave. . .there the Persian, your eye

trusty in all things, who reviewed ten thousand, ten thousand"
(Aeschylus, *Pers*. 978-84); μίαν μίαν· ἀντὶ τοῦ κατὰ μίαν.
Σοφοκλῆς "Εριδι, "Μίαν μίαν: instead of κατὰ μίαν. Sophocles
in *Eris*" (The Antiatticist, *Anecdota Graeca* 1.108).[362]

It is doubtful, however, that in these two texts the
numeral is repeated to express the distributive idea because
such a construction never occurs again in the lengthy writings
of either Aeschylus or Sophocles. It may be repeated for
emphasis. The repetition of μυρία in the Aeschylus text is
probably an example of anadiplosis (rhetorical doubling) as is
the double ἔλιπες ἔλιπες in the same text. The text of Sophocles
is an alleged fragment of the lost play *Eris* recorded by the
Antiatticist in the sixth century A.D. The phrase μίαν μίαν,
when found elsewhere is used adverbially and means: "once in a
while, occasionally"[364] or "together."[365]

In Hellenistic Greek a distributive numeral is very rarely
expressed by repetition of a cardinal numeral, and never in a
literary text: τοὺς κλάδους ἔνικον (= ἔνεγκον) εἰς τὴν ὁδὸν
πάντα εἴνα δήσῃ τρία τρία κὲ ἐλκύσῃ, "carry all the branches
into the road so that he might bind them together three by three
and drag them along" (*POxy*. 121.19). In this text the numerals
are neuter plurals in the accusative case and are most probably
used adverbially, since they cannot be in apposition to the
masculine noun κλάδους. Another example: ἐπίγρ<αφον> ἐν ἑκάστῳ
τῶν φύλλων τὰ τῶν θεῶν ὀνόματα κὲ ἐπευθάμενος ἔρε (= αἷρε) κατὰ
δύο δύο, "Write on each of the leaves (of palm) the names of
the gods and, having prayed, lift them up two by two" (*POxy*.
886.16-20). In this text the repeated numeral (δύο) is in the
accusative case after the preposition κατά. The third and final
example: ἔστιν τάραχοι (= τάριχοι?) δεκαδύο καὶ κοπταὶ
εἰκοσιδύο τῇ μικρᾷ καὶ δίδι (= δίδου) αὐτῇ ἀνὰ ἓν ἕν, "There
are twelve smoked fish and twenty-two sesame cakes for the
little (girl), (and) give (them) to her one by one" (Preisigke,
Sammelb. 7660.31).[366] In this text the repeated numeral (ἕν)
is in the accusative case after the preposition ἀνά. The fact
that the neuter form ἕν is used when the items to be given are
masculine (τάραχοι) and feminine (κοπταί) shows that the phrase
ἀνὰ ἕν came to be regarded as a single word much like καθ' εἷς,
which is discussed below. However, the doubling of the numeral

in this text and the two papyri cited above requires an explanation. In Coptic the distributive is expressed with a repetition
of the cardinal number.[367] Since repetition of a cardinal to
express a distributive does not seem to occur in classical or
Hellenistic Greek, outside of a few documents written in Egypt,
the three examples of it cited above may be explained as due to
the confusion of the Greek idiom with that of the Egyptian
language.[368] Hence the repetition of the numeral in Mk 6:7 and
14:19 does not seem to be in accord with normal Greek usage.

    In Hebrew, on the other hand, distributive numerals may
be expressed by the repetition of the cardinal number,[369] e.g.,
šĕnayim šĕnayim bāʾû, "They went in two by two" (Gen 7:9) Qumran
Hebrew: šnym šnym bʾw ʾl htbh, "They entered the ark two by two"
(CD 5:1, a paraphrase of Gen 7:9); Proto-Mishnaic Hebrew:
wprwṭ kl ʾḥd wʾḥ[d], "and the exact total of all (the treasures)
one by one" (3Q15 12:12-13). Here the numeral is repeated with
the conjunction waw.[370]

    No distributive numeral ever turns up in biblical Aramaic.
In Middle Aramaic the distributive idea is expressed in one text
by repetition of the cardinal with the conjunction waw: lkwl
ḥd wḥd [mn ʿwbdyhwn], "with regard to all [of their deeds] one by
one (4QEn[c] 1 vi 1). In Late Aramaic distributives are regularly
expressed by the repetition of the cardinal numeral.[371]

    The OG usually translates the Hebrew construction in ques-
tion in literal fashion, e.g., δύο δύο, "two by two" (Gen 7:9;
cf. 7:2, 3, 15), but may also use the correct Greek construction
as in 3 Kgdms 18:13--ἀνὰ πεντήκοντα, "fifty by fifty" (for
Hebrew ḥămiššîm ḥămiššîm).

    Hence the repetition of the numeral δύο in Mk 6:7 is due
to Semitic interference, from imitation of the OG, from contemporaneous Hebrew, or (at least possibly) from contemporaneous
Aramaic.

    In the case of Mk 14:19, the expression εἷς κατὰ εἷς is
also unparalleled in non-biblical Hellenistic Greek. It is the
result of a mixture of the Semitic idiom in which the cardinal
is repeated, and the Hellenistic pronominal expression καθεῖς/
κατὰ εἷς, "one by one, each one."[372]

    There are also two verses in the Gospel of Mark in which
the distributive idea is expressed by repetition of a noun (and

we mention it here to fill out the picture): καὶ ἐπέταξεν αὐτοῖς
ἀνακλιθῆναι πάντας συμπόσια συμπόσια, "And he ordered them to
sit down company by company (literally "And he ordered them that
all, companies, companies, sit down," Mk 6:39; here the accusative neuter plurals συμπόσια συμπόσια are in apposition with
πάντας, the subject of the infinitive); καὶ ἀνέπεσαν πρασιαὶ
πρασιαί, "and they sat down group by group (literally "and they,
groups, groups, sat down," Mk 6:40; here the nominative plurals
πρασιαὶ πρασιαί would be the subject of ἀνέπεσαν, or would stand
in apposition to the pronoun "they" contained in the verb).
Matthew omits the repeated word in Mk 6:39 and the entire verse
40. Luke avoids the repeated words in both verses.

The repetition of a noun to express the distributive idea
never occurs in Greek. The usual construction for this is the
preposition κατά (or ἀνά) with the accusative of the noun.[373]

In biblical Hebrew single words, and even whole groups of
words, may be repeated in a variety of ways to express the
distributive idea:[374]

(i) simple repetition of the word: hayyōṣē᾿ haśśādeh šānâ
šānâ, "(seed) coming forth (from) the field year by year"
(Deut 14:22);

(ii) with the prepositions b or l before each word:
wayyilqĕṭû ᾿ōtô babbōqer babbōqer, "and they gathered it
morning by morning (every morning)" (Exod 16:21);
labbōqer labbōqer, "morning by morning" (1 Chr 9:27);

(iii) with the preposition b before the second word only:
tō᾿kĕlennû šānâ bĕšānâ, "you shall eat it year by year"
(Deut 15:20);

(iv) with the two words joined by copulative waw:
bĕ᾿omram ᾿ēlāy(w) yôm wāyôm, "when they spoke to him day
by day" (Esth 3:4).

In Qumran Hebrew a type of distributive is expressed by
repetition of a noun with the preposition b on the second word,
as in biblical Hebrew (iii) above: kkh yᶜśw šnh bšnh, "Thus
they shall do year by year" (1QS 2:19; also 1QM 2:8), or with
the repeated word joined to the first word by the copulative
waw, as in biblical Hebrew (iv) above: ltkwn ᶜt wᶜt wlmšql ᾿yš
w᾿yš, "in accordance with the arrangement of season by season
and the weight of man by man" (1QS 9:12).

There is no distributive construction attested in biblical
Aramaic. In Middle Aramaic a type of distributive construction
turns up with repetition of a noun with the copulative *waw:*
ḥd lkwl gbr wgbr, "one for each man" (2Q24 4:8; also 11QtgJb
38:7-8).

The OG translates the Hebrew distributive construction of
simple repetition of a noun in various ways:

(i) by simple repetition of the noun in Greek, e.g.
καὶ ἦσαν ποιοῦντες ἔθνη ἔθνη θεοὺς αὐτῶν, "But nation
after nation kept making their (own) gods" (4 Kgdms 17:29,
for Hebrew *gôy gôy;* cf. Num 9:10; Exod 8:10[14]);

(ii) by inserting the preposition κατά before the repeated
nouns, e.g., κατὰ φυλὰς φυλάς, "tribe by tribe" (Zech
12:12, for Hebrew *mišpāḥōt mišpāḥōt;* cf. Deut 14:22);

(iii) by the normal Greek construction: κατά with a single
noun, e.g., καθ' ἡμέραν, "day by day" (Prov 8:30, for
Hebrew *yôm yôm*).

Hence the distributives expressed by repetition in Mk 6:39
συμπόσια συμπόσια, "company by company") and Mk 6:40 (πρασιαὶ
πρασιαί, "group by group") are due to Semitic interference,
possibly from imitation of the OG. The simple repetition of a
noun in a distributive sense as in these Marcan verses does not
occur in contemporaneous Semitic literature. However, since
the distributive idea may be expressed in Qumran Hebrew and
Middle Aramaic by repetition of the noun with the conjunction
waw (and in Qumran Hebrew also with the preposition *b*), it is
possible that the Marcan expressions in question may derive
from contemporaneous Semitic, although not by word-for-word
translation.

(d) Εἷς. . .καὶ εἷς = ὁ μέν (ἕτερος). . .ὁ δέ (ἕτερος)

Hebrew and Aramaic express the correlative idea: "one. . .
another/the other" (or: "one. . .one," also possible in English) by repetition of the numeral "one" with the conjunction
waw, "and" (examples given below). In classical Greek, this
idea is usually expressed by the definite article (with a
demonstrative force) repeated with the particles μέν. . .δέ,[375]
e.g., τὸ μὲν γὰρ αὐτῶν διὰ διδαχῆς, τὸ δ' ὑπὸ πειθοῦς ἡμῖν
ἐγγίγνεται, "for one of them arises in us by teaching, the

other by persuasion" (Plato, *Ti*. 51E). Hence it has been
claimed that the use of εἷς. . .καὶ εἷς (. . .καὶ εἷς), "one
. . .and one (. . .and one)" in three Marcan texts is due to
Semitic interference:[376]

καὶ ποιήσωμεν τρεῖς σκηνάς, σοὶ μίαν καὶ Μωϋσεῖ μίαν καὶ
'Ηλίᾳ μίαν, "Now let us make three tents, one for you
and one for Moses and one for Elijah" (Mk 9:5);
δὸς ἡμῖν ἵνα εἷς σου ἐκ δεξιῶν καὶ εἷς ἐξ ἀριστερῶν
καθίσωμεν ἐν τῇ δόξῃ σου, "Grant us that we may sit, one
at your right and one at your left, in your glory" (Mk
10:37);
καὶ σὺν αὐτῷ σταυροῦσιν δύο λῃστάς, ἕνα ἐκ δεξιῶν καὶ ἕνα
ἐξ εὐωνύμων αὐτοῦ, "And they crucified two robbers with
him, one on his right and one on his left" (Mk 15:27).[377]

As we have seen above (in section [a] "Use of the Cardinal
for the Ordinal"), the numeral εἷς, "one," is used in Greek to
indicate the first in a list or a series when the second item is
enumerated by the ordinal δεύτερος, "second," or by ἕτερος or
ἄλλος, "(the) other." Moreover, in a few texts, the enumeration
of a duality or a quantity may be made by the repetition of
the numeral εἷς with the particles μέν. . .δέ,[378] e.g., ἓν μὲν
γάρ ἐστι παραδείγματος εἶδος τὸ λέγειν πράγματα προσγεγενημένα,
ἓν δὲ τὸ αὐτὸν ποιεῖν, "(There are two forms of argument:)
namely, one form of argument is to relate things that have
(actually) happened before, the other (literally "and one") is
to invent (them) oneself" (Aristotle, *Rh*. 2.20.2 [1393a]; also
En 6.1.5 [1139a]); τούτων δ' ἔστιν ἓν μὲν παισίν, ἓν δὲ ἐφήβοις,
ἄλλο τελείοις ἀνδράσιν, ἄλλο τοῖς ὑπὲρ τὰ στρατεύσιμα ἔτη
γεγονόσι, "(four parts of a square:) one of these is for boys,
one for youths, another for mature men, another for those past
the age of military service" (Xenophon, *Cyr*. 1.2.4); ἐπιστόλια
β, ἓν μὲν περὶ Ταύγχιος, ἓν δὲ περὶ Τετειμούθιος, "two letters,
one about Taugchis and one about Teteïmuthis (*PGoodsp*. 3.11-14);
καρποδέσμια μικτὰ δύο, ἓν μὲν σανδύκινον καὶ ἓν πορφυροῦν,
"two motley armlets, one red and one purple" (*POxy*. 1153.13-14).
The example from Oxyrhynchus seems to have combined the classical usage of μέν. . .δέ with the simple copulative καί. We
note, however, that the precise Marcan usage εἷς. . .καί εἷς
is never found in non-biblical Greek.

On the other hand, the idiom used to express the enumeration "one. . .and one" in both Hebrew and Aramaic is the numeral
"one" repeated after the conjunction *waw*. Examples:

biblical Hebrew: *tāmĕkû bĕyādāy(w) mizzeh ʾeḥād ûmizzeh
ʾeḥād*, "they held up his hands, one (ʾeḥād) on this (side)
and one (ʾeḥād) on that (side)" (Exod 17:12); *ʾeḥād nōśēʾ
šĕlōšâ gĕdāyîm wĕʾeḥād nōśēʾ šĕlōšet kikkĕrōt leḥem wĕʾeḥād
nōśēʾ nēbel yāyin*, "(three men:) one carrying three kids,
and one carrying three loaves of bread, and one carrying
a skin of wine" (1 Sam 10:3; also Lev 12:8; 15:15);

Qumran Hebrew: *wšʿrym šnym lm[g]dl ʾḥd l[ymyn wʾ]ḥd
lśmʾwl*, "and a tower has two gates, one to [the right and
o]ne to the left" (1QM 9:14); *ʾḥt ʾhb ʾl lkwl ʿdy ʿwlmym
. . . ʾḥt tʿb swdh*, "(two spirits:) God loves one for all
eternity. . .the other (literally "one"), he loathes its
counsel" (1QS 3:26--4:1). This example lacks the copula.

Proto-Mishnaic Hebrew: no examples;

biblical Aramaic: no examples:

Middle Aramaic: *[try mgd]lyn ḥd m[n y]mynʾ wḥd mn śm[ʾl]*,
"[two tow]ers, one o[n the r]ight and one on the le[ft]"
(5Q15 1 i 12); *[. . .]t ʾrʿʾ ḥd mnhwn lmdbr bh bny ʾnšʾ wḥd
mnhwn [lk]l [ymyn wlnhryn wḥd mnhwn] lmdbryn*, "[And I saw
three section]s of the earth: one of them (was) for the
dwelling of the sons of men in it, and one of them (was)
[for al]l [the seas and rivers, and one of them] (was)
for the deserts" (4QEnastr[b] 23 8-9; also 4QEnastr[c] 1 ii 19
[restored]).

The OG translates the Hebrew usage in question literally,
e.g., ἐστήριζον τὰς χεῖρας αὐτοῦ, ἐντεῦθεν εἷς καὶ ἐντεῦθεν εἷς,
"they propped up his arms, one here and one there" (Exod 17:12);
ἕνα αἴροντα τρία αἰγίδια καὶ ἕνα αἴροντα τρία ἀγγεῖα ἄρτων καὶ
ἕνα αἴροντα ἀσκὸν οἴνου, "(three men:) one carrying three kids,
and one carrying three baskets of loaves and one carrying a
skin of wine" (1 Kgdms 10:3; also Lev 12:8; 15:15).

Although we have seen a few instances of Greek usage which
is rather similar to that in the Marcan texts in question, the
exact usage itself never turns up in non-biblical Greek. Since
Hebrew and Aramaic usage corresponds exactly to that of Mark,
the use of εἷς. . .καὶ εἷς in Mk 9:5; 10:37; 15:27 is most

probably due to Semitic interference, whether from imitation
of the OG, or from contemporary Hebrew or Aramaic.

4. The Noun
(a) Nominative Case

(i) Article + Nominative = Vocative

In the Greek language many masculine and feminine singular
nouns have a separate form for the vocative case, which is used
in exclamations and in direct address. Other nouns, which have
no distinct vocative form, use the nominative form to express
the vocative idea. Since it is already determined, a vocative
(of either type) normally does not take the definite article.[379]
In several Marcan texts, however, the nominative (with the definite article) is used in direct address where one would expect
the vocative:

ἔξελθε τὸ πνεῦμα τὸ ἀκάθαρτον ἐκ τοῦ ἀνθρώπου, "Unclean
spirit, come out of the man!" (Mk 5:8);

τὸ κοράσιον, σοὶ λέγω, ἔγειρε, "Little girl, I say to
you, arise!" (Mk 5:41);

τὸ ἄλαλον καὶ κωφὸν πνεῦμα, ἐγὼ ἐπιτάσσω σοι, ἔξελθε ἐξ
αὐτοῦ, "Deaf and dumb spirit, I order you, come out of
him!" (Mk 9:25);

καὶ ἔλεγεν· ἀββά ὁ πατήρ, πάντα δυνατά σοι, "And he kept
saying, 'Abba, Father, all things (are) possible for you'"
(Mk 14:36);

ὁ θεός μου, ὁ θεός μου, εἰς τί ἐγκατέλιπές με, "My God,
my God, why have you forsaken me?" (Mk 15:34); cf. ὁ θεός,
ὁ θεός μου, πρόσχες μοι· ἵνα τί ἐγκατέλιπές με, "God my
God give heed to me, why have you abandoned me?" Ps 21
[22]:2 OG).[380]

In classical Greek, nominative forms are sometimes used in
direct address instead of vocatives in poetry (seldom in
prose).[381] This occurs only in the following cases:[382]

(1) where a second substantive (in the nominative) is
joined to a prior vocative by the conjunctions τε or καί, or
when the nominative stands in apposition to the prior vocative,
e.g., ὦ δέσποτ᾽ ἄναξ. . .λαμπρός τ᾽ αἰθήρ, "O Master, King. . .
and glowing Ether" (Aristophanes, *Nu.* 264-65); ὦ Κῦρε καὶ οἱ

ἄλλοι Πέρσαι, "O Cyrus and other Persians" (Xenophon, *Cyr.*
3.3.20); ὑμεῖς δὲ οἱ ἡγεμόνες. . .πρὸς ἐμὲ πάντες συμβάλλετε,
"You, O leaders. . .come to me, all (of you)" (Xenophon, *Cyr.*
6.2.41);

(2) an attributive adjective in the nominative may modify
a vocative, e.g., ὦ τλήμων ἄνερ κακῶν τοσούτων οὐχ ὁρᾷς ἐπιρροάς,
"O wretched man, do you not see floods of such evils?" (Euripides,
Andr. 348; compare ὦ γενεὰ ἄπιστος, "O faithless generation!"
[Mk 9:19]);

(3) in a few instances a nominative with the article may
replace a vocative when the verb is in the imperative mood,
e.g., ὁ παῖς, ἀκολούθει δευρο, "Slave, follow (me) hither!"
(Aristophanes, *Ra.* 521; also *Av.* 665-66; *Ach.* 242; Plato, *Smp.*
218B). But, as has been pointed out, this rare usage occurs
only when inferiors are commanded;[383]

(4) in a very few other instances a nominative form is
used without the article where a vocative would be expected,
e.g., ὦ φίλος, εἶπε, "O friend, speak!" (Aeschylus, *Prom.* 545;
also Euripides, *Supp.* 277; Aristophanes, *Nu.* 1168).

In Hellenistic Greek there are a few examples in which a
nominative is joined to a vocative by a conjunction or by
apposition, e.g., ὦ δέσποτ᾽ Ὀσεράτι κα<ὶ> θεοί, "O master
Oseratis and gods" (UPZ 1.1); κύριε ὁ θεός, "Lord God" (Epictetus
2.16.13--but this text merely repeats a formula from Jewish
Christian magic[384]). There are also a few "unsure" examples
in non-literary Greek cited by Mayser, in which a nominative
(without the definite article) is used where a vocative might
be expected:[385] Δημήτριος Δημητρίου χρηστὲ χαῖρε, "Demetrius,
gracious (son) of Demetrius, hail" (Preisigke, *Sammelb.* 4013;
also 439); Ἀπολλώνιος, λαβὲ τοὺς χαλκούς, "Apollonius, take
the coins" (*PLeid.* C p. 118 2.7; also *PPar.* 43 *conclusio*).
However, the fact is that in no Hellenistic Greek text, which
has not been influenced by Jewish or Christian writings, and
which can be dated to the first century A.D. or before,[386] is
the arthrous nominative used in place of the vocative, as it
is in the Marcan texts presently under discussion.

In biblical Hebrew the vocative idea is very frequently
expressed with substantives other than proper names by means
of the definite article on the noun,[387] e.g., *hōšíᶜā hammelek*,

"Help, O king!" (2 Sam 14:4); $wayy\bar{o}{}^{\jmath}mer$ ${}^{\jmath}\bar{e}l\hat{e}k\bar{a}$ $ha\acute{s}\acute{s}\bar{a}r$, "And he
said '(It is) to you, O commander'" (2 Kgs 9:5). When a vocative
has a suffixal pronoun, it may not take the article since it is
already determined by the suffix,[388] $b\breve{e}s\bar{o}d\bar{a}m$ ${}^{\jmath}al$ $t\bar{a}b\bar{o}{}^{\jmath}$ $nap\breve{s}\hat{\imath}$,
"Come not into their council, my soul" (Gen 49:6). In Qumran
Hebrew, on the contrary, the article is not used with vocatives,
e.g., $qwmh$ $gbwr$, "Arise, O Mighty One!" (1QM 12:10); $\breve{s}m^{c}w$
$\d{h}kmym$. . .$wnmhrym$, "Hear, O wise men. . .and you that are quick!"
(1QH 1:34-35); $hwsypw$ ${}^{c}rmh$ $\d{s}dyqym$, "Redouble prudence, O you
just!" (1QH 1:35-36). There are no examples of direct address
in the Proto-Mishnaic Hebrew texts.

In biblical Aramaic the vocative idea with nouns other than
proper names is usually expressed by the emphatic state of the
noun,[389] e.g., ${}^{\jmath}ant(h)$ $malk\bar{a}{}^{\jmath}$ $h\bar{a}z\bar{e}h$ $h\breve{a}wayt\bar{a}$, "You saw, O king"
(Dan 2:31; also 2:29, 37; 3:9, 10); $l\breve{e}k\hat{o}n$ ${}^{\jmath}\bar{a}m\breve{e}r\hat{\imath}n$ ${}^{c}ammayy\bar{a}{}^{\jmath}$
${}^{\jmath}ummayy\bar{a}{}^{\jmath}$ $w\breve{e}li\breve{s}\breve{s}\bar{a}nayy\bar{a}{}^{\jmath}$, "You are commanded, O peoples, nations,
and languages" (Dan 3:4). In the published Middle Aramaic texts
there is no example of a vocative consisting of a simple noun.
Vocatives in this literature always have a suffix or are followed
by a "genitive" in a construct chain (and therefore are in the
construct state). As in Hebrew, when an Aramaic vocative has a
suffixal pronoun, it is determined by that pronoun and lacks the
emphatic ending (= the article in Hebrew), e.g., biblical
Aramaic: $m\bar{a}r\hat{\imath}$ $\d{h}elm\bar{a}{}^{\jmath}$ $l\breve{e}\breve{s}\bar{a}n\breve{e}{}^{\jmath}ayk$, "My lord, (may) the dream (be)
for those who hate you" (Dan 4:16); Middle Aramaic: $wk^{c}n$ $lkwn$
${}^{\jmath}nh$ ${}^{\jmath}mr$ bny [. . .], "And now I say to you, my sons. . ."
(4QEn^{g} 1 v 24 = *1 Enoch* 94:1; also 1QapGn 2:13, 24; 22:32).

The OG frequently translates the Hebrew vocative in literal
fashion, that is, with the article and the nominative, e.g.,
ὁ ἄρχων, "O commander" (4 Kgdms 9:5). But the proper, vocative,
case is also used, e.g., Βασιλεῦ, "O king" (2 Kgdms 14:4). In
the case of one word, θεός, "God," as J. C. Doudna has pointed
out,[390] the arthrous nominative used as a vocative (ὁ θεός)
seems to be a fixed phrase in the OG. Curiously enough, although
the arthrous vocative $h\bar{a}{}^{\jmath}\breve{e}l\bar{o}h\hat{\imath}m$, "O God," never occurs in the
Hebrew Old Testament, the anarthrous vocative ${}^{\jmath}el\bar{o}h\hat{\imath}m$ (which
occurs frequently in Psalms) is almost always translated by
ὁ θεός, e.g., Ps 41:2; 42:2; 43:2 (some fifty-one times in
Psalms).

With regard to a vocative which is determined only by a
suffix in Hebrew, the OG frequently translates with an arthrous
nominative and a possessive pronoun, e.g., ἡ ψυχή μου, "O my
soul" (Gen 49:6; Hebrew: *napšî*); ὁ θεός μου, "My God" (Ps
21[22]:3; Hebrew: *ʾĕlōhay*).

In translating biblical Aramaic vocatives both the OG and
Theodotion always use the proper vocative case in Greek (for
the Aramaic texts see above): βασιλεῦ, "O king" (Dan 2:29, 31,
37; 3:9, 10); ἔθνη καὶ χῶραι, λαοὶ καὶ γλῶσσαι, "O nations and
places, peoples and tongues" (Dan 3:4 OG): λαοί, φυλαί, γλῶσσαι
(Theodotion); βασιλεῦ (Dan 4:19 OG = Masoretic Text 4:16); κύριε
(Dan 4:19 Theodotion = Masoretic Text 4:16).

Hence the use of arthrous nominatives to express direct
address (where a vocative would be correct in Hellenistic Greek)
in Mk 5:8, 41; 9:25; 14:36; 15:34 has probably been caused by
Semitic interference in Marcan Greek. Although the interference
may possibly be due to Hebrew, Aramaic, or to imitation of the
OG in Mk 5:8, 41; 9:25; 14:36, it is most probably due to Aramaic
in Mk 5:41 and 14:36 where the evangelist cites the Aramaic
saying. However, since Hebrew and Aramaic both lack the article
when a suffix is used with a noun, in Mk 15:34 ὁ θεός μου is
probably the result of imitation of the OG, especially since the
Marcan text refers to OG Ps 21[22]:2.

(ii) Nominative in Time Designations

In classical Greek the accusative case was used to express
the extent of time over which an action took place, e.g.,
ἐνταῦθα ἔμεινεν ἡμέρας ἑπτά, "he remained there for seven days"
(Xenophon, *An.* 1.2.6). In Hellenistic Greek the accusative
case, and sometimes even the dative case were used to express
extent of time,[391] e.g., accusative: ἔγνων ἐγὼ ἤδη τρίτην
ἡμέραν ἔχοντος αὐτοῦ τῆς ἀποχῆς, "I learned (about it) when he
was keeping his fast already for a third day" (Epictetus 2.15.5);
ἦν ἐν τῇ ἐρήμῳ τεσσεράκοντα ἡμέρας, "he was in the desert (for)
forty days" (Mk 1:13); dative: τ[ετραε]τεῖ ἤδη χρόνωι ἐν τῇ
χρ[είᾳ] πονούμενος ἐξησθένησα, "having labored at the post for
a four year period, I became weak" (*PFay.* 106.12-14). Yet in
one verse in the Gospel of Mark the nominative case is apparently
used to indicate extent of time: σπλαγχνίζομαι ἐπὶ τὸν ὄχλον

ὅτι ἤδη ἡμέραι τρεῖς προσμένουσίν μοι, καὶ οὐκ ἔχουσιν τί
φάγωσιν, "I have compassion on the crowd because they have remained with me now three days, and they do not have anything to
eat" (Mk 8:2). The awkwardness of the use of the nominative for
extent of time is evidenced by the several variant readings of
the text,[392] although Matthew has taken over the entire sentence
in word for word fashion (Luke omits the entire pericope). Now
since in Hebrew and Aramaic a substantive without preposition
or any "case" designation may express extent of time, J. C.
Doudna and N. Turner have claimed that the Marcan usage in
question is the result of the evangelist's translating an
undifferentiated form used to express extent of time in Semitic
by the nominative case in Greek.[393]

Several scholars have attempted to explain the Marcan
nominative in question as a parenthetical nominative, that is,
an elliptical nominal clause (with the verb "to be" omitted)
which has been intruded into the sentence without any conjunction
(i.e., asyndetically).[394] Thus ὅτι ἤδη (εἰσίν) ἡμέραι τρεῖς
προσμένουσιν would be translated ". . .because they have remained
with me--(it is) now three days."[395] It is true that parenthetical nominatives occur in both classical and Hellenistic Greek,
mostly in expressions which name something,[396] e.g., οὗτος ὁ
πεμφθεὶς ὑφ' ἡμῶν, 'Αριστοφῶν ὄνομ' αὐτῷ. . .ἠργολάβηκεν αὐτός,
"This (man) who was sent by us--his name (being) Aristophon. . .
has himself entered into an agreement" (Demosthenes 32.11);
τῶν παρθένων μία τῶν φυλαττουσῶν τὸ ἱερὸν πῦρ, 'Οπιμία ὄνομα
αὐτῇ, τὴν παρθενίαν ἀφαιρεθεῖσα μιαίνει τὰ ἱερα, "One of the
virgins who guarded the sacred fire--Opimia (being) her name--
having lost her virginity was polluting the sacred rites"
(Dionysius Halicarnassus 8.89.4). However, apart from one fixed
expression, ὅσαι ἡμέραι, "as many as (there are) days" = "daily,
quotidie,"[397] no parenthetical nominative ever occurs as a
temporal designation in either classical Greek or in any
Hellenistic literary author.[398]

In the non-literary papyri, parenthetical nominatives with
οὐλή, "scar," and γείτονες, "adjacent areas" are frequently
used "in descriptions of persons and places respectively."[399]
In one text among the papyri a nominative is used to express
extent of time, but here the verb "to be" is expressed, making

the text a separate clause and not a parenthetical nominative
(which construction some have claimed occurs in Mk 8:2);
κατα[δε]δυναστεύομαι. . .μῆνές εἰσιν δέκα, "I have been
holding power. . .it is ten months" (Mitteis, *Chrestomathie*
5.3). Finally, there are five texts "with asyndetic quasi-
clausal temporal designation in the nom.":[400]

> with a nominative after ἰδού, "behold": ἰδοῦ δύο μῆνες
> σήμερον οὐδὲν δέδωκάς μοι, "you have given me nothing,
> behold, two months today" (*PPrincet.* 2.98.17);
>
> ἡ μήτηρ σου Κοφαήνα ἀσθενῖ (= ἀσθενεῖ) εἰδοῦ δέκα τρῖς
> (= ἰδοῦ δέκα τρεῖς) μῆνες, "your Mother Kophaena is sick,
> behold thirteen months" (*BGU* 948.6);
>
> with a nominative standing alone: ἐνιαυτὸς σήμερον ἐκτὸς
> σοῦ εἰμι, "I am without you, a year today" (*POxy.* 1216.8-9);
>
> πολλαὶ ἡμέραι προσκαρτερουμεν Φιλέα τῷ μοσχομαγείρῳ ,
> "Many days we have been waiting for Phileas the butcher"
> (*POxy.* 1764.4-5);
>
> φερνὴν ἓν καὶ ἐγγυῶνται ἀλλήλους εἰς ἔκτισιν, διετὴς
> χρόνος ἤδηι, "the dowry which they also pledge one another
> as payment, already a two-year period" (*BGU* 1848.9-11).

Since the extent of time is normally expressed by the accusative
case in the papyri,[401] the usage in these five texts is probably
due to Egyptian interference.[402]

In biblical Hebrew, the extent of time over which some
action has taken place may be expressed by the *nota accusativi*
ᵓēt with a noun, e.g., *maṣṣ ̯ôt yē ᵓākēl ᵓēt šib ᶜat hayyāmîm*,
"Unleavened bread shall be eaten for the seven days" (Exod 13:7),
or by a noun standing alone,[403] e.g., *šēšet yāmîm ta ᶜăbōd*, "Six
days you shall work" (Exod 20:9). In Qumran Hebrew the particle
ᵓēt is not used to indicate extent of time, but this idea is
frequently expressed by the substantive standing alone, e.g.,
wn ᶜnš šsh ḥwdšym, "and he shall be punished (for) six months"
(1QS 7:4; also 7:3, 4b, 5, 6, 8 [*bis*]); [*l*]*hywt zr ᶜm lpnyk kwl
hymym*, ". . .[that] their seed be before your face (for) all
days" (1QH 17:14). In Proto-Mishnaic Hebrew extent of time is
expressed by a noun with the particle ᵓēt: [*ḥkrty*]. . .ᵓt ḥmš
[*šnym*], "[I lease (it)]. . .for five [years]" (Mur 24 B 7-10).

To express extent of time, biblical Aramaic also uses a
substantive standing alone, e.g., *dî hăwā ᵓ bĕnēh miqqadmat dĕnâ*

šĕnîn saggîʾān, "(the temple) which was built many years ago"
(literally "from before this [for] many years," Ezra 5:11).
The same is true in Middle Aramaic, e.g., trty ᶜśrh šnyn hwwʾ
yhbyn mdthwn lmlk ᶜylm, "Twelve years they kept paying their
tribute to the king of Elam" (1QapGn 21:26-27); wqwšṭʾ kwl ywmy
dbrt, "and (during) all my days I have practiced the truth"
(1QapGn 6:2; also 20:18 and 4QEn^b l i l = 1 Enoch 5:9).

The OG always uses the proper accusative case when translating a Hebrew or Aramaic substantive which expresses extent
of time, e.g., ἄζυμα ἔδεσθε τὰς ἑπτὰ ἡμέρας, "You shall eat
unleavened bread for the seven days" (Exod 13:7 [Masoretic Text
cited above]; also in 20:9); ὃς ἦν ᾠκοδομημένος πρὸ τούτου ἔτη
πολλά, "(the temple) which has been built many years before
this" (2 Esdr 5:11).

As we have seen, the use of the nominative case in Mk 8:2
to express extent of time is unparalleled in non-biblical
Hellenistic literary Greek. The few examples of it in the non-
literary papyri are most probably the result of Egyptian (Hamitic)
interference. A probable explanation for the unusual Marcan
usage is that it is a literal rendering of an undifferentiated
Hebrew or Aramaic substantive in a written or oral source used
by the writer of the Gospel of Mark.[404] The Hebrew phrase
kbr šlšt ymym or the Aramaic kbr ywmyn tltʾ, "already three
days" could thus have been translated ἤδη ἡμέραι τρεῖς in Greek.
Imitation of the OG may be ruled out since the Semitic expressions
in question have always been translated by the correct (accusative) case of the noun in that version of the Old Testament. If,
however, the Marcan text owes its present form to the evangelist
himself or to a Greek source, it is the result of Semitic interference in its author's Greek.

(b) Genitive Case

    (i) The "Hebraic" Genitive

It is well known that adjectives in Hebrew and Aramaic are
few in number. Writers in these languages frequently used a
second substantive (nomen rectum) in a construct chain with a
first substantive (nomen regens) in order to express some
attribute of the first substantive, e.g., laʾ ăḥuzzat ᶜōlām,

"as an eternal possession" (literally "a possession of eternity,"
Gen 17:8). As a result, attributes of a substantive in biblical
Greek are frequently expressed by a substantive in the genitive
case (the normal case for the translation into Greek of the
nomen rectum in a Semitic construct chain), e.g., βασιλεῖς
ἐλέους, "merciful kings" (literally "kings of mercy," 3 Kgdms
21:31 = Masoretic Text 1 Kgs 20:31 *malkê ḥeṣed*).[405] Hence
scholars have claimed a Semitic provenience for such "Hebraic"
genitives (genitives of quality) in New Testament Greek.[406]
There are two texts in the Gospel of Mark which interpreters
have discussed as possible examples of this so-called Hebraic
genitive.[407] They are:

> κηρύσσων βάπτισμα μετανοίας εἰς ἄφεσιν ἀμαρτιῶν, "(John
> the Baptist) preaching a baptism of repentance for the
> forgiveness of sins" (Mk 1:4; μετανοίας is the genitive
> meant);
> καὶ τοὺς ἄρτους τῆς προθέσεως ἔφαγεν, "and (David) ate
> the presentation bread"[408] (literally "loaves of presenta-
> tion," Mk 2:26).[409]

At the outset it should be noted that Mk 1:4 probably contains
a genitive expressing purpose, rather than a genitive of quality.

In classical Greek "the genitive to denote quality occurs
chiefly as a predicate,"[410] e.g., τὸν εὕρισκε οἰκίης μὲν ἐόντα
αγαθῆς τρόπου δὲ ἡσυχίου, "(Cambyses) whom he found to be of a
good house and of a quiet temper" (Herodotus 1.107). Its
attributive use is limited to poetry, e.g., λευκης χιόνος
πτέρυγι, "with snow-white pinion" (literally "with pinion of
white snow," Sophocles, *Ant.* 114), and to expressions of the
exact size or age of something (genitive of measure),[411] e.g.,
ὀκτὼ σταδίων. . .τεῖχος, "a wall. . .eight stadia long"
(literally "of eight stadia," Thucydides 7.2.4); compare:
ἀπελθόντες ἀγοράσωμεν δηναρίων διακοσίων ἄρτους, "Shall we go
and buy bread worth (literally "of") two hundred denarii?"
(Mk 6:37).[412] In Hellenistic Greek the rule is that a genitive
of quality occurs only in the predicate position,[413] unless
the specific age, size, or price of something is given (genitive
of measure).[414] Radermacher has adduced a few (late) exceptions
to this rule:[415] οὐ γὰρ ἔπρεπε Περικλεῖ. . .λόγους εἰρωνείας
καὶ πανουργίας περιτιθέναι, "for it was not fitting. . .to

attribute to Pericles words of irony and (other) villanies"
(Marcellinus, *Vita Thucydidis* 97, second century A.D. or later;
also Demosthenes, *In Midiam* 93 [a Hellenistic interpolated
document]; pseudo-Chion, *Ep.* 16.3; pseudo-Hippocrates, *Ep.* 10.5).
However, since such a genitive of quality never occurs in the
papyri, or in Hellenistic literary Greek before the second century
A.D., we must conclude that a genitive of quality (which is not
a genitive of exact measure) in the attributive position is
incorrect in first-century Greek prose.

Whereas the genitive in the phrase τοὺς ἄρτους τῆς
προθέσεως (Mk 2:26) is clearly such a genitive of quality (see
above),[416] we may not be sure that the genitive in the phrase
βάπτισμα μετανοίας (Mk 1:4) denotes simply a quality of the
βάπτισμα: "repentance-baptism." The noun βάπτισμα can be
understood as expressive of action (the washing involved in a
baptism); in this case the genitive could be a genitive of
purpose, expressing the goal of the action: "baptism to/for
repentance." The genitive of purpose (a rare use of the genitive alone where the preposition ἕνεκα, "for the sake of," with
a genitive would normally be used) is known in Greek, e.g., ἃς
ἁπάσας ἡ πόλις τῆς τῶν ἄλλων 'Ελλήνων ἐλευθερίας καὶ σωτηρίας
πεποίηται, "all of which the city did (for the sake) of the
freedom and salvation of the Greeks" (Demosthenes 18.100).
However, such a genitive is always used predicatively as in the
above example,[417] and never as the attribute of a noun, as in
Mk 1:4. N. Turner has said that the genitive μετανοίας in Mk
1:4 may possibly be a kind of genitive of material: "baptism
involving (or "consisting of") repentance."[418] But this is
hardly correct.

In biblical Hebrew "merely formal genitives are those added
to the construct state as nearer definitions."[419] These "genitives" may denote a quality of a person or thing, e.g.,
ᵓǎḥuzzat ᶜōlām, "a possession of eternity" (= "an eternal
possession," Gen 17:8; also 1 Kgs 20:31, cited above), and even
the purpose for which something is intended, e.g., ṣōᵓn ṭibḥâ,
"sheep for slaughter" (Ps 44:23); mûsar šĕlōmēnû, "the
chastisement (designed) for our peace" (Isa 53:5).[420] Such
"genitives" also occur in Qumran Hebrew, e.g., qualitative:
ḳᶜṣt ṣdqw, "the counsel of his righteousness" (= "his righteous

counsel," 1QS 1:13); ᵓnšy ḥyl, "men of strength" (= "valiant
men," 1QM 2:8); expressing purpose: ḥṣwṣrwt mqrᵓ, "the trumpets
of summons" (1QM 3:7, namely, the trumpets used to summon the
community; frequently in the War Scroll: 1QM 2:16; 3:1, 2, 3, 4,
5, etc.); ḥlyl thlh, "the flute of praise" (1QH 11:23). These
"genitives" (expressed by a construct chain or with the particle
šl) also o-cur in Proto-Mishnaic Hebrew: qualitative: wlᶜlm
bny yhnw ᵓth ršt šlᶜlm, "and for ever my sons shall benefit
from this possession of eternity" (= "everlasting possession,"
Mur 22 1-9 6); šny [m]ksh, "years of tax" (= "fiscal years,"
Mur 24 E 10; cf. F 11-12); expressing purpose: wttqn lhn mqwm
pnyw, "and you shall prepare for (each one of) them the place
of his presence" (= his guest quarters," Mur 44:4-5).

In biblical and Middle Aramaic the "genitive of quality"
may be expressed with the construct chain, as well as with the
particle dî, e.g., biblical Aramaic: ᵓattûn nûrāᵓ, "oven of
fire" (= "fiery oven," Dan 3:6; also 2:9); ḥezwāᵓ dî lēlĕyāᵓ,
"vision of the night" (= "nocturnal vision," Dan 2:19); Middle
Aramaic: mrh rbwtᵓ, "the lord of greatness" (= "the great
lord," 1QapGn 2:4; also 20:26; 4QEnᵃ 1 i 6; 1 ii 10); ᵓrḥᵓ dy
mdbrᵓ, "the way of the desert" (= "the desert route," 1QapGn
21:28; also 21:8). The "genitive of purpose" occurs in Middle
Aramaic: qrb ᵓbdn, "a war for destruction" (4QEnᵇ 1 iv 6);
[ḥrb] ᵓbdn, "[sword] for destruction" (4QEnᶜ 1 vi 16-17).

Although the OG (and Theodotion) sometimes translate these
"genitives" with an attributive adjective (e.g., εἰς κατάσχεσιν
αἰώνιον, "for an eternal inheritance," Gen 17:8; Masoretic Text
cited above), they frequently translate such "genitives" of
quality or purpose with the genitive case in Greek, e.g.,
qualitative: τὴν κάμινον τοῦ πυρός, "the oven of fire" (Dan
3:6 OG and Theodotion; also 3 Kgdms 21:31; Masoretic Text cited
above); expressing purpose: πρόβατα σφαγῆς, "sheep for slaughter"
(Ps 43[44]:23; Masoretic Text cited above).

Hence the genitive of quality προθέσεως in Mk 2:26 is
incorrect in Hellenistic Greek. Although it could possibly be
the result of interference from contemporaneous Hebrew or
Aramaic, it is most probably a secondary Hebraism as in OG
1 Kgdms 21:7, since this text is explicitly referred to in the
Marcan verse. The phrase βάπτισμα μετανοίας, in Mk 1:4 is

incorrect in Hellenistic Greek whether it contains a genitive of
quality or a genitive of purpose, since the genitive is attributive. While such genitives are not attested in Hellenistic
Greek prose of or before the first century A.D., they are
perfectly normal in contemporaneous Hebrew and Aramaic.

(ii) Υἱός and a Genitive in a Figurative Sense

In Hebrew and Aramaic a characteristic or condition of a
person may be expressed by a phrase made up of the construct
form of the word for "son" (Hebrew *ben*, Aramaic *bar*) followed
by a common noun in a construct chain, e.g., Hebrew: *ben ḥayil*,
"a hero" (literally "a son of strength," 1 Kgs 1:52); Aramaic:
brḥryn (here written as one word), "freeman" (literally "a son
of freedom," 11QtgJb 32:4). Hence it has been claimed that in
the New Testament the phrase "son of X" (υἱός + a genitive),
which indicates a characteristic of a person, is the result of
Semitic interference.[421] Prescinding from the phrases ὁ υἱός
τοῦ ἀνθρώπου and (ὁ) υἱός (τοῦ) θεοῦ (on which see below),
there are two instances in the Gospel of Mark:

μὴ δύνανται οἱ υἱοὶ τοῦ νυμφῶνος, ἐν ᾧ ὁ νυμφίος μετ'
αὐτῶν ἐστιν, νηστεύειν, "Can the wedding guests (literally
"the sons of the bridal chamber") fast while the bride-
groom is with them?" (Mk 2:19);

καὶ ἐπέθηκεν αὐτοῖς ὄνομα Βοανηργές, ὅ ἐστιν υἱοὶ βροντῆς,
"and he surnamed them Boanerges, that is, sons of thunder"
(Mk 3:17).[422]

In classical Greek there are a few texts in which the word
υἱός is followed by a similar genitive; it is used, however, in
a more figurative way: ὀδύνης γὰρ ὑὸς [= υἱός] ἢ κακοδαιμ(ον)ῶν
τις ἢ μελαγχολῶν ἄνθρωπος, "For he (is) a son of pain or one
possessed or a melancholy man" (Menander, *Dysc.* 88-89);
Διόνυσος, υἱός σταμνίου, "Dionysus, son of a wine pot"
(Aristophanes, *Ra.* 22); κόρον, ὕβριος υἱόν, δεινὸν μαιμώοντα,
"insolence, son of pride, eager for danger" (Herodotus 8.77,
in an oracle of one of the Bacis prophets written in poetic
verse). However, these few texts are examples of a highly
poetic style, whereas such usage is not found in classical
prose.[423] Moreover, the "genealogical metaphor," which this
literary figure has been called, generally uses the word παῖς

with a genitive ("child of X"), and not υἱός, the word in
question.[424]

    In Hellenistic Greek there are a few inscriptions in which
an honorary civic title is conferred by the phrase "son of
X":[425] Τιβ. Κλαύδιος υἱὸς πόλεως Κλεόμαχος φιλόκαισαρ,
"Tib(erius) Claudius, son of the city of Cleomachus, a friend
of Caesar" (Dittenberger, *SIG* 813 A 4; also 804.10; 854.3, all
from the first century A.D.); γνώμη Γαίο[υ 'Ι]ουλίου. . .τοῦ
δήμου τοῦ Σαρδι[αν]ῶν υἱοῦ, "resolution of Caius Julius. . .
son of the people of the Sardians" (Dittenberger, *OGI* 2.470.10,
second century B.C.).[426] The classical figurative expression
with υἱός explained above does not occur in Hellenistic Greek.
In one text, the literary technique of personification is used
to extol the values of Law (ὁ νόμος). Among other things, Law
is called "king of men and gods" [an allusion to Pindar, *frag.*
169], "the convener of national festival gatherings, the possessor
of invincible might, a schoolmaster of youth, a fellow laborer
of poverty, and ὁ τοῦ Διὸς ὄντως υἱός ("the veritable Son of
Zeus": Dio Chrysostom 75 [58].8; see 11[3].8-9). Hence this
text is not an example of the figurative meaning of υἱός in
question, but a clear instance of the literary personification
of an abstract idea.

    In biblical Hebrew a common periphrasis used to indicate
"a person (poetically even a thing) possessing some object or
quality, or being in some condition" is the phrase "son of X,"[427]
e.g., ben mešeq, "heir" (literally, "son of inheritance," Gen
15:2); ben qāšet, "arrow" (literally, "son of a bow," Job 41:20);
bĕnê rešep, "sparks" (literally "sons of flame," Job 5:7). The
expression also occurs in Qumran Hebrew: bn nkr, "foreigner"
(literally, "son of a foreign land," 4QFlor 1:4; bn hnkr CD 11:2);
bny knp, "birds" (literally, "sons of a wing," 1QM 10:14); bny
hmhnh, "members (literally "sons") of the camp" (CD 13:13).
The expression does not occur in the Proto-Mishnaic Hebrew
material.

    The same usage occurs in Aramaic with the word bar, "son"
(plural bĕnê),[428] e.g., biblical Aramaic: bĕnê gālûtā᾿, "the
exiles" (literally "the sons of the exile," Dan 2:25; Ezra 6:16);
Middle Aramaic: brhryn (written as one word), "freeman"
(literally "son of freedom," 11QtgJb 32:4 = Hebrew ḥopšî

"freeman," Job 39:5); *bny byty*, "my household servants"
(literally "sons of my house," 1QapGn 22:33).

The OG frequently translates the figurative expression
"son of X" with the word υἱός and a genitive, e.g., υἱός
δυνάμεως, "son of power" (3 Kgdms 1:52 for Hebrew *ben ḥayil*);
υἱῶν ἀποικεσίας, "of the sons of emigration" (2 Esdr 6:16 for
Aramaic *bĕnê gālûtāʾ*). Sometimes, too, *ben* is rendered by the
Greek word τέκνον, "child," e.g., τὰ τέκνα ἀδικίας, "the children
of injustice" (Hos 10:9 = Hebrew *bĕnê ʿalwâ*). In the Pentateuch,
Joshua, Isaiah, and 1-2 Chronicles, the OG frequently translates
into Greek idiomatically, with a single substantive,[429] e.g.,
ἀλλογενής, "foreigner" (Exod 12:43 = Hebrew *ben nēkār*, "son of
a foreign land").

As we have seen, a characteristic or condition of a person
is not normally conveyed in non-biblical Greek by the phrase
"son of X" (υἱός + genitive), with a few exceptions in classical Greek writings of high poetic style, and, in Hellenistic
Greek, in the phrase υἱὸς θεοῦ, and in a few honorary civic
titles (in some inscriptions, never in the non-literary papyri).
Since the Marcan phrases οἱ υἱοὶ τοῦ νυμφῶνος (= "the wedding
guests," Mk 2:19) and υἱοὶ βροντῆς (literally "sons of thunder,"
a translation of the enigmatic Greek transliteration of a
probably Semitic βοανηργές[430] in Mk 3:17) are unparalleled in
non-biblical Greek, they seem to be the result of Semitic
interference in Marcan Greek, whether from contemporaneous
Hebrew or Aramaic. Imitation of the OG is less probable because
the phrases are not found in that translation, and especially
in Mk 3:17 because the alleged Semitic original is given in the
same verse.

(iii) The Phrase ὁ υἱὸς τοῦ ἀνθρώπου

It is almost universally claimed that the phrase ὁ υἱὸς
τοῦ ἀνθρώπου (plural οἱ υἱοὶ τῶν ἀνθρώπων), "the son of man,"
is a literal translation from Semitic,[431] since in Hebrew and
Aramaic, unlike Greek, an individual of a gruop may be expressed
by the phrase made up of the word "son" (Hebrew *ben*, Aramaic
bar) followed by the "genitive" of the group to which he belongs
(construct chain). The phrase occurs in the singular fourteen

times in the Gospel of Mark (Mk 2:10, 28; 8:31, 38; 9:9, 12,
31; 10:33, 45; 13:26, 14:21 [bis], 41, 62--usually in a saying
of Jesus and referring to himself) and once in the plural:
πάντα ἀφεθήσεται τοῖς υἱοῖς τῶν ἀνθρώπων τὰ ἁμαρτήματα, "All
sins will be forgiven the sons of men" (Mk 3:28--the only
instance of the plural of the phrase in the entire New Testament).[432]

     The expression ὁ υἱὸς τοῦ ἀνθρώπου (and its plural) does
not occur in non-biblical Greek. In classical and Hellenistic
Greek the individual members of a guild or any large and
coherent group are sometimes called παῖδες (followed by a genitive), "children of X,"[433] e.g., οἷα πολλὰ ῥητόρων παῖδες ἐπὶ
τοὺς δικαστὰς μηχανῶνται, "rhetoricians (literally "children
of rhetoricians") devise many such things for the judges"
(Lucian, Anach. 19; also Dionysius Halicarnassus, Comp. 22);
ὅ τι δή ποτε καλοῦσι τὸ τοιοῦτον οἱ ζωγράφων παῖδες, "whatever
the professional painters (literally "the children of painters")
call such a thing" (Plato, Leg. 769B; also R. 407E); Ἰώνων
παῖδας δούλους εἶναι ἀντ' ἐλευθέρων ὄνειδος καὶ ἄλγος μέγιστον
μὲν αὐτοῖσι ἡμῖν, "That the Ionians (literally "children of
Ionians") are slaves rather than free is very much a burden to
us ourselves" (Herodotus 5.49; also 1.27; 3.21).[434] Hence the
phrase ὁ υἱὸς τοῦ ἀνθρώπου would simply mean "the man's son" or
"the son of the man" (plural "the men's sons") in non-biblical
Greek of the first century A.D. This is hardly the meaning of
the phrase in the New Testament.

     In biblical Hebrew the construct form of the word for "son"
(ben, and its plural bĕnê) may be followed by a "genitive"
(which may or may not have the article) in order to express an
individual member (or, in the plural, individual members) of a
society, tribe, or any definite class,[435] e.g., determinate
(nomen rectum with article); bĕnê hāʾĕlōhîm, "the sons of God"
(= "beings of the class of God," Gen 6:2; also Lev 25:45; Neh
3:8; 1 Kgs 20:35); indeterminate (nomen rectum without article);
ben hăkāmîm, "a son of wise men" (= "a wise individual," Isa
19:11; also Gen 17:12; Qoh 10:17; Ps 72:4). The following
phrases using the ben + "genitive" construction occur in biblical Hebrew which could be translated "(the) son(s) of man/men":

(1) *ben ᵓādām*, "son of men" (always indeterminate) and its
plural *bĕnê ᵓādām*, "sons of men" (indeterminate) and *bĕnê
hā᾿ādām*, "the sons of men" (determinate). In this phrase
the noun *ᵓādām* is used in its collective sense: "men, mankind."[436] The singular form always occurs in a poetic or
solemn context,[437] e.g., it occurs ninety-three times in
Ezekiel as God's address to the prophet (Ezek 2:1, 3, 6,
etc.); *lō᾿ ᵓîš ᵓēl wîkazzēb ûben ᵓādām wĕyitneḥām*, "God
is not a man, that he should lie, or a son of men, that he
should change his mind" (Num 23:19). Its determinate form
ben hā᾿ādām, "the son of man" is not attested in biblical
Hebrew. Plural: indeterminate: *wĕhōkaḥtîw bĕšēbeṭ ᵓānāšîm
ûbĕnigᶜê bĕnê ᵓādām*, "I will chasten him with a rod of men
and with stripes of sons of men" (2 Sam 7:14); determinate:
wĕ᾿im bĕnê hā᾿ādām ᵓărûrîm hēm, "and if (it be) the sons
of men, may they be cursed" (1 Sam 26:19). Both plural
forms (determinate and indeterminate) are common terms for
"men."

(2) *bĕnê ᵓîš*, "sons of man." This phrase occurs only four
times, and is always plural and indeterminate: *wayyaggeh
bĕnê ᵓîš*, "and he does not grieve sons of man" (Lam 3:33;
also Ps 4:3); *gam bĕnê ᵓādām gam bĕnê ᵓîš yaḥad ᶜāšîr
wĕ᾿ebyôn*, "(Hear this) both sons of men and sons of man,
rich and poor alike" (Ps 49:3; also 62:10. Perhaps
bĕnê ᵓîš refers to men of high estate in the latter two
texts, because of the parallels in verse 3b of Psalm 49
[cited above]).[438]

(3) *ben ᵓĕnôš*, "son of man." This phrase occurs only once
in biblical Hebrew: *māh ᵓādām wattēdāᶜēhû ben ᵓĕnôš
wattĕḥaššĕbēhû*, "What is man that you regard him, a son
of man that you think of him?" (Ps 144:3; note the
parallelism between *ᵓādām* and *ben ᵓĕnôš*). In this phrase
the "genitive" *ᵓĕnôš* has a collective meaning "man, mankind."[439]

In the Qumran Hebrew texts the following forms of the
phrase in question occur: singular: *bn ᵓdm* (indeterminate)
and *bn h᾿dm* (determinate), plural: *bny ᵓdm* (indeterminate)
and *bny h᾿dm* (determinate); *bny ᵓyš* (plural indeterminate only);
bny ᵓnwš (plural indeterminate only). Examples:

(1) *bn ᵓdm*, "a son of men": *wᵓny ydᶜty ky lwᵓ lᵓnwš ṣdqh wlwᵓ lbn ᵓdm twm drk*, "And I, I know that righteousness does not belong to mankind nor perfection of way to a son of men" (1QH 4:30);

bn hᵓdm, "the son of men": *wmh ᵓp hwᵓh bn hᵓdm bmᶜśy plᵓkh*, "And what indeed is the son of men amidst your marvellous works?" (1QS 11:20);[440]

bny ᵓdm, "the sons of men": *nstrh mᵓnwš dᶜh wmzmt ᶜrmh mbny ᵓdm*, "knowledge is hidden from mankind and the counsel of prudence from sons of men" (1QS 11:6; also 11:15; 1QH 2:24; 4:32; 5:11, 15; 6:11; 11:6);

bny hᵓdm, "the sons of men": *wlbny hᵓdm ᶜbwdt ᶥhᶜwwn*, "but to the sons of men (is) the service of iniquity" (1QH 1:27; also CD 12:4). In all these texts the various forms of the phrase have the generic meaning "man, mankind."

(2) *bny ᵓyš*, "sons of man": *lmśkyl lhbyn wllmd ᵓt kwl bny ᵓwr btwldwt kwl bny ᵓyš*, "For the man of understanding, that he may instruct and teach all sons of light concerning the nature of all sons of man" (1QS 3:13; also 4:15, 20, 26; 1QM 11:14; 1Q*36* 25:5). In all these texts the phrase has the generic meaning "human being(s), mankind."

(3) *bny ᵓnwš*, "sons of men": *lbny ᵓnwš kwl nplᵓwtykh*, "(And I will recount. . .) to sons of men all your marvels" (1QH 1:34). Here, too, the expression is generic and means "men, mankind."

None of the Hebrew phrases in question turn up in the Proto-Mishnaic Hebrew material.

In biblical and Middle Aramaic the phrase *br ᵓnš*, "son of man,"[441] occurs in the singular only in the indeterminate form. It is also attested once in Old Aramaic (but never in non-biblical Imperial Aramaic): *bkl mh zy ymwt br ᵓnš*, "in whatever way a son of man (= "someone") shall die" (Sefire 3.16); biblical Aramaic: *waᵓărû ᶜim ᶜănānê šĕmayyāᵓ kĕbar ᵓĕnāš ᵓātēh hăwāh*, "and behold, with the clouds of heaven there came (someone) like a son of men" (= "a human being," Dan 7:13); Middle Aramaic: *dy lᵓ yṣkh kwl br ᵓnwš lmmnyh*, "which no son of man (= "no one") can number" (1QapGn 21:13; the spelling *ᵓnwš* [with medial *waw*] is most likely a Hebraism);[442] [. . .b]*r ᵓnš twlᶜ[tᵓ. . .]*, "(How much less a man, a maggot), [a so]n of man, a wor[m]," (11QtgJb 9:9 = Hebrew *ben ᵓădām*, Job 25:6); *wlbr ᵓnš ṣdqtk*, "and to a son of man your justice" (11QtgJb 26:3 = Hebrew *ben ᵓādām*, Job 35:8). Thus the indeterminate form *br ᵓnš* has both a generic ("a human being") and an indefinite ("one") meaning in Aramaic prior to and contemporaneous to the writing of the New Testament.[443]

The plural form *bny ᵓnš(ᵓ)* usually occurs in the determinate form: biblical Aramaic: *ûmin bĕnē ᵓănāšāᵓ ṭĕrîd*, "and he was expelled from among the sons of men" (Dan 5:21; also 2:38; in both instances *bny ᵓnš* = "mankind, human beings"); Middle Aramaic: *[wk]l ᵓnšᵓ ᶜlwhy ḥzyn wbny ᵓnšᵓ mrḥyq [b]h ybqwn*, "[and al]l men (are) gazing upon it (an injustice) and the sons of men will examine it" (11QtgJb 28:2-3 = Hebrew *ᵓĕnôš*, Job 36:25); *[hww ᵓklyn] ᶜml kl bny ᵓnšᵓ*, "[they were devouring] the labor of all the sons of men" (4QEn[a] 1 iii 18 = *1 Enoch* 7:3; the Greek version has τῶν ἀνθρώπων for *bny ᵓnš*): *[npš]t kl bny ᵓnšᵓ*, "[. . .the soul]s of all the sons of men" (4QEn[e] 1 xxii 1 = *1 Enoch* 22:3; Greek: τῶν ἀνθρώπων); *ḥd mnhwn lmdbr bh bny ᵓnšᵓ*, "one of them (sections of the earth) (was) for the dwelling of the sons of men in it" (4QEnastr[b] 23:8). There is only one certain instance of the indeterminate plural form: *wb[ny] ᵓnwš ᵓtw wbᶜwn lmqṣ wlmᶜqr l[ᵓ]rzᵓ*, "and some men (literally "s[ons] of men") came intending (literally "and they sought") to cut down and uproot the cedar" (1QapGn 19:15; the spelling *ᵓnwš* is a Hebraism as in 1QapGn 21:13 [see above]).[444] In all these texts the determinate form *bny ᵓnšᵓ* has a generic meaning: "mankind," whereas, in the one certain instance of the indeterminate form (1QapGn 19:15), the meaning is indefinite.

In the OG the following translations occur for the various forms of the phrase in Hebrew and Aramaic:

singular: υἱὸς ἀνθρώπου, "son of man" for Hebrew *ben ᵓādām*, e.g., Num 23:19 and throughout Ezekiel; for Hebrew *ben ᵓĕnôš* in Ps 143[144]:3; for Aramaic *bar ᵓĕnāš* in Dan 7:13. The arthrous form ὁ υἱὸς τοῦ ἀνθρώπου never occurs in the OG.

plural: υἱοὶ ἀνθρώπων (without article) both for Hebrew *bĕnē ᵓādām*, e.g., 2 Kgdms 7:14, and *bĕnē hāᵓādām*, e.g., 1 Kgdms 26:19; for Hebrew *bĕnē ᵓîš* in Ps 4:3; οἱ υἱοὶ τῶν ἀνθρώπων (with article) both for Hebrew *bĕnē ᵓādām*, e.g., Ps 61[62]:10, and *bĕnē hāᵓādām*, e.g., Gen 11:5; for Hebrew

bĕnê ᵓîš in Ps 48[49]:3 and 61[62]:10; for Aramaic bĕnê
ᵓǎnāšāᵓ in Dan 2:38 (Theodotion: OG is different here);
plural: υἱοὺς ἀνδρός, a literal translation of Hebrew
bĕnê ᵓîš in Lam 3:33;

plural: τῶν ἀνθρώπων for Aramaic bĕnê ᵓǎnāšā in Dan 5:21
(Theodotion; OG omits this verse).

Hence the phrase ὁ υἱὸς τοῦ ἀνθρώπου (fourteen times in
the Gospel of Mark) and its plural οἱ υἱοὶ τῶν ἀνθρώπων (Mk 3:28)
are the result of Semitic interference. The plural form in
Mk 3:28 may be due to the influence of contemporaneous Hebrew
or Aramaic, or to imitation of OG usage. With regard to the
singular form (which does not occur in the OG), if it is a
literal translation from the Semitic, it would represent the
Hebrew determinate form bn hᵓdm (attested only once--and then
with the article added above the line) or the Aramaic determinate
form br ᵓnšᵓ (unattested). The Hebrew determinate phrase has
a generic meaning "a human being" (as does the indeterminate
form bn ᵓdm). The only attested Aramaic form (indeterminate)
br ᵓnš, may have a generic ("a human being") or an indefinite
("one") meaning. However, neither of these two meanings seems
to fit the context, since ὁ υἱὸς τοῦ ἀνθρώπου is usually in a
saying attributed to Jesus. It is debated whether it is ever
used for an ordinary human being. Thus it is most likely that
a special titular meaning has been attached to the phrase in its
use in the canonical gospels. To go into the development or
origin of this usage is not the function of this study.

(iv) The Phrase (ὁ) υἱὸς (τοῦ) θεοῦ

In the phrase (ὁ) υἱὸς (τοῦ) θεοῦ the noun υἱός is used
with a genitive in a figurative sense: the activity of a human
father is transferred to God. The phrase occurs in four Marcan
texts:

ἀρχὴ τοῦ εὐαγγελίου ᾽Ιησοῦ Χριστοῦ υἱοῦ θεοῦ, "Beginning
of the gospel of Jesus Christ, son of God" (Mk 1:1);[445]
σὺ εἶ ὁ υἱὸς τοῦ θεοῦ, "You are the son of God" (Mk 3:11);
τί ἐμοὶ καὶ σοί, ᾽Ιησοῦ υἱὲ τοῦ θεοῦ ὑψίστου, "What is it
to me and to you, Jesus, son of God the Most High?"
(Mk 5:7);

ἀληθῶς οὗτος ὁ ἄνθρωπος υἱὸς θεοῦ ἦν, "Truly this man
was a son of God" (Mk 15:39).[446]

The phrase υἱὸς θεοῦ in a figurative sense, that is, used
to designate an historical person, is unknown in classical Greek.
On the other hand, in the writings of some Hellenistic philosophers, whose doctrines of the unity of mankind led to the idea
of divine sonship for all men, man is called a "son of God,"[447]
e.g., διὰ τί μὴ εἴπη αὐτὸν. . .υἱὸν τοῦ θεοῦ, "Why should he
(the attentive student) not call himself. . .a son of God?"
(Epictetus 1.9.6; also 1.3.2); υἱὸς θεοῦ ὁ ταῦτα μόνα τιμῶν ἃ
καὶ ὁ θεός, "A son of God (is) one who esteems only these things
which God also (esteems): (Sextus Pythagoreus, *Sent*. 135; also
58; 60; 376a). Moreover, in the Hellenistic world, Roman
emperors were considered to be divine "sons of God" (θεοῦ υἱός =
Latin *divi filius*),[448] e.g., Καῖσαρ θεοῦ υἱὸς Σεβαστός, "Caesar
Augustus, son of God" (*IG* 12.3.174); ὄμνυμι Καίσαρα ᾿Αυτοκράτορα
θεοῦ υἱόν, "I swear by Caesar Autokrator, son of God" (*BGU*
543.3; also Dittenberger, *OGI* 328.3; 470.13). Hence, from the
point of view of grammar, the anarthrous phrase υἱὸς θεοῦ in a
figurative sense in Mk 1:1 (B ℵ[corr] D W) and 15:39 is attested
in non-biblical Hellenistic Greek, although the word order differs from the imperial title. However, the phrase either
determined by the article (ὁ υἱὸς τοῦ θεοῦ, "the son of God")
or used in the vocative case (υἱὲ τοῦ θεοῦ, "son of God"), is
unattested in Greek with reference to an historical person.

As we have seen above (in section [iii]), in Hebrew and
Aramaic the word for "son" may be used with a "genitive" in a
figurative sense to indicate a member of a society, tribe, or
definite class. The term "the sons of God" (always plural and
determinate) occurs in biblical Hebrew as a designation for
heavenly beings (angels): *wayyirʾû bĕnê hāʾĕlōhîm ʾet bĕnōt
hāʾādām kî ṭōbōt*, "And the sons of God saw that the daughters
of men were fair" (Gen 6:2; also 6:4; Job 1:6; 2:1); *wayyārîʿû
kol bĕnê ʾĕlōhîm*, "and all (the) sons of God shouted for joy"
(Job 38:7); *mî. . .yidmeh lyhwh bibĕnê ʾēlîm*, "Who. . .among
the sons of God is like YHWH?" (Ps 89:7; also 29:1; *ʾēl*, and its
plural *ʾēlîm*, never take the article in the Old Testament).
God's people, Israel, are called "His (my) sons" in Deut 32:5,
19; Isa 43:6; 45:11 (cf. *bānîm ʾattem lyhwh ʾĕlōhêkem*, "You are

sons of YHWH, your God" [Deut. 14:1]). Finally, God calls the
Davidic king "my son" in 2 Sam 7:14; Ps 2:7; 1 Chr 17:13; 22:10;
28:6. The term "sons of God" turns up once in the Qumran Hebrew
material: [. . .] *bny ᵓlym*, "(the) sons of God" (1QH f 2 3).
In this fragmentary text the phrase *bny ᵓlym* probably refers to
heavenly beings, since it is paralleled by *bny šmym*, "sons of
heaven," in the same line. The phrase does not occur in the
Proto-Mishnaic Hebrew documents.

    The expression "son of God" (indeterminate singular) occurs
once in biblical Aramaic: *wĕrēwēh dî rĕbîᶜāyᵓā* (read *rĕbîᶜāyāᵓ*)
dāmēh lĕbar ᵓĕlāhîn, "and the appearance of the fourth (is)
similar to a son of (the) gods" (Dan 3:25). Here the expression
refers to an angelic or heavenly being. In Middle Aramaic the
phrase turns up in the singular, determinate form: *brh dy ᵓl*
ytᵓmr wbr ᶜlywn yqrwnh, "He shall be hailed (as) the Son of God,
and they shall call him Son of the Most High" (4Q246 2:1). The
word *bar* has the suffix *h* which is further determined by the
phrase *dî ᵓĒl*. Whether the text refers to a past historical
figure or a future apocalyptic one is disputed.[449]

    The OG translates the Hebrew expression *bĕnê (hā)ᵓelōhîm*
by the phrase οἱ υἱοὶ τοῦ θεοῦ in Gen 6:2, 4, and by a paraphrase
with ἄγγελοι, "angels," in Job 1:6; 2:1; 38:7). The anarthrous
Hebrew expression *bĕnê ᵓēlîm* is translated by υἱοὶ θεοῦ in
Ps 30[29]:1 and 88[89]:7. The Aramaic phrase *bar ᵓĕlāhîn*, "a
son of God" (Dan 3:25), is translated by υἱὸς θεοῦ by Theodotion
(Dan 3:92) and paraphrased by ἄγγελος θεοῦ by the OG (Dan 3:92).

    Finally, in the Hellenistic deutero-canonical text, the
Wisdom of Solomon, a righteous man is called a "son of God":
εἰ γάρ ἐστιν ὁ δίκαιος υἱὸς θεοῦ, ἀντιλήμφεται αὐτοῦ, "For if
the just man is a son of God, he will help him" (Wis 2:18).

    Whatever the origins of the phrase (ὁ) υἱὸς (τοῦ) θεοῦ,
and its theological meaning in the Gospel of Mark (questions
beyond the scope of this study), the following may be stated
about the grammatical aspect of the phrase: (1) the anarthrous
form of the phrase, υἱὸς θεοῦ, in Mk 1:1 (B ℵ^corr D W) and 15:39
is also attested in non-biblical Hellenistic Greek. (2) The
determinate phrase (either with the article as in Mk 3:11 or
determined by the vocative case as in Mk 5:7) is never used
with reference to an historical figure in non-biblical Greek.

(3) The determinate (suffixal) form of the same phrase does occur in an Aramaic text which may speak of a (past or present) historical person of an apocalyptic figure.

(c) Dative Case

(i) Frequency of the Simple Dative

R. A. Martin has claimed that in Hebrew and Aramaic the preposition *b* is used to express many ideas ("dative, locative, and instrumental case ideas")[450] which, in normal Greek style, would be expressed by the dative case alone or with some preposition other than ἐν.[451] Since the Semitic preposition *b* is usually translated by the Greek preposition ἐν in the OG, Martin claims that the frequency of the preposition ἐν with the dative case is extremely high in translation Greek in comparison with that in original Greek composition. To demonstrate this, he has counted simple datives (exluding "datives used with forms of λέγω, εἶπον, and δίδωμι")[452] in several OG passages as well as in several Hellenistic literary writers and selected papyri. He then compared those figures with the number of datives with ἐν in the same passages. The results show that the proportion of simple datives to datives with ἐν in translation Greek (about 1 to 1) is significantly lower than in original Greek composition (at least 3 to 1).[453]

An examination of the Gospel of Mark reveals that there are 227 simple datives (excluding datives with λέγω, εἶπον and δίδωμι) in comparison with 126 datives following the preposition ἐν, or a proportion of about 1.8 to 1. Hence according to the statistical method of Martin, the Gospel of Mark does not seem to be influenced by Semitic nearly as much as the OG in its use of the dative with ἐν.

Martin has overlooked one fact, however, and this diminishes the effective application of his study of the Greek of Mark. With the exception of the datives with the three verbs, Martin has counted every simple dative in his texts. However, as we have seen above (in section 2.a.i), personal pronouns in the oblique cases are used much more frequently in the Gospel of Mark than in non-biblical Greek because of Semitic interference. For example (again omitting datives with λέγω, εἶπον, and δίδωμι), the dative of αὐτός used as a personal pronoun occurs

103 times in Mark (96 times as a simple dative, 3 times with
ἐν, and 4 times with other prepositions), whereas, in a similar
amount of text of Epictetus (Book 3, chapters 1 through 21) it
turns up only 10 times.[454] Hence, in order that Martin's
statistical study be effective in the Gospel of Mark, some
qualification for personal pronouns would have to be made in
his totals.

The only clear instances in which biblical Greek frequently
uses the preposition ἐν with a dative where non-biblical Greek
would normally use the simple dative are the instrumental and
associative datives.

Smyth defines the instrumental and associative datives
(which represent the Indo-European instrumental case in Greek)
as "that *by which* or *with which* an action is done or accompanied."[455] The instrumental dative proper denotes the instrument
or manner of the action, e.g., ἔβαλλέ με λίθοις, "he was pelting
me with stones" (Lysias 3.8). The associative (comitative)
dative denotes persons or things which accompany or take part
in an action,[456] e.g., ὀλίγον γὰρ χρόνον ἀλλήλοις διειλέγμεθα,
"for we have conversed with each other only a little while"
(Plato, *Ap*. 37A); βιαίῳ θανάτῳ ἀποθνῄσκειν, "to die by a violent
death" (Xenophon, *Hier*. 4.3). Although these datives were
normally used without prepositions in classical Greek, it has
been pointed out repeatedly that there are occasional instances
in which the preposition ἐν was added,[457] e.g., instrumental:
ἐν ἀργύρῳ ἢ χρυσῷ πίνειν, "to drink with a silver or gold (cup)"
(Lucian, *Merc. cond*. 26); associative: ἐν θεραπείᾳ εἶχον πολλῇ,
"they were treating (them) with much consideration" (Thucydides
1.55.1). Similarly, there are examples of these datives in
Hellenistic Greek with the preposition ἐν even though they
normally occurred without it.[458] Examples: instrumental:
διαλυόμεναι ἐν τῶι λιμῶι, "being destroyed by the famine"
(*PPar*. 28.13; but cf. [by the same writer] τῶι λιμῶι διαλυθῆναι,
"to be destroyed by the famine" [*PPar*. 22.21]); associative:
Μαρρείους σὺν ἄλλοις πλείοσι ἐν μαχαίραις παραγινομένου, "when
Marreios arrived with many others with swords" (*PTebt*. 41.4).
Nevertheless, several grammarians have pointed out that the
influence of the Hebrew and Aramaic preposition *b* has greatly

extended the use of ἐν with the instrumental and associative
datives in the OG and New Testament.[459]

In Hebrew the preposition *b* may be used to represent "the
means or instrument (or even the personal agent), as something
with which one has associated himself in order to perform an
action."[460] This usage corresponds to both the instrumental
and associative datives in Greek. Examples:

biblical Hebrew: *baššēbeṭ yakkû*, "they will strike with a
rod" (Mic 4:14); *bĕšimĕkā nābûš qāmēnû*, "in your name we
tread down our assailants" (Ps 44:6);

Qumran Hebrew: *w'ny ᶜbdk ydᶜty brwḥ*, "And I, your servant,
have known in the spirit (which you have given me)" (1QH
13:18-19); *ymym wthwmwt [. . .] byhm hkynwth bhwkmtkh*, "and
you have established the seas and the deeps [. . .] in your
wisdom: (1QH 1:14);

Proto-Mishnaic Hebrew: *[. . .] m'lw 'bdw bhrb* "[The
majority] of them perished by the sword" (Mur 45:7).

The same range of instrumental and associative meanings
exists for the corresponding Aramaic preposition *b*.[461] Examples:

biblical Aramaic: *wĕhatmah malkā' bĕᶜizqĕtēh*, "And the
king sealed it (the rock) with his signet ring" (Dan 6:18);
wahăṭāyāk bĕṣidqâ pēruq, "and expiate your sins by righteousness" (Dan 4:24);

Middle Aramaic: *w'ḥy btlyky wtplṭ npšy bdylyky*, "and I
shall live with your help and my life will be saved because
of you" (1QapGn 19:20); *wywpᶜ b[tqp] gbrw[th mn šmy šmyh]*,
"And he will appear in [the strength of His] might [from
the heaven of heavens]" [4QEn^a 1 i 6 = *1 Enoch* 1:4]).

The OG translates both Hebrew and Aramaic *b* quite frequently
with the preposition ἐν, as it does in its translations of all
four biblical texts cited above: ἐν ῥάβδῳ, "with a rod" (Mic
4:14); ἐν τῷ ὀνόματί σου, "in your name" (Ps 43[44]:6); ἐν τῷ
δακτυλίῳ ἑαυτοῦ, "with his own signet ring" (Dan 6:18); ἐν
ἐλεημοσύναις, "by means of alms" (Dan 4:27 [= Masoretic Text
4:24]).

Now in the Gospel of Mark instrumental and associative
datives turn up 20 times with the preposition ἐν (3:22, 23;
4:2, 24, 30; 5:25; 9:1, 29 [*bis*], 38, 41, 50 [*bis*]; 11:10
[= OG Ps 117:26], 28, 29, 33; 12:1, 36; 14:1) and 23 times

without ἐν (1:8 [bis], 34; 2:8; 3:33; 5:3, 4 [bis], 5, 29;
6:13; 7:2, 3, 5, 6 [= OG Isa 29:13]; 8:31; 9:49; 12:13, 40;
14:65; 15:19, 34, 46). The number of these datives with ἐν
is extremely high in comparison to the occasional instance of
them in non-biblical Greek. Since the instrumental and associative ideas are expressed in Hebrew and Aramaic by the preposition
b, "in," the conclusion is that at least the frequency of the
preposition ἐν with these datives in the Marcan Gospel should be
ascribed to Semitic interference, whether from imitation of the
OG, or from contemporaneous Hebrew or Aramaic.

In response, therefore, to the question of the frequency
of the dative case posed by R. A. Martin: on the one hand, the
preposition ἐν is used at least 20 times with datives in the
Gospel of Mark where normal Greek would probably use simple
datives; on the other hand, the frequency of the simple dative
of the third person pronoun is extremely high in the same gospel.

(ii) Dative after γίνομαι

J. Jeremias has claimed that "in our passage [ἐκείνοις δὲ
τοῖς ἔξω ἐν παραβολαῖς τὰ πάντα γίνεται (Mk 4:11)] γίνεσθαι
'to happen' used as an impersonal verb with the person in the
dative is not idiomatic Greek but a semitism. It renders an
Aramaic h^awa l^e [hắwắ ᵓlẽ] 'to belong to somebody, to happen to
somebody, to be assigned to somebody.'"[462] He translates the
phrase: "But to those who are without all things are imparted
in riddles."[463] In fact, however, the passage contains the verb
γίνομαι used impersonally ("to happen") and what is called a
dative of advantage/disadvantage in Greek.

The dative of advantage or disadvantage (dativus commodi or
incommodi), in which the person for whose advantage or disadvantage something is done is put in the dative,[464] occurs in
classical Greek with the impersonal verb γίγνομαι, e.g., ἃ τοῖσι
δυσσεβοῦσι γίγνεται βροτῶν, "those things which happen to the
ungodly among mortals" (Euripides, Med. 755). The same usage
obtains in Hellenistic Greek,[465] e.g., ἀποκλεισμὸς ἐμοὶ οὐ
γίνεται, ἀλλὰ τοῖς βιαζομένοις, "There is no enclosure for me,
but for those who would force themselves in" (Epictetus 4.7.20);
μὴ ἀνάπλασσε. . .ὅσαι διαχύσεις ἦσαν ἐκεῖ διάγοντι, ὅσαι γένοιντ᾿
ἂν ἐπανελθόντι, "Don't picture. . .how many relaxations there

were for someone living there, how many there might be for someone returning" (Epictetus 3.24.109; also 2.21.17).

In Hebrew a "dative of advantage/disadvantage" may be expressed by the preposition *lĕ* with a substantive in a sentence
with the verb *hāyāh*, "to be, to happen" e.g., biblical Hebrew:
wayĕhî dĕbar šĕmûʾēl lĕkōl yiśrāʾēl, "And the word of Samuel
was for all Israel" (1 Sam 4:1); *wĕhāyāh lĕkā wĕlāhem lĕʾoklâ*,
"and it (the stored food) shall be as food for you and for them"
(Gen 6:21); Qumran Hebrew: *whyth lw lbryt yhd*, "and for him it
(expiation) shall be as a covenant of the community" (1QS 3:11);
hyyth ly lhwmt ʿwz, "You have become as a strong wall for me"
(1QH 3:37). The "dative of advantage/disadvantage" does not
occur with the verb "to be" in the Proto-Mishnaic Hebrew documents.

The "dative of advantage/disadvantage" may also be expressed in Aramaic by means of the preposition *lĕ* with a
substantive, e.g., biblical Aramaic: *yitʿăbēd ʾadrazdāʾ lĕbêt
ʾĕlāh šĕmayyāʾ*, "let it be done in full for the house of the God
of heaven" (Ezra 7:23); *ûmāzôn lĕkōllāʾ bēh*, "and food for all
(was) in it" (Dan 4:9); Middle Aramaic: [*ʾdyn lhwwn šmhtk*]*n
llwt ʿlm l*[*kl qšytyn*], "[Then shall you]r [names be] as an
eternal curse for [all the righteous]" (4QEn[a] 1 ii 6 = *1 Enoch*
5:6; the Greek text has τότε ἔσται τὰ ὀνόματα ὑμῶν εἰς κατάραν
αἰώνιον πᾶσιν τοῖς δικαίοις, "Then shall your names be as an
eternal curse for all the righteous"). Although the "dative of
advantage/disadvantage" is attested in Aramaic, it never occurs
with the verb *hăwāʾ* in biblical Aramaic, and only once, if
restored correctly, in Middle Aramaic.

Hence, although the dative ἐκείνοις τοῖς ἔξω with the verb
γίνεται in Mk 4:1 may be a translation from Semitic, such a
dative of advantage/disadvantage with the impersonal verb
γίνομαι is perfectly normal in Greek. The Marcan verse should
be translated: "But for those (who are) outside all happens
in riddles."

(iii) The Phrase τί ἐμοί (ἡμῖν) καί σοί

There has been a good deal of discussion on the possible
Semitic provenience of the phrases τί ἡμῖν καί σοί (Mk 1:24)

and τί ἐμοί καί σοί (Mk 5:7), literally translated: "What to
us/me and to you?"[466] The phrase occurs in classical Greek and
is really a nominal clause made up of the subject τί, the verb
"to be" (ἐστίν) omitted by ellipsis, and two datives of possession.[467] N. Turner claims, however, that "the Hebraic idiom is
not quite in accordance with the classical idiom," in which
"the element of interference and concern is not always present,"
as it is in Mk 1:24 and 5:7.[468]

    Such elliptical clauses with τί and two datives are not
uncommon in both classical and Hellenistic Greek, and should be
translated: "What has X to do with Y?"[469] or "What have X and
Y in common?"[470] Examples:

    classical Greek: τί τῷ νόμῳ καί τῇ βασάνῳ, "What has the
    law to do with interrogation by torture?" (Demosthenes
    29.36; see also Anacreon 17.4 and 10); (with the verb "to
    be" expressed) σοί δέ καί τούτοισι τοῖσι πρήγμασι τί ἐστι,
    "But what have you to do with these matters?" (Herodotus
    5.33; this enraged remark is followed by: τί πολλά
    πρήσσεις, "Why are you so meddlesome?"; compare Aristophanes,
    Eq. 1022);

    Hellenistic Greek: τί ἡμῖν καί σοί, ἄνθρωπε, "What have we
    to do with you, knave?" (who has just made a joke during a
    shipwreck--Epictetus 2.19.16); τί ἐμοί καί σοί, ἄνθρωπε;
    ἀρκεῖ ἐμοί τά ἐμά κακά, "What have I to do with you, knave?
    My own evils are enough for me!" (Epictetus 2.19.19; also
    20.11; similarly 1.1.16; 22.15; 27.13; 3.18.7; 22.99).

    This type of nominal clause also turns up in biblical Hebrew:
mah lî wālāk, (literally) "What to me and to you" (that you have
come to fight against my land)? (Judg 11:12; also 1 Kgs 17:18;
2 Kgs 3:13; 2 Chr 35:21); mah lî wĕlākem, "What to me and to you
(you sons of Zeruiah, that you should this day be as an adversary
to me?" (2 Sam 19:23; also 16:10). As Turner has pointed out,
in all these texts, the idea of an irate rebuke of someone
meddling in another's affairs is prominent.[471]

    The phrase does not occur in the Qumran or Proto-Mishnaic
Hebrew material, nor in biblical or Middle Aramaic, but there
is no reason to believe that it would not be possible in those
languages.

The OG consistently renders the Hebrew phrases cited above
exactly as in the Marcan texts under discussion: τί ἐμοὶ καὶ
σοί (ὑμῖν), (literally) "What to me and to you?"

Although a literal translation of the biblical Hebrew
phrase *mah lî wālāk* (as translated in the OG: τί ἐμοὶ καὶ σοί)
may be behind Mk 1:24 and 5:7, the idiom is perfectly acceptable
in contemporaneous Greek usage. Indeed, there are almost perfect
parallels to the setting of the Marcan texts, with the idea of
an irate rebuke to someone about to meddle in another's affairs,
in Epictetus (especially 2.19.16, 19, and 20.11 cited above).

(iv) Dative of Cognate Noun with Finite Verb for Emphasis

In biblical Hebrew emphasis may be added to a finite verb
by placing the infinitive absolute of the same verb before or
after that verb. Since the OG frequently translated such an
expression with the dative of a noun which was cognate (either
in etymology or in meaning) to the verb in the sentence, it has
often been claimed that at least the frequency of such usage in
the New Testament is due to imitation of this stylistic feature
of the OG.[472] The texts in question in the Gospel of Mark are:

καὶ ἐξέστησαν εὐθὺς ἐκστάσει μεγάλῃ, "and immediately
they were utterly amazed" (literally "they were amazed
with great amazement," Mk 5:42);

ὁ κακολογῶν πατέρα ἢ μητέρα θανάτῳ τελευτάτω, "He who
speaks evil of father or mother, let him surely die" (Mk
7:10 = OG Exod 21:16A; Manuscript B has τελευτήσει θανάτῳ,
cf. Lev. 20:9).[473]

In classical Greek when a cognate noun is used with a verb
to emphasize that verb, it is usually an accusative form (cognate accusative or accusative of content or internal object;
see below in section [d]). The dative case of a cognate noun is
used more rarely. It can be placed either before or after the
verb, and expresses the cause, manner, or means of the action of
the verb,[474] e.g., ὑπὲρ τοῦ μηδένα τῶν πολιτῶν βιαίῳ θανάτῳ
ἀποθνήσκειν, "in order that none of the citizens die by a
violent death" (Xenophon, *Hier.* 4.3); ὃ δὲ παραλαβὼν ἡμέας
λυμαίνεται λύμῃσι ἀνηκέστοισι, "having taken us, he afflicts
(us) with incurable afflictions" (Herodotus 6.12). These cognate datives themselves are usually modified by an attribute of

some sort, and thus do not merely emphasize the verb, but add a
particular nuance to the action of the verb:[475] "he afflicts us
with *incurable* afflictions"; "to die by a *violent* death." However, in a very few cases a cognate dative (without attribute)
seems merely to emphasize the verb: φεύγων φυγῇ τὸ γῆρας,
"fleeing old age completely" (literally "fleeing. . .by flight,"
Plato, *Smp*. 195B; also *Phdr*. 265C); γάμῳ γεγαμηκὼς τὴν ἐμὴν
μητέρα, ἑτέραν εἶχε γυναῖκα, "having lawfully married my mother,
he kept another woman" (literally "having married by marriage,"
Demosthenes 39.26; also Hippocrates, *Art*. 10.13).

In Hellenistic Greek the use of a cognate dative is rare,
and such a dative almost always has an attribute of its own, and
thus expresses the occasion, manner, or means by which the action
of the verb is carried out,[476] e.g., βουλευομένοις κοινῆι βουλῆι,
"for those planning with *common* counsel" (*PEleph*. 1.5); βεβαιώσω
πάσῃ βεβαιώσει ἐπὶ τὸν ἅπαντα χρόνον, "I shall guarantee with
every assurance for all time" (*PLond*. 2.262.6; the same expression also occurs in *BGU* 427.22; 584.7; 667.12); ᾿Αυρ(έλια)
Δομέτια βιώσασα βιῷ κουριδία<ς> σεμνῆς γυνεκὸς ἀνέστησε στήλ(ην),
"Aurelia Domitia, having lived with (the) life of a solemnly
wedded wife, raised up this stele" (*Stud.Pont*. 3.71a. 1-4).
There is only one undisputed Hellenistic text in which a cognate
dative (without attribute) seems merely to emphasize the verb:[477]
Δέων πρεσβύτερος τοῖς. . .πρεσβυτέροις καὶ διακώνοις ἀγαπετοῖς
ἀδελφοῖς ἐν κ(υρί)ῳ θ(ε)ῷ χαρᾷ χαίρειν,"Leon, prebyter to the
. . .presbyters and deacons, beloved brothers in the Lord God,
fullness of joy" (*POxy*. 1162.4-5). However, this is a fourth
century A.D. Christian document which probably uses the cognate
dative χαρᾷ in imitation of Jn 3:29--χαρᾷ χαίρει διὰ τὴν φωνὴν
τοῦ νυμφίου, "he rejoices greatly at the voice of the bride-
groom." Hence ἐξέστησαν. . .ἐκστάσει μεγάλη (Mk 5:42), in which
a cognate dative with an attributive adjective expresses the
manner of the action of the verb, is possible in Hellenistic
Greek, though such usage is not common. On the other hand,
the simple cognate dative θανάτῳ in Mk 7:10 which serves merely
to emphasize the verb is unparalleled in profane Hellenistic
Greek.[478]

In biblical Hebrew one manner in which a finite verb may
receive emphasis is by the addition of the infinitive absolute

either before or after the verb,[479] e.g., *wĕnimṣāʾ bĕyādô môt yûmāt*, "and (should a stolen slave) be found in his possession, he shall surely be put to death" (Exod 21:16); *wĕhinnēh bēraktā bārēk*, "and behold, you have truly blessed" (Num 24:10). This biblical Hebrew usage does not occur in any of the Qumran Hebrew sectarian documents,[480] nor in any of the Proto-Mishnaic Hebrew material. There is no such form as an infinitive absolute in biblical or Middle Aramaic.[481]

The OG usually employs one of two constructions to translate a finite verb which has received emphasis by means of the infinitive absolute of the same verb stem: (1) the verb plus the dative of a cognate or similar noun (about 200 times, mainly in the Pentateuch), e.g., Exod 21:16 (OG and Masoretic Text cited above), or (2) the verb plus the present or aorist participle of the cognate or similar verb (also about 200 times, but chiefly outside of the Pentateuch), e.g., πληθύνων πληθυνῶ τὰς λύπας σου, "I will greatly multiply your pains" (Gen 3:16; Hebrew: *harbāh ʾarbeh ʿiṣṣĕbônēk*).[482] The OG translators probably used the cognate dative to translate the infinitive absolute because of the (rare) use of the cognate dative in classical Greek explained above, since literal translation (infinitive plus finite verb) would have been incomprehensible in Greek.[483]

The force of the verb may also be strengthened in biblical Hebrew by the addition of an object (internal or absolute object) which is a noun derived from the same stem as the verb, placed either before or after the verb,[484] *ûmalkêhem śāʿărû śaʿar*, "and their kings trembled violently" (literally "shuddered a shudder," Ezek 27:35); very frequently with an attributive adjective: *wayyeḥĕrad yiṣḥāq ḥărādâ gĕdôlâ*, "and Isaac trembled severely" (literally "trembled a great trembling," Gen 27:33). There are no instances of the accusative of internal object in the Qumran Hebrew sectarian documents[485] or in the Proto-Mishnaic Hebrew material.

Something resembling the accusative of internal object occurs in Aramaic,[486] e.g., Middle Aramaic: *wᶜl kwl nšyn šwpr šprh*, "and above all women she is beautiful indeed" (1QapGn 20:6-7; here the peal active participle *šprh* is the predicate of the clause, modified by the abstract noun *šwpr*; *wḥlmt ʾnʾ ʾbrm ḥlm*, "and I, Abram, dreamed a dream" (1QapGn 19:14; also

19:17-18). Otherwise this cognate noun is accompanied by an
attribute and shows the manner by which the action of the verb
is carried out,[487] e.g., *wbkyt ᵓnh ᵓbrm bky tqyp*, "and I, Abram,
wept bitterly" (literally "a vehement weeping," 1QapGn 20:10-11).
Some grammarians, including C. Brockelmann, H. Bauer, and P.
Leander think that when a qualitative adjective is used, the
cognate substantive can be omitted, with the result that the
adjective appears to be and functions as an adverb,[488] e.g.,
malkā᷉ᵓ bĕnas ûqĕṣap śaggîᵓ, "the king was angered and became
quite furious" (Dan 2:12); *wĕᵓattûnā᷉ᵓ ᵓēzēh yattîrā᷉ᵓ*, "and the
furnace was exceedingly hot" (Dan 3:22). However, one can also
explain these instances as simply the adverbial use of an adjective (especially when they have the ending -ā) without recourse
to understood cognates.

The OG usually translates the Hebrew internal object with
the accusative of the cognate noun (cognate accusative, accusative of content), e.g., ἁμαρτίαν ἥμαρτεν, "she sinned greatly"
(literally "she sinned a sin" Lam 1:8); ἐξέστη δὲ Ισαακ ἔκστασιν
μεγάλην, "Isaac was greatly confused" (Gen 27:33, 34; 2 Kgdms
12:16; 3 Kgdms 1:12; Isa 21:7; 42:17; 45:17; Prov 21:26). In a
few cases, however, a cognate dative has been used, e.g., οἱ
βασιλεῖς αὐτῶν ἐκστάσει ἐξέστησαν, "their kings were greatly
astonished" (literally "were astonished with astonishment,"
Ezek 27:35); ἐδειλίασαν φόβῳ, "they feared with fear" (Ps
13[14]:5).

Hence, since in Mk 7:10 the cognate dative without attribute
expressing emphasis is unparalleled in profane Hellenistic Greek,
and since that Marcan verse explicitly cites OG Exod 21:16, we
conclude that the use of θανάτῳ in Mk 7:10 is a Semitism which
reflects the OG translation of a Hebrew infinitive absolute in
that text of Exodus. The use of a cognate dative (ἐκστάσει)
with an attributive adjective (μεγάλῃ) in Mk 5:42 is possible
in normal Hellenistic Greek, though such usage is rare. The
Marcan usage may be due to a conflation of OG Ezek 27:35
(ἐκστάσει ἐξέστησαν, cf. Ezek 26:16; 32:10) and Gen 27:33
(ἐξέστη ἔκστασιν μεγάλην) since cognate nouns with attributive
adjectives which express the quality of the action of the verb
are almost always in the accusative case in profane Greek and
the New Testament alike.[489] It is possible, too, that Mk 5:42

translates a Hebrew or Aramaic accusative of internal object,
even though the OG usually translates such a construction with
the Greek accusative of content.

(d) Accusative of Cognate Noun with Finite Verb for Emphasis

As we have seen (above in section c.iv) the force of a
verb may be strengthened in Hebrew and Aramaic by the addition
of an object (internal or absolute object) which is a noun
derived from the same stem as the verb. Since this usage is
very common in the Old Testament, several authors have claimed
that the frequency of cognate accusatives in the Greek of the
New Testament is due to Semitic interference, especially from
imitation of the OG (which usually translates the Hebrew construction with a cognate accusative in Greek).[490] There is only one
instance of a cognate accusative in the Gospel of Mark: καὶ
ἐφοβήθησαν φόβον μέγαν, "and they feared greatly" (literally
"and they feared a great fear," Mk 4:41).[491]

In both classical and Hellenistic Greek the accusative of
a substantive which is cognate (either in etymology or in meaning) with a verb form may be added to that verb in order to
strengthen its force (cognate accusative, accusative of internal
object, or, of content).[492] Usually the cognate accusative has
an attribute of its own,[493] as in the Marcan text in question
(μέγαν), e.g., γάμους τε τοὺς πρώτους ἐγάμεε Πέρσῃσι ὁ Δαρεῖος,
"Darius made the most noble marriages with the Persians"
(Herodotus 3.88); οὐχ ὀλίγην ζημείαν μοι ἐζημιώσαμεν, "I used
to suffer not a little loss to myself" (BGU 146.10). This
construction, however, is rare in Hellenistic Greek.[494]

As we have seen above (in section c.iv) the cognate accusative of the internal object occurs in biblical Hebrew (frequently)
as well as in Aramaic. We have also seen that the OG usually
translates such a cognate accusative by a cognate accusative in
Greek.

The cognate accusative φόβον μέγαν in Mk 4:41 is possible
in Hellenistic Greek. Such usage is rare, however, and the
expression φοβέομαι φόβον μέγαν never occurs in profane Greek.
It does occur once in the OG, and with exactly the same verb
form: καὶ ἐφοβήθησαν οἱ ἄνδρες φόβον μέγαν, "and the men

feared greatly" (Jonah 1:10, for Hebrew *wayyîr'û hā'ǎnāsîm yir'â
gǝdōlâ*, "and the men feared greatly" (literally "feared a great
fear") compare: καὶ ἐφοβήθησαν οἱ ἄνδρες φόβῳ μεγάλῳ,(Jonah
1:16, for the same Hebrew text as at 1:10!). Hence it is
probable that the evangelist or his source chose the rare Greek
cognate accusative in Mk 4:41 in imitation of the style of the
OG.

(ē) The Use of the Plural οὐρανοί

     Because the word for "heaven" or "sky" in Hebrew and
Aramaic is always used in the plural, it has been claimed that
the use of the Greek plural οὐρανοί in the New Testament is the
result of Semitic interference.[495] In the Gospel of Mark the
word οὐρανός occurs seventeen times: 1:10, 11; 4:32; 6:41;
7:34; 8:11; 10:21; 11:25, 30, 31; 12:25; 13:25 (*bis*), 27, 31,
32; 14:62. In thirteen of these texts it is used in the
singular, following normal Greek usage, but in the following
four texts the plural is used:
     εἶδεν σχιζομένους τοὺς οὐρανούς, "he saw the heavens torn
     open" (Mk 1:10);
     καὶ φωνὴ ἐγένετο ἐκ τῶν οὐρανῶν, "and there was a voice
     from the heavens" (Mk 1:11);
     ἀλλ' εἰσὶν ὡς ἄγγελοι ἐν τοῖς οὐρανοῖς, "but they are like
     angels in the heavens" (Mk 12:25);
     καὶ οἱ ἀστέρες ἔσονται ἐκ τοῦ οὐρανοῦ πίπτοντες, καὶ αἱ
     δυνάμεις αἱ ἐν τοῖς οὐρανοῖς σαλευθήσονται, "and the
     stars will be falling from heaven (singular) and the
     powers in the heavens (plural) will be shaken" (Mk 13:25;
     the last part of the verse is similar to καὶ τακήσονται
     πᾶσαι αἱ δυνάμεις τῶν οὐρανῶν, "and all the powers of the
     heavens shall be dissolved" [OG Isa 34:4, Manuscript B]--
     not in the Masoretic Text).[496]
     In classical Greek (mainly in poetry) the plural may be
used to lend dignity to something (plural of majesty, a *pluralis
poeticus*), [497] e.g., ἐς Διὸς θρόνους, "(man is borne) to the
throne (literally "thrones") of Zeus" (Sophocles, *Ant.* 1041).
The fact is, however, that the plural of οὐρανός is never so
used in classical Greek. Furthermore, the plural οὐρανοί

occurs only rarely, and when it does, it always has the true
plural meaning "heavens" (more than one) or "worlds,"[498] e.g.,
περιέχειν φασὶ πάντας τοὺς οὐρανοὺς ἄπειρον ὄν, "they say that
(the element), being boundless, embraces all the heavens"
(Aristotle, *Cael*. 3.5; p. 303b, lines 12-13; cf., in the same
treatise, τὸ γὰρ ὅλον καὶ τὸ πᾶν εἰώθαμεν λέγειν οὐρανόν, "for
we are accustomed to call the whole and the all 'οὐρανός'"
[1.9; p. 278b, lines 21-22]).

    With the exception of the OG, the plural οὐρανοί does not
occur in Hellenistic Greek in the singular sense ("heaven")
until the second or third century A.D.[499] Hence the use of the
plural οὐρανοί in the New Testament for the idea of "heaven"
or "sky" is quite unusual.

    In biblical Hebrew the word for "sky" or "heaven" is always
plural: *šāmayim*.[500] This is probably an example of the Hebrew
plural of extension, "the idea of a whole composed of innumer-
able separate parts or points."[501] The plural *šmym* is always
used in Qumran Hebrew (e.g., 1QS 4:22; 1QM 12:1; 1QH 1:9, etc.)
and in Proto-Mishnaic Hebrew (e.g., Mur 43:4; 3Q*14* 3:3).

    The corresponding Aramaic word, *šĕmayin/šĕmayyāᵓ*, "heaven,
sky," is always used in the plural,[502] in both biblical Aramaic
(e.g., Ezra 5:11; Dan 4:8, etc.) and Middle Aramaic (e.g.,
1QapGn 2:5; 22:16; 4QEn[g] 1 iv 23, 24, etc.).

    The OG translates Hebrew *šāmayim* and Aramaic *šĕmayin*
with the singular of the Greek word οὐρανός about 90% of the
time. Yet in 10% of the translated texts the plural οὐρανοί
occurs.[503] The best explanation of this phenomenon has been
given by P. Katz:[504] The OG usually translates with the
singular form οὐρανός, but in some texts of poetic style the
translator made use of the Greek idea of the plural of majesty
(*pluralis poeticus*), because of the elevated style of the
Hebrew poetry, and especially when the parallelism of the
Hebrew phrase demanded a plural substantive. H. Traub points
out that there is only one prose text in which the plural
οὐρανοί occurs in the OG, but that it is a prophetic saying:[505]
ἕως τῶν οὐρανῶν ἔφθακεν, "(The prophet Oded said). . .'(the rage)
reaches up to the heavens'" (2 Chr 28:9).

    Hence the use of the plural οὐρανοί for the idea "heaven"
or "sky" in Mk 1:10, 11; 12:25; 13:25 is the result of Semitic

interference, whether from contemporary Hebrew or Aramaic, or
(especially in the case of Mk 13:25) from imitation of OG
usage.

5. The Adjective: Positive Degree for Comparative

     Unlike Greek, which has a special form for the comparative
degree of the adjective, Hebrew and Aramaic have no special
form of the adjective to indicate comparison. For this reason
the frequent use of the positive degree of adjectives in New
Testament Greek, where one would expect the comparative degree,
has been considered to be the result of Semitic interference.[506]
The following texts in the Gospel of Mark have been cited as
instances of this phenomenon:[507]

     καλόν ἐστίν σε κυλλὸν εἰσελθεῖν εἰς τὴν ζωὴν ἢ τὰς δύο
     χεῖρας ἔχοντα ἀπελθεῖν εἰς τὴν γέενναν, "It is better
     (literally "good") that you enter into life maimed than
     having two hands to go to gehenna" (Mk 9:43);
     καλόν ἐστίν σε εἰσελθεῖν εἰς τὴν ζωὴν χωλὸν ἢ τοὺς δύο
     πόδας ἔχοντα βληθῆναι εἰς τὴν γέενναν, "It is better
     (literally "good") that you enter into life lame than
     having two feet to be thrown into gehenna" (Mk 9:45);
     καλόν σέ ἐστιν μονόφθαλμον εἰσελθεῖν εἰς τὴν βασιλείαν
     τοῦ θεοῦ ἢ δύο ὀφθαλμοὺς ἔχοντα βληθῆναι εἰς τὴν γέενναν,
     "It is better (literally "good") that you enter into the
     kingdom of God with one eye than having two eyes to be
     thrown into gehenna" (Mk 9:47);
     καλὸν αὐτῷ εἰ οὐκ ἐγεννήθη ὁ ἄνθρωπος ἐκεῖνος, "It (would
     be) well for him if that man had not been born" (Mk 14:21).[50?]

     In all four texts we are dealing with the neuter nominative
of the adjective καλός, "good," used with the verb "to be"
(understood in Mk 14:21). The expression καλόν ἐστιν (frequently
with the verb "to be" omitted) is one of many impersonal expressions (e.g., δίκαιόν ἐστιν, "it is just," ἀναγκαῖόν ἐστιν, "it
is necessary," αἰσχρόν ἐστιν, "it is shameful," καιρός ἐστιν,
"it is advantageous") used in both classical and Hellenistic
Greek to indicate the necessity, advantage, duty, etc. which
results from a given situation.[509] These expressions are
usually completed by an infinitive,[510] e.g., καλόν μοι τοῦτο
ποιούσῃ θανεῖν, "It (would be) well for me to die while doing

this" (Sophocles, *Ant.* 72); καλὸν δὲ καὶ τὸ εἰδέναι τὴν αὐτοῦ
παρασκευήν, "It (is) good to know one's own preparation"
(Epictetus 2.6.3). But such an impersonal expression may also
be followed by a conditional clause, e.g., καὶ ἔστι γε νὴ Δί´,
ἔφη ὁ Σωκράτης, καλόν, ἐὰν δύνῃ ταῦτα ποιῆσαι, "Socrates said:
'And it is good, by Zeus, if you can do these things'" (Xenophon,
Mem. 3.3.2); καὶ γὰρ αἰσχρόν, εἰ πύθοιτό τις λόγοις κολάζειν,
"For it (would be) shameful if someone should learn to chastise
with words" (Sophocles, *Aj.* 1159). Hence Mk 14:21, in which
the impersonal expression καλόν (ἦν ἄν), in the positive degree,
is completed by a conditional clause, is perfectly normal in
Greek: "It (would be) well for him if that man had not been
born."

With regard to Mk 9:43, 45, 47, there are two possible
explanations of the use of καλόν: (1) the positive degree of
the adjective is used for the comparative, βέλτιον: "It is
better that you enter. . .than to go";[511] (2) the adjective
καλόν is used in the positive sense, but the particle μᾶλλον
has been omitted from before ἤ by ellipsis. In this case the
particle ἤ ("than") alone would have the meaning of μᾶλλον ἤ
("rather than"), which is the normal comparative phrase used
after the positive degree of an adjective.[512] The texts in
question would be translated "It is good that you enter. . .
rather than to go/be thrown."

(1) In classical and Hellenistic Greek scholars have
adduced only two texts in which the positive degree of an adjective may possibly be used for the comparative: ἐμοὶ πικρὸς
τέθνηκεν ἤ κείνοις γλυκύς, αὐτῷ δὲ τερπνός, "His death was
(literally "he died") more bitter (literally "bitter") to me
than sweet to them, but for himself (it was) pleasant"
(Sophocles, *Aj.* 966); οὕτω ἂν δίκαιον ἡμέας ἔχειν τὸ ἕτερον
κέρας ἤ περ ᾿Αθηναίους, "Thus (it is) more just (literally "just")
that we hold the second wing than that the Athenians (hold it"
(Herodotus 9.26). Hence, if καλόν is used in a comparative
sense ("better") in Mk 9:43, 45, 47, it is not normal Hellenistic
Greek, since there are only two possible examples of such usage
in classical Greek and none at all in non-biblical Hellenistic
Greek.

(2) The particle ἤ alone can have the sense of μᾶλλον ἤ
("rather than") after verbs of wishing or choosing,[513] e.g.,
ὅστις δ' ᾑρεῖτο καὶ σὺν τῷ γενναίῳ μειονεκτεῖν ἤ σὺν τῷ ἀδίκῳ
πλέον ἔχειν, "Whoever chose even with the noble man to be poor
rather than to have more with the unjust. . ." (Xenophon, *Ag.*
4.5); μέγαν σε θέλει γενέσθαι ἤ πολλὰς πληγὰς λαβεῖν, "(God)
wishes you to become great rather than to receive many stripes"
(Epictetus 3.22.53; also *BGU* 846.15). In rare instances the
particle ἤ may also be used without μᾶλλον after a verb which
expresses a judgment in a doubtful situation,[514] e.g., τεθνάναι
νομίσασα λυσιτελεῖν ἤ ζῆν. . .κατεκωλύθη, "Thinking it (more)
profitable to die rather than to live. . .she was detained"
(Andocides 1.125); τούτους ἂν ὀρθῶς καὶ δικαίως προσαγορεύσειε
συνάρχοντας καὶ συστρατήγους ἤ ἐκείνους, "(If one regards
political careers. . .) he will rightly and justly call these
men co-rulers and soldiers rather than those men" (Plutarch,
Pel. 4.2). However, there is only one text in Greek in which
the particle ἤ (without μᾶλλον), following an adjective in the
positive degree, may have the force of μᾶλλον ἤ:[515] οὕτω ἂν
δίκαιον ἡμέας ἔχειν τὸ ἕτερον κέρας ἤ περ 'Αθηναιους, "Thus
(it is) just that we hold the second wing rather than the
Athenians" (Herodotus 9.26).[516] Hence, if in Mk 9:43, 45, 47
καλόν is used in the positive sense and is followed by the
particle ἤ with an adversative sense ("It is good to enter. . .
rather than to go"), it is not normal usage in Hellenistic Greek.

Biblical Hebrew, which has no special form for the comparative degree of an adjective, usually expresses comparison by
means of the simple form of an adjective followed by the preposition *min* (which usually means "from"),[517] e.g., *ṭôb tittî ᵓōtāh
lāk mittittî ᵓōtāh lᵓîš ᵓaḥēr*, "(It is) better (literally
"good") that I give her to you than that I should give (literally
"from my giving") her to another man" (Gen 29:19); *ṭôb môtî
mēhayyāy*, "(It is) better (literally "good") that I die than
that I live" (literally "my death is good from my life," Jonah
4:3; also Ps 118:8). There are no instances of this comparative
expression in either the Qumran Hebrew or the Proto-Mishnaic
Hebrew documents.

Aramaic also uses the adjective plus *min* to express a comparative,[518] e.g., biblical Aramaic: *ḥezwah rab min ḥabrātah*,

"the sight of it (the horn) (was) greater (literally "great")
than its fellows" (Dan 7:20); Middle Aramaic: [wby⁾ ⁾whrn dy]
mn dn rb, "[and another house which] (was) greater than this"
(4QEn^c 1 vi 28 = 1 Enoch 14:15); [d⁾nw]n tqypyn mny, "[for the]y
(are) stronger than I" (4QEnGiants^c 7; also 4QEn^d 1 xii 5 =
1 Enoch 26:3).[519]

The OG renders the Hebrew and Aramaic construction (adjective plus min comparative) in a variety of ways:

(1) with the comparative degree of the adjective and the
particle ἤ, e.g., βέλτιον δοῦναί με αὐτὴν σοὶ ἤ δοῦναί με
αὐτὴν ἀνδρὶ ἑτέρῳ, "(It would be) better that I give her
to you than that I give her to another man" (Gen 29:19);

(2) with the comparative and a genitive of comparison,
e.g., τί γλυκύτερον μέλιτος, "What (is) sweeter than
honey?" (Judg 14:18);

(3) with the positive degree of the adjective and a
preposition: with ὑπέρ: οὐκ ἦν ἐν υἱοῖς Ισραηλ ἀγαθὸς
ὑπέρ αὐτόν, "among the sons of Israel there was not a
better man than he" (literally "good over him," 1 Kgdms
9:2); with παρά: μέγας κύριος παρὰ πάντας τοὺς θεούς,
"Great is the Lord above all gods" (Exod 18:11);

(4) with the positive degree of the adjective and the
particle ἤ (as in Mk 9:43, 45, 47), e.g., ἀγαθὸν πεποιθέναι
ἐπὶ κύριον ἤ πεποιθέναι ἐπ᾿ ἄνθρωπον, "(It is) better
(literally "good") to rely on the Lord than to rely on
man" (Ps 117[118]:8); καλὸν τὸ ἀποθανεῖν με ἤ ζῆν με,
"(It is) better (literally "good") that I die than that I
live" (Jonah 4:3);

(5) with the positive degree of the corresponding adverb
and ἤ, e.g., καλῶς μοι ἦν τότε ἤ νῦν, "It was better (literally "well") for me then than now" (Hos 2:9).

The use of the positive degree of the adjective καλόν and
the particle ἤ in Mk 9:43, 45, 47 is not normal in non-biblical
Hellenistic Greek whether the positive degree is being used for
the comparative, or whether the particle ἤ has the sense of
μᾶλλον ἤ ("rather than") after the positive form καλόν. It
is most probably an attempt to render into Greek a Hebrew or
Aramaic comparative (adjective followed by the preposition
min). Such a translation of the Semitic comparative into Greek

is attested in the OG. Hence the expression καλόν. . .ἤ in
Mk 9:43, 45, 47 should be translated "It is better. . .than. . ."
It is probably the result of Semitic interference from contemporary Aramaic or (possibly) Hebrew, or may be an imitation of
certain OG texts. Mk 14:21 uses καλόν normally as in non-
biblical Greek.

NOTES

CHAPTER III

[1]Cf. E. Schwyzer, *Griechische Grammatik*, Vol. 2, p. 693,
and M. Zerwick, *Untersuchungen zum Markus-stil* (Scripta Pontificii
Instituti Biblici; Rome: Pontifical Biblical Institute, 1937),
p. 75. This observation has been corroborated by several statistical studies which show the percentage of main clauses in which
the subject precedes the verb:
    86% in Polybius and 82% in Xenophon according to E. Kieckers,
*Die Stellung des Verbs im Griechischen und in den verwandten
Sprachen* (Strassburg: Trübner, 1911), p. 5;
    from 71% to 87% in Herodotus, Thucydides, Xenophon, Lysias,
Demosthenes, and Polybius according to H. Frisk, *Studien zur
griechischen Wortstellung* (Göteborgs Högskolas Årsskrift 39:1;
Göteborg: Elanders, 1932), p. 16;
    78% in Epictetus according to E. C. Colwell, *The Greek of
the Fourth Gospel*, p. 23;
    72% in the papyri selected for study by Frisk, *Studien*,
p. 16;
    about 65% for the papyri studied by Schwyzer, *Griechische
Grammatik*, Vol. 2, p. 695;
    only 42% in the papyri studied by Colwell, *The Greek of the
Fourth Gospel*, p. 23, but he considers the figure exceptionally
low and explains the frequent verb--subject word order in these
papyri as "due to formulas of legal and business papyri" (p. 23,
n. 2).

[2]Blass-Debrunner-Funk, #472.

[3]"Wortstellung," K. Brugmann, *Griechische Grammatik* (4th
ed.; rev. by A. Thumb; Munich: Beck, 1913), p. 659.

[4]*Studien*, pp. 28-31.

[5]According to Frisk (*Studien*, pp. 28-31), in Mark the
predicate precedes the subject in relative clauses 50% of the
time, in temporal clauses 67%, and in conditional clauses 43%.

[6]*Untersuchungen*, pp. 97-104.

[7]Cf. Zerwick, *Untersuchungen*, p. 97.

[8]Another five sentences are asyndetic and have the word
order verb--subject. Five sentences have post-positive *gar* and
one each is introduced by the adverbs ὡσαύτως, πάλιν, and
ὁμοίως. These eight have subject--verb order. We omit these
thirteen sentences, too, from the study.

[9]Verb--subject word order is "gewöhnlich" in these sentences
(Zerwick, *Untersuchungen*, p. 75). Lagrange claimed that when a
predicative participle in Mark's Greek precedes the main verb
(e.g., καὶ ἀναστὰς ἠκολούθησεν αὐτῷ, "and having stood up he
followed him" [Mk 2:14], "le sujet précède réellement, sous la

197

forme d'un participe" (*Saint Marc*, p. xciv). Now these participles precede the main verb in 100 texts where no subject is
expressed, and in another 27 texts precede the subject and the
verb where the subject is expressed. If these two types of
sentences are to be considered as having subject--verb word
order, then that word order would predominate in the texts we
are considering in Mark. However, these participles are not
"le sujet réellement," but are conjunctive (not attributive)
participles, the equivalent of an adverbial clause which applies
to the whole sentence (L. Hartman, *Testimonium linguae* [Coniec-
tanea neotestamentica 19; Lund: Gleerup, 1963], pp. 9-10, and
Blass-Debrunner-Funk ##412 and 418). Such conjunctive participles
have no counterpart in Hebrew or Aramaic, but would be expressed
by a finite verb coordinated with a second verb in the sentence,
e.g., Hebrew: *wayyāqām wayyēlek*, "and he rose and went" (Gen
22:3); Aramaic: *wqn wbhr ᶜbdwhy*, "and he rose and chose from
his servants" (1QapGn 22:5). This Semitic usage is translated
precisely by a conjunctive participle and finite verb in the OG,
as in the case of the Hebrew example given above, ἀναστὰς
ἐπορεύθη, "having stood up he went" (Gen 22:3). Hence, sentences
with these participles (where no subject is expressed) do not
show subject--verb word order, or the opposite, and are omitted
from this study. When, however, the subject is expressed in
sentences with conjunctive participles with the word order: καί--
conjunctive participle--subject--verb (e.g., καὶ σπαράξαν αὐτὸν
τὸ πνεῦμα...ἐξῆλθον ἐξ αὐτοῦ, "and the spirit having convulsed
him...came out of him" [Mk 1:26], in Mark 27 times), the word
order should be taken to be verb--subject, "denn der Satz ist
zurückzuführen auf die ihm gedanklich zugrunde liegende Form
καὶ ἐσπάραξεν αὐτὸν τὸ πνεῦμα καὶ..." (Zerwick, *Untersuchungen*,
p. 75). Furthermore, as we have seen above, a Semitic *Vorlage*
for this type of Greek sentence would also have the form: finite
verb--subject--coordinating conjunction--finite verb, e.g.,
Hebrew: *wayyāqām yaᶜᵃqōb wayyiśśāʾ ʾet bānāy(w)*, "and Jacob
rose and placed his sons" (Gen 31:17; cf. Old Greek: ἀναστὰς
δὲ Ιακωβ ἔλαβεν, "having risen Jacob took..."); Aramaic: *bʾdyn
ʾth ᶜly hrqnwš wbᶜʾ mny*, "then Hirqanos came me and begged me"
(1QapGn 20:21).

[10]Cf. Schwyzer, *Griechische Grammatik*, Vol. 2, pp. 694-95.

[11]Cf. Kieckers, *Die Stellung des Verbs*, p. 142.

[12]#472.1. Cf. Kieckers, *Die Stellung des Verbs*, p. 64.

[13]According to Lagrange, *Saint Marc*, p. xciv. Cf. Smyth,
Greek Grammar, #966.

[14]Gesenius-Kautzsch-Cowley, ##141(1) and 142(f).

[15]This is most likely due to the influence of Akkadian.
Cf. Bauer-Leander #99(a) and (c), and S. Segert, *Altaramäische
Grammatik* (Leipzig: VEB Verlag Enzyklopädie, 1975), p. 422.

[16]Black, *Aramaic Approach*, p. 51.

[17]E. Mayser, *Grammatik*, 2:2:53.

[18]*Ibid.*, 2:2:54.

[19]*Syntactical Evidence*, p. 30.

[20]The form ἀνὴρ ὁ ἀγαθός is a Hellenistic development
whereby "das zunächst unbestimmt gefasste Nomen erst nachträglich
durch einen attributiven Zusatz determiniert werden soll" (Mayser,
Grammatik 2:2:52). This form, however, does not occur in the
Gospel of Mark.

[21]Gesenius-Kautzsch-Cowley, #132(b). Cf. #132(a).

[22]Fitzmyer, *Genesis Apocryphon*, p. 222.

[23]Cf. Bauer-Leander #94(f).

[24]The adjectives are postpositive in Mk 1:6 (*bis*), 8, *11*,
23, *26*, 26, 27, *27*, 34; 2:21 (*bis*), 22 (*quater*); 3:8, *11*, *29*, 29;
4:1, 2, 5, *8*, *20*, 32, 33, *34*, 37, 39, 41; 5:2, 7, *7*, *8*, 11, *13*,
21, 24, 42; 6:*7*, 13, 20, 35 (*bis*); 7:4, 13, 25; 8:7, *38* (*bis*);
9:2, *7*, 14, 17, 19, *25*, 42; 10:17 (*bis*), 22, 30, 46 (*bis*); 12:6,
36, 42, *43*; 13:*11*, 26; 14:3, 15; 15:17, 34, 37, 40, 41; 16:5.
The italicized verses contain articular adjectives (all in the
form article--substantive--article--adjective) while in the rest
of the verses neither substantive nor adjective is articular.
Prepositive adjectives are found in Mk 1:35, 45; 2:15, 21; 3:7,
29; 4:*34*; 5:26; 6:5, 13, 31, 32, 34, *39*; 7:2, 5; 8:1; 9:*25*, 12:4,
5, 31, *37*, 40, 41; 13:2; 14:6; 15:17, 43. Several of these
examples, however, may be considered as emphatic usage, and thus
could translate a Semitic source with the same word order, e.g.,
χεῖρον σχίσμα, "a *worse* tear" (Mk 2:21; cf. 3:29; 4:34; 12:4,
31, 40; 14:6). Both Matthew and Luke keep the Marcan word order
when they take over an adjective from Mark.

[25]Mayser, *Grammatik*, 2:2:143.

[26]*Ibid.*, 2:2:143.

[27]In the first twenty papyri of G. Milligan's *Selections
from the Papyri* (Cambridge: Cambridge University Press, 1927)
which vary in content and range from the third century B.C. to
the first A.D., of over 60 genitives dependent on anarthrous
substantives, only 7 are prepositive.

[28]Cf. G. D. Kilpatrick, "The Order of Some Noun and Adjective
Phrases in the New Testament," *NovT* 5 (1962), p. 112.

[29]Both Matthew (ἀγέλη χοίρων πολλῶν, "a herd of many swine"
[8:30]) and Luke (ἀγέλη χοίρων ἱκανῶν, "a herd of large swine"
[8:32]) seem to have had difficulty with the phrase and have
changed it.

[30]For a discussion of the phrase in Mk 1:11 and 9:27, see
Kilpatrick, "The Order of Some Noun and Adjective Phrases,"
p. 113 and H. Schlier, *Der Brief an die Epheser* (Düsseldorf:
Patmos, 1957), pp. 56-57.

[31]*The Eucharistic Words of Jesus* (New York: Scribner's
Sons, 1966), p. 172.

[32]See Mayser, *Grammatik*, 2:2:61.

[33]See, for example, J. A. Emerton, "The Aramaic Underlying *to haima mou tēs diathēkēs* in Mk. XIV. 24," *JTS* 6 (1955), pp. 238-40; "*TO HAIMA MOU TĒS DIATHĒKĒS:* The Evidence of the Syriac Versions," *JTS* 13 (1962), pp. 111-17; "Mark xiv. 24 and the Targum to the Psalter," *JTS* 15 (1964), pp. 58-59; J. Dupont, "'Ceci est mon corps,' 'Ceci est mon sang,'" *La nouvelle revue théologique* 80 (1958), pp. 1030-32; H. Gottlieb, "*TO HAIMA MOU TĒS DIATHĒKĒS,*" *Studia theologica* 14 (1960), pp. 115-18; Jeremias, *The Eucharistic Words of Jesus*, pp. 193-95; E. Haenchen, *Der Weg Jesu* (Sammlung Töpelmann 2/6; Berlin: Töpelmann, 1966), p. 482; J. E. David, "*To haima mou tēs diathēkēs.* Mt 26, 28: Un faux problème," *Bib* 48 (1967), pp. 291-92; D. Dormeyer, *Die Passion Jesu als Verhaltensmodell* (Neutestamentliche Abhandlungen 11; Münster: Aschendorff, 1974), p. 103, n. 266.

[34]Gesenius-Kautzsch-Cowley #129(e) for Hebrew; for Aramaic, see Bauer-Leander #89(d).

[35]Mayser, *Grammatik*, 2:2:64.

[36]The difficulty of the phrase in Greek has been pointed out by Gottlieb ("*TO HAIMA MOU TĒS DIATHĒKĒS*, p. 115), David ("*To haima mou tēs diathēkēs*," p. 291), and Dupont ("'Ceci est mon corps,'" p. 1031).

[37]Gesenius-Kautzsch-Cowley, #129(e).

[38]However, in this text the preposition *l* may simply mean "into": "in your entering *into* the small basin."

[39]Bauer-Leander, #90(a) and (j).

[40]See R. H. Fuller, *The Mission and Achievement of Jesus* (Studies in Biblical Theology 12; London: SCM, 1954), p. 69. H. Gottlieb ("*TO HAIMA MOU TĒS DIATHĒKĒS*," p. 116) maintains that the construction also turns up in biblical Aramaic at Dan 2:32: *rēʾšēʾ dî dĕhab ṭāb*, but this is really a "freier Genitiv," not dependent, but predicative: "its head was of fine gold" (see Bauer-Leander, #90 [f]). The verse is translated in the OG ἧν ἡ κεφαλὴ αὐτῆς ἀπὸ χρυσίου χρηστοῦ, "its head was of fine gold," and by Theodotion: ἧς ἡ κεφαλὴ χρυσίου χρηστοῦ, "(the image) whose head (was) of fine gold."

[41]See Emerton, "Mark xiv. 24," p. 58.

[42]For the several attested word orders of a phrase which includes an arthrous noun, an attributive participle, and another attribute, see Mayser, *Grammatik*, 2:2:61-64.

[43]In this example the noun ʾnšy, its genitive hyl, and its attributive participle mlwmdy are indefinite and lack the article, but, as in Mk 14:24, the dependent genitive hyl comes between the noun and the participle.

[44]That šlp ("the fallow land"), and not the place name haš-Šoʾ, is modified by the participle is clear from the next line of the text: brwy šl hšwʾ bṣwyh šb , "In the irrigated land of haš-Šoʾ, under the cippus that is there..." (line 14).

[45]The Greek version of the book of Enoch translates with
the following text (= *1 Enoch* 9:1): καὶ θεασάμενοι (or
ἐ εάσαντο) αἷμα πολὺ ἐκχυννόμενον (or ἐκκεχυμένον) ἐπὶ τῆς γῆς,
"and seeing (or "they saw") much blood poured out upon the earth."

[46]See, for example, Jeremias, *The Eucharistic Words of
Jesus*, pp. 170, n. 1, 194, 226; Lagrange, *Saint Marc*, p. 379;
Taylor, *Saint Mark*, p. 545.

[47]The Middle Aramaic retroversion of Mk 14:24 given above
is to be preferred to the Late Aramaic retroversions of Dalman:
ᵓidmî dĕliqĕyāmāᵓ dĕmiŝtĕpek ᶜal saggîᵓîn, "my blood of the
covenant which (is) shed in behalf of many" (*Jesus-Jeshua*,
pp. 160 and 171), and Jeremias: ᵓādām qĕyāmî, "(literally) the
blood of my covenant" (*The Eucharistic Words of Jesus*, p. 195).
For the Middle Aramaic form *dam* (as opposed to Dalman's "Galilean
Aramaic" form ᵓdm [cf. *Grammatik des JPA*, p. 202]), compare
4QEn[a] 1 iv 7 and 4QEn[b] 1 iii 8 cited above. In the same texts
occurs the peal passive participle ŝpyk [note the Greek translation of this verb (= *1 Enoch* 9:1) given in note 45 above]. The
hitpael participle of the same verb turns up in 4QEnGiants[e] 1:2:
[bh dm] hwh mŝtpk, "[upon it blood] was being shed." The
Aramaic word qĕyām is used to translate Hebrew bĕrît in 11QtgJb
35:7 (= Job 40:28). The adjective saggîᵓ is spelled in Middle
Aramaic either with initial *samek* (e.g., 11QtgJb 26:4; 4QEn[a] 1
iv 7) or *śin* (e.g., 1QapGn 20:33, 34).

[48]Mayser, *Grammatik*, 2:2:168.

[49]"The Mechanics of Translation Greek," *JBL* 52 (1933),
p. 248.

[50]*Syntactical Evidence*, p. 21.

[51]ʿΟ, ἡ, τό represent a pronoun in Mk 1:36, 45; 2:25; 3:4,
20; 4:10, 15; 5:27, 34, 40; 6:24, 37, 38, 49, 50; 7:6, 28; 8:5,
28, 33 (*ter*); 9:12, 19, 21, 32, 34; 10:3, 4, 20, 22, 26, 36, 37,
39, 48, 50; 11:6; 12:15, 16 (*bis*), 17 (*bis*); 13:14, 15, 16;
14:11, 20, 31, 46, 52, 61, 68, 70, 71; 15:2, 13, 14; 16:6.

[52]Namely in Mk 1:30, 32, 38; 2:17, 18, 26; 3:3, 22, 34;
4:5, 6, 16, 18 (*bis*), 19, 20, 34; 5:4, 26, 30, 33; 6:19, 20, 22,
39, 41 (*ter*), 55; 7:3, 6, 16, 18, 20, 26; 8:6, 19; 9:10, 23, 27,
37, 39, 43, 45; 10:5, 13, 18, 21, 23, 24 (*bis*), 38, 39, 40, 51;
11:10, 13, 29; 12:17, 23, 37; 13:2, 5, 13, 17, 26, 31; 14:6,
12, 21, 29, 38 (*ter*), 55, 62, 63, 64; 15:4, 5, 9, 11, 12, 14,
15, 16, 34, 37, 40, 44, 47.

[53]The *frequency* of such personal pronouns will be discussed
in section B.2(a)ii.

[54]*Selections from the Papyri*, pp. 1-119.

[55]Gesenius-Kautzsch-Cowley, #117(a), (e), and (n).

[56]In this phase of Aramaic the independent pronoun as direct
object has been found only in the third plural form.

[57]Gesenius-Kautzsch-Cowley, #117(x).

[58]In lQapGn 2:13--*wly t³mr*, "and she was saying to me," the indirect object represented by *ly* probably comes before its verb because of parallelism to the previous *ᶜmy tmll*, "she was speaking with me."

[59]This may mean "You must make me know!"

[60]Mayser, *Grammatik*, 2:2:80.

[61]Joüon, *Grammaire*, #143(i).

[62]Bauer-Leander, #73(c).

[63]Cf. Blass-Debrunner-Funk, #458; Colwell, *The Greek of the Fourth Gospel*, pp. 17-18; Deissmann, *Light from the Ancient East*, p. 133; H. Ljungvik, *Beiträge zur Syntax der spätgriechischen Volkssprache* (Skrifter utgivna av Kungl. Humanistiska Vetenskaps-Samfundet 27; Uppsala: Almqvist & Wiksell, 1932), pp. 54-55; Mayser, *Grammatik*, 2:3:184; Moulton, *Prolegomena*, p. 12; Radermacher, *Neutestamentliche Grammatik*, p. 218; N. Turner, *Syntax*, p. 334; Zerwick, *Graecitas*, #450.

[64]Examples are given by Deissmann, *Light from the Ancient East*, pp. 134-35; Ljungvik, *Beiträge*, pp. 83-84; Mayser, *Grammatik*, 2:3:184-86; Moulton-Milligan, p. 314.

[65]For examples in Strabo and Diodorus, see Radermacher, *Neutestamentliche Grammatik*, pp. 218-19, and in Xenophon, see Conybeare and Stock, *Selections*, p. 51.

[66]Unfortunately, L. Rydbeck (*Fachprosa*) has not researched paratactic καί in his study of the so-called *Zwischenprosa* (see chapter 1 above), but a careful examination of all the examples of this type of Greek writing which he does cite in other contexts reveals that these texts almost always employ the hypotactic style.

[67]The statistics are from L. Wohleb, "Beobachtungen zur Erzählungsstil des Markusevangeliums," *Römische Quartalschrift* 36 (1928), p. 189 and have been taken over by Zerwick, *Untersuchungen*, p. 2.

[68]*Syntactical Evidence*, p. 19.

[69]The statistics given by N. Turner, "The Relation of Luke i and ii to the Hebraic Sources and to the Rest of Luke-Acts," *NTS* 2 (1955-56), p. 108 are: Romans--.5 uses of καί for every use of δέ, 1 and 2 Corinthians--.6 to 1, and Galatians--.3 to 1.

[70]Martin, *Syntactical Evidence*, p. 19.

[71]Gesenius-Kautzsch-Cowley, #154. We will discuss the Hebrew and Middle Aramaic evidence for the various types of parataxis as they come up in the discussion below.

[72]J. C. Hawkins considers that there are 88 sections and subsections in Mark, which are denoted in the Westcott-Hort edition of the gospel by fresh paragraphs for sections and

spaces for subsections (*Horae Synopticae* [2nd rev. ed.; Oxford: Clarendon Press, 1909], p. 151). Zerwick says that the figure should be 89 (*Untersuchungen*, p. 1).

[73]Beyer considers that Mk 4:12, 20; 5:4, 26; 9:39; 10:11; 11:23; 12:19 contain conditional (-temporal) parataxis between subordinate clauses. He sees a high possibility of Semitic interference here since both Hebrew and Aramaic avoid double subordination where possible (*Semitische Syntax*, p. 259).

[74]Howard considers that this verse contains a "conditional parataxis of the imperative" ("Semitisms," p. 421).

[75]For parallels to the temporal use of καί as in Mk 15:25, see Liddell-Scott, p. 857, where they give several classical examples of καί which is "used to express simultaneity." For Hellenistic examples of this temporal use of καί, namely, when it means "when, until, before," see Ljungvik, *Beiträge*, pp. 76-79, 84-86, and Moulton, *Prolegomena*, p. 12, n. 2. The consecutive use of καί is "ausserordentlich häufig" (Ljungvik, *Beiträge*, p. 60). Examples are given by Ljungvik, *ibid.*, pp. 59-68; Mayser, *Grammatik*, 2:3:145 and 186; Colwell, *The Greek of the Fourth Gospel*, pp. 88-89. For examples of καί and a future indicative after an imperative see Beyer, *Semitische Syntax*, pp. 251-52; Blass-Debrunner-Funk, #369.3; Colwell, *The Greek of the Fourth Gospel*, pp. 26-27; Radermacher, *Grammatik*, p. 216. Καί stands for a relative in the examples given by L. Radermacher, "Besonderheiten der Koine-Syntax," *Wiener Studien* 31 (1909), p. 5; Ljungvik, *Beiträge*, pp. 86-87; Radermacher, *Grammatik*, p. 218. The adversative use of καί is very common; cf. Bauer-Arndt-Gingrich, p. 393 (under καί 2.g) and the examples in Ljungvik, *Beiträge*, pp. 55-57.

[76]Gesenius-Kautzsch-Cowley, #112(ff).

[77]*Ibid.*, #155(b).

[78]Cf. *ibid.*, #163(a).

[79]Cf. Bauer-Leander, #107(c).

[80]Bauer-Arndt-Gingrich (p. 393) mention *Hermetic Writings* 13.1 as a text in which καί introduces an apodosis. It is the apodosis, however, of a temporal protasis expressed by a genitive absolute: ἐμοῦ τε σοῦ ἱκέτου γενομένου. . ., καὶ ἔφης, "When I became your supplicant. . ., and [= "and then, at that point"] you said. . . ." Καί introduces the apodosis of a conditional sentence only in Homer, and there very infrequently (cf. Liddell-Scott-Jones, p. 857 under καί B.3). Radermacher (*Grammatik*, p. 218) gives examples of καί plus a finite verb following a genitive absolute and following a temporal clause with ἐπεί, but no real parallel in Greek to this New Testament use of καί has yet been found.

[81]Gesenius-Kautzsch-Cowley, #112(ff).

[82]Even though Beyer (*Semitische Syntax*, p. 67) says that *waw* of the apodosis in the Aramaic language occurs "selten," we make this conclusion because of the clear parallel in *Middle*

Aramaic, which we cite above, and point out that the construction is infrequent also in the Gospel of Mark.

[83]Matthew and Luke take over into their gospels only the latter three verses. Of these, Matthew does not change Mk 11:28 (if this is the correct reading), and Luke retains the καί in his parallels to Mk 10:26 and 12:37.

[84]Cf. Lagrange, *Evangile selon Saint Jean* (6th ed.; Etudes bibliques; Paris: Gabalda, 1936), p. cvi. Liddell-Scott-Jones (under καί II. 2, p. 857) give classical examples of καί "in questions, to introduce objection or express surprise." For Hellenistic examples see Colwell, *The Greek of the Fourth Gospel*, p. 88, and Ljungvik, *Beiträge*, p. 56.

[85]Gesenius-Kautzsch-Cowley, #150(a).

[86]Howard, "Semitisms," p. 420.

[87]Cf. Smyth, *Greek Grammar*, #2220(b), and Moulton-Milligan, p. 455, col. 2.

[88]This is the text found in the manuscripts B ℵ[corr] and Ψ. The word με, omitted in C Θ λ φ 565, is considered dubious (it is placed in square brackets) in the Nestle-Aland edition of the New Testament. The Old Latin omits θέλετέ με and reads: *quid faciam.* Codex Bezae has only ποιήσω. The Koine text family, A Γ and Φ have τί θέλετε ποιῆσαι με, and L W have, similarly, τί θέλετέ με ποιῆσαι.
The texts which have the infinitive ποιῆσαι (A Γ Φ L W) are generally inferior to the other codices, and are so in this case where they correct the text so that it has the very common infinitive construction after θέλειν (cf. Smyth, *Greek Grammar*, #1869). Codex Bezae avoids the problem by omitting everything except ποιήσω, thus making the affirmative statement "I will do it," instead of the more probable question, witnessed in the Matthean parallel (20:21--τί θέλεις). The Old Latin manuscripts simplify the text by omitting θέλετε (με), and are also secondary witnesses here. We prefer the text of B ℵ[corr] and Ψ, τί θέλετέ με ποιήσω to that of C Θ λ Φ 565, which omit the word με, for two reasons: (a) the text of Codex B is generally superior to that of C Θ etc.; (b) the text τί θέλετέ με ποιήσω is the *lectio difficilior* here, since when the subject of a verb dependent on θέλειν is expressed, one would normally expect that verb to be an infinitive, e.g., θέλω δέ σε ἀναγνοῦναι, "I want you to read" (*POxy.* 4.743.2a). Codices C Θ λ φ 565 have avoided this difficulty by omitting the superfluous pronoun με.

[89]See Howard, "Semitisms," p. 421.

[90]Moulton, *Prolegomena,* p. 185. Cf. Blass-Debrunner-Funk, #366. For examples in which βούλεσθαι and θέλειν take a subjunctive without ἵνα see Howard, "Semitisms," p. 421, and Moulton-Milligan, p. 286.

[91]Cf. Taylor, *St. Mark,* p. 440.

[92]None of these instances resemble the phenomenon found in Official Aramaic where a finite modal verb takes a finite verbal complement (usually in the imperfect, but occasionally in the perfect), e.g., *lᵓ ᵓkl ᵓnṣl lplṭy mn tḥt lbbk*, "I shall not be able to take Palti away from you" (literally, "from under your heart") *BMAP* 2:13. See further *BMAP* 3:14; *AP* 1:4, 5, 6; 5:6, 9, 12; 6:12; 8:15, etc.; *AP* 18:3; *BMAP* 7:42 (with perfect).

[93]*Aramaic Approach*, p. 55; cf. pp. 55-61.

[94]The lists of examples we give here are not completely exhaustive, but are intended to demonstrate the high frequency of the construction in Mark.

[95]Most of the asyndeta in Mark occur in the discourses of Jesus or of the other characters in the gospel. The examples that occur in the narrative part have been italicized.

[96]Blass-Debrunner-Funk, #458. Cf. Schwyzer, *Grammatik*, Vol. 2, pp. 632-33.

[97]Blass-Debrunner-Funk, #461.1. Cf. Colwell, *The Greek of the Fourth Gospel*, pp. 15-16.

[98]Colwell discusses its high frequency in Epictetus' *Discourses* (in both narrative and discourse sections) and the papyri (*ibid.*, pp. 11-16). For numerous examples in the papyri see Ljungvik, *Beiträge*, pp. 87-102 and Radermacher, *Grammatik*, pp. 221-22.

[99]For numerous examples in Epictetus and the papyri see Colwell, *The Greek of the Fourth Gospel*, pp. 16-17.

[100]Gesenius-Kautzsch-Cowley, #120(h).

[101]Joüon, *Grammaire*, #177(a).

[102]Gesenius-Kautzsch-Cowley, #120(g).

[103]Cf. C. Brockelmann, *Grundriss der vergleichenden Grammatik der semitischen Sprachen* (2 vols.; Hildesheim: Olms, 1913), Vol. 2, p. 475.

[104]*Ibid.*, Vol. 2, p. 476.

[105]Bauer-Leander, #106(b).

[106]Lagrange, *Saint Marc*, p. lxxi.

[107]*The Greek of the Fourth Gospel*, p. 17.

[108]Cf. Blass-Debrunner-Funk, #461.1 and Moulton, *Prolegomena*, p. 14.

[109]There is a text problem here: the manuscripts W and ff[2] sa bo[pt] read ἐγένετο δέ, but this is an assimilation to Lk 3:21, its parallel--ἐγένετο δέ. Θ omits the word ἐγένετο, but both Matthew and Luke witness to the authenticity of this word

(Mt 3:13--τότε παραγίνεται, Lk 3:21--ἐγένετο δέ). Codex
Vaticanus omits the initial καί, but in the light of the strong
witness of all the other manuscripts to the word καί, and because
of the fact that Mark prefers to begin a new paragraph with καί
in 80 out of 88 or 89 instances (see section A.2.b on "Καί
Beginning a New Paragraph in Mark"), we opt, along with the
Nestle-Aland edition, for the text καί ἐγένετο at Mk 1:9.

[110]Robertson, *Grammar*, p. 1043; cf. Smyth, *Greek Grammar*,
##1982 and 1985, and Goodwin-Gulick, #887.

[111]For other examples, see Mayser, *Grammatik*, 2:1:307;
Liddell-Scott, p. 1674 (under συμβαίνω III.1.b); and Moulton-
Milligan, p. 597.

[112]For other examples, see Mayser, *Grammatik*, 2:1:307; and
Moulton-Milligan, p. 126.

[113]Cf. Beyer, *Semitische Syntax*, p. 30. Beyer claims that
ἐγένετο and an accusative with infinitive construction approaches
the normal Greek construction of γίνεται, γένηται, or γίνοιτο
with an infinitive (p. 56, n. 2), but even Moulton realized that
it was "a step" from those forms to the aorist narrating a
single, past event (*Prolegomena*, p. 17). Zerwick, too, qualifies
his opinion of ἐγένετο with an infinitive by calling it a
"constructio 'graeca'" (Note his quotation marks! *Graecitas*,
#389, n. 1).

[114]Cf. Gesenius-Kautzsch-Cowley, #111(f), (g), and (b). The
temporal expression is most frequently a preposition (usually *b*)
and a substantive, e.g., *wayĕhî bitĕhillat šibtām*, "and it happened at the beginning of their dwelling" (2 Kgs 17:25). The
temporal expression may also take the following forms: (a) a
preposition with an infinitive, e.g., *wayĕhî bĕšahēt ᵓelōhîm*,
"And it happened in God's destruction" (Gen 19:29); (b) a
subordinate clause (most frequently with the particle *kaᵓăšer*
e.g., *wayĕhî kaᵓăšer šamaᶜ*, "And it happend when he heard"
(Neh 3:33); (c) a nominal clause (usually a substantive with a
participle), e.g., *wayĕhî hēm yōšĕbîm*, "And it happened (while)
they were sitting" (1 Kgs 13:20). (M. Johannessohn, "Das
biblische *kai egeneto* und seine Geschichte," *Zeitschrift für
vergleichende Sprachforschung indogermanischer Sprachen* 53
[1925], pp. 161-212, esp. p. 164. Cf. Beyer, *Semitische Syntax*,
p. 32).

[115]Beyer, *Semitische Syntax*, p. 52.

[116]*Ibid*., p. 53. The past action introduced by *wayĕhî* may
also be expressed by (a) a perfect with *waw* copulative, e.g.,
wayĕhî hēmmāh badderek wĕhaššĕmuᶜā bāᵓâ ᵓel dāwid, "And it
happened (when) they were on the way that the report came to
David" (2 Sam 13:30); (b) the perfect without *waw* (about 15% of
the time), e.g., *wayĕhî bitĕhillat šibtām šam lōᵓ yārᵓû*, "And it
happened at the beginning of their dwelling there (that) they
did not fear" (2 Kgs 17:25); (c) a noun clause introduced by
wĕhinnēh, e.g., *wayĕhî hûᵓ terem killāh lĕdabbēr wĕhinnēh ribqâ
yōṣēt*, "And it happened before he finished speaking that
Rebekah came out" (Gen 24:15). Cf. *ibid*., pp. 53-58.

[117]Cf. Gesenius-Kautzsch-Cowley, #111(o) and 112(d).

[118]*Semitische Syntax*, p. 52, n. 2.

[119]Gesenius-Kautzsch-Cowley, #112(ee).

[120]Other Greek translations of *wayĕhî*, which occurs about 400 times in the Old Testament, are with δέ instead of καί (about 50 times), and καὶ ἐγενήθη (the aorist passive, about 70 times according to Beyer, *Semitische Syntax*, p. 31). The temporal expression with the preposition *b* and an infinitive in Hebrew is translated by ἐν τῷ and the infinitive, e.g., καὶ ἐγένετο ἐν τῷ ἐκτρῖψαι κύριον (Gen 19:29); with a subordinate clause introduced by *ka'ăšer* in Hebrew: καὶ ἐγένετο ἡνίκα ἤκουσεν (2 Esdr 13:33 = MT Neh 3:33); with a nominal clause in Hebrew, almost always a genitive absolute in the Greek, e.g., καὶ ἐγένετο αὐτῶν καθημένων, "And it happened as they were sitting. . ." (3 Kgdms 13:20).

[121]Naturally, when the construction is asyndetic in Hebrew (i.e., *wayĕhî* and a perfect without *waw*) it is translated literally in the Greek.

[122]Johannessohn, "Das biblische καὶ ἐγένετο," p. 163; cf. Beyer, *Semitische Syntax*, p. 31, n. 1.

[123]Unless, as is very unlikely, Codex Vaticanus is correct at 3 Kgdms 11:43--καὶ ἐγενήθη ὡς ἤκουσεν Ιεροβοαμ υἱὸς Ναβατ κατευθύνειν, "And it happened as Jeroboam son of Nabat heard that he made straight (for his city)." The other manuscripts have the more probable text with the finite verb κατευθύνει.

[124]Gesenius-Kautzsch-Cowley, #122(bb).

[125]J. T. Milik, *The Books of Enoch*, p. 165.

[126]Beyer considers that Mk 1:9 and 4:4 contain a Hebraism (*Semitische Syntax*, p. 303).

[127]According to Beyer, αὐτὸν ἐν τοῖς σάββασιν παραπορεύεσθαι διὰ τῶν σπορίμων is a *Zwischensatz* which may have been mistaken, in a Hebrew *Vorlage*, for the action introduced by καὶ ἐγένετο (*ibid.*, p. 59).

[128]*Ibid.*, p. 56.

[129]Beyer also considers Mk 2:23 to be a "gräzisiert" form which is "weder semitisch noch griechisch, sicherer LXXismus" (*ibid.*, pp. 296 and 303).

[130]Scholars are quick to point out what they consider a parallel to this verse: γίνεται γὰρ ἐντραπῆναι, "for it happens that one feels ashamed" (literally, "for to feel ashamed happens," *PPar.* 49.29), but this is no true parallel. The papyrus is speaking of a general condition of man, but the Marcan γίνεται equals a past tense and introduces a past event.

[131]Beyer claims that Mk 2:15 is "im Semitischen nicht zu belegen, sicherer Gräzismus" (*ibid.*, pp. 296 and 303), but since

there is no non-biblical evidence for καί γίνεται (as a historical present) introducing a past event, we strongly disagree.

[132]Cf. Blass-Debrunner-Funk, #466, Mayser, *Grammatik*,
2:1:343 and 2:3:189; Radermacher, *Grammatik*, p. 219; Zerwick,
Graecitas, #25.

[133]Blass-Debrunner-Funk, #466(1).

[134]Colwell, *The Greek of the Fourth Gospel*, pp. 37-38.

[135]For further examples see Bauer-Arndt-Gingrich, p. 238
(under ἐκεῖνος 1.b) and p. 601 (under οὗτος 1.a.*e*); Colwell,
The Greek of the Fourth Gospel, pp. 38-40 (very frequent in
Epictetus); Ljungvik, *Beiträge*, pp. 6-9; Lagrange, *Evangile
selon Saint Matthieu* (Etudes bibliques; Paris: Gabalda, 1927),
p. xcvii.

[136]These are mainly from Aelian, *De natura animalium:*
οἱ δὲ ὀδόντες μεμυκότος, οὐκ ἂν αὐτοὺς ἴδοις, "but as for the
teeth of the growling (horned ray), you would not see them"
(1.19); ὁ κόραξ, ὄρνιν αὐτόν φασίν ἱερόν, "As for the raven,
they call it a sacred bird" (1.48); ἡ ἄγρα, εἰπεῖν αὐτὴν οὐ
χεῖρόν ἐστι, "As for the catch, it is not bad (i.e., it would
be good) to explain it" (1.55); ὁ κόραξ, οὐκ ἂν αὐτὸν ἐς τόλμαν
ἀθυμότερον εἴποις τῶν ἀετῶν, "As for the raven, you might say
that it is no less faint-hearted in daring than the eagles"
(2.51); ὑπεριδόντα δὲ τοῦ νόμου καί ἐσελθόντα ἀνάγκη πᾶσα αὐτὸν
ἐνιαυτοῦ πρόσω μὴ βιῶναι, "whoever disregards the law and
enters, it is of all necessity that he not live longer than a
year" (Pausanias 8.38.6).

[137]Other examples are given by Colwell, *The Greek of the
Fourth Gospel*, pp. 38-39; Mayser, *Grammatik*, 2:3:197; Howard,
"Semitisms," p. 425.

[138]"Grec biblique," col. 1355. Cf. Gignac, "The Language
of the Non-Literary Papyri," p. 151. Abel (*Grammaire*, p. 133)
points out that the construction is very frequent in the Coptic
versions of the Old Testament.

[139]Gesenius-Kautzsch-Cowley, #143(a); cf. (b), (c), and
116(w), and Beyer, *Semitische Syntax*, p. 146.

[140]*Semitische Syntax*, pp. 75-295.

[141]Above in section A.2.d.

[142]*Semitische Syntax*, p. 97.

[143]*Ibid.*, p. 96; cf. Gesenius-Kautzsch-Cowley, #159(ff).

[144]*Semitische Syntax*, p. 96.

[145]*Ibid.*, pp. 96-97.

[146]*Ibid.*, p. 96. The examples are Ps 138[139]:8; Prov 9:12;
Job 10:15; 16:6; 35:6. The OG understands the sentence differently in Isa 43:2 and Job 22:23.

[147]Cf. Smyth, *Greek Grammar*, #2777 and #2966; Beyer, *Semitische Syntax*, p. 104; Mayser, *Grammatik*, 2:3:116 and 118.

[148]Smyth, *Greek Grammar*, #2346; cf. Mayser, *Grammatik*, 2:3:116.

[149]Kühner-Gerth, #577.8; cf. Robertson, *Grammar*, p. 1025; Smyth, *Greek Grammar*, #2783; Mayser, *Grammatik*, 2:3:205.

[150]Smyth, *Greek Grammar*, #2966.

[151]*Semitische Syntax*, p. 105. He claims that the frequency of εἰ μή = "except" in Mark is about the same as that of the exceptive *ᵓellā̄ᵓ* in Jewish Palestinian Aramaic (p. 104, n. 3).

[152]Cf. J. T. Milik, *DJD* II p. 164 (note on Mur 45:8); Segal, *Mishnaic Hebrew Grammar*, p. 147. The Proto-Mishnaic form *ᵓlh* (and thus probably also the Mishnaic form *ᵓlᵓ*) is not from the Late Aramaic particle *ᵓlᵓ* (the conditional particle *ᵓyn* and the negative *lᵓ*) because the contemporary (Middle) Aramaic form of the conditional was *hn* as in biblical and earlier Aramaic (cf. lQapGn 2:5; 20:19; Mur 18:7; 20:9; 21 1-3 10).

[153]Beyer, *Semitische Syntax*, p. 104.

[154]The three instances are the same type of sentence in both Hebrew and Greek: *ᵓên. . .kî ᵓim* and a substantive, οὐκ ἔστιν . . .εἰ μή, "this is not (anything). . .except X."

[155]*Semitische Syntax*, p. 106.

[156]*Ibid.*, p. 105.

[157]*Ibid.*, p. 106.

[158]*Ibid.*, p. 304.

[159]*Ibid.*, pp. 303 and 304.

[160]*Ibid.*, p. 129.

[161]*Ibid.*, pp. 130 and 304.

[162]*Ibid.*, pp. 138 and 305.

[163]Kühner-Gerth, 2:2:487.

[164]*Semitische Syntax*, p. 107.

[165]Thus Beyer's claim "dieser Sprachgebrauch ist aus dem *Griechischen* nicht zu belegen" (*ibid.*, p. 130) is simply false.

[166]*Semitische Syntax*, p. 145.

[167]*Ibid.*, pp. 145 and 142.

[168]*Ibid.*, p. 163; cf. p. 169. This construction is described fully above in section A.4, *Casus Pendens*.

[169] *Semitische Syntax*, pp. 163-64.

[170] *Ibid.*, p. 176; cf. p. 304.

[171] Blass-Debrunner-Funk, #293; Zerwick, *Graecitas*, #216; Mayser, *Grammatik*, 2:1:76.

[172] *Ibid.*, 2:1:261.

[173] Blass-Debrunner-Funk, #380.1; cf. Smyth, *Greek Grammar*, #2506.

[174] Turner, *Syntax*, p. 109; cf. Mayser, *Grammatik*, 2:1:266.

[175] Turner, *Syntax*, p. 110.

[176] General relative clauses in Epictetus: 1.2.31; 4.4; 11.19; 12.27; 16.21; 25.14, 24; 27.2; 28.8, 10; 29.28, 39, 62; 2.1.24; 2.21; 3.4; 4.7; 10.23; 12.4; 13.3; 15.9; 16.42; 21.4; 22.3, 15, 34. Indefinite conditional clauses (εἴ/ἐὰν τις): 1.4.2, 27; 19.1, 21; 2.2.18; 9.22; 20.2, 21; 21.7; 23.36.

[177] *Grammatik*, 2:1:262-67.

[178] Cf. Gesenius-Kautzsch-Cowley, #138(f).

[179] The restoration is fairly certain here because the text translates Gen 20:13--ᵓel kol hammāqôm ᵓǎšer nābôᵓ šammāh ᵓimrî lî, "in whatever place we enter, say about me. . . ."

[180] Namely, in Mk 3:29, 35; 4:9, 25a,b; 6:11, 22b, 23; 8:35a, b, 38; 9:37a, b, 40, 41, 42; 10:9, 11, 15, 43, 44; 11:23 (with ὅς or ὅστις); 6:56b and 11:24 (with ὅσος); 6:10, 56a; 9:18; 14:9 (with ὅπου [ἐ]άν).

[181] Namely, in Mk 4:23; 7:16; 8:23, 34; 9:22, 35; 11:3, 13; 12:19; 13:21.

[182] See n. 176 above.

[183] *Einleitung*, p. 19.

[184] *Aramaic Approach*, p. 93.

[185] *Ibid.*, p. 94.

[186] *Style*, p. 21.

[187] *The Parables of Jesus*, p. 11.

[188] "Die aramäische Vorgeschichte unserer Evangelien," *TLZ* 94 (1949), p. 530.

[189] *The Parables of Jesus*, p. 11, n. 2.

[190] *Einleitung*, p. 19.

[191] *Aramaic Approach*, p. 95.

[192]*The Parables of Jesus*, p. 11, n. 2.

[193]Smyth, *Greek Grammar*, #1120; cf. Winer-Moulton, p. 131.

[194]Smyth, *Greek Grammar*, #1122; cf. Goodwin-Gulick, #948.

[195]Smyth, *Greek Grammar*, #1121; cf. Schwyzer, *Griechische Grammatik*, 2:25; Mayser, *Grammatik*, 2:2:44-47.

[196]Gesenius-Kautzsch-Cowley, #126(q); cf. S. R. Driver, *Notes on the Hebrew Text and the Topography of the Books of Samuel* (2nd ed.; Oxford: Clarendon Press, 1913), p. 6.

[197]Segal, *Grammar of Mishnaic Hebrew*, p. 180.

[198]Fitzmyer, *Genesis Apocryphon*, p. 221.

[199]*Ibid.*, p. 221; cf. Bauer-Leander, #88(1).

[200]Cf. *ibid.*, #88(h).

[201]T. Muraoka ("Notes on the Aramaic of the Genesis Apocryphon [1]," *RevQ* 8 [1972-76], p. 13) has argued that there is a difference of meaning between the emphatic form *bqwšt$^{\supset}$* and the absolute form *bqwšt* in the Genesis Apocryphon. He claims that the emphatic form in 2:5 and 22, following the pronoun *kwl$^{\supset}$*, "everything," the direct object of a verb meaning "to make known," has the meaning "to make known everything *in its truth*.." On the other hand, the absolute form in 2:7, 10, and 18 means simply "honestly," being used with the intransitive verb *mll* in 2:7 and 18, while it is followed by *kwl$^{\supset}$* in 2:10. This kind of argument can only be regarded as tendentious in light of the evidence of other Middle Aramaic documents. Abstract nouns are used indiscriminately in either the emphatic or absolute state. Note the following examples of *qwšt*, the noun in question: emphatic state as nomen rectum: [*n*]*šbt qwšt$^{\supset}$*, "the plant of truth" (4QEn^{c} 1 v 4); absolute state as nomen rectum in the same phrase: *n*[*šbt*] *qšt*, "the pl[ant of] truth" (4QEn^{g} 1 iv 12-13); emphatic state as subject of a nominal clause: *w^{c}d ^{c}ly qšt$^{\supset}$ kb*[*r hwh mtqym*], "and until my time truth [was] stil[l enduring]" (4QEn^{g} 1 iii 24); absolute state as subject of the nominal sentence: *wkl* [*šl*]*m wqšwt nhyr*[*yn*], "and all [pea]ce and truth give light" (4Q^{c}-Amram^{e} 12).

[202]*Grammatik des biblisch-aramäischen* (Leipzig: Vogel, 1884), #79(f).

[203]Although the use of ἄρτος/ἄρτοι to mean "food" is most probably a lexical Semitism, grammatically speaking, the use of the article with it in place of a possessive pronoun ("*their* food") is normal in Greek, and is found in both the Matthean and Lucan parallels.

[204]*Einleitung*, p. 11.

[205]#259.

[206]*Aramaic Approach*, pp. 94-95.

[207]Mayser, *Grammatik*, 2:2:39; cf. Blass-Debrunner-Funk, #259.1; Radermacher, *Grammatik*, p. 116.

[208]Smyth, *Greek Grammar*, #1183; cf. Blass-Debrunner-Funk, #248.1; Mayser, *Grammatik*, 2:2:66.

[209]Blass-Debrunner-Funk, #259.1.

[210]In their parallels both Matthew and Luke use the phrases exactly as Mark does, i.e., without the article.

[211]In only one Synoptic parallel to these four Marcan texts is the phrase in question taken over. In Mt 21:42 (= Mk 12:11 = Ps 117:23) the phrase appears, as in Mark, without the article.

[212]Cf. H. B. Swete, *The Gospel According to St. Mark* (London: Macmillan, 1898), p. 46; A. H. McNeile, *The Gospel According to St. Matthew* (London: Macmillan, 1915), p. 123; V. Taylor, *St. Mark*, p. 213.

[213]*Einleitung*, p. 22.

[214]*Syntax*, p. 38.

[215]Blass-Debrunner-Funk, #278; cf. Smyth, *Greek Grammar*, #1214; Doudna, *The Greek of the Gospel of Mark*, p. 36.

[216]For example, according to R. A. Martin (*Syntactical Evidence*, p. 26), dependent genitive pronouns occur only once per 38 lines of text in the first two books of Polybius, once per 46 lines in books 3 and 4 of Epictetus, and once per 40 lines in selections from Plutarch. By contrast a dependent genitive pronoun occurs every 2 to 5 lines in the various books of the OG (roughly equivalent to Marcan usage). Unemphatic pronouns occur very infrequently also in Rydbeck's *Zwischenprosa*. For example, one can read whole pages of Galen's citations of ancient pharmacologists (*Zwischenprosa* writers according to Rydbeck [*Fachprosa*, p. 22]) without coming across a single example.

[217]The possessive genitives μου, σου, and αὐτοῦ occur in the papyri "je vulgärer der Stil ist, desto stärker in den Vordergrund" (Mayser, *Grammatik*, 2:1:63).

[218]*Ibid.*, 2:1:63.

[219]Blass-Debrunner-Funk, #278.

[220]Vergote, "Grec biblique," col. 1356.

[221]See M. Johannessohn, *Der Gebrauch der Präpositionen in der Septuaginta* (Mitteilung des Septuaginta-Unternehmens 3/3; Berlin: Weidmann, 1926), pp. 369-70.

[222]#278.

[223]*Einleitung*, p. 19; cf. Zerwick, *Graecitas*, #205.

[224]Manuscripts ℵ B D read αὐτοῦ (= "of Herod") here, but A C are probably correct even though they have the more difficult reading αὐτῆς τῆς, because the daughter was Herodias' and not Herod's. Matthew omits αὐτός (αὐτῆς) in his parallels to Mk 6:17, 22; 12:36, 37. Luke omits αὐτός in his parallels to Mk 6:17 and 12:37, retains it in his parallel to 12:36, and has no verse parallel to Mk 6:22.

[225]*Aramaic Approach*, p. 96. See Turner, *Syntax*, p. 41, for the same opinion. Taylor (*St. Mark*, p. 311) would also translate Mk 6:17 "For he, Herod. . . ."

[226]Smyth, *Greek Grammar*, #1204 and Mayser, *Grammatik*, 2:2:75.

[227]Smyth, *Greek Grammar*, #1207 and Mayser, *Grammatik*, 2:2:76.

[228]Smyth, *Greek Grammar*, #1204 and Mayser, *Grammatik*, 2:2:77.

[229]Moulton-Milligan, p. 94.

[230]Mayser, *Grammatik*, 2:2:76; cf. Moulton, *Prolegomena*, p. 91; Ljungvik, *Beiträge*, pp. 8-9; Robertson, *Grammar*, p. 709; H. Riesenfeld, "Nachträge. 1. Lagercrantz' Beiträge zum N.T.," *ConNT* 3, p. 24.

[231]Mayser, *Grammatik*, 2:2:76.

[232]Colwell (*The Greek of the Fourth Gospel*, p. 49) claims that *POxy*. 480.2 (cited above) is an example of a pronoun "anticipating a genitive" in Hellenistic Greek, but this is also an example of the use of αὐτός widely recognized in Hellenistic Greek. Compare *PRein*. 26.11 (also cited above).

[233]See Brown-Driver-Briggs, p. 215 (under *hû* 1.e), Koehler-Baumgartner 1:227 (under *hû* 7), Joüon, *Grammaire*, #146(e).

[234]Joüon, *Grammaire*, #146(e).

[235]*Aramaic Approach*, p. 96. Contrary to Black's statement in the following sentence, Burney (*Aramaic Origins*, pp. 85-86) does not give any Aramaic examples of an independent pronoun used proleptically before a noun for the sake of emphasis.

[236]See, for example, T. Nöldeke, *Compendious Syriac Grammar* (2nd rev. ed.; London: Williams & Norgate, 1904), #227.

[237]In Middle Aramaic, as in biblical Aramaic, a first person pronoun may precede a proper name in order to add emphasis (Fitzmyer, *Genesis Apocryphon*, p. 217; cf. Bauer-Leander #93[i]), e.g., *ᵓnh lmk ᵓtbhlt*, "I, Lamech, became frightened" (1QapGn 2:3); *ᵓǎnāᵓ dāryāweš šamet tĕᶜēm*, "I, Darius, make a decree" (Ezra 6:12). In these texts, however, the pronoun is not used prepositively, but we have proper names in apposition to a pronoun.

[238]Bauer-Leander #72(e). Segert (*Altaramäische Grammatik*, p. 325) considers that *hû* in this verse is an anaphoric pronoun in a nominal clause: "This (is) the image: its head. . . ." This, too, is incorrect.

[239]Cf. F. Rosenthal, *Grammar of Biblical Aramaic* (Porta linguarum orientalium, Neue Serie 5; Wiesbaden: O. Harrassowitz, 1968), #32. In similar fashion to this usage of the independent form of the personal pronoun as a demonstrative, the suffixal form of the personal pronoun may function as a demonstrative (prepositively), e.g., *bah ša^cătā*, "at this (very) moment" (Dan 3:6, 15; 4:30; 5:5; cf. Rosenthal, *ibid.*, #89).

[240]Bauer-Leander, #90(j).

[241]Blass-Debrunner-Funk (#277.3) give this translation for Mk 6:17.

[242]This is different from the perfectly normal Greek construction in which a second clause, logically parallel to a relative clause, is linked to the latter by means of a personal pronoun. See Blass-Debrunner-Funk, #297 and Howard, "Semitisms," p. 435.

[243]"This usage [a relative pronoun further qualified by a personal pronoun] parallels that of Coptic, in which a specification of a relative by a pronominal suffix is required by the indeclinability of the relative *et/ete*." (Gignac, "The Language of the Non-Literary Papyri," p. 151). See also Vergote, "Grec biblique," col. 1356.

[244]Segal, *Mishnaic Grammar*, p. 204.

[245]Thackeray, *Grammar*, p. 46. For further examples of this usage in the OG see Exod 29:33; 4 Kgdms 17:29; Jer 48:3 (= MT 42:3).

[246]In this verse οὗ is a relative adverb ("where"), not the genitive of the relative pronoun. It is resumed by the pleonastic phrase ἐν αὐτῷ, which has been literally translated from the Hebrew.

[247]Black (*Aramaic Approach*, p. 102) claims that Mk 8:36 is an example of this usage. Blass-Debrunner-Funk (#283.4) and Turner (*Syntax*, p. 43) include Mk 10:45, and Bauer-Arndt-Gingrich (p. 902, under ψυχή 1.f) include Mk 14:34.

[248]Matthew takes over all three Marcan verses in literal fashion. Luke changes τὴν ψυχὴν αὐτοῦ (Mk 8:36) to the reflexive pronoun ἑαυτόν, "himself" in Lk 9:25. He omits Mk 10:45 and 14:34.

[249]Liddell-Scott-Jones, pp. 2026-27; cf. E. Jacob, "Ψυχή," *TDNT* 9:608-17.

[250]The basic meaning of Hebrew *nepeš*, like Akkadian *napištu*, is "throat," where the breath makes a sound. This meaning turns up in the Old Testament: "Save me, O God, for

the waters have come up to my neck (nepeš)" (Ps 69:2). See
L. Dürr, "Hebr. nepeš = akk. napištu = Gurgel, Kehle," ZAW 43
(1925), pp. 262-69.

[251]Koehler-Baumgartner 2:626-27 and Gesenius-Kautzsch-
Cowley, #139(f). Cf. Jacob, "Ψυχή," pp. 617-31.

[252]Cf. Gesenius-Kautzsch-Cowley, #135(a), (i), and (k).

[253]Ibid., #139(f), n. 5.

[254]The phrase ᶜl npšh, "for himself" (with the masculine
third person singular suffix "taken from Aramaic orthography"
[J. T. Milik, DJD 2, p. 158]) is common in these contracts (see
also Mur 24 C 19; D 20; 36 1-2 6; 42:10; ᶜl npšh, "for herself"
in Mur 29 verso 3, cited above). The phrase is formulaic and
always follows the name of a witness at the end of a contract
or letter: "X, for him/herself."

[255]Of 755 instances of the word nepeš in the Old Testament,
the OG translates with ψυχή over 600 times (Koehler-Baumgartner
2:626), e.g., καὶ ζήσεται ἡ ψυχή μου ἕνεκεν σοῦ, "and my soul
shall live because of you" (Gen 12:13, for Hebrew: wĕḥāyĕtâ
napšî biglālēk). Cf. N. Bratsiotis, "Nepeš--psychē, ein
Beitrag zur Erforschung der Sprache und der Theologie der
Septuaginta," Volume du congrès (VTSup 15; Leiden: Brill,
1966), p. 58.

[256]For example: ὥστε τρέχων περὶ τῆς ψυχῆς πρό τε τοῦ
θανάτου πεισόμενος πολλά τε καὶ λυγρά, "inasmuch as he was
running a race for his life and about to suffer much misery
before death" (Herodotus 9.37); in the following text the commander of the Assyrian army says to his soldiers just before
they are to go into battle: νῦν γὰρ ὑπὲρ ψυχῶν τῶν ὑμετέρων
ἀγών, "For now the struggle (concerns) your lives" (Xenophon,
Cyr. 3.3.44).

[257]"Even there [Lk 9:25] it would be truer to say that
ἑαυτόν has been levelled up to τὴν ψυχὴν αὐτοῦ, than that ψυχή
has been emptied of its meaning" (Moulton, Prolegomena, p. 87).

[258]The idea of "giving one's life" occurs in Isa 53:12
(also Sir 29:15 and 1 Macc 2:50 in a text which even lacks a
canonical Hebrew Vorlage), of "one's life as a ransom" in
Isa 53:10, and justifying and bearing the sin of "many (=all)"
in Isa 53:11-12.

[259]Liddell-Scott-Jones, p. 2027.

[260]For a similar conclusion on the meanings of the word
ψυχή, see Bratsiotis, "Nepeš--psychē," pp. 87-89.

[261]Mayser, Grammatik, 2:2:79 and 82.

[262]See the "index verborum" in H. Schenkl, Epicteti dissertationes ab Arriani digestae (Bibliotheca scriptorum graecorum
et romanorum Teubneriana; Stuttgart: Teubner, 1965), pp. 563-64.

[263]N. Turner, "The Unique Character of Biblical Greek,"
VT 5 (1955), p. 209. By contrast, Hebrews, James, and 2 Peter
use ἐκεῖνος with equal frequency as a pronoun and as an adjective. The Pauline corpus shows a proportion of 1 to 0.5.

[264]Gesenius-Kautzsch-Cowley, #136(a).

[265]Cf. Bauer-Leander, #73(f).

[266]Cf. Rosenthal, *Grammar of Biblical Aramaic*, #89.

[267]See Turner, "Unique Character," p. 209 for the exact
statistics.

[268]"Merito notatum est, in LXX. . .distinctionem illam
inter οὗτος et ἐκεῖνος stricte grammaticaliter observari, idque
quamvis haec distinctio in textu hebraico non habeat quod ei
correspondeat" (Zerwick, *Graecitas*, #214).

[269]It is translated by ἐκεῖνος only 9 times: Gen 17:23,
26; Exod 12:51; Deut 2:7; 3:12; Jos 6:26(25); Jer 8:3; 45(38):4;
Ezek 40:1.

[270]·Εκεῖνος translates independent *hû²* (plural *hemmâ*) only
six times: Gen 6:4; Exod 12:42; 19:3; Isa 57:6; Ezek 40:46;
Mic 7:12.

[271]Cf. Doudna, *Greek*, pp. 126-27.

[272]*The Eucharistic Words of Jesus*, pp. 183-84 and p. 184,
n. 3.

[273]Mayser, *Grammatik*, 2:2:79.

[274]*Ibid.*, 2:2:79.

[275]Dalman, *Grammatik des JPA*, p. 113; cf. Brockelmann,
Grundriss 2:79. Dalman (*Jesus-Jeshua*, pp. 62-63) claims that
such an Aramaic pleonastic demonstrative lies behind τούτων
in Mt 5:19: μίαν τῶν ἐντολῶν τούτων τῶν ἐλαχίστων, "one of
these least commandments."

[276]In addition to several Late Aramaic examples of the
pleonastic demonstrative, Jeremias (*Eucharistic Words*, p. 184,
n. 2) cites a single biblical Hebrew text in which he claims that
a demonstrative is used pleonastically: *wĕ⁽al mî nāṭaštā mĕ⁽aṭ
hassō²n hāhēnnâ bammidbār*, "And with whom have you left those
few sheep in the wilderness?" (1 Sam 17:28). The demonstrative
hāhēnnâ in the phrase "those sheep," however, clearly refers
to the sheep mentioned in 17:20 and is not pleonastic.

[277]As we have pointed out in the conclusion to section (i),
ἐκεῖνος as in Mk 2:20; 13:17, 19, 24; 14:25 may have been used
in imitation of an Old Testament eschatological phrase.

[278]*Aramaic Approach*, p. 105. The texts which Black cites
are Mk 5:22; 6:15; 8:28; 9:17; 12:28; 13:1; 14:10, 20, 43, 66.

[279]*Graecitas*, #155.

[280]*Syntax*, p. 196.

[281]#247.2

[282]The use of εἷς with τις as in Mk 14:47: εἷς δέ τις τῶν
παρεστηκότων, "one of (those) standing by," is found in classical Greek. See Schwyzer, *Griechische Grammatik*, 2:215.*i*;
Liddell-Scott-Jones, p. 492 (under εἷς 4); Blass-Debrunner-
Funk, #247.2; Turner, *Syntax*, p. 196. Luke copies εἷς τις (in
Lk 22:50), but Matthew drops τις (Mt 26:51) in favor of the more
usual New Testament construction of εἷς alone plus a genitive.

[283]Smyth, *Greek Grammar*, #1267.

[284]For example, Jannaris, *Historical Greek Grammar*, #622;
Moulton, *Prolegomena*, p. 97; Mayser, *Grammatik*, 2:2:86, n. 1;
Liddell-Scott-Jones, p. 492 (under εἷς 4).

[285]For the same opinion, see M. Johannessohn, "Das
biblische καὶ ἰδού in der Erzählung samt seiner hebräischen
Vorlage," *Zeitschrift für vergleichende Sprachforschung indogermanischer Sprachen* 67 (1940), p. 69, and Blass-Debrunner-
Funk, #247.2. The following classical texts have been cited
by various authors as examples in which εἷς = τις, the indefinite pronoun: παρελθὼν δὲ Σθενελάδας τελευταῖος εἷς τῶν ἐφόρων
τότε ὤν, "Finally Sthenelaides, who was one of the ephors then,
came forward" (Thucydides 1.85.3); πρέπεις δὲ Κάδμου θυγατέρων
μορφὴν μία, "You are like one of the daughters of Cadmus in
form" (Euripides, *Ba.* 917); Isaeus, *Pyrrhi hered.* 37; Thucydides
4.40.2; 50.1; Aeschines 1.180; 3.89; Alexis 220.5; Herodotus
4.3. In the following texts, cited by various authors as
examples where adjectival εἷς = τις the numerical value is still
retained, and thus they are not true examples of εἷς as the
indefinite article: μία καὶ ἕνα λόγον ἔχουσα ἀρχαῖον, "(What
conduct is dear to God?) inferring one (kind of conduct) inferring one
ancient phrase" (Plato, *Lg.* 4.716C); Aeschines 1.165, 182;
Xenophon, *Mem.* 3.3.12; Plato, *Lg.* 9.8555E; Thucydides 4.57.2;
6.34.2; Aristophanes, *Av.* 1292; Demosthenes 21.87; Aristotle,
Pol. [7.3.6 1325b].

[286]Robertson, *Grammar*, p. 292.

[287]Various texts have been cited to prove the opposite,
but εἷς has numerical force ("one") in each case: τῶν ἐφόρων
ἕνα, "one of the ephors" (Plutarch, *Cleom.* 7.2; "ephors" are
mentioned just a few lines before in this text, and so ἕνα
clearly retains its numerical force: "*one* of the ephors [about
which we have just been speaking]"); Herodian 7.5.4; Dio
Chrysostom 21.15; Josephus, *AJ.* 9.106; Plutarch, *Arat.* 5.3;
Eunapius, *VS* (ed. Boissonade), p. 484, l. 28; Polybius 1.78.1.

[288]W. C. Till, *Koptische Grammatik* (Leipzig: Harrassowitz,
1955), #225; cf. L. Stern, *Koptische Grammatik* (Leipzig: Weigel,
1880), #264.

[289]Vergote, "Grec biblique," col. 1356, and Gignac, *An Introductory New Testament Greek Course* (Chicago: Loyola University, 1973), p. 170.

[290]Robertson, *Grammar*, p. 674.

[291]Abel, *Grammaire*, #36.c; cf. Jannaris, *Historical Greek Grammar*, #623; Moulton, *Prolegomena*, p. 97; Mayser, *Grammatik*, 2:2:85.

[292]However, in every other instance in Epictetus εἷς has a numerical force, whether used as a substantive or as an adjective.

[293]*Wyqm ḥd [dmy]*, "And someone will avenge [my blood]" (Sefire 3:22). An example from Late Aramaic: *whwh mṣtᶜr ᶜl ḥd dhwh gby bᶜyynyh*, "and he was troubled about someone who was exalted in his (own) eyes" (*y. Ned.* x 10, folio 42 recto, col. b, line 16; this text is cited incompletely by Black, *Aramaic Approach*, p. 105).

[294]When Matthew takes over the phrases in question (only from Mk 8:28 and 14:43) he also uses εἷς. Luke changes εἷς to τις in his parallels to Mk 6:15 and 8:28, thus changing the meaning to "any of the prophets." He paraphrases in his parallel to Mk 14:10, but takes over εἷς from Mk 14:43: "one of the Twelve."

[295]In their parallels to these verses Matthew abbreviates Mk 5:22 (ἔρχεται εἷς τῶν ἀρχισυναγώγων) to εἷς προσελθών, "someone coming up"; Luke follows another tradition: ἦλθεν ἀνὴρ ᾧ ὄνομα Ἰάϊρος, "a man by the name of Jairus came." Matthew changes Mk 13:1 to οἱ μαθηταί, while Luke omits the verse. At Mk 14:66 Matthew changes to μία παιδίσκη and Luke to παιδίσκη τις. Neither evangelist takes over Mk 12:28.

[296]In their parallels to Mk 9:17, Matthew changes εἷς ἐκ τοῦ ὄχλου to ἄνθρωπος, "a man," and Luke changes to ἀνήρ, "a man." At Mk 10:17 Matthew also has εἷς (εἷς προσελθών) while Luke changes to τις.

[297]So Taylor, *St. Mark*, p. 470; Lagrange, *Evangile selon Saint Marc*, p. 302; Swete, *St. Mark*, p. 263.

[298]So Winer-Schmiedel, #26.5.b and Swete, *St. Mark*, p. 293. In their parallels to Mk 11:29 Matthew retains, while Luke drops, ἕνα. Only Luke takes over Mk 12:42, and drops μία.

[299]*Aramaic Approach*, p. 106.

[300]Black includes another text: ἀπαντήσει ὑμῖν ἄνθρωπος κεράμιον ὕδατος βαστάζων, "A man carrying a jar of water will meet you" (Mk 14:13). According to his explanation of the text the person referred to would merely be "someone carrying a jar of water." In the usual explanation of the text, however, the fact that this was "a *man* carrying a jar of water" would be an unusual phenomenon which would be easily recognizable by the disciples. For, whereas women carried jars of water, a man

would have carried a leather bottle (Lagrange, *Saint Marc*, p. 373; cf. Taylor, *St. Mark*, p. 537). Even though the more usual word for "an adult male" was ἀνήρ, the word ἄνθρωπος was used to indicate a man, a male, even in classical Greek, e.g., ὁ ἄνθρωπος. . .ὁ δοὺς τὸ φάρμακον. . .ἐπεσκόπει τοὺς πόδας καὶ τὰ σκέλη, "The man. . .who had administered the poison. . . examined (his) feet and legs" (Plato, *Phd.* 117E; cf. Bauer-Arndt-Gingrich, p. 67, under ἄνθρωπος 2.b.*a*).

[301]Blass-Debrunner-Funk, #242.2; cf. Kühner-Gerth, 2:1:272; Liddell-Scott-Jones, p. 141 (under ἄνθρωπος 4); Turner, *Syntax*, p. 195.

[302]Smyth, *Greek Grammar*, #986; cf. Schwyzer, *Griechische Grammatik*, 2:613. New Testament examples of this usage include: ἄνδρες ἀδελφοί, "brothers" (Acts 1:16); ἄνδρες Ἰουδαῖοι, "Men of Judea (literally "men, Jews")" (Acts 2:14); ἄνδρες Ἀθηναῖοι, "Athenians" (Acts 17:22).

[303]Smyth, *Greek Grammar*, #986.c.

[304]Only one exception is to be noted, and it is found in a very illiterate papyrus letter: οὐκ οἶδες ὅτι θέλω πηρὸς γενέσται εἰ γνοῦναι (= γενέσθαι ἢ γνῶναι) ὅπως ἀνθρώπῳ ἔτι ὀφείλω ὀβολόν, "Do you not know that I would rather be maimed than know that I s[till] owe someone (literally "a man") an obol?" (*BGU* 846.15-16). Bauer-Arndt-Gingrich cite Pausanius 5.7.3, but ἄνθρωπος does not occur in that text. In 5.7.2: καὶ ἐνταῦθα ἐξ ἀνθρώπου γενέσθαι πηγήν, "(They say that. . . Arethusa, unwilling to marry, crossed to Ortygea) and there changed from a human being to a spring," ἀνθρώπου clearly means "human being."

[305]Cf. Bauer-Leander, #87(d). ᵓyš is also used in Official Aramaic as an indefinite pronoun in Cowley, *AP* 20:10, 12, 13, 14; 42:6; Kraeling, *BMAP* 8:4, 5, 6. ᵓyš ḥd means "a certain man, someone" in the Behistun Inscription 3.38 (Cowley, *AP*, p. 253). ᵓyš plus a negative means "no one" in Cowley, *AP* 30:14; Aḥiqar 116 (*bis*).

[306]Fitzmyer (*Genesis Apocryphon*, p. 143), following Ginsberg (*Theological Studies* 28 [1967], p. 577), restores the end of this line as ynpq[wnny. . .], "they escort me out." Such a restoration would be in harmony with the text of Gen 12:20: wayĕṣaw ᶜālāy(w) parᶜōh ᵓănāšîm wayĕšallĕḥû ᵓōtô , "and Pharaoh commanded (his) men concerning him that (literally "and") they sent him away." The difficulty with such a restoration is that ᵓnwš is a singular form ("a man"), as in 1QapGn 19:15; 21:13. The restored form should be ynpq[ny].

[307]Thackeray, *Grammar*, p. 45, e.g., ἀποστέλλω πρὸς σὲ ἄνδρα ἐκ γῆς Βενιαμιν, "I shall send you a man from Benjamin" (1 Kgdms 9:16). See also Black, *Aramaic Approach*, p. 106, n. 2.

[308]For a table showing the Synoptic parallels to the texts in question, see page 135.

[309]*Style*, p. 15; cf. *Syntax*, p. 208.

[310]*Aramaic Approach*, p. 107.

[311]It is also possible that ἀπ' ἀγορᾶς in this text is a *constructio praegnans* (cf. Winer-Moulton, pp. 776-77; Blass-Debrunner-Funk, #209.4; Bauer-Arndt-Gingrich, p. 86, under ἀπό 5). In this case Mk 7:4 could be translated: "(coming) from the market, they do not eat unless they wash themselves," or even "And unless they wash themselves from (contact with) the marketplace, they do not eat."

[312]Smyth, *Greek Grammar*, #1341; Schwyzer, *Griechische Grammatik*, 2:102; Robertson, *Grammar*, p. 515; Kühner-Gerth, 2:1:345.

[313]Schwyzer, *Griechische Grammatik*, 2:102; Robertson, *Grammar*, p. 515; Kühner-Gerth, 2:1:345.

[314]Moulton, *Prolegomena*, p. 72; Blass-Debrunner-Funk, #164; Mayser, *Grammatik*, 2:2:348.

[315]*Ibid.*, 2:2:351.

[316]Mayser (*ibid.*, 2:2:351) gives only two examples of the phrase in question used as the subject of the sentence, and these are from the same document!

[317]M. Johannessohn, *Der Gebrauch der Kasus und der Präpositionen in der Septuaginta* (Diss. Berlin, 1910), p. 18; cf. Gesenius-Kautzsch-Cowley, #119(w), n. 2.

[318]Matthew does not take over Mk 5:35; 6:43; 7:4, but in his parallel to Mk 12:2 he changes ἀπὸ τῶν καρπῶν, "some of the fruits" to a simple accusative: τοὺς καρπούς, "the fruits." Luke omits Mk 6:43 and 7:4. In his parallel to Mk 5:35 he adds the indefinite pronoun τις to the Marcan phrase: τις ἀπὸ τοῦ ἀρχισυναγώγου, "someone from the leader of the synagogue." He retains the basic construction of Mk 12:2 in Lk 20:10: ἵνα ἀπὸ τοῦ καρποῦ τοῦ ἀμπελῶνος δώσουσιν αὐτῷ, "in order that they give him (some) of the fruit of the vineyard."

[319]See C. H. Turner, "Marcan Usage: Notes, Critical and Exegetical, on the Second Gospel," *JTS* 25 (1924), pp. 378 and 380; Blass-Debrunner-Funk, #130.2; N. Turner, *Syntax*, p. 292; Taylor, *St. Mark*, p. 293.

[320]The verse is taken over by Matthew in literal fashion (Mt 24:22) and omitted entirely by Luke.

[321]Cf. J. H. Moulton, "Grammatical Notes from the Papyri," *Classical Review* 15 (1901), p. 442 and *Prolegomena*, p. 246.

[322]For a list of about twenty examples of this use of πᾶς with negative prepositions in the papyri, see Ljungvik, *Beiträge*, pp. 19-20.

[323]*Beiträge*, pp. 20-21. As Ljungvik (*ibid.*, p. 18) has pointed out, the Hellenistic literary text adduced by Rader-macher (*Grammatik*, pp. 219-20) is not truly an example of the

usage in question: οὐκ ἀπὸ τοῦ βελτίστου πάντα περὶ αὐτῶν γράφων ἀλλ' εἰ βούλει, καὶ ἀπὸ φιλοτιμίας, "writing all things about them not from the best (motive), but, if you wish, even from love of honor" (Dionysius Halicarnassus, *Pomp.* 756). It is clear that in this text the negative οὐκ goes only with ἀπὸ τοῦ βελτίστου (in contrast [ἀλλ'] with ἀπὸ φιλοτιμίας), whereas πάντα retains its normal meaning "all."

[324]Αὐτή<ν> is so read by the editors of the Oxyrhynchus papyri, B. P. Grenfell and A. S. Hunt. Αὐτῇ, the dative form, would also be correct in Greek.

[325]It is very unlikely that the few instances of οὐ . . . πᾶς = οὐδεὶς in the papyri are due to Egyptian interference, since, unlike Semitic, Coptic has words for "no one/nothing." In the Sahidic dialect *laaw* ("anyone/anything") with a negative particle means "no one/nothing." Thus the Marcan text in question is translated correctly: *nemn̄ laaw n̄sarx naoujai pe*, "not anyone of flesh will be saved/safe" (Mk 13:20). In the Bohairic dialect the word *hli* ("anyone/anything") used with a negative particle means "no one/nothing," e.g., *mpehli eimi*, "no one knows" (Jn 13:28; Greek: οὐδεὶς ἔγνω). However, the Bohairic text of Mk 13:20 does not use *hli* with a negative, but has *nawnanohem an pe n̄jesarx niben*, "All flesh will be saved." But this is the result of literal translation of the Greek text.

[326]"Πολλοί," *TDNT* 6:543-45. Jeremias has established that Hebrew *rabbîm* in chapter 53 of Isaiah (to which both Mk 10:45 and 14:24 refer) "is interpreted inclusively not only by later Judaism but also by Paul and John. It is taken to refer to the whole community, comprised of many members, which has fallen under the judgment of God." He concludes that "there is no support for the idea that Jesus [or, we may add, the author of Mark] interpreted Is. any differently" (*ibid.*, 6:545). For πολλοί = πάντες see also Jeremias, *Eucharistic Words of Jesus*, pp. 181-82; P. Joüon, *L'Evangile de Notre-Seigneur Jésus-Christ. Traduction et Commentaire* (VS 5; Paris: Beauchesne, 1930), p. 125, and O. Cullmann, "Nt.liche Wortforschung. *HYPER (ANTI) POLLON*," *TZ* 4 (1948), pp. 471-73.

[327]Mk 10:45 is taken over word for word by Matthew and omitted entirely by Luke. Matthew follows Mark at 14:24 with περὶ πολλῶν for the Marcan ὑπὲρ πολλῶν, whereas Luke has ὑπὲρ ὑμῶν.

[328]See the two examples cited above and the following texts of Epictetus: 1.29.30; 2.13.4; 3.23.7; 4.8.32.

[329]Jeremias, "Πολλοί," 6.537. According to Joüon (*L'Evangile*, p. 125), the idea of totality ("all") comes about because the sum of *all* consists of *many* individuals.

[330]Jeremias, "Πολλοί," 6:538. See 1QS 6:1, 7, 8, 9, 11 (*bis*), 12 (*bis*), etc.

[331]Jeremias claims that both Mk 10:45 and 14:24 are based on the Hebrew, and not the Greek, text of Isa 53:10-12.

[332]In a text concerning the saving work of Jesus Christ
(Rom 5:12-21), Paul also uses (οἱ) πολλοί in the inclusive sense
"all" in vss. 15 and 19. This is proved by the fact that in
verses surrounding these texts (namely in vss. 12 and 18 [bis]),
πάντες, "all," is used in similar statements. The explanation
for the use of πολλοί = πάντες in vss. 15 and 19 is that there
Paul is alluding to Isa 53:12e and 11c, in which (hā)rabbîm is
used inclusively in Hebrew (and πολλοί in the OG). Hence this
Pauline usage is due to the interference of Hebrew, whether
directly from the Hebrew Old Testament or indirectly from the
OG. Cf. Jeremias, "Πολλοί," pp. 542-43. See also C. K. Barrett,
A Commentary on the Epistle to the Romans (New York: Harper,
1957), p. 114 and E. Brandenburger, *Adam und Christus.
Exegetisch-religionsgeschichtliche Untersuchung zu Rom 5, 12-21*
(Neukirchen: Neukirchener Verlag, 1962), pp. 221 and 242.

[333]*Aramaic Approach*, p. 121; cf. Turner, *Syntax*, p. 22.

[334]In his parallels to Mk 2:7, 24, and 8:12, Matthew drops
interrogative τί and makes the sentences declarative. At Mk
2:8 and 15:34 he changes τί and εἰς τί to another interrogative
particle, ἱνατί, "Why?" He omits Mk 4:40 entirely, and retains
τί at Mk 10:18. Luke changes τί to τίς in his parallel to Mk
2:7--τίς ἐστιν οὗτος, "Who is this man?" At Mk 2:8 he makes
τί function as a pronoun by dropping the accusative ταῦτα:
τί διαλογίζεσθε, "What are you considering?" He takes over τί
in the Marcan sense of "why?" from Mk 2:24 and 10:18, whereas
by omitting τί in Mk 8:12 he makes the sentence declarative.
Luke has no parallels to either Mk 4:40 or 15:34.

[335]*Aramaic Approach*, pp. 122-23.

[336]Goodwin-Gulick, #1059; cf. Schwyzer, *Griechische
Grammatik*, 2:77; Blass-Debrunner-Funk, #299.4.

[337]Gesenius-Kautzsch-Cowley, #148.

[338]This is Black's translation (following Wensinck). He
also cites *y. Kil.* ix 4, folio 32b, lines 7 and 54, but one
looks in vain to find interrogative *mah* in these texts (*Aramaic
Approach*, pp. 121-22).

[339]Abel, *Grammaire*, #35(1); cf. Liddell-Scott-Jones, p.
1798 (under τίς B.8.g).

[340]The word "Sabbath" (from Hebrew šabbāt, the "Sabbath"·
of the Old Testament) appears in the Greek of the OG, New
Testament, and of the Jewish writers Josephus and Philo in two
forms: τὸ σάββατον, a neuter singular noun (from Hebrew
šabbāt with the neuter ending of the Greek o-declension: -ον),
and a neuter plural form: τὰ σάββατα. There are several explanations for the latter form: (a) it is a true plural of
the alternate form τὸ σάββατον (a *pluralis abundantiae* or
majestatis; cf. M. Black, "*EPHPHATHA* (Mk 7.34), [*TA*] *PASCHA*
(Mt 26.18W), [*TA*] *SABBATA* (passim), [*TA*] *DIDRACHMA* (Mt 17.24
bis)," *Mélanges bibliques en hommage au R. P. Béda Rigaux*
[ed. by A. Descamps and A. de Halleux; Gembloux: Duculot, 1970],
p. 61). (b) σάββατα was not a plural in origin, but rather is

Hebrew "šabbāt plus a to make it pronounceable in Greek" (Blass-
Debrunner-Funk, #141.3; cf. E. Schwyzer, *Griechische Grammatik*,
1:409). (c) A third explanation is that σάββατα is an Aramaizing
form in Greek (from the Aramaic word for "Sabbath" in the emphatic
state: šabbĕtāʾ), according to Black, "*EPHPHATHA*," p. 61; cf.
A. Pelletier, "*Sabbata*: Transcription grecque de l'araméen,"
VT 22 (1972), pp. 436-47, and F. Bussby, "A Note on *Sabbata* and
Sabbaton in the Synoptics," *BJRL* 30 (1946), pp. 157-58. Whatever
the provenience of the plural form σάββατα may have been, in
Mk 16:2 and similar New Testament phrases the words σάββατα and
σάββατον are equivalent to "week," as in Late Aramaic and Mishnaic Hebrew (see G. Dalman, *Aramäisch-Neuhebräisches Handwörter-
buch*, p. 414).

[341]Cf. Blass-Debrunner-Funk, #247.1; Doudna, *Greek of the
Gospel of Mark*, pp. 95-96; Turner, *Syntax*, p. 187; Zerwick,
Graecitas, #154.

[342]Moulton-Milligan (p. 187, under εἷς; cf. Moulton,
Prolegomena, pp. 95-96) claim that εἷς is used as an ordinal in
a non-literary papyrus: τῇ μίᾳ καὶ εἰκαίδι (= εἰκάδι) τοῦ
Ἐπιφ, "on the twenty-first (literally "on the one and twentieth
day of the month") of Epiph" (*BGU* 623.4). The noun εἰκάς (the
name of the number "twenty") means "the twentieth day of the
month" and is used in combination with the ordinal numbers (with
καί) in naming the twenty-second to the twenty-ninth days of
the month in the papyri (Mayser, *Grammatik*, 1:2:78). The fact
that for the twenty-first day the cardinal μία is used with
καὶ εἰκάς reflects a similar phenomenon in the Greek non-literary
papyri. In the papyri the ordinals "twenty-second" to "twenty-
ninth" are expressed by the ordinals δεύτερος, τρίτος, etc. with
καὶ εἰκοστός, the ordinal "twentieth," whereas the ordinal
"twenty-first" is expressed by the cardinal εἷς with καὶ εἰκοστός
(Mayser, *Grammatik*, 1:2:78), e.g., ἓν καὶ εἰκοστόν, "twenty-
first" (*UPZ* 41.16); δευτέρου καὶ εἰκοστοῦ, "of the twenty-
second" (*PTebt*. 109.7). As Blass-Debrunner-Funk (#247.1) point
out, the latter usage (εἷς καὶ εἰκοστός = "twenty-first")
"merely betrays an incomplete development of ordinals (from the
cardinal εἷς καὶ εἴκοσι taken as one word) like Lat. *unus et
vicesimus*, German *der ein-und-zwanzigste*, etc." A. Debrunner
(review of L. Radermacher, *Neutestamentliche Grammatik* in *GGA*
4 [1926], p. 142) suggests that εἷς καὶ εἰκάς is treated exactly
like εἷς καὶ εἰκοστός because "εἰκάς ist völlig gleichwertig mit
εἰκοστή. . .sowie attisch und hellenistisch τετράς [the name of
the number "four" which, like εἰκάς, is used for the name of
that day: "the fourth day of the month"] mit τετάρτη [the
ordinal "fourth"]." At any rate, this Hellenistic use of εἷς
with καὶ εἰκοστός and καὶ εἰκάς where classical Greek would have
used πρῶτος is limited to these two expressions and sheds little
light on the problem of the use of the cardinal μία in Mk 16:2.

[343]Bauer-Arndt-Gingrich (p. 231 under εἷς 4) cite Callimachus *frag*. 482 (ed. Schneider; ed. Pfeiffer *frag*. 550): ὃ πρὸ
μιῆς ὥρης θηρίον οὐ λέγεται, "the beast which is not mentioned
before the first hour." This text is probably corrupt because
of metathesis of M and I in the uncial Mss. (ΠΡΟΜΙΗΣΩΡΗΣ for
ΠΡΟΙΜΗΣΩΡΗΣ). Nauck (*Hermes* 24 [1889], p. 454) emends πρὸ μιῆς
ὥρης to προίμης ὥρης, "at an early hour." Liddell-Scott-Jones

accept this emendation (p. 1543 under πρώιμος [πρόιμος, with
short *o*, is the Ionic form of the word]), as does A. W. Mair
(*Callimachus and Lycophron* [Loeb Classical Library] p. 348).
Compare Lucian, *Amor.* 39: θηρίων τῶν πρωίας ὥρας ὀνομασθῆναι
δυσκληδονίστων, "of the beasts which it is ill-omened to name
at an early hour." Bauer-Arndt-Gingrich adduce another text
in this context: ἕνα καὶ εἰκοστόν, "twenty-first" (Joannes
Lydus, *Mag.* 3.4 W; ed. Wuensch 3.26, p. 113, 1.6). This use
of the cardinal εἷς in the ordinal expression for "twenty-first"
has been discussed in the previous footnote.

[344]In Hebrew (and Aramaic) the ordinals above "ten" have no
form of their own, but are expressed by the cardinals.

[345]The following have translated *hkwhn h⁾ḥd* (1QM 7:12)
as "the first priest": A. Dupont-Sommer, *The Essene Writings
from Qumran* (Gloucester: Smith, 1973), p. 181; G. Vermes,
The Dead Sea Scrolls in English (Baltimore: Penguin, 1968),
p. 133; J. Carmignac and P. Guilbert, *Les textes de Qumran*
(Paris: Letouzey & Ané, 1961), p. 103; J. Carmignac, *La Règle
de la Guerre* (Paris: Letouzey & Ané, 1958), p. 110.

[346]This is the translation of J. van der Ploeg (*Le rouleau
de la guerre. Traduit et annoté, avec une introduction* [Studies
on the Texts of the Desert of Judah 2; Leiden: Brill, 1959],
p. 117) "Un des prêtres." E. Lohse (*Die Texte aus Qumran*
[Munich: Kösel, 1971], p. 197) and T. H. Gaster (*The Dead Sea
Scriptures* [Garden City: Doubleday, 1957], p. 290) translate:
"The one priest. . .the six (others)." The priest in question
is probably the same as "the priest appointed for the hour of
vengeance" (*hkwhn hhrws lmwᶜd nqm*) in 1QM 15:6-7, who is
distinguished from the chief priest (*kwhn hr⁾š*) in the same
context (1QM 15:4).

[347]F. Boll, "Hebdomas," *Paulys Realencyclopädie der class-
ischen Altertumswissenschaft* (ed. G. Wissowa; Stuttgart:
Metzler, 1912) 7:2, col. 2550.

[348]*Ibid.*, col. 2573. "The custom of referring the days to
the seven stars called planets was instituted by the Egyptians,
but is now found among all man kind" (Dio Cassius 36.18.1; see
also Plutarch, *Mor.*, *Questiones conviviales* 4.7 [672]). Cf.
E. Schürer, "Die siebentägige Woche im Gebrauch der christlichen
Kirche der ersten Jahrhunderte," *ZNW* 6 (1905), pp. 1-66, and J.
Finegan, *Handbook of Biblical Chronology* (Princeton: Princeton
University Press, 1964), pp. 15-16.

[349]Gesenius-Kautzsch-Cowley, #134(p).

[350]There are no ordinals above "tenth" attested in Aramaic.
Hence in 1QapGn 21:27 the cardinal numerals in the following
phrases may be understood as ordinals: *wbšnt tlt ᶜšrh. . .wbšnt
⁾rbᶜ ᶜšrh*, "and in the year thirteen. . .and in the year fourteen."

[351]C. Levias, "Numbers and Numerals," *The Jewish Encyclopedia* (New York: Ktav, 1970) 9:348.

^{352}See Dalman, *Grammatik des JPA*, p. 247.

^{353}Except in Gen 8:5; 2 Chr 29:17; 2 Esdr 7:9, where πρώτη is used.

^{354}Doudna, *Greek*, p. 94.

^{355}The same system for the days of the week turns up in the Didache: δευτέρᾳ σαββάτων καὶ πέμπτῃ, "on the second and fifth (days) of the week" (8:1), namely, the ordinals followed by σαββάτων are used for days of the week other than "the first."

^{356}H. B. Swete, *Mark*, p. 74. For M.-J. Lagrange (*Saint Marc*, p. 97) ΕΙΣ. . .ΕΝ. . .ΕΝ would be "d'une écriture bizarre"; for V. Taylor (*St. Mark*, p. 254) it would be "intolerable."

^{357}Cf. B. M. Metzger, *A Textual Commentary on the Greek New Testament* (New York: United Bible Societies, 1971), p. 83.

^{358}They were added to Codex Vaticanus, for example, only in the ninth century (H. Follieri, *Codices graeci Bibliothecae Vaticanae selecti* [Exempla scripturarum 4; Rome: Vatican Library, 1969], p. 8).

^{359}Matthew changes the Marcan verses to read ὃ μὲν ἑκατόν, ὃ δὲ ἑξήκοντα, ὃ δὲ τριάκοντα, "some one hundred, some sixty, and some thirty" (Mt 13:8 and 23). In his parallel to Mk 4:8 Luke uses only one number and makes it the correct Greek multiplicative ἑκατονταπλασίονα, "a hundredfold" (Lk 8:8). He changes the phrase in Mk 8:20 completely to ἐν ὑπομονῇ, "in patience" (Lk 8:15).

^{360}Gesenius-Kautzsch-Cowley, #134(r).

^{361}Blass-Debrunner-Funk, #248; cf. Smyth, *Greek Grammar*, #354.a; Schwyzer, *Griechische Grammatik*, 1:598-99; Mayser, *Grammatik*, 2:2:402 and 436.

^{362}"The expression μίαν μίαν ["one by one"] introduces an idiom which. . .is, except here, totally unknown in classical Greek" (R. J. Walker, *The Ichneutae of Sophocles* [London: Burns & Oates, 1919], p. 357.

^{363}Thus H. W. Smyth (*Aeschylus* [Loeb Classical Library; New York: Putnam's Sons, 1922], p. 192) translates: "Didst thou in very truth leave there thine Eye, in all things trusty, that numbered tens upon tens of thousands."

^{364}Χρὴ οὖν μίαν μίαν συγκαταβαίνειν τοῖς ἀδελφοῖς, "Therefore it is necessary occasionally to come down with the brothers" (*Apophthegmata patrum, Anton.* 13; see E. A. Sophocles, *Greek Lexicon*, 1:427).

^{365}Τὸν δὲ Φοιβάμμωνα τὸν φροντιστὴν μεταστειλάμενος ἔχε ἐγγύς, σοῦ μίαν μίαν, "having summoned Phoibammon the steward, keep him at hand together with you" (*POxy.* 940.6). The editors of this document (B. P. Grenfell and A. S. Hunt, *The Oxyrhynchus Papyri* [London: Egypt Exploration Fund, 1898], 6:310) point out that the context shows clearly that μίαν μίαν here means "together."

[366]This is the papyrus that Turner (*Syntax*, p. 187) following Blass-Debrunner-Funk, #248.1, identifies as "P. Columb. no. 318." There is no number 318 among the Columbia papyri.

[367]Till, *Koptische Grammatik*, ##109, 168, and 226; cf. Stern, *Koptische Grammatik*, #273.

[368]So Vergote, "Grec biblique," col. 1356; cf. Gignac, "The Language of the Non-Literary Papyri," p. 151.

[369]Gesenius-Kautzsch-Cowley, #134(q).

[370]In Mishnaic Hebrew: ᵓḥd ᵓḥd, "one by one" (*m. Ma^caś* 3.2); ᵓḥt ᵓḥt, "one by one" (*m. Ma^caś* 3.3).

[371]Dalman, *Grammatik des JPA*, p. 135, e.g., tryn tryn, "two by two" (*b. Soṭa* 17b): ḥmyš ḥmyš, "five by five" (*Tg. Onq.* Num 3:47).

[372]Hellenistic Greek made extensive adverbial use of several phrases composed of a preposition and a noun or pronoun. One of these was καθ᾽ ἕν(α): e.g., ἄν τε ὁμοῦ ἄν τε καθ᾽ ἕνα ὁμοίως κακόν ἐστιν, "whether (they die) all together or one by one it is equally an evil" (Epictetus 3.22.33; note the parallel use of καθ᾽ ἕνα and the adverb ὁμοῦ; cf. *PPar.* 62.2.6; 8.11; *PTebt.* 190; see Mayser, *Grammatik*, 1:3:205). The formulaic phrase καθ᾽ ἕν was widely used with the definite article (τὸ καθ᾽ ἕν) as a kind of substantive, with the meaning: "list, detailed account" (*ibid.*, 1:3:205; see Preisigke, *Wörterbuch* vol. 1, col. 426 for copious examples; an example in the OG is 1 Esdr 1:31). The phrase καθ᾽/κατὰ ἕν(α) came to be used as a type of pronoun in its own right, and even assumed case endings corresponding to its use in a sentence: nominative: ἦ ἄρα καθ᾽ εἷς λανθάνει σε περιιών, "Then does each (mistake) in turn escape your notice?" (Lucian, *Sol.* 9; see also 3 Macc 5:34). Commenting on this second-century A.D. text of Lucian, M. D. Macleod says: καθ᾽ εἷς or καθεῖς is an illogical alternative for ἕκαστος and only found in late vulgar Greek" (*Lucian* [Loeb Classical Library; Cambridge: Harvard University Press, 1967] 8:30, n. 1). By his use of the "vulgar" καθ᾽ εἷς in this text, Lucian is making fun of a sophist's lack of grammatical knowledge. The phrase καθ᾽ ἕν(α) is also found in the genitive case: Ὦ νεανίαι, φιλοφρόνως ἐγὼ καθ᾽ ἑνὸς ἑκάστου ὑμῶν θαυμάζω, "O young men, I marvel at each one of you benevolently" (4 Macc 8:5); accusative: καθ᾽ ἕνα στρεβλούμενον καὶ φλεγόμενον ὁρῶσα μήτηρ οὐ μετεβάλλετο, "Having seen each one being tortured and set on fire, the mother did not turn away" (4 Macc 15:14). On the subject, see Winer-Schmiedel, p. 246; Blass-Debrunner-Funk, #305; Bauer-Arndt-Gingrich, p. 231, under εἷς 5.e; Turner, *Syntax*, p. 198).

[373]Cf. Mayser, *Grammatik*, 2:2:402 and 436; Smyth, *Greek Grammar*, ##1682 and 1690.

[374]Gesenius-Kautzsch-Cowley, #123(c).

[375]Cf. Smyth, *Greek Grammar*, ##1106 and 1107, and Goodwin-Gulick, #979.

[376]Black, *Aramaic Approach*, p. 108, and Turner, *Syntax*, p. 36, *Style*, p. 36; cf. A. Hilhorst, *Sémitismes et latinismes dans le Pasteur d'Hermas* (Graecitas christianorum primaeva 5; Nijmegen: Dekker & van de Vegt, 1976), pp. 129-31.

[377]In his parallels to all three Marcan verses, Matthew uses εἷς. . .καὶ εἷς as in Mark, as does Luke in his parallel to Mk 9:5. Luke does not take over Mk 10:37 and 15:27.

[378]Bauer-Arndt-Gingrich, p. 231 (under εἷς 5.a) and Blass-Debrunner-Funk, #247.3; cf. Mayser, *Grammatik*, 2:1:57.

[379]Cf. Schwyzer, *Griechische Grammatik*, 2:60.

[380]Mark uses the proper vocative forms (or, in words which have no distinct vocative form, the nominative/vocative form without the article) in the following texts: Ἰησοῦ Ναζαρηνέ (1:24); τέκνον (2:5); διδάσκαλε (4:38; 9:38; 10:17 [διδάσκαλε ἀγαθέ], 20, 35; 12:14, 19, 32; 13:1); Ἰησοῦ, υἱὲ τοῦ θεοῦ (5:7); θυγάτηρ (5:34 B D W; ℵ ℵ A Θ use the classical vocative θυγάτερ. The preferred text in Mk 5:34, θυγάτηρ, is probably nothing more than a "scribal slip" [Blass-Debrunner-Funk, #147.3], since by the first century A.D. there was no distinction in pronunciation between η and ε. Such vocatives in -ηρ for the nouns πατήρ, μήτηρ, and θυγάτηρ are well-attested in both classical and Hellenistic Greek [see Schwyzer, *Griechische Grammatik*, 1:567; Blass-Debrunner-Funk, #147.3; Mayser, *Grammatik*, 2:1:55; and Moulton, *Prolegomena*, p. 71]. Moreover, in words which have a distinct vocative form, Mark never uses the nominative form without the article elsewhere as a vocative); σατανᾶ (8:33); ὦ γενεὰ ἄπιστος (9:19; the nominative form of an attributive adjective is frequently joined to a vocative noun form in Greek [see below]); τέκνα (10:24); υἱὲ Δαυὶδ Ἰησοῦ (10:47); υἱὲ Δαυίδ (10:48); Σίμων (14:37); βασιλεῦ (15:18).

In their parallels to the Marcan texts of the present discussion, Matthew changes the nominative ὁ πατήρ in Mk 14:36 to the vocative πατέρ μου, and the nominatives ὁ θεός μου *(bis)* in Mk 15:34 to θεέ μου *(bis)*, whereas he omits Mk 5:8, 41, and 9:25 entirely. Luke changes the nominative τὸ πνεῦμα τὸ ἀκαθαρτόν in Mk 5:8 to the dative case, and the nominative ὁ πατήρ in Mk 14:36 to the vocative πατέρ. In the parallel to Mk 5:41 he changes the Marcan text to another arthrous nominative form, ἡ παῖς, which he uses as a vocative. Luke also uses the nominative with article for a vocative in texts which are not in the triple tradition, e.g., μὴ φοβοῦ, τὸ μικρὸν ποίμνιον, "Do not fear, little flock" (Lk 12:32; also 10:21). He omits Mk 9:25 and 15:34 entirely.

[381]Kühner-Gerth, 2:1:47.

[382]For this schema, see Schwyzer, *Griechische Grammatik*, 2:63-64; cf. Kühner-Gerth, 2:1:46-50, and Smyth, *Greek Grammar*, #1287.

[383]Schwyzer, *Griechische Grammatik*, 2:26 and Blass-Debrunner-Funk, #147.3; cf. J. Wackernagel, "Über einige antike Anredeformen," *Kleine Schriften* (Göttingen: Akademie der Wissenschaften, 1953), pp. 970-99, esp. p. 974.

[384]The usage is formulaic, and therefore not without influence from the Jewish or Christian sacred writings (G. Breithaupt, "Über zwei Anredeformen bei Epiktet," *Hermes* 62 [1927], p. 255).

[385]Mayser, *Grammatik*, 2:1:55; cf. Doudna, *Greek*, p. 14, n. 1.

[386]In some late papyri the words ὁ θεός are used as a vocative, e.g., ῾Ο θ[εὸ]ς ὁ παντοκράτωρ ὁ ἅγιος. . .ὁ π[ατ]ήρ, "O God, holy ruler of all things. . .Father [of our Lord]," (*POxy.* 925.1; fifth/sixth century A.D.). On the subject, see Breithaupt ("Über zwei Anredeformen," p. 255), who points out that these texts are either Jewish or Christian in origin, and thus influenced by biblical Greek usage.

[387]Gesenius-Kautzsch-Cowley, #126(e).

[388]Cf. *ibid.*, #126(u).

[389]Cf. Bauer-Leander, #92(a).

[390]*Greek*, pp. 77-78.

[391]Cf. Moulton, *Prolegomena*, pp. 75-76; Robertson, *Grammar*, p. 527; Blass-Debrunner-Funk, #201; and Turner, *Syntax*, p. 243.

[392]Codex B emends to the dative case (ἡμέραις τρίσιν), whereas Δ (λ) Φ have the accusative (ἡμέρας τρεῖς). Codex D attempts to correct the text by adding εἰσίν after τρεῖς and substituting a temporal clause for the main verb, προσμένουσιν: ἤδη ἡμέραι τρεῖς εἰσιν ἀπό ποτε ὧδέ εἰσιν, literally, "it is already three days since they are here."

[393]Doudna, *Greek*, p. 76; Turner, *Style*, p. 17.

[394]See Moulton, *Prolegomena*, p. 70; Robertson, *Grammar*, p. 460; Blass-Debrunner-Funk, #144; Taylor, *St. Mark*, p. 358; Lagrange, *Saint Marc*, p. 201.

[395]As we have seen above (in section A.2.c "Paratactic καί to Introduce Logically Subordinate Clauses") a nominal clause (with or without the verb "to be") may be used to express a temporal idea when it is joined to the sentence in syndetic fashion, i.e., with the conjunction καί, e.g., νὺξ ἐν μέσῳ καί παρῆμεν τῇ ὑστεραίᾳ εἰς τὴν ἐκκλησίαν, "Night intervened (literally "[was] in the middle"), and we came into the assembly the next day" (Aeschines, *In Ctes.* 71); compare ἦν δὲ ὥρα τρίτη καί ἐσταύρωσαν αὐτόν, "It was the third hour and they crucified him" (Mk 15:25).

[396]Cf. Schwyzer, *Griechische Grammatik*, 2:66; Smyth, *Greek Grammar*, ##1478 and 940; Blass-Debrunner-Funk, #144; Turner, *Syntax*, p. 230.

[397]Cf. Kühner-Gerth 2:2:418 and Blass-Debrunner-Funk, #144.
For example: οὐδὲν κωλύει ἐπᾴδεσθαι ὑπὸ σοῦ ὅσαι ἡμέραι, "I
have nothing against (literally "Nothing hinders") being charmed
by you every day" (Plato, *Chrm.* 176B). However, one has to
consider the proper function of the relative ὅσαι in this
elliptic phrase; it may betray a subordinate clause relationship.

[398]Moulton (*Prolegomena*, p. 70) cites, without translation,
a fifth century B.C. Attic inscription as evidence of a parenthetical nominative expressing extent of time: [παρέδοσαν]. . .
[ἐπὶ τῆς 'Αιαν]τίδος πρυτανείας, πρώτης πρυ[τανευούσης τ]ρεῖς
καὶ δέκα ἡμέραι ε<ί>δεληλυ[θυίας. . . .] (*IG* 1.179.10-12).
This is the restoration of K. Meisterhans (*Grammatik der attischen
Inschriften* [3rd ed.; Berlin: Weidmann, 1900], p. 203), and it
is not necessarily correct (see Blass-Debrunner-Funk, #144).
Dittenberger restores [ἐπὶ τῆς 'Αιαν]τίδος πρυτανείας πρώτης
πρυ[τανευούσης τ]ρεῖς καὶ δέκα ἡμέραι ἐσεληλυ[θυῖαι ἦσαν],
"[during the] presidency [of Aian]tis, which was the first one
rei[gning, th]irteen days had expired" (*SIG* 1.72.10-12 [my
translation]). Compare ἐπὶ τῆς 'Ακαμαντίδος πρυτανεία[ς ὀγδόης
πρυταγευούσο]ης πέντε ἡμέραι ἐσεληλύ[θασι τῆ]ς πρυτανείας,
(*IG* 1².324.9-10) and [ἐπὶ τῆς Κεκροπίδο]ς πρυτανείας δευτέ[ρας
πρυ]τανευούσης τέτταρες ἡμέραι ἦσ[αν ἐλ]η[λυθυῖαι] (*IG* 1.273.4).

[399]Moulton, "Grammatical Notes from the Papyri, *Classical
Review* 18 (1904), p. 152 (with examples). For more examples,
see Mayser, *Grammatik*, 2:3:197 and 18.

[400]Blass-Debrunner-Funk, #144.

[401]Cf. Mayser, *Grammatik*, 2:2:327.

[402]In Coptic, the idea of extent of time is frequently
expressed by the particle *eis* (Sahidic)/*is* (Bohairic), "behold"
(= Greek ἰδού, Stern, *Koptische Grammatik*, #229; see Vergote,
"Grec biblique," col. 1357). We may take as an example the
Marcan text in question: *je ēdē eis šomn̄t n̄hoou seproskarterei
eroi*, literally ". . .because already, behold three days they
wait upon me" (Mk 8:2 Sahidic); *je is g n̄ehoou seohi saroi*,
". . .because, behold 3 days they remain with me" (Mk 8:2
Bohairic). In this type of expression in Coptic the noun has
the definite article n̄/n̄e, but is otherwise undifferentiated.
Hence it is easy to suppose that an Egyptian writing Greek
might translate *eis šomn̄t n̄hoou*, "behold three days" by ἰδού
and the nominative τρεῖς ἡμέραι. This would account for the
unusual expressions in *PPrincet.* 2.98.17 and *BGU* 948.6. On
the other hand, the Egyptian might drop the particle *eis* (= ἰδού
in Greek) because it is not correct in Greek, and translate the
undifferentiated substantive by the nominative alone as in *POxy.*
1216.8; 1764.4; *BGU* 1848.11 (cited above).

[403]Gesenius-Kautzsch-Cowley, #118(i).

[404]Such a translation is not without precedent. The
literal translator Aquila has used a nominative to translate a
temporal expression in his version of Josh 1:11. The Hebrew
text is as follows: *kî bĕ‘ōd šĕlōšet yāmîm ᵓattem ᶜōbĕrîm ᵓet
hayyardēn*, "for within (literally "in the duration of") three

days you are to pass over the Jordan." Having translated the
combination bĕʿôd with the adverb ἔτι, "still," Aquila then
translated the undifferentiated noun phrase šĕlōšet yāmîm by
the nominative case: τρεῖς ἡμέραι. Thus Aquila's translation
of Josh 1:11, ὅτι ἔτι τρεῖς ἡμέραι ὑμεῖς διαβήσεσθε, ". . .
because still three days (or "three days longer") you will pass
over." It is without parallel in normal Greek writing. The
OG also translates with ἔτι and the nominative τρεῖς ἡμέραι,
but adds the conjunction καί in order to avoid the incorrect
asyndeton, as in Aquila's version. In this way the OG translates with more idiomatic Greek: ὅτι ἔτι τρεῖς ἡμέραι καί
ὑμεῖς διαβαίνετε, ". . .because (there are) still three days
and you will pass over."

[405]By contrast, the OG translates Gen 17:8 (Hebrew text
cited above) with the proper attributive adjective: εἰς
κατάσχεσιν αἰώνιον, "for an eternal possession."

[406]See Abel, *Grammaire*, #44(e); Blass-Debrunner-Funk,
#165; Howard, "Semitisms," p. 440; U. Holzmeister, "Die
katholischen deutschen Übersetzungen des Neuen Testaments seit
Schluss des vorigen Jahrhunderts," *Zeitschrift für katholische
Theologie* 41 (1917), pp. 317-18; Moule, *Idiom-Book*, pp. 175-76;
Radermacher, *Grammatik*, p. 111; Schwyzer, *Griechische Grammatik*,
2:122; Turner, *Syntax*, pp. 212-13; Zerwick, *Graecitas*, #40.

[407]Taylor (*St. Mark*, p. 154) considers Mk 1:4 to have a
genitive of quality, whereas Turner (*Syntax*, p. 213) lists it
under genitives of quality with a question mark. Blass-
Debrunner-Funk (#165) also list Mk 1:4 in the section on the
genitive of quality, but remark: "where it was not even possible
to use an equivalent adj." Howard ("Semitisms," p. 440) lists
οἱ ἄρτοι τῆς προθέσεως (Mk 2:26) as a "Hebraic" genitive,
considering it to be "a t. t. [technical term] from the Old
Testament."

[408]This Marcan verse refers to a story about King David
in 1 Sam 21:1-7 in which he and his men eat the leḥem happānîm,
literally "the bread of the face." This bread was placed every
Sabbath on a table in the Tabernacle in the presence of God
(see Lev 24:5-9). The phrase ἄρτοι (τῆς) προθέσεως in Mk 2:26
reflects the OG version of 1 Sam 21:7, where it occurs as a
paraphrase for Hebrew qōdeš, "the holy (bread)." Elsewhere in
the OG the phrase is used to translate leḥem hammaʿăreket, "the
bread of the row" or "layer" (="the layer-bread," 1 Chr 9:32;
23:29; cf. 2 Chr 13:11). Once it is used to translate ʿērek leḥem,
"given amount of bread" (Exod 40:23), and once to translate
leḥem happānîm, "the bread of the presence" (2 Chr 4:19). Note
that the phrase ἄρτοι (τῆς) προθέσεως does not translate any
corresponding Hebrew phrase in literal fashion: ἄρτοι is plural
(leḥem is [probably collective] singular) and πρόθεσις refers
to the action of "setting out" whereas the Hebrew word maʿăreket
refers to the result of the setting out (cf. the root verb ʿrk
"put, set in rows"), namely, the actual "layer" or "row" (cf.
Koehler-Baumgartner, p. 550 under maʿăreket). The OG term
obviously refers to the bread described at length in Lev 24:5-9,
but, as Swete has pointed out, it "points to the ordered rows
upon the table rather than to their ceremonial import" (*St. Mark*,

p. 49). Hence the Greek phrase is a technical term (cf. Howard, "Semitisms," p. 440), which literally means "the loaves of (the) presentation" or "setting out." The attributive genitive προθέσεως is a genitive of quality which would normally be expressed by an attributive adjective or participle, e.g., οἱ ἄρτοι οἱ προτεθέντες, "the loaves which have been set out (in rows)."

[409]In their parallels to these Marcan verses, Matthew drops the entire phrase κηρύσσων. . .ἁμαρτιῶν in Mk 1:4 and replaces it with λέγων μετανοεῖτε, "saying 'Repent!'" Luke takes over the Marcan text in word for word fashion. Both Matthew and Luke take over the OG technical term τοὺς ἄρτους τῆς προθέσεως literally from Mk 2:26.

[410]Smyth, *Greek Grammar*, #1320.

[411]Cf. *ibid.*, ##1320-21; Goodwin-Gulick, ##1082(e) and 1085; Schwyzer, *Griechische Grammatik*, 2:122; Kühner-Gerth, 2:1:264.

[412]Moulton (*Prolegomena*, p. 235) considers that genitives after negative adjectives belong to this category of genitives which he calls the "genitive of definition" (*ibid.*, p. 73), e.g., ἀδιστάστους [= ἀδιστάκτους] ὄντας πάσης αἰτίας, "being undoubted of any guilt" (*PTebt.* 124.26). This type of genitive, however, is an ablative genitive (genitive of separation, cf. Smyth, *Greek Grammar*, #1427 and Kühner-Gerth, 2:1:394 and 401). These genitives do not have much in common with the genitives of quality under discussion.

[413]Cf. Mayser, *Grammatik*, 2:2:218; Blass-Debrunner-Funk, #165.

[414]Mayser, *Grammatik*, 2:2:134-36.

[415]*Grammatik*, p. 109.

[416]Compare τὴν γέενναν τοῦ πυρός, "the fiery gehenna" (literally "the gehenna of fire," Mt 5:22; 18:9), τῶν οἰκονόμων τῆς ἀδικίας, "the unjust steward" (Lk 16:8), ὁ κριτὴς τῆς ἀδικίας, "the unjust judge" (Lk 18:6).

[417]Cf. Smyth, *Greek Grammar*, #1408; Goodwin-Gulick, #1122.

[418]*Syntax*, p. 214.

[419]Gesenius-Kautzsch-Cowley, #128(k).

[420]Cf. *ibid.*, #128(p) and (q).

[421]Blass-Debrunner-Funk, #162.2; Winer-Schmiedel, p. 264, n. 6; Winer-Moulton, p. 298; Zerwick, *Graecitas*, #47; Bauer-Arndt-Gingrich, p. 842 (under υἱός 1.c.*d*); Hilhorst, *Sémitismes*, pp. 145-47.

[422]Both Matthew and Luke take over the phrase οἱ υἱοὶ τοῦ νυμφίος in their parallels to Mk 2:19; they both omit Mk 3:17b.

232   SEMITIC INTERFERENCE

[423]Winer-Schmiedel, p. 246; cf. Kühner-Gerth 2:1:280.

[424]Cf. Liddell-Scott-Jones, p. 1847 (under υἱός 5), S.
Boscherini, "*ODYNES UOS* (Menandri, *Dysc.* v. 88)," *Studi
italiani di filologia classica* 31 (1959), p. 253. Some examples
of the figurative expression with παῖς: ἐγὼ δ' ἐμαυτὸν παῖδα
τῆς Τύχης νέμων τῆς εὖ διδούσης οὐκ ἀτιμασθήσομαι, "I, who rank
myself as the child of Fortune, shall not be shamed" (Sophocles,
OT 1080-81); ἀργυρέαισι δὲ νωμάτω φιάλαισι βιατὰν ἀμπέλου παῖδ',
"let him hand around the potent child of the vine in silver
cups" (Pindar, *N.* 9.51-52).

[425]Cf. Liddell-Scott-Jones, p. 1847 (under υἱός 7); W. von
Martitz, "υἱός," *TDNT* 8:337 (with a few more examples).

[426]The Greek phrase υἱὸς θεοῦ, "son of God," is used by
some Hellenistic philosophers about individual men, and, in
other Hellenistic documents, it refers to certain Roman emperors.
This is a figurative use of υἱός whereby the activity of a human
father is transferred by analogy to God as creator. However,
apart from the few honorary civic titles discussed above, this
use of υἱός in a figurative sense is unique in Hellenistic Greek
prose, and occurs only in the phrase υἱὸς θεοῦ, "son of God."
It will be discussed below in section iv ("The Phrase [ὁ] υἱὸς
[τοῦ] θεοῦ).

[427]Gesenius-Kautzsch-Cowley, #128(s); cf. L. Koehler and
W. Baumgartner, *Hebräisches und aramäisches Lexikon zum Alten
Testament* (3rd rev. ed.; Leiden; Brill, 1967--), p. 132 (under
bēn 7).

[428]Cf. Bauer-Leander, #89(h); Vogt, *Lexicon*, p. 31 (under
bar 2).

[429]Thackeray, *Grammar*, p. 42.

[430]Whatever the Semitic phrase behind the transliteration
Βοανηργές in Mk 3:17 might be (see the discussions of Taylor,
St. Mark, pp. 231-32 and Dalman, *Words of Jesus*, p. 49), the
Greek expression υἱοὶ βροντῆς in the same verse should be translated according to the Semitic idiom at work in the phrase.
In similar expressions in Hebrew in which the "genitive" after
ben is a concrete object, the "son (daughter) of X" is the pro-
duct of the object expressed by the "genitive," e.g., "as the
sparks (*bĕnê rešep*, literally "sons of flame") fly upward"
(Job 5:7); "an arrow (*ben qāšet*, literally "son of a bow")
cannot make him flee" (Job 41:2); "He drove his arrows (*bĕnê
ʾašpātô*, literally, "sons of his quiver") into my heart" (Lam
3:13); "Joseph is a fruitful bough" (*ben pōrāt*, literally "son
of a fruit-bearing [tree]," Gen 49:22); "the sound of the grind-
ing is low. . .and all the voices/notes (*bĕnôt haššîr*, literally
"daughters of the song") are brought low" (Qoh 12:4). Hence
the phrase υἱοὶ βροντῆς (Mk 3:17) may best be translated
"thunderbolts/thunderclaps." On the subject see A. Fridrichsen,
"Exegetisches zum Neuen Testament," *Symbolae Osloenses* 13 (1934),
p. 40.

[431]Some of the more recent literature dealing with the linguistic background of the phrase: F. H. Borsch, *The Son of Man in Myth and History* (Philadelphia: Westminster, 1967), pp. 21-32; C. Colpe, "ὁ υἱὸς τοῦ ἀνθρώπου," *TDNT* 8:400-77 (extensive bibliography, pp. 400-401); J. B. Cortes and F. M. Gatti, "The Son of Man or the Son of Adam," *Bib* 49 (1968), pp. 457-502; J. A. Fitzmyer, review of Black, *Aramaic Approach*, *CBQ* 30 (1968), pp. 417-28, esp. 424-28, and "The New Testament Title 'Son of Man' Philologically Considered," *A Wandering Armean: Collected Aramaic Essays* (Missoula: Scholars Press, 1978), pp. 143-60; R. E. C. Formesyn, "Was there a Pronominal Connection for the 'Bar Nasha' Selfdesignation?" *NovT* 8 (1966), pp. 1-35; A. J. B. Higgins, *Jesus and the Son of Man* (Philadelphia: Fortress, 1964), pp. 16-17; J. Jeremias, "Die älteste Schicht der Menschensohn-Logien," *ZNW* 58 (1967), pp. 159-62; R. Marlow, "The *Son of Man* in Recent Journal Literature," *CBQ* 28 (1966), pp. 20-30 (recent bibliography [annotated]); S. Schulz, "Die Bedeutung der neuen Targumforschung für die synoptische Tradition," *Abraham unser Vater* (ed. by O. Betz; Leiden: Brill, 1963), pp. 425-36; E. Sjöberg, "*Bn ᵓdm* und *br ᵓnš* im Hebräischen und Aramäischen," *Acta orientalia* 21 (1950-53), pp. 57-65, 91-107; G. Vermes, "The Use of *br nš/br nšᵓ* in Jewish Aramaic," in M. Black, *Aramaic Approach*, pp. 310-30 (surveys philological study of the phrase from 1896 to 1951, and the evidence of the Late Aramaic of the classical targums and other rabbinic materials), and *Jesus the Jew: A Historian's Reading of the Gospels* (New York: Macmillan, 1973), pp. 188-91 ("Excursus II: Debate on the Circumlocutional Use of the Son of Man").

[432]In the texts in question which Matthew and Luke take over from Mark, the singular of the phrase almost always appears; there is one exception: Mt 16:21 has αὐτόν for τὸν υἱὸν τοῦ ἀνθρώπου in Mk 8:31). Matthew changes the plural form τοῖς υἱοῖς τῶν ἀνθρώπων in Mk 3:28 to τοῖς ἀνθρώποις (Mt 12:31), and Luke omits the entire verse.

[433]Cf. Kühner-Gerth, 2:1:281; Liddell-Scott-Jones, p. 1289 (under παῖς 1.3); Bauer-Arndt-Gingrich, p. 841 (under υἱός 1.c.*a*).

[434]Homer uses υἱός in this sense, e.g., υἱὲς 'Αχαιῶν, "sons of Achaeans" (= "the Greeks," *Il.* 1.162), but this ancient usage does not occur in later Greek; therefore it is scarcely relevant in a discussion of first century A.D. Greek. Bauer-Arndt-Gingrich (p. 841, under υἱός 1.c.*a* and *b*) adduce two texts in which they claim that υἱός (with a genitive) is used to indicate a member of a coherent group of some kind: οἶμαι γὰρ ἐρωτᾶν σε ὅτου υἱός ἐστιν, "For I suppose you were asking whose son he is" (Dio Chrysostom 21[75].15); ἐδόκει οι (read οὐ?) τοὺς υἱ[οὺς τοῦ θ]εοῦ ἐπιδαμοῦντος αὐτοῦ ἀλλ' ἐν 'Επιδαύρωι ἐόντος τὰγ κεφα[λὰν ἀπο]ταμεῖν, "it does not seem best that the so[ns of the g]od (Asclepius), since he is not at home but is in Epidaurus, cut [off] the hea[d]" (Dittenberger, *SIG* 1169.11-13). However, in the text of Dio Chrysostom the question "whose son he is" is asked literally (ὅτου, "whose," is singular). The reply does refer to a group, but the phrase used is "one of the Spartans" (ἀλλ' ἦ τῶν Σπαρτῶν ἐστιν εἷς, "Well, is he one of

the Spartans?"), and not υἱός with a genitive. In the second
text (*SIG* 1169) the restoration is far from certain, in this
account of a sick woman's dream, especially since nothing like
υἱὸς τοῦ θεοῦ indicating a member of a group ever occurs again
in non-biblical Hellenistic Greek. Finally, Bauer-Arndt-
Gingrich (p. 841, under υἱός l.c.*a*) cite the following text
as an example of members of a guild who are called "sons"
(υἱοί): μηδὲν οὖν ἥγου τοὺς υἱέας τοὺς ἐμούς, τὸν Μαχάονα
ἐκεῖνον καὶ Ποδαλείριον ἥττον τι εἶναι δεξιωτέρους, "Do not
suppose that my sons, the last mentioned Machaon and Podaleirius,
were any less excellent (than later physicians)" (Maximus of
Tyre 10[4].2). Of course, the phrase υἱός + a genitive does
not occur here, in this rhetorical reply put on the lips of the
god Asclepius.

[435]Gesenius-Kautzsch-Cowley, #128(v); E. Schweizer, "Huios,"
TDNT 6:346.

[436]Koehler-Baumgartner (3rd rev. ed.), p. 14 (under *ʾādām*
l.c).

[437]Colpe, "'Ο υἱὸς τοῦ ἀνθρώπου," 6:402; cf. Sjöberg,
"*Bn ʾdm* und *br ʾnš*," pp. 57-59.

[438]Cf. Koehler-Baumgartner (3rd rev. ed.), p. 42 (under
ʾiš 3a).

[439]Cf. *ibid.*, p. 68 (under ʾěnōš 1 and 3a).

[440]In this instance the article is written above the line,
obviously added.

[441]In the phrase the word ʾěnāš has a collective meaning
"man, mankind." Cf. Vogt, *Lexicon*, pp. 12-13.

[442]Fitzmyer, *Genesis Apocryphon*, p. 151.

[443]The phrase may be used in some instances in Late Aramaic
as a surrogate for "I" (the speaker), but this data can be used
only in a confirmatory way should the same meaning be found in
some as yet unpublished Middle Aramaic text. See Vermes, "The
Use of *br nš/br nšʾ*," pp. 320-28 and the remarks of Fitzmyer
(review of Black, *Aramaic Approach*, pp. 426-28). Fitzmyer
discusses in great detail the lateness of the phrase *br nš/nšʾ*
in "The New Testament Title 'Son of Man,'" pp. 145-55.

[444]In another text the restoration is not certain: *ʾw mnw
hwʾ* [*mn kwl bny ʾ*]*nwš dy ykl* [. . .], "Or who is there [among
all the sons of m]en who is able. . ." (4QEn[g] 1 v 20 = *1 Enoch*
93:13). The Greek text is lacking here; the Ethiopic text
has: "And who is there of all men (*běʾěsi*) that could know."

[445]There is a text problem here. Although manuscripts B
ℵ[corr] D W have υἱοῦ θεοῦ, "son of God," the early textual
witnesses ℵ* and Θ omit the phrase. The omission of the phrase
may be the result of a scribal error (the endings of the previous word Χριστοῦ and the last word of the phrase, θεοῦ, are
the same). On the other hand "there was always a temptation to

expand titles and quasi titles of books" (B. M. Metzger, *A Textual Commentary on the Greek New Testament*, p. 73). We include the longer text in this study for the sake of completeness; the phrase does turn up again in Mk 15:39 (see below).

[446]In their parallels to the Marcan texts both Matthew and Luke omit Mk 1:1 and 3:11. Both take over the vocative υἱε τοῦ θεοῦ from Mk 5:7. In their parallels to Mk 15:39, Matthew changes the word order of the phrase υἱὸς θεοῦ to θεοῦ υἱός, whereas Luke changes the phrase to the adjective δίκαιος: "This man was just."

[447]See von Martitz, "υἱός," 8:337; Bauer-Arndt-Gingrich, p. 841 (under υἱός 1.c.*g*).

[448]See *ibid.*, p. 842 (under υἱός 2.b); von Martitz, "υἱός," 8:336; Moulton-Milligan, p. 649; Liddell-Scott-Jones, p. 1847 (under υἱός 9.c). The anarthrous form of the Greek phrase may be the result of translation from the Latin; note the word order.

[449]On the question see J. A. Fitzmyer, "The Contribution of Qumran Aramaic to the Study of the New Testament," *NTS* 20 (1974), pp. 392-93 (where the text made public by J. T. Milik in a lecture at Harvard University in December 1972 is cited). Cf. M. Hengel, *The Son of God* (Philadelphia: Fortress, 1976), pp. 44-45.

[450]*Syntactical Evidence*, p. 36.

[451]*Ibid.*, p. 36.

[452]*Ibid.*, p. 36, n. 1. Martin does not say why he omits datives with these verbs from his counting. These verbs frequently take indirect objects in Greek, as do their equivalents in Semitic. Whereas the indirect object is expressed by a simple dative in Greek, in Hebrew and Aramaic indirect object nouns usually have the preposition *l* and indirect object pronouns most frequently occur without any preposition as suffixes on the verb. Hence, an indirect object in Hebrew or Aramaic would rarely be translated into Greek with the preposition ἐν. We must surmise, then, that by eliminating datives with the verbs λέγω, εἶπον, and δίδωμι, Martin has attempted to exclude from his totals a large number of indirect object datives which have little possibility of taking either the preposition ἐν in Greek, or *b* in Semitic.

[453]Martin gives the following statistics for the proportion of simple datives to datives with ἐν in selections from the following books of the OG: Genesis 1.5 to 1; 1 Kingdoms .83 to 1; 3 Kingdoms 1.6 to 1; 4 Kingdoms .6 to 1; Daniel (Hebrew sections) .82 to 1; Daniel (Aramaic sections) 1.7 to 1; Ezra (Hebrew sections) .82 to 1; Ezra (Aramaic sections) .76 to 1. In contrast to these known translations, Martin gives the following proportions for selections from these Hellenistic Greek writings: Plutarch's *Lives* 3.3 to 1; Polybius 12.3 to 1; Epictetus 4.5 to 1; select papyri 7 to 1.

[454]Forms of αὐτός turn up as simple datives in Epictetus
in 3.1.22, 32; 2.10; 3.34; 10.15; 13.12, 22; 17.8; 21.21, and
once with a preposition in 3.20.14 (ἐν αὐτῇ).

[455]Smyth, *Greek Grammar*, #1503.

[456]Cf. *ibid.*, #1503.

[457]See J. Humbert, *La disparition du datif en grec (du
Ier au Xe siècle)* (Collection linguistique de la Société
Linguistique de Paris; Paris: Champion, 1930), p. 99; cf.
Smyth, *Greek Grammar*, #1511; Schwyzer, *Griechische Grammatik*,
2:169-70; Blass-Debrunner-Funk, #195; Kühner-Gerth, 2:1:464-65.

[458]Cf. Humbert, *La disparition du datif*, p. 106; Moulton,
Prolegomena, p. 62; Doudna, *Greek*, p. 24; Mayser, *Grammatik*,
2:2:357 and n. 3. Most of the Hellenistic examples of instrumental and associative ἐν occur in papyri where Egyptian
interference has been suspected, since "in Coptic the preposition h^e n has the same functions" in this regard as Semitic *b*
(Gignac, "Language of the Non-Literary Papyri," p. 151; cf.
Vergote, "Grec biblique," col. 1357).

[459]See Blass-Debrunner-Funk, #195; Turner, *Syntax*, pp. 240,
241, and 252; Robertson, *Grammar*, pp. 533-34; Martin, *Syntactical Evidence*, p. 36; Winer-Moulton, p. 485; Humbert, *La
disparition du datif*, p. 110.

[460]Gesenius-Kautzsch-Cowley, #119(o).

[461]Cf. Rosenthal, *Grammar of Biblical Aramaic*, #77; and
Vogt, *Lexicon*, p. 23 (under the preposition *b* 4).

[462]*The Parables of Jesus*, p. 16.

[463]*Ibid.*, p. 16.

[464]Smyth, *Greek Grammar*, #1481; cf. Schwyzer, *Griechische
Grammatik*, 2:150.

[465]Cf. Mayser, *Grammatik*, 2:2:270-71; Blass-Debrunner-
Funk, #188; Turner, *Syntax*, p. 238.

[466]See N. Turner, *Grammatical Insights*, pp. 43-47;
Lagrange, *Saint Marc*, p. 22; Taylor, *St. Mark*, p. 174; Blass-
Debrunner-Funk, #127.3; O. Bächli, "Was habe ich mit Dir zu
schaffen?" *TZ* 33 (1977), pp. 69-80, esp. pp. 76-77. The phrase
also occurs in Jn 2:4 (see also R. E. Brown, *The Gospel According
to John I-XII* [Anchor Bible; Garden City: Doubleday, 1966],
p. 99 for a discussion of the Johannine use of the expression).

[467]Cf. Smyth, *Greek Grammar*, #1479; Schwyzer, *Griechische
Grammatik*, 2:143; Kühner-Gerth, 2:1:417; Winer-Moulton, p. 731.

[468]*Grammatical Insights*, p. 46.

[469]Liddell-Scott-Jones, p. 488 (under εἰμί C. III. 2); cf.
Smyth, *Greek Grammar*, #1479.

470Kühner-Gerth, 2:1:417.

471*Grammatical Insights*, p. 96. R. E. Brown (*Gospel According to John I-XII*, p. 99) claims that in two Old Testament texts, the expression in question does not have the nuance of a hostile refusal of an inopportune involvement with another person, but "implies simple disengagement": *mah lî wālāk*, "What to me and to you?" (2 Kgs 3:13); *ᵓeprayim mah lî ᶜôd laᶜăṣabbîm*, literally "Ephraim, what to me any longer, to idols?" (Hos 14:8). Elisha's reply to the king of Israel in 2 Kgs 3:13 certainly appears to be hostile; in the following verse he ex-claims: "As the Lord of hosts lives, were it not that I respect the king of Judah, I should neither look at you nor notice you at all!" In the second text adduced by Brown, we may query whether the expression in question is the same (the copula *wĕ*, "and" is missing, and the adverb ᶜôd is present).

472See H. St. J. Thackeray, "Renderings of the Infinitive Absolute in the LXX," *JTS* 9 (1908), pp. 597-601, and *Grammar of the Old Testament in Greek*, p. 49; Abel, *Grammaire*, #45(r); Colwell, *Greek of the Fourth Gospel*, p. 31; H. Kaupel, "Beobachtungen zur Übersetzung des Infinitivus absolutus in der Septuaginta," *ZAW* 20 (1945-48), pp. 191-92; Radermacher, *Grammatik*, p. 129; Howard, "Semitisms," p. 444; Blass-Debrunner-Funk, #198.6; Turner, *Syntax*, p. 241; Zerwick, *Graecitas*, #60; Hilhorst, *Sémitismes*, p. 152.

473Matthew has no parallels to these Marcan texts. He does cite OG Exod 21:16 in another context (Mt 15:4), and has the same text as in Mk 7:10. Luke omits the cognate dative ἐκστάσει in his parallel to Mk 5:42. He omits Mk 7:10 entirely. But cf. ἐπιθυμίᾳ ἐπεθύμησα τοῦτο τὸ πάσχα φαγεῖν μεθ᾽ ὑμῶν, literally, "With desire I have desired to eat this Passover with you" (Lk 22:15).

474Smyth, *Greek Grammar*, #1577; cf. Schwyzer, *Griechische Grammatik*, 2:166; Kühner-Gerth, 2:1:308, Anmerkung 4.

475Cf. Hilhorst, *Sémitismes*, pp. 150-51.

476Mayser, *Grammatik*, 2:2:319, Anmerkung 2.

477There are two Hellenistic texts in which some manuscripts have cognate datives: ἁψάμενον ἁφῇ, literally "having been touched with a touch" (Galen, *Temp.* 2.6.627), νίκη ἐνίκησε, "he won with a victory" (Aelian, *VH* 8.15); these, however, are not the standard texts given in most editions (see Hilhorst, *Sémitismes*, p. 151). There are two examples in which cognate datives occur with verbal adjectives: φυγῇ φευκτέον, literally "(a book) ought to be fled with flight" (Lucian, *Ind.* 16); ὅτι δοχῇ δεκτικόν ἐστιν [. . .], literally "that (the body of Christ) be received with a reception" (*POxy*.5.16, a Christian document!).

478The following authors insist that the cognate dative as in Mk 7:10 is not the same thing as a cognate dative (with an attribute) expressing manner or means: Blass-Debrunner-Funk (#198.6); Abel (*Grammaire*,#45[s]); Howard ("Semitisms," p. 444);

Hilhorst (*Sémitismes*, pp. 151-52); cf. Zerwick, #62.

[479]Cf. Gesenius-Kautzsch-Cowley, #113(n).

[480]The infinitive absolute, of course, does not occur in
1QIsa[a] (a copy of the Old Testament book of Isaiah): $šm^c w$ $šmw^c$,
"Listen attentively" (1QIsa[a] 6:3 = Masoretic Text Isa 6:9;
also 15:30; 19:18; 34:2 = Masoretic Text Isa 19:22; 24:19; 40:30,
respectively).

[481]Note that this infinitive absolute construction does
occur in Old Aramaic, e.g., *hskr thskrhm*, "you must hand them
over" (Sefire 3:2; also 3:6, 12-13, 18; see Fitzmyer, *Genesis
Apocryphon*, p. 122; and *The Aramaic Inscriptions of Sefîre*
[Biblica et Orientalia 19; Rome: Pontifical Biblical Institute,
1967], p. 174). Unfortunately, no text in the Old Testament
book of Job in which the infinitive absolute construction
occurs (Job 6:2; 13:5, 17; 15:35; 21:2; 37:2) is preserved in
the Aramaic targum of Job from Qumran (11QtgJb).

[482]For a full explanation of all the possible translations
by the OG of the infinitive absolute used with a finite verb of
the same stem, see Thackeray, "Renderings of the Infinitive
Absolute," pp. 597-601, or *Grammar of the Old Testament in
Greek*, pp. 47-50.

[483]So Thackeray, *ibid.*, pp. 49-50. The OG translates
literally only once: ἐξολεθρεῦσαι δὲ αὐτοὺς οὐκ ἐξωλέθρευσαν,
"They did not drive them out utterly" (Josh 17:13).

[484]Gesenius-Kautzsch-Cowley, #117(p) and (q).

[485]It does, of course, occur in 1QIsa[a] in those texts which
correspond to those which have the construction in the Old
Testament book of Isaiah: *hqšb qšb*, "let him listen very attentively" (1QIsa[a] 16:22 = Masoretic Text Isa 21:7; also 19:14,
22; 28:19; 35:28-29; 38:24 = Masoretic Text Isa 24:16, 22; 35:2;
42:17; 45:17, respectively).

[486]Cf. Bauer-Leander, #100(d), and Brockelmann, *Grundriss*,
2:294; see Fitzmyer, *Genesis Apocryphon*, p. 122.

[487]Bauer-Leander, #100(d); cf. Brockelmann, *Grundriss*,
2:294.

[488]*Ibid.*, 2:301 (examples on p. 303); cf. Bauer-Leander,
#100(d).

[489]Cf. Blass-Debrunner-Funk, #198.6 and Turner, *Syntax*,
p. 242.

[490]Turner, *Syntax*, p. 245; Abel, *Grammaire*, #43(f), rem. 2;
cf. Howard, "Semitisms," p. 445; Blass-Debrunner-Funk, #153.1.

[491]In their parallels to Mk 4:41 both Matthew and Luke
avoid the cognate accusative: οἱ δὲ ἄνθρωποι ἐθαύμασαν, "the
men marveled" (Mt 8:27); φοβηθέντες δὲ ἐθαύμασαν, "fearing
they marveled" (Lk 8:25).

[492]Smyth, *Greek Grammar*, #1564, Kühner-Gerth, 2:1:305;
Blass-Debrunner-Funk, #153.1; Moule, *Idiom Book*, p. 32;
Robertson, *Grammar*, p. 478; Mayser, *Grammatik*, 2:2:317.

[493]Cf. Smyth, *Greek Grammar*, #1570; Blass-Debrunner-Funk,
#153.1; Mayser, *Grammatik*, 2:2:318.

[494]Cf. Moulton, "Grammatical Notes from the Papyri,"
p. 436; Robertson, *Grammar*, p. 478; Moulton-Milligan, p. 273,
under ζημία.

[495]Schwyzer, *Griechische Grammatik*, 2:44; Blass-Debrunner-
Funk, #4.2 and 141.1; H. Traub, "οὐρανός," *TDNT* 5:513; Doudna,
Greek, p. 74; Turner, *Syntax*, p. 25; Hilhorst, *Sémitismes*, pp.
126-28.

[496]The following table shows the Matthean and Lucan
parallels to the Marcan texts in which οὐρανός/οὐρανοί appears.
Those instances in which either evangelist has changed the
Marcan usage from singular or plural, or the reverse, will be
pointed out by an asterisk:

Mark	Matthew	Luke	Mark	Matthew	Luke
1:10 plur.	plur.	*sing.	11:31 sing.	sing.	sing.
1:11 plur.	plur.	*sing.	12:25 plur.	*sing.	--
4:32 sing. (OG)	sing.	sing.	13:25 sing.	sing.	--
6:41 sing.	sing.	sing.	13:25 plur.	plur.	plur.
7:34 sing.	--	--	13:27 sing. (OG)	*plur.	--
8:11 sing.	sing.	sing.	13:31 sing.	sing.	sing.
10:21 sing.	*plur.	*plur.	13:32 sing.	*plur.	--
11:25 sing.	*adjective	--	14:62 sing.	sing.	--
11:30 sing.	sing.	sing.			

[497]Cf. Smyth, *Greek Grammar*, #1006; Schwyzer, *Griechische
Grammatik*, 2:44.

[498]Liddell-Scott-Jones, p. 1273, under οὐρανός; H. Traub,
"οὐρανός," *TDNT* 5:497; Hilhorst, *Sémitismes*, pp. 126-27. F. Torm
("Der pluralis οὐρανοί," *ZNW* 33 [1934], p. 48) has presented a
few late traditions concerning Anaximander in which the plural
of οὐρανός occurs. However, in these texts the true plural is
always meant: Α. ἀπεφήνατο τοὺς ἀπείρους οὐρανοὺς θεούς,
"A(naximander) declared that the boundless heavens were gods"
(Aetius, *De placitis philosophorum* 1.7.12 [Diels, *Vorsok.*[6]
1.86.13]; also Pseudo-Plutarch, *Strom.* 2 [*Vorsok.*[6] 1.82.29];
Hippolytus, *Ref.* 1.6.2 [*Vorsok.*[6] 1.84.5]).

[499]Hilhorst, *Sémitismes*, p. 126, e.g., εἷς θεὸς ἐν
οὐρανοῖς μέγας Μὴν Οὐράνιος, μεγάλη δύναμις τοῦ ἀθανάτου θεοῦ,
"There is one great god in (the) heavens, Men Ouranios, great
power of the immortal God" (E. Lane, *Corpus monumentorum
religionis dei Menis* [Leiden: Brill, 1971], 1.83, second or
third century A.D.); also Achilles Tatius (fourth century A.D.)
2.36.4; 2.37.2, etc.; see Hilhorst, *Sémitismes*, p. 126, n. 2.

[500]This may appear to be a dual form, but it is really a plural (cf. Gesenius-Kautzsch-Cowley, #88[d]; L. Koehler and W. Baumgartner, *Lexicon in veteris testamenti libros* (Leiden: Brill, 1951), p. 986, under *sāmayim*).

[501]Gesenius-Kautzsch-Cowley, #124(b).

[502]Cf. Bauer-Leander, #87(e); Vogt, *Lexicon*, p. 170.

[503]Hilhorst, *Sémitismes*, p. 126; cf. Doudna, *Greek*, p. 74.

[504]*Philo's Bible* (Cambridge: Cambridge University Press, 1950), pp. 141-46; cf. Hilhorst, *Sémitismes*, p. 127.

[505]"οὐρανός," 5:512.

[506]Wellhausen, *Einleitung*, p. 21; Howard, "Semitisms," p. 441; Abel, *Grammaire*, #37(g); Blass-Debrunner-Funk, #245.3; Doudna, *Greek*, p. 32; Schwyzer, *Griechische Grammatik*, 2:183, n. 6; Turner, *Style*, p. 22; Moulton-Milligan, p. 276 (under ἥ); Black, *Aramaic Approach*, p. 117.

[507]Only Black (*Aramaic Approach*, p. 117) considers Mk 14:21 as a text in which the positive degree (καλόν) is used for the comparative (βέλτιον). Unlike the first three examples it does not contain the comparative particle ἥ. Evidently Black considers that the conditional clause may suggest the comparative idea, but see the discussion below.

[508]The Matthean parallels use καλόν (. . . ἥ) in exactly the same manner as the Marcan texts under discussion. Luke omits all the Marcan texts in question.

[509]Cf. Schwyzer, *Griechische Grammatik*, 2:308.

[510]*Ibid.*, 2:308; cf. G. Bertram, "Καλός," *TDNT* 3:357; Liddell-Scott-Jones, p. 870 (under καλός II.1); Bauer-Arndt-Gingrich, p. 401 (under καλός 3.c).

[511]An example of the normal usage with the comparative (βέλτιον): βέλτιον ὀλιγάκις πλημμελεῖν ὁμολογοῦντα σωφρονεῖν πλεονάκις ἥ ὀλιγάκις ἁμαρτάνειν λέγοντα πλημμελεῖν πολλάκις, "It is better to err seldom while frequently confessing to be wise than seldom to miss the mark while frequently saying that one errs" (Epictetus, *Gnom.* C 4).

[512]An example with the normal adversative (μᾶλλον ἥ) after the impersonal expression καλόν (ἐστιν): καλόν μοι τοῦδ' ὑπερπονουμένῳ θανεῖν προδήλως μᾶλλον ἥ τῆς σῆς ὑπὲρ γυναικός, "It (would be) good for me to die suffering for that man in public view rather than (to die) for the sake of your wife" (Sophocles, *Aj.* 1310-12; cf. Epictetus 2.2.26).

[513]Cf. Kühner-Gerth, 2:2:303; Winer-Moulton, p. 302; Smyth, *Greek Grammar*, #2863.

[514]Cf. Kühner-Gerth, 2:2:302.

[515]Quite different, of course, is the case in which the
comparative particle ἤ is used after an adjective in the positive
degree which implies comparison (ἄλλος, ἕτερος, διάφορος, etc.)
e.g., ὥστ' ἄλλα χρῄζειν ἤ τὰ σὺν κέρδει καλά, ". . .so as to
grasp other (things) than those profitable with gain" (Sophocles,
OT 595). See Schwyzer, *Griechische Grammatik*, 2:565; Smyth,
Greek Grammar, #2863.

[516]In a text adduced in this context by Winer-Moulton
(p. 301), Aristotle, *Pr.* 29.6, the accepted text has the
comparative αἴσχίον ("more shameful") before the comparative
particle ἤ, rather than the variant reading which they cite:
αἰσχρόν, "shameful." In other texts adduced in this context,
the particle ἤ has its other normal, disjunctive meaning, e.g.,
αἰσχρὸν δὲ βιασθέντας ἀπελθεῖν ἤ ὕστερον ἐπιμεταπέμπεσθαι τὸ
πρῶτον ἀσκέπτως βουλευσαμένους, "(It would be) shameful to be
forced to go away *or* later to send for reinforcements having
made our plans at first without due consideration" (Thucydides
6.21). On the matter see Kühner-Gerth, 2:2:303.

[517]Cf. Gesenius-Kautzsch-Cowley, #133(a).

[518]Bauer-Leander, #94.

[519]The Greek text of Enoch translates with the comparative
degree of the adjective where the Aramaic has the adjective
with *min*: καὶ ὁ οἶκος μείζων τούτου, "and a house greater than
this" (En 14:15); καὶ <ε>ἶδον πρὸς ἀνατολὰς ἄλλο ὄρος ὑψηλότερον
τούτου, "and I saw to the east another mountain higher than
this" (En 26:3).

CHAPTER IV

CONCLUSION

The body of this study has been the detailed grammatical
analysis of more than half the alleged Semitisms in the Gospel
of Mark. We have employed a methodology which uses as control
literature the Greek, Hebrew, and Aramaic documents, and only
those documents, which are witnesses of those languages at the
time when the New Testament was composed. This general conclusion includes a chart in which are set down all the alleged
Semitisms examined in this study. After each Semitism the
Marcan verse or verses in which it occurs are given in a second
column. A third column states the relative frequency with which
that syntagmeme occurs in Hellenistic Greek (G), Qumran and
Proto-Mishnaic Hebrew (H; these are the types of Hebrew which
were being written [and spoken?] at the time of the writing of
the New Testament), Middle Aramaic (A), and in the Greek Old
Testament (OG), as follows:

G1 -- attested, though extremely rare, in Hellenistic
    Greek

$G1^E$ -- G1, but the few instances are probably the result
    of Egyptian (Hamitic) interference

G2 -- attested, but infrequent, in Greek

G3 -- frequent in Greek

G4 -- normal Greek usage

H1 -- possible in Hebrew (By this we mean that the usage
    occurs in earlier [biblical] Hebrew, although it does
    not turn up in Qumran or Proto-Mishnaic Hebrew.)

H2 -- attested, but infrequent, in Qumran and Proto-
    Mishnaic Hebrew

H3 -- frequent in H

H4 -- normal usage in H

A1 -- possible in Aramaic (By this we mean that the usage
    occurs in earlier [Official] Aramaic, although it
    does not turn up in Middle Aramaic.)

A2 -- attested, but infrequent, in Middle Aramaic

A3 -- frequent in A

243

A4 -- normal usage in A

OG1 -- found in the OG, though rarely

OG2 -- frequent in the OG

OG3 -- common OG usage

OG4 -- neither Greek nor Semitic usage, probable imitation
       of OG style

OG5 -- quotation or conflation of OG text(s)

In a fourth column in the chart, we present a conclusion about
the provenience of each alleged Semitism.

Some notes on the explanation of the chart follow. Whenever
a Semitism may be the result of any of the three possible sources
for Semitic interference, namely, Hebrew, Aramaic, or imitation
of the OG, the conclusion is "Semitism: H A OG" (without punc-
tuation). When, however, one of the Semitic sources is more
likely to lie behind the Marcan usage, its abbreviation is given
first and followed by a comma, e.g., "Semitism: H, OG, or
(possibly) A." When specific phrases occur in the Gospel of
Mark which are not normal in Greek and do not occur in the OG,
we have concluded that imitation of the OG is less likely than
Semitic interference from contemporaneous Hebrew or Aramaic.
Whenever an alleged Semitism has been understood incorrectly
by the various authors, and is really some other type of Greek
usage, we have marked it with an asterisk (*) in the first column
of the chart. When only one verse in the gospel has been thus
incorrectly explained, we have marked only that verse (in the
second column) with an asterisk. The frequencies given in the
third column are those for the correctly described syntactical
feature.

The chart summarizes the conclusions of the body of the
study and with them a much clearer picture of Semitic interference in Marcan syntax has emerged: (1) We have found that much
grammatical usage in Marcan Greek which various authors have
claimed to be the result of Semitic interference is, in fact,
quite possible in Hellenistic Greek. At times, those who have
falsely claimed a necessary Semitic provenience for some Marcan
construction have not properly analyzed the Greek usage (in
B.1.a, b; 2.a.ii; b; c.ii; d.iii [Mk 5:35 only]; 5 [Mk 14:21
only]). More frequently, however, the error has been made
because of insufficient knowledge of Hellenistic Greek grammar

(in A.1.c [anarthrous genitives], h; 2.e, f.i, ii; g; 4 [with demonstrative pronoun]; 5.a, b; 6; B.2.d.i [εἷς as indefinite article], ii [ἄνθρωπος with adjective or article], iii; f; 4.c.ii, iii).

(2) On the other hand, certain constructions which various authors have argued are acceptable in Greek have been shown to be quite abnormal, or even totally unattested in Hellenistic Greek, whereas their appearance in Semitic is normal (sometimes only possible). These are true Semitisms: A.1.d, e; 2.b, d; 3; 4 (with resumptive personal pronoun); B.2.a.iii; d.i (εἷς as an indefinite pronoun), ii (ἄνθρωπος [alone] = τις), iv; e; 3.a, b, c, d; 4.a.i, ii; b.i, ii, iii; 4.c.iv; d, e; 5.

(3) As has long been known, certain constructions in the Gospel of Mark which are attested in Hellenistic Greek are most likely due to Semitic interference at least in the frequency of their occurrence. (When this is the case the fourth column in the chart has "Frequency due to H A OG.") This study has confirmed this fact with additional statistics on the various constructions: A.1.a, b, c, f, g; 2.a, c; B.2.a.i; c.i; 4.c.i. Of course, no individual instance of any of these constructions can be claimed definitely as a Semitism. At the same time, the presence of any individual instance of them is equally probable as owing either to Hebrew or Aramaic interference or as imitation of the style of the OG.

(4) Furthermore, we have found that nine definite Semitisms (A.1.d; 2.b; 4 [with unemphatic personal pronoun]; B.2.a.iii; d.i [εἷς as indefinite pronoun]; e; 3.a, c [Mk 6:7], d) and four probable Semitisms (A.4 [with emphatic personal pronoun]; B.2.d. iv; 4.d; 5) can also be the result of Semitic interference from any of the three possible sources (H A OG).

(5) We have confirmed that there are several types of Semitism in the Gospel of Mark (H A OG, H A, A OG, H OG, OG, A) and that syntactical Semitic interference permeates every page of the gospel.

Type of Alleged Semitism	Marcan Vss.	Frequency in G, H, A, OG	Conclusion
A. General Style and Structure of Sentence			
1. Word Order			
(a) Position of Verb (before Subject)	*passim*	G2 H4 A4 OG3	Frequency due to A, OG (or possibly) H
(b) Position of Attributive Adjective			
arthrous	*passim*	G2 H4 A4 OG3	Frequency due to H A OG
anarthrous	*passim*	G3 H4 A4 OG3	Frequency prob. due to H A OG
(c) Position of Dependent Genitive			
arthrous	*passim*	G3 H4 A4 OG3	Frequency prob. due to H A OG
anarthrous	*passim*	G3 H4 A4 OG3	Both Greek and Semitic usage
(d) Phrase: Substantive-Genitive-Adjective	5:11; 14:24 (1:11; 9:27?)	-- H4 A1 OG3	Semitism: H, OG, or (possibly) A
(e) Phrase: Subst.-Poss. Pron.-Genitive	14:24	-- H2 A1 --	Semitism: H or (possibly) A
(f) (Lack of) Separation of Subst. from Article	*passim*	G3 H4 A4 OG3	Infrequency prob. due to H A OG
(g) Position of Unemphatic Pers. Pronouns as Direct and Indir. Objects	*passim*	G3 H4 A4 OG3	Frequency prob. due to H A OG
(h) Position of Demonstrative Adjectives	*passim*	G4 H4 A4 OG3	Both Greek and Semitic usage
2. Parataxis			
(a) Coordination of Indep. Clauses w. καί	*passim*	G2 H4 A4 OG3	Frequency due to H A OG

		G	H	A	OG	
(b) Καί Beginning New Paragraph	*passim* (80X)	--	H4	A3	OG3	Semitism: H A OG
(c) Καί + Logically Subord. Clauses	*passim*	G3	H4	A4	OG3	Frequency prob. due to H A OG
(d) Καί + Apodosis of Condit. Sentence	7:11-12; 8:38; 14:9	--	H3	A2	OG1	Semitism: H or A
(e) Καί Introducing Incredulous Question	4:13; 9:12; 10:26; 11:28; 12:37	G3	H3	A3	OG1	Both Greek and Semitic usage
(f) Subjunctive after (i) imperative	1:44	G3	--	--	--	Grecism
(ii) θέλειν	10:36, 51; 14:12	G3	--	--	--	Grecism
(g) Asyndeton between sentences	*passim* (49X)	G3	H3	A2	OG1	Both Greek and Hebrew usage
between imperatives	2:11; 4:39; 6:38; 8:15; 10:14; 14:42	G3	H3	A3	OG1	Both Greek and Semitic usage (but 2:11; 14:42 are lexical Semitisms)
3. Καί ἐγένετο followed by finite verb	1:9; 4:4	--	--	A2	OG2	Semitism: OG or A
infinitive	2:15, 23	--	--	--	--	Mixture of OG Semitism and Greek usage (infinitive after γίνομαι)
4. *Casus pendens* followed by demonstrative pronoun	3:35; 6:16; 7:20; 12:10, 40; 13:11, 13	G4	--	--	OG1	Grecism
emphatic personal pronoun	8:38; 14:44	G1	H4	A1	OG3	Probable Semitism: H, OG, or (possibly) A
unemphatic personal pronoun	4:25a, b; 9:42; 11:23	G1^E	H4	A1	OG3	Semitism: H, OG, or (possibly) A

5. Conditional Sentence			
(a) Shortening of Parallel Condit. Sentences	11:31-32	G3 H3 -- --	Both Greek and Hebrew usage
(b) Abridged Exceptive Clauses	2:26; 4:22a, b; 6:4; 8:14; 9:9; 13:32	G3 H2 A1 OG1	Greek usage attested in H and possible in A
6. General Relative Clause	4:25a, b; 8:38; 9:42; 11:23	G3 H3 A3 OG3	Frequency both Greek and Semitic
B. The Several Parts of Speech			
1. Definite Article			
(a) Unusual Insertion of Article*	*passim* (25X)	G3 H1 A3 OG3	Both Greek and Semitic (A, OG, and possibly H) usage
(b) Unusual Omission of Article*	1:2; 2:21; 8:3, 26; 9:31; 12:11, 14	G3 H4 A4 OG3	Both Greek and Semitic usage
2. Pronouns			
(a) Personal Pronouns			
(i) Unusual Frequency in Oblique Cases	*passim*	G1E H4 A4 OG3	Frequency due to H A OG
(ii) Prepositive Use for Emphasis*	6:17; 12:36, 37; 6:22	G4 H1 A1 OG1; G4 H2 A4 --	Grecism (only possible in Semitic); Both Greek and Semitic (common in A, rare in H) usage
(iii) Redundant Use after Relative	1:7; 7:25; 13:19	G1E H3 A3 OG2; -- H3 A3 OG5	Semitism: H A OG; Semitism: conflation of OG texts
(b) Ψυχή = Reflexive Pronoun*	8:36; 10:45; 14:34	G4 H4 A4 OG3	Both Greek and Semitic usage

		G	H	A	OG	Frequency due to
(c) Demonstrative Pronoun						
(i) Frequency of ἐκεῖνος	*passim*	G2	H3	A3	OG3	Frequency due to H A OG
(ii) Pleonastic Use of Demonstratives*	4:11; 9:42; 13:24; 14:21, 25	G3	H3	A3	OG3	Both Greek and Semitic usage
(d) Indefinite Pronoun						
(i) Εἷς = τις						
as indefinite pronoun (+ genitive)	5:22; 12:28; 13:1; 14:66	G1^E	H4	A4	OG3	Semitism: H A OG
as indefinite pronoun (alone)	9:17; 10:17	--	H2	A1	--	Semitism: H or (possibly) A
as indefinite article	11:29; 12:42	G2	H4	A4	OG3	Both Greek (rare) and Semitic
(ii) Ἄνθρωπος = τις						
used alone	1:23; 4:26; 5:2; 12:1	--	H4	A4	OG1	Semitism: H or A
with attrib. participle or adj.	3:1; 13:34	G3	H4	A4	OG3	Both Greek and Semitic usage
with definite article*	7:15 (*bis*), 18, 20 (*bis*), 23	G4	H4	A4	OG3	Both Greek and Semitic usage
(iii) Ἀπό + Genitive = Indefinite Plural	6:43; 7:4(?); 12:2	G3	H1	A1	OG2	Greek and (possibly) Semitic
	5:35*	G4	H4	A4	OG3	Both Greek and Semitic usage
(iv) Οὐ...πᾶς = οὐδείς	13:20	G1	H4	A4	OG2	Probable Semitism: H, A, or (possibly) OG
(e) Πολλοί = πάντες	10:45; 14:24	--	H4	A1	OG3	Semitism: H, OG, or (possibly) A

	Reference	G	H	A	OG	Both Greek and Hebrew usage / Remarks
(f) Interrogative Pron. Introducing Question Expressing Wonder or Indignation	2:7, 8, 24; 4:40; 8:12; 10:18; 15:34	G4	H3	--	OG1	Both Greek and Hebrew usage
3. Numerals and Distributives						
(a) Cardinal for Ordinal	16:2	--	H4	A4	OG3	Semitism: OG, H, A
(b) "Εν + Cardinal = Multiplicative	4:8, 20	--	--	A4	--	Aramaism
(c) Distributives Expressed by Repetition						
δύο δύο	6:7	G1E	H3	A1	OG3	Semitism: H, OG, or (possibly) A
εἷς κατὰ εἷς	14:19	--	--	--	--	Mixture of Semitic (doubling) and Hellenistic Greek καθεῖς
repetition of substantive	6:39, 40	--	H1	--	OG2	Semitism: OG or (possibly) H
(d) Εἷς...καὶ εἷς = ὁ μέν...ὁ δέ	9:5; 10:37; 15:27	--	H4	A4	OG3	Semitism: H A OG
4. The Noun						
(a) Nominative Case						
(i) Article + Nominative = Vocative						
article + nominative	5:8, 41; 9:25; 14:36	--	--	A1	OG2	Semitism: A or OG (prob. A in Mk 5:41; 14:36, where A is cited)
article + nominative + possessive pronoun	15:34	--	--	--	OG4	Semitism: reference to OG text
(ii) Nominative in Time Designations	8:2	G1E	H4	A4	--	Semitism: H or A
(b) Genitive Case						
(i) "Hebraic" Genitive	1:4	--	H4	A4	OG2	Semitism: H or A
	2:26	--	H4	A4	OG5	Semitism: reference to OG text

Description	Reference	G	H	A	OG	Notes
(ii) υἱός + Genitive	2:19; 3:17	G1	H4	A4	OG2	Semitism: H or A
(iii) 'Ο υἱὸς τοῦ ἀνθρώπου	passim (14X)	--	H2	A1	--	Semitism: H or (possibly) A
οἱ υἱοὶ τῶν ἀνθρώπων	3:28	--	H4	A4	OG3	Semitism: H A OG
(iv) ('Ο) υἱὸς (τοῦ) θεοῦ undetermined	1:1; 15:39	G2	H1	A2	--	Both Greek and Semitic usage
determined	3:11; 5:7	--	H1	A2	--	Attested in A, but grammatically possible in G and H
(c) Dative Case						
(i) Frequency of Dative dative with ἐν	passim	G2	H4	A4	OG3	Frequency due to H A OG
dative of third person pronoun	passim	G2	H4	A4	OG3	Frequency due to H A OG
(ii) Dative after γίνομαι	4:1	G4	H4	A3	OG3	Both Greek and Semitic usage
(iii) Τί ἐμοί (ἡμῖν) καὶ σοί	1:24; 5:7	G3	H1	A1	OG3	Both Greek and Semitic usage
(iv) Cognate Dative simple	7:10	--	--	--	OG4	Semitism from OG
with attributive adjective	5:42	G1	--	--	OG5	Probable imitation of OG, but possible in G
(d) Cognate Accusative	4:41	G1	H3	A3	OG3	Probably due to OG, H, or A, but possible in G
(e) Plural of οὐρανός	1:10, 11; 12:25; 13:25	--	H4	A4	OG2	Semitism: H A OG

5. Adjective Positive Degree for Comparative	9:43, 45, 47	G1 H4 A4 OG2	Probable Semitism due to H A OG, but attested in G (very rarely)
	14:21*	G4 H4 A4 OG3	Both Greek and Semitic usage

BIBLIOGRAPHY

Greek Grammars and Grammatical Studies

Abel, Félix-Marie. "Coup d'oeil sur le *koinē*." *Revue biblique*
    35 (1926) 5-26.

_____. *Grammaire du grec biblique suivie d'un choix de*
    papyrus. Etudes bibliques. Paris: J. Gabalda et Fils,
    1927.

Angus, Samuel. "The *koinē*, the Language of the New Testament."
    Princeton Theological Review 8 (1910) 44-92.

Bauer, Walter. "An Introduction to the Lexicon of the Greek
    New Testament." *A Greek-English Lexicon of the New*
    Testament and Other Early Christian Literature. Trans-
    lated and adapted by William F. Arndt and F. Wilbur
    Gingrich. Chicago: University of Chicago Press, 1957,
    pp. ix-xxv.

Blass, Friedrich and Debrunner, Albert. *A Greek Grammar of the*
    New Testament and Other Early Christian Literature.
    Translated and revised by Robert W. Funk. Chicago:
    University of Chicago Press, 1961.

Brugmann, Karl. *Griechische Grammatik*. 4th ed. Revised by
    Albert Thumb. Handbuch der klassischen Altertumswissen-
    schaft 2/1. Munich: Beck, 1913.

Colwell, Ernest Cadman. "The Greek Language." *Interpreter's*
    Dictionary of the Bible. Edited by G. A. Buttrick. New
    York: Abingdon Press, 1962. Vol. 2. Pp. 479-87.

Debrunner, Albert. *Geschichte der griechischen Sprache II.*
    Grundfragen und Grundzüge des nachklassischen Griechisch.
    Sammlung Göschen 114. Berlin: W. de Gruyter, 1954.

_____. Review of *Über die Sprache und Stil des Diodors*,
    by J. Palm. *Gnomon* 28 (1956) 586-89.

Deissmann, Adolf. "Hellenistisches Griechisch." *Realencyclo-*
    pädie für protestantische Theologie und Kirche. Edited
    by J. J. Herzog and A. Hauck. Leipzig: J. C. Hinrichs,
    1899. Vol. 7. Pp. 627-39.

Foucault, Jules Albert de. *Recherches sur langue et le style*
    de Polybe. Collection d'études anciennes. Paris: Belles
    Lettres, 1972.

Gignac, Francis T. *A Grammar of the Greek Papyri of the*
    Roman and Byzantine Periods. Vol. I: *Phonology*. Testi
    e documenti per lo studio dell'antichità 55. Milan:
    Istituto editoriale Cisalpino--La Goliardica, 1976.

253

_____. "The Language of the Non-Literary Greek Papyri."
    *Proceedings of the Twelfth International Congress of
    Papyrology.* Edited by D. H. Samuel. American Studies
    in Papyrology. 7. Toronto: A. M. Hakkert, Ltd., 1970.
    Pp. 139-52.

Goodwin, William Watson. *Greek Grammar.* Revised by Charles
    Burton Gulick. Boston: Ginn & Company, 1930.

Hatzidakis, Georgios N. "Ziel und Methode der neugriechischen
    Sprachforschung." *Einleitung in die neugriechischen
    Grammatik.* Bibliothek indogermanischer Grammatiken 5.
    Leipzig: Breitkopf & Härtel, 1892. Pp. 1-49.

Higgins, Martin J. "The Renaissance of the First Century and
    the Origin of Standard Late Greek." *Traditio* 3 (1945)
    49-100.

Kapsomenos, Stylianos G. "Das Griechisch in Ägypten." *Museum
    Helveticum* 10 (1953) 248-63.

Kühner, Raphael. *Ausführliche Grammatik der griechischen
    Sprache.* 2 vols. 3rd ed. Edited by Bernhard Gerth.
    Hannover and Leipzig: Hahnsche Buchhandlung, 1898-1904.

Jannaris, Anthony Nicholas. *An Historical Greek Grammar.*
    London: Macmillan, 1897.

Maldfeld, Georg. "Der Beitrag ägyptischer Papyruszeugen für
    den frühen griechischen Bibeltext." *Mitteilungen aus der
    Papyrussammlung der österreichischen Nationalbibliothek* 5
    (1955) 79-84.

Mayser, Edwin. *Grammatik der griechischen Papyri aus der
    Ptolemäerzeit: Mit Einschluss der gleichzeitigen Ostraka
    und der in Ägypten verfassten Inschriften.* 2 vols. 2nd
    ed. Berlin-Leipzig: W. de Gruyter, 1926-38.

Meecham, Henry George. *The Letter of Aristeas.* Manchester:
    Manchester University Press, 1935.

Meillet, Antoine. *Aperçu d'une histoire de la langue grecque.*
    Paris: Hachette, 1955.

Meisterhans, Konrad. *Grammatik der attischen Inschriften.*
    3rd rev. ed. Edited by E. Schwyzer. Berlin: Weidmann,
    1900.

Milligan, George. *Selections from the Papyri.* Cambridge:
    Cambridge University Press, 1912.

Montevecchi, Orsolina. "Continuità ed evoluzione della lingua
    greca nella Settanta e nei Papiri." *Actes du congrès
    internationale de papyrologie.* Warsaw/Krakow: Wroclaw,
    1961. Pp. 39-49.

Moulton, James Hope. *A Grammar of New Testament Greek.* Vol. I:
    Prolegomena. 3rd rev. ed. Edinburgh: T. & T. Clark,
    1908.

_____, and Howard, Wilbert Francis. *Grammar of New
    Testament Greek.* Vol. II: *Accidence and Word Formation.*
    Edinburgh: T. & T. Clark, 1929.

O'Callaghan, Jose. "Koiné." *Enciclopedia de la Biblia.*
    Barcelona: Garriga, 1963-65. Vol. 4. Cols. 848-52.

Palm, Jonas. *Über die Sprache und Stil des Diodoros von
    Sizilien.* Lund: Gleerup, 1955.

Peremans, Willy. "Uber die Zweisprachigkeit im ptolemäischen
    Ägypten." *Studien zur Papyrologie und antiken Wissen-
    schaftsgeschichte.* Festschrift F. Oertel. Edited by
    H. Braunert. Bonn: Habelt, 1964. Pp. 49-60.

Radermacher, Ludwig. *Neutestamentliche Grammatik: Das
    Griechisch des Neuen Testaments im Zusammenhang mit der
    Volkssprache dargestellt.* 2nd ed. Handbuch zum Neuen
    Testament 1. Tübingen: J. C. B. Mohr, 1925.

_____. *Koine.* Sitzungsberichte der Wiener Akademie,
    Philosophische-historische Klasse 224/5. Vienna:
    R. M. Rohrer, 1947.

Richards, George Chatterton. Review of *A Grammar of New
    Testament Greek.* Vol. I: *Prolegomena,* 2nd ed., by
    James Hope Moulton. *Journal of Theological Studies* 10
    (1908-09) 283-90.

Robertson, Archibald Thomas. *A Grammar of the Greek New
    Testament in the Light of Historical Research.* 4th ed.
    London: Hodder and Stoughton, 1923.

Salonius, Aarne Henrik. *Zur Sprache der griechischen
    Papyrusbriefe.* Vol. I: *Die Quellen.* Helsinki:
    Helsingfors Akademische Buchhandlung, 1927.

Schmiedel, Paul Wilhelm. *Georg Benedikt Winer's Grammatik des
    neutestamentlichen Sprachidioms. I. Theil: Einleitung
    und Formenlehre.* 8th ed. Göttingen: Vandenhoeck &
    Ruprecht, 1894.

Schubart, Wilhelm. *Einführung in die Papyruskunde.* Berlin:
    Weidmann, 1918.

Schwyzer, Eduard. *Dialectorum graecarum exempla epigraphica
    potiora.* Leipzig: S. Hirzel, 1923. Reprinted Hildesheim:
    G. Olms, 1960.

_____. *Griechische Grammatik.* 2 vols. Handbuch der
    Altertumswissenschaft 2:1. Munich: C. H. Beck'sche
    Verlagsbuchhandlung, 1953.

Shenkl, H. *Epicteti dissertationes ab Arriani digestae.*
    Bibliotheca scriptorum graecorum et romanorum teubneriana.
    Stuttgart: B. G. Teubner, 1965.

Smyth, Herbert Weir. *Greek Grammar.* Revised by Gordon M.
    Messing. Cambridge, MA: Harvard University Press, 1956.

Thackeray, Henry St. John. *A Grammar of the Old Testament in
    Greek.* Vol. I. Cambridge: Cambridge University Press,
    1909.

Thomson, George D. *The Greek Language.* Cambridge: Heffer &
    Sons, 1960.

Thumb, Albert. *Die griechische Sprache im Zeitalter des
    Hellenismus.* Strassburg: Trübner, 1901.

_____. "On the Value of the Modern Greek for the Study
    of Ancient Greek." *Classical Quarterly* 8 (1914) 181-205.

Turner, Nigel. *A Grammar of New Testament Greek by James Hope
    Moulton.* Vol. III: *Syntax.* Edinburgh: T. & T. Clark,
    1963.

_____. *A Grammar of New Testament Greek by James Hope
    Moulton.* Vol. IV: *Style.* Edinburgh: T. & T. Clark,
    1976.

Vergote, Joseph. "Het probleem van de Koine in het licht
    der moderne linguistiek." *Philologische Studien* 6
    (1934-35) 81-107.

Völker, Franz. *Syntax der griechischen Papyri. I. Der Artikel.*
    Münster: Westfälische Vereinsdruckerei, 1903.

Wackernagel, Jakob. "Die griechische Sprache." *Die griechische
    und lateinische Literatur und Sprache.* Berlin/Leipzig:
    Teubner, 1905. Pp. 286-318.

Wifstrand, Albert. "Det grekiska prosapraket: en historisk
    översikt." *Eranos* 50 (1952) 149-63.

_____. "The Homily of Melito on the Passion." *Vigiliae
    christianae* 2 (1948) 201-23.

Winer, Georg Benedikt. *A Treatise on the Grammar of New
    Testament Greek.* Translated by W. F. Moulton. Edinburgh:
    T. & T. Clark, 1882.

Zerwick, Maximilian. *Graecitas biblica Novi Testamenti exemplis
    illustratur.* 5th ed. Rome: Pontifical Biblical Insti-
    tute, 1966.

Grammatical Studies of Hebrew and Aramaic

Bagatti, Bellarmino, and Milik, József Tadeusz. *Gli scavi del "Dominus flevit."* I. *La necropoli del periodo romano.* Pubblicazione dello Studium Biblicum Franciscanum 13. Jerusalem: Tipografia del PP. Francescani, 1958.

Bauer, Hans, and Leander, Pontus. *Grammatik des Biblisch-Aramäischen.* Tübingen: Max Niemeyer Verlag, 1927.

Ben-Ḥayyim, Z. "Traditions in the Hebrew Language, with Special Reference to the Dead Sea Scrolls." *Aspects of the Dead Sea Scrolls.* Edited by C. Rabin and Y. Yadin. Scripta Hierosolymitana 4. Jerusalem: Magnes Press, 1958. Pp. 200-14.

Beyer, Klaus. Review of *Altaramäische Grammatik*, by Rainer Degen. *Zeitschrift der deutschen morgenländischen Gesellschaft* 120 (1970) 198-204.

Black, Matthew. "The Aramaic Spoken by Christ and Lc 14,5." *Journal of Theological Studies* 1 (1950) 60-62.

_____. "The Development of Aramaic Studies since the Work of Kahle." *In Memoriam Paul Kahle.* Edited by G. Fohrer and M. Black. Beihefte zur *Zeitschrift für die alttestamentliche Wissenschaft* 103. Berlin: A. Töpelmann, 1968. Pp. 17-28.

_____. "ΕΦΦΑΘΑ (Mk. 7. 34)." *Mélanges bibliques en hommage au R. P. Béda Rigaux.* Edited by A. Descamps and A. de Halleux. Gembloux: Duculot, 1970. Pp. 57-60.

Brock, Sebastian. "The Phenomenon of the Septuagint." *Oudtestamentische Studiën* 17 (1972) 11-36.

Dalman, Gustaf. *Aramäische Dialektproben.* 2nd rev. ed. Leipzig: J. C. Hinrichs, 1927.

_____. *Grammatik des jüdisch-palästinischen Aramäisch.* 2nd ed. Leipzig: J. C. Hinrichs, 1905.

Degen, Rainer. *Altaramäische Grammatik der Inschriften des 10.-8. Jahrhunderts vor Christi.* Abhandlungen für die Kunde des Morganlandes 38/3. Wiesbaden: F. Steiner, 1969.

Delcor, M. "Le Targum de Job et l'araméen du temps de Jésus." *Revue des sciences religieuses* 47 (1973) 232-61. Also in *Exégèse biblique et Judaisme.* Edited by J.-E. Ménard. Strasbourg: Faculté de théologie catholique, 1973. Distributed by Brill, Leiden.

Díez Macho, Alexandro. *Neophyti I: Targum palestinense I. Génesis.* Textos y estudios 7. Madrid: Consejo superior de investigaciones científicas, 1968.

_____. "The Recently Discovered Palestinian Targum: Its Antiquity and Relationship with the Other Targums" *International Organization for the Study of the Old Testament Congress Volume. Vetus Testamentum,* Supplements 7. Leiden: Brill, 1959. Pp. 222-45.

_____. "Le targum palestinien." *Exégèse biblique et judaïsme.* Edited by J. E. Ménard. Strasbourg: Faculté de théologie catholique, 1973. Pp. 15-77.

Drijvers, H. J. W. *Old-Syriac (Edessean) Inscriptions.* Semitic Study Series 3. Leiden: Brill, 1972.

Dupont-Sommer, André. *Les Araméens.* L'orient ancien illustré Paris: Maisonneuve, 1949.

Eiss, Werner. "Zur gegenwärtigen aramäistischen Forschung." *Evangelische Theologie* 16 (1956) 170-81.

Emerton, John Adney. "*MARANATHA* and *EPHPHATHA.*" *Journal of Theological Studies* 18 (1967) 427-31.

Fitzmyer, Joseph A. *The Genesis Apocryphon of Qumran Cave I.* 2nd rev. ed. Biblica et Orientalia 18a. Rome: Pontifical Biblical Institute, 1971.

_____. "The Phases of the Aramaic Language." *A Wandering Aramean: Collected Aramaic Essays.* Society of Biblical Literature Monograph Series. Missoula: Scholars Press, 1979. Pp. 57-84.

_____. "Some Observations on the Targum of Job from Qumran Cave XI." *Catholic Biblical Quarterly* 36 (1974) 503-24.

_____. Review of *The New Testament and the Palestinian Targum to the Pentateuch,* by Martin McNamara. *Theological Studies* 29 (1968) 322-26.

_____. Review of *Neofiti I,* by Alexandro Díez Macho. *Catholic Biblical Quarterly* 32 (1970) 107-12.

Ginsberg, Harold Louis. Review of *The Genesis Apocryphon,* 1st ed., by Joseph A. Fitzmyer. *Theological Studies* 28 (1967) 574-77.

Grelot, Pierre. Review of *The Genesis Apocryphon,* 1st ed., by Joseph A. Fitzmyer. *Revue biblique* 74 (1967) 102-105.

Joüon, Paul. *Grammaire de l'hébreu biblique.* Rome: Pontifical Biblical Institute, 1923.

Kahle, Paul. *The Cairo Geniza.* 2nd ed. Oxford: B. Blackwell, 1959.

_____. *Masoreten des Westens.* 2 vols. Stuttgart: Kohlhammer, 1927. Reprinted Hildesheim: G. Olms, 1967.

Kaufman, S. A. "The Job Targum from Qumran." *Journal of the American Oriental Society* 93 (1973) 317-27.

Kautzsch, E., ed. *Gesenius' Hebrew Grammar.* 2nd ed. Revised by A. E. Cowley. Oxford: The Clarendon Press, 1910.

Kittel, Gerhard. *Die Probleme des palästinischen Spätjudentums und das Urchristentum.* Beiträge zur Wissenschaft vom Alten und Neuen Testament 3/1. Stuttgart: Kohlhammer, 1926.

Klausner, Joseph. *Mwṣ'h šl lšwn hmšnh [The Origin of the Mishnaic Language].* Scripta universitatis atque bibliothecae hierosolymitanarum, orientalia et judaica 1. Jerusalem: Hebrew University Press, 1923.

Kutscher, Eduard Yechezkel. "Aramaic." *Current Trends in Linguistics: Volyme 6. Linguistics in Southwest Asia and North Africa.* Edited by T. A. Sebeok. The Hague: Mouton, 1970. Pp. 347-412.

_____. "Aramaic." *Encyclopaedia judaica.* Jerusalem: Keter Publishing House Ltd., 1971. Vol. 1. Cols. 259-87.

_____. "The Language of the Genesis Apocryphon." *Aspects of the Dead Sea Scrolls.* Edited by C. Rabin and Y. Yadin. Scripta Hierosolymitana 4. Jerusalem: Magnes Press, 1958. Pp. 1-35.

_____. "The Languages of the Hebrew and Aramaic Letters for Bar Cocheba and His Contemporaries." *Leshonenu* 25 (1961) 117-33; 26 (1962) 7-23.

_____. "Mišnisches Hebräisch." *Rocznik Orientalistyczny* 28 (1964) 33-48.

Le Déaut, Roger. "The Current State of Targumic Studies." *Biblical Theology Bulletin* 4 (1974) 3-32.

_____. *Introduction à la littérature targumique.* Rome: Pontifical Biblical Institute, 1966.

_____. *Liturgie juive et le Nouveau Testament.* Rome: Pontifical Biblical Institute, 1965.

_____. "Targumic Literature and New Testament Interpretation." *Biblical Theology Bulletin* 4 (1974) 243-89.

Malina, Bruce. *The Palestinian Manna Tradition.* Arbeiten zur Geschichte des späteren Judentums und des Urchristentums. Leiden: Brill, 1968.

Manson, Thomas Walter. Review of *The Cairo Geniza,* by Paul Kahle. *Dominican Studies* 2 (1949) 183-92.

McNamara, Martin. *The New Testament and the Palestinian Targum to the Pentateuch.* Analecta Biblica 27. Rome: Pontifical Biblical Institute, 1966.

Metzger, Bruce M. "A Comparison of the Palestinian Syriac
    Lectionary and the Greek Gospel Lectionary." *Neotesta-
    mentica et semitica.* Festschrift M. Black. Edited by
    E. E. Ellis and M. Wilcox. Edinburgh: T. & T. Clark,
    1969. Pp. 209-20.

Meyer, Rudolf. "Der gegenwärtige Stand der Erforschung der in
    Palästina neugefundenen hebräischen Handschriften: 47.
    Die vier Höhlen von Murabbaᶜāt." *Theologische Literatur-
    zeitung* 88 (1963) cols. 19-28.

_____. "Geschichte des Hebräischen." *Hebräische Grammatik.*
    3rd rev. ed. Sammlung Göschen 763. Berlin: W. de Gruyter,
    1966. Vol. 1. Pp. 27-36.

Miller, M. "Targum, Midrash and the Use of the Old Testament
    in the New Testament." *Journal for the Study of Judaism
    in the Persian, Hellenistic and Roman Period* 2 (1971)
    29-82.

Muraoka, Takamitsu. "The Aramaic of the Old Targum of Job
    from Qumran Cave XI." *Journal of Jewish Studies* 25 (1974)
    425-43.

_____. "Notes on the Aramaic of the Genesis Apocryphon
    (1)." *Revue de Qumran* 8 (1972-76) 7-51.

Nöldeke, Theodor. *Die semitischen Sprachen.* 2nd rev. ed.
    Leipzig: Tauchnitz, 1899.

Rabin, Chaim. "The Historical Background of Qumran Hebrew."
    Aspects of the Dead Sea Scrolls. Edited by C. Rabin and
    Y. Yadin. Scripta Hierosolymitana 4. Jerusalem: Magnes
    Press, 1958. Pp. 144-61.

_____. *Qumran Studies.* Oxford: University Press, 1957.

Rosenthal, Franz. *Die aramäistische Forschung seit Th. Nöldeke's
    Veröffentlichungen.* Leiden: Brill, 1939.

_____. *A Grammar of Biblical Aramaic.* Porta Linguarum
    Orientalium, New Series 5. 3rd printing. Wiesbaden:
    Otto Harrassowitz, 1968.

Schulz, Siegfried. "Die Bedeutung der neuen Targumforschung
    für die synoptische Tradition." *Abraham unser Vater.*
    Festschrift O. Michel. Leiden-Cologne: Brill, 1963.
    Pp. 425-36.

Schultze, Martin. *Grammatik der aramäischen Muttersprache Jesu.*
    Berlin: Calvary, 1899.

Segal, Moses Hirsch. *A Grammar of Mishnaic Hebrew.* Oxford:
    The Clarendon Press, 1927.

_____. "Hebrew in the Period of the Second Temple." *Inter-
    national Journal of Apocrypha* 6/23 (1910) 79-82.

_____. "Mishnaic Hebrew and its Relation to Biblical Hebrew and to Aramaic." *Jewish Quarterly Review* 20 (1908) 647-737.

Segert, Stanislaus. "Die Sprachenfragen in der Qumrāngemeinschaft." *Qumran-Probleme*. Edited by H. Bardtke. Berlin: Akademie-Verlag, 1963. Pp. 313-39.

_____. "Sprachliche Bermerkungen zu einigen aramäischen Texten von Qumran." *Archiv orientální* 33 (1965) 190-206.

_____. "Zur Orthographie und Sprache der aramäischen Texte von Wadi Murabbaᶜat." *Archiv orientální* 31 (1963) 122-37.

Thomas, David Winton. "The Language of the Old Testament." *Record and Revelation*. Edited by H. W. Robinson. Oxford: The Clarendon Press, 1938. Pp. 374-402; 490-91.

Vaux, Roland de. "Les grottes de Murabbaᶜat et leurs documents." *Revue biblique* 60 (1953) 245-67.

_____. "Quelques textes hébreux de Murabbaᶜat." *Revue biblique* 60 (1953) 268-75.

Vogt, Ernst. *Lexicon linguae aramaicae veteris testamenti*. Rome: Biblical Institute, 1971.

Wagner, Max. *Die lexikalischen und grammatikalischen Aramäismen im alttestamentlichen Hebräisch*. Beihefte zur *Zeitschrift für die alttestamentliche Wissenschaft* 96. Berlin: A. Töpelmann, 1966.

York, A. D. "The Dating of Targumic Literature." *Journal for the Study of Judaism in the Persian, Hellenistic and Roman Period* 5 (1974) 49-62.

Semitic Interference in Biblical Greek

Abbott, Edwin Abbott. *Johannine Grammar*. London: C. Black, 1906.

Allen, Willoughby Charles. "The Aramaic Background of the Gospels." *Studies in the Synoptic Problem*. Edited by W. Sanday. Oxford: The Clarendon Press, 1911. Pp. 287-312.

_____. "The Aramaic Element in St. Mark." *Expository Times* 13 (1901-02) 328-30.

_____. *The Gospel According to St. Mark*. Oxford Church Biblical Commentary. New York: Macmillan, 1915.

_____. "The Original Language of the Gospel according to St. Mark." *Expositor* 6/1 (1900) 436-43.

Allis, Oswald Thompson. "The Alleged Aramaic Origin of the Fourth Gospel." *Princeton Theological Review* 26 (1928) 531-72.

Angus, Samuel. "Modern Methods in New Testament Philology."
    Harvard Theological Review 2 (1909) 446-64.

Antoniadis, Sophie L. *L'évangile de Luc: Esquisse de grammaire
    et de style.* Paris: Belles Lettres, 1930.

Argyle, Aubrey William. *An Introductory Grammar of New Testa-
    ment Greek.* Ithaca: Cornell University Press, 1965.

_____. "The Theory of an Aramaic Source in Acts 2,14-40."
    Journal of Theological Studies 4 (1953) 213-14.

Atkinson, Basil Ferris Campbell. *The Greek Language.* London:
    Faber & Faber, 1931.

Aytoun, Robert Alexander, "The Ten Lucan Hymns of the Nativity
    in Their Original Language." *Journal of Theological
    Studies* 18 (1916-17) 274-88.

Bacon, Benjamin Wisner. "More Philological Criticism of Acts."
    American Journal of Theology 22 (1918) 1-23.

Ball, Charles James. "Had the Fourth Gospel an Aramaic Arche-
    type?" *Expository Times* 21 (1909-10) 91-93.

Barton, George Aaron. "Prof. Torrey's Theory of the Aramaic
    Origin of the Gospels and the First Half of the Acts of
    the Apostles." *Journal of Theological Studies* 36 (1935)
    357-73.

Beyer, Klaus. *Semitische Syntax im Neuen Testament. I. Satz-
    lehre Teil 1.* Revised 2nd ed. Studien zur Umwelt des
    Neuen Testaments 1. Göttingen: Vandenhoeck & Ruprecht,
    1968.

Bishop, Eric Francis Fox. *"Ap' agoras:* Mark 7:4." *Expository
    Times* 61 (1949-50) 219.

Black, Matthew. *An Aramaic Approach to the Gospels and Acts.*
    3rd ed. Oxford: The Clarendon Press, 1967.

_____. "Aramaic Studies and the New Testament: the Un-
    published Work of the Late A. J. Wensinck of Leyden."
    Journal of Theological Studies 49 (1948) 157-65.

_____. "Language and Script. 1. The Biblical Languages."
    Cambridge History of the Bible. Cambridge: Cambridge
    University Press, 1970. Vol. 1. Pp. 1-11.

_____. "The Recovery of the Language of Jesus." *New
    Testament Studies* 3 (1956-57) 305-13.

_____. "Second Thoughts: IX. The Semitic Element in the
    New Testament." *Expository Times* 77 (1965-66) 20-23.

_____. "Semitismos del Nuevo Testamento." *Enciclopedia
    de la Biblia.* Barcelona: Garriga, 1963-65. Vol. 6.
    Cols. 594-96.

_____. "Unresolved New Testament Problems. The Problem of the Aramaic Element in the Gospels." *Expository Times* 59 (1947-48) 171-76.

Boatti, Abele. *Grammatica del greco del Nuovo Testamento.* Venice: Libreria Emiliana, 1910.

Boismard, M. E. "Importance de la critique textuelle pour établir l'origine araméenne du quatrième évangile." *L'Evangile de Jean: Etudes et problèmes.* Louvain: Desclée de Brouwer, 1958. Pp. 41-57.

Bonaccorsi, Giuseppe. *Primi saggi di filologia neotestamentaria. I. Introduzione, Vangeli, Atti degli Apostoli.* Turin: Società editrice internationale, 1933.

Bonsirven, Joseph. "Les aramaïsmes de S. Jean l'Evangéliste?" *Biblica* 30 (1949) 405-32.

Born, Adrianus van den, and McGuire, Martin Rawson Patrick. "Biblical Greek." *Encyclopedia Dictionary of the Bible.* Edited by L. F. Hartman. New York: McGraw-Hill Book Company, 1963. Cols. 245-46.

Botte, Bernard. *Grammaire grecque du Nouveau Testament.* Paris: J. de Gigord, 1933.

Bratsiotis, Nikolaus P. "*Nepeš -- psychē,* Ein Beitrag zur Erforschung der Sprache und der Theologie der Septuaginta." *Volume du Congress. Genève 1965. Vetus Testamentum,* Supplement 15. Leiden: E. J. Brill, 1965. Pp. 58-89.

Brown, Schuyler. "From Burney to Black: The Fourth Gospel and the Aramaic Question." *Catholic Biblical Quarterly* 26 (1964) 323-39.

Büchsel, Friedrich. "Die griechische Sprache der Juden in der Zeit der Septuaginta und des Neuen Testaments." *Zeitschrift für die alttestamentliche Wissenschaft* 60 (1944) 132-49.

Burkitt, Francis Crawford. "Professor Torrey on 'Acts.'" *Journal of Theological Studies* 20 (1918-19) 320-29.

Burney, Charles Fox. *The Aramaic Origin of the Fourth Gospel.* Oxford: The Clarendon Press, 1922.

Burrows, Millar. "The Johannine Prologue as Aramaic Verses." *Journal of Biblical Literature* 45 (1926) 57-69.

_____. "Mark's Transitions and the Translation Hypothesis." *Journal of Biblical Literature* 48 (1929) 117-23.

_____. "The Original Language of the Gospel of John." *Journal of Biblical Literature* 49 (1930) 95-139.

_____. "Principles for Testing the Translation Hypothesis in the Gospels." *Journal of Biblical Literature* 53 (1934) 13-30.

_____. "The Semitic Background of the New Testament."
    The Bible Translator 2 (1951) 67-73.

Bussby, Frederick. "A Note on *Sabbata* and *Sabbaton* in the
    Synoptics." *Bulletin of the John Rylands Library* 30
    (1946) 157-58.

Cadbury, Henry Joel. "Luke -- Translator or Author?" *American
    Journal of Theology* 24 (1920) 436-55.

_____. *The Making of Luke-Acts.* New York: Macmillan, 1927.

    The Style and Literary Method of St. Luke. Harvard
    Theological Studies 6. Cambridge, MA: Harvard University
    Press, 1920.

_____. "The Vocabulary and Grammar of New Testament Greek."
    The Bible translator 2 (1951) 153-59.

Chajes, Hirsh Perez. *Markus--Studien.* Berlin: Schwetschke,
    1899.

Charles, Robert Henry. *A Critical and Exegetical Commentary on
    the Revelation of St. John.* International Critical Com-
    mentary. Edinburgh: T. & T. Clark, 1920.

_____. *Studies in the Apocalypse.* Edinburgh: T. & T.
    Clark, 1913.

Chase, Frederic Henry. *The Old Syriac Element in the Text of
    Codex Bezae.* London: Macmillan, 1893.

Clarke, William Kemp Lowther. "The Use of the Septuagint in
    Acts." *The Beginnings of Christianity.* 2 vols. Edited
    by F. J. Foakes-Jackson and K. Lake. London: Macmillan,
    1922. Vol. 1. Part 2. Pp. 66-105.

Colwell, Ernest Cadman. "A Definite Rule for the Use of the
    Article in the Greek New Testament." *Journal of Biblical
    Literature* 52 (1933) 12-21.

_____. *The Greek of the Fourth Gospel.* Chicago: Chicago
    University Press, 1931.

Connolly, Hugh. "The Appeal to Aramaic Sources of our Gospels."
    Downside Review 66 (1948) 25-37.

_____. "Syriacisms in St. Luke." *Journal of Theological
    Studies* 37 (1936) 374-85.

Conybeare, Frederick Cornwallis, and Stock, St. George. *Selec-
    tions from the Septuagint.* Boston: Ginn & Company, 1905.

Cranfield, C. E. B. *The Gospel According to St. Mark.* Cambridge
    Greek Testament Commentary. Cambridge: Cambridge Univer-
    sity Press, 1959.

Dalman, Gustaf. *Jesus-Jeschua. Studies in the Gospels.* Trans-
    lated by P. P. Levertoff. London: S.P.C.K., 1929.

_____. *The Words of Jesus*. Translated by D. M. Kay. Edinburgh: T. & T. Clark, 1902.

_____. Review of *The Aramaic Origin of the Fourth Gospel*, by C. F. Burney. *Theologische Literaturzeitung* 48 (1923) 7-8.

Danker, Frederick W. "The *huios* Phrases in the New Testament." *New Testament Studies* 7 (1960-61) 94.

Daube, David. "Concerning the Reconstruction of 'the Aramaic Gospels.'" *Bulletin of the John Rylands Library* 29 (1945) 3-39.

Debrunner, Albert. Review of *Neutestamentliche Grammatik*, by L. Radermacher. *Göttingsche Gelehrte Anzeigen* 4 (1926) 129-52.

_____. Review of *La langue des Evangiles*, by H. Pernot. *Gnomon* 4 (1928) 441-44.

Deissmann, Adolf. *Bible Studies*. Translated by A. Grieve. Edinburgh: T. & T. Clark, 1901.

_____. *Light from the Ancient East*. Translated by L. R. M. Strachan. London: Hodder & Stoughton, 1927.

_____. *New Light on the New Testament from Records of the Greco-Roman Period*. Edinburgh: T. & T. Clark, 1907.

_____. *The Philology of the Greek Bible. Its Present and Future*. London: Hodder & Stoughton, 1908.

_____. "Die Sprache der griechischen Bibel." *Theologische Rundschau* 1 (1898) 463-72; 5 (1902) 58-69; 9 (1906) 210-29; 15 (1912) 339-64.

Dey, Joseph. "'Ad Graecam originem revertentes.' Literatur zur neutestamentlichen Philologie." *Bibel und Leben* 2 (1961) 120-31.

_____. "Von der Sprache des Neuen Testaments." *Bibel und Leben* 1 (1960) 39-50.

Dibelius, Martin. Review of *Das biblische* kai egeneto, by M. Johannessohn. *Gnomon* 3 (1927) 646-50.

Dodd, Charles Harold. "The First Epistle of John and the Fourth Gospel." *Bulletin of the John Rylands Library* 21 (1937) 129-56.

Doudna, John Charles. *The Greek of the Gospel of Mark. Journal of Biblical Literature* Monograph Series. Philadelphia: Society of Biblical Literature, 1961.

Dressler, H. "Greek Language, Early Christian and Byzantine." *New Catholic Encyclopedia*. New York: McGraw-Hill, 1967. Vol. 6. Pp. 730-31.

Emerton, John Adney. "Mark xiv.24 and the Targum to the
    Psalter." *Journal of Theological Studies* 15 (1964) 58-59.

_____. Review of *The Semitisms of Acts*, by M. Wilcox.
    Journal of Semitic Studies 13 (1968) 282-97.

Evans, D. Emrys. "Case-Usage in the Greek of Asia Minor."
    Classical Quarterly 15 (1921) 22-30.

Falconer, James William. "The Aramaic Source of Acts I-XV and
    Paul's Conversion." *Expositor* 8/19 (1920) 271-85.

Feigin, Samuel Isaac. "The Original Language of the Gospels."
    Journal of Near Eastern Studies 2 (1943) 187-97.

Fitzmyer, Joseph A. "The Contribution of Qumran Aramaic to the
    Study of the New Testament." *New Testament Studies* 20
    (1974) 382-407.

_____. "Methodology in the Study of the Aramaic Substratum
    of Jesus' Sayings in the New Testament." *Jésus aux ori-
    gines de la christologie.* Edited by J. Dupont. Biblio-
    theca ephemeridum theologicarum lovaniensium 40. Gembloux:
    Duculot, 1975. Pp. 73-102.

_____. "The New Testament Title 'Son of Man' Philological-
    ly Considered." *A Wandering Aramean: Collected Aramaic
    Essays.* Society of Biblical Literature Monograph Series.
    Missoula: Scholars Press, 1979. Pp. 143-60.

_____. "The Study of the Aramaic Background of the New
    Testament." *A Wandering Aramean: Collected Aramaic Essays.*
    Society of Biblical Literature Monograph Series. Missoula:
    Scholars Press, 1979. Pp. 1-28.

_____. Review of *An Aramaic Approach to the Gospels and
    Acts,* by Matthew Black. *Catholic Biblical Quarterly* 30
    (1968) 418-28.

Foakes, Jackson, Frederick John. "Professor C. C. Torrey on
    the *Acts.*" *Harvard Theological Review* 10 (1917) 352-61.

Frisk, Hjalmar. *Studien zur griechischen Wortstellung.*
    Göteborgs Högskolas Årsskrift 39/1. Göteborg: Elanders,
    1933.

Gander, G. "Le texte du Nouveau Testament." *Revue de théologie
    et de philosophie* 34 (1946) 153-74.

Gehman, Henry S. "The Hebraic Character of Septuagint Greek."
    Vetus Testamentum 1 (1951) 81-90. Also in *Septuagintal
    Lexicography.* Edited by R. A. Kraft. Septuagint and
    Cognate Studies 1. Missoula: Society of Biblical Litera-
    ture, 1972. Pp. 92-101.

Gignac, Francis T. "Semitic Interference in New Testament
    Greek." *An Introductory New Testament Greek Course.*
    Chicago: Loyola University Press, 1973. Pp. 167-71.

Goguel, Maurice. *Introduction au Nouveau Testament*.   Paris:
     Leroux, 1923.

Gonzaga, M. "Paratactic *kai* in the New Testament." *Classical
     Journal* 21 (1925-26) 580-86.

Goodspeed, Edgar Johnson. "The Origin of Acts." *Journal of
     Biblical Literature* 39 (1920) 83-101.

_____. "The Origin of Acts." *New Solutions of New Testa-
     ment Problems*. Chicago: Chicago University Press, 1927.
     Pp. 65-93.

_____. "The Original Language of the Gospels." *Atlantic
     Monthly* 154 (1934) 474-78.

_____. "The Original Language of the New Testament."
     New Chapters in New Testament Study. New York: Macmillan,
     1937. Pp. 127-68.

_____. "The Possible Aramaic Gospel." *Journal of Near
     Eastern Studies* 1 (1942) 315-40.

Grant, E. L. "Hebrew, Aramaic and the Greek in the Gospels."
     Greece and Rome 20 (1951) 115-22.

Grimme, Hubert. "Studien zum hebräischen Urmatthäus."
     Biblische Zeitschrift 23 (1935-36) 244-65, 347-57.

Haenchen, Ernst. *Der Weg Jesu*. Sammlung Töpelmann 2/6.
     Berlin: A. Töpelmann, 1966.

_____. "Zum Text der Apostelgeschichte." *Zeitschrift für
     Theologie und Kirche* 54 (1957) 22-55.

_____. Review of *The Semitisms of Acts*, by M. Wilcox.
     Theologische Literaturzeitung 91 (1966) 355-57.

Halévy, Joseph. "Notes pour l'évangile de Marc." *Revue
     sémitique* 8 (1900) 115-49.

Harder, Günther. "Miszelle zu 1. Kor 7,17." *Theologische
     Literaturzeitung* 79 (1954) 367-72.

Harris, James Rendel. "The So-Called Biblical Greek." *Exposi-
     tory Times* 25 (1913) 54-55.

Hawkins, John C. *Horae Synopticae*. *Contributions to the Study
     of the Synoptic Problem*. 2nd rev. ed. Oxford: The
     Clarendon Press, 1909.

Heinrici, C. F. Georg. *Der literarische Character der neutesta-
     mentlichen Schriften*. Leipzig: Dürr, 1908.

Helbing, Robert. *Die Kasussyntax der Verba bei den Septuaginta*.
     Göttingen: Vandenhoeck & Ruprecht, 1928.

Higgins, Martin J.   "Greek Language, Biblical." *New Catholic Encyclopedia*. New York: McGraw-Hill, 1967. Vol. 6. Pp. 729-30.

Hilhorst, A.   *Sémitismes et latinismes dans le Pasteur d'Hermas*. Graecitas christianorum primaeva 5. Nijmegen: Dekker & van de Vegt, 1976.

Howard, Wilbert Francis.   "The Language of the New Testament." *A Companion to the Bible*. Edited by T. W. Manson. Edinburgh: T. & T. Clark, 1939. Pp. 23-30.

_____.   "Semitisms in the New Testament." *Accidence and Word-Formation*. Volume 2 of *A Grammar of New Testament Greek*, by James Hope Moulton. Edinburgh: T. & T. Clark, 1929. Pp. 411-85.

Hudson, J. T.   "The Aramaic Basis of St. Mark." *Expository Times* 53 (1941-42) 264-70.

Humbert, Jean.   *La disparition du datif en grec (du Ier au Xe siècle)*. Collection linguistique publiée par la Société de Linguistique de Paris. Paris: Champion, 1930.

Irmscher, Johannes.   "Der Streit um das Bibelgriechisch." *Acta antiquae academiae hungaricae* 7 (1959) 127-34.

Jeremias, Joachim.   "Die aramäische Vorgeschichte unserer Evangelien." *Theologische Literaturzeitung* 74 (1949) 527-32.

_____.   *The Eucharistic Words of Jesus*. Rev. ed. Trans-lated by N. Perrin. New York: Scribner's Sons, 1966.

_____.   "Die Lampe unter dem Scheffel." *Zeitschrift für die neutestamentliche Wissenschaft* 39 (1940) 237-40.

_____.   "Markus 14, 9." *Abba. Studien zur neutestament-lichen Theologie und Zeitgeschichte*. Göttingen: Vanden-hoeck & Ruprecht, 1966. Pp. 115-20.

_____.   "Die Muttersprache des Evangelisten Matthäus." *Zeitschrift für die neutestamentliche Wissenschaft* 50 (1959) 270-74.

_____.   *The Parables of Jesus*. Rev. ed. Translated by S. H. Hooke. London: SCM, 1963.

_____.   "Die Salbungsgeschichte Mk. 14, 3-9." *Zeitschrift für die neutestamentliche Wissenschaft* 35 (1936) 75-82.

_____.   "Zum Gleichnis vom verlorenen Sohn, Luk. 15, 11-32." *Theologische Zeitschrift* 5 (1949) 228-31.

Johannessohn, Martin.   "Die biblische Einführungsformel *kai estai*. *Zeitschrift für die alttestamentliche Wissenschaft* 18 (1942-43) 129-84.

_____. "Das biblische *kai egeneto* und seine Geschichte."
*Zeitschrift für vergleichende Sprachforschung auf dem
Gebiete der indogermanischen Sprachen* 53 (1925) 161-212.

_____. *Der Gebrauch der Kasus und der Präpositionen in
der Septuaginta. I. Gebrauch der Kasus.* Dissertation,
University of Berlin, 1910.

_____. *Der Gebrauch der Präpositionen in der Septuaginta.*
Mitteilung des Septuaginta-Unternehmens 3/3. Berlin:
Weidmann, 1926.

Johnson, Sherman Elbridge. "The Septuagint and the New Testament." *Journal of Biblical Literature* 56 (1937) 331-45.

Johnston, George. "The Biblical Languages. (B) The Language
of the New Testament." *A Companion to the Bible.* 2nd ed.
Edited by H. H. Rowley. Edinburgh: T. & T. Clark, 1963.
Pp. 19-25.

Joüon, Paul. *L'Evangile de Nôtre Seigneur Jésus-Christ:
Traduction et commentaire.* Verbum salutis 5. Paris:
Beauchesne, 1930.

_____. "Notes philologiques sur les Evangiles."
Recherches de science religieuse 17 (1927) 537-40; 18
(1928) 345-59, 499-502.

_____. "Quelques aramaïsmes sousjacents au grec des
Evangiles." *Recherches de science religieuse* 17 (1927)
210-29.

Katz, Peter. "Zur Übersetzungstechnik der Septuaginta." *Welt
des Orients* 2 (1954-56) 267-73.

Kaupel, Heinrich. "Beobachtungen zur Überzetzung des Infinitivus absolutus in der Septuaginta (G)." *Zeitschrift für
die alttestamentliche Wissenschaft* 20 (1945-48) 191-92.

Kieckers, Ernst. *Die Stellung des Verbs im Griechischen und
in den verwandten Sprachen.* Strassburg: K. J. Trübner,
1911.

Kilpatrick, George Dunbar. "Atticism and the Text of the
Greek New Testament." *Neutestamentliche Aufsätze.* Fest-
schrift J. Schmid. Edited by J. Blinzler, O. Kuss, and
F. Mussner. Regensburg: F. Pustet, 1963. Pp. 125-37.

_____. "Language and Text in the Gospels and Acts."
Vigiliae christianae 24 (1970) 161-71.

_____. "The Order of Some Noun and Adjective Phrases."
Novum Testamentum 5 (1962) 111-14.

_____. "The Order of Some Noun and Adjective Phrases
in the New Testament." *The Bible Translator* 16 (1965)
117-19.

_____. "The Possessive Pronouns in the New Testament."
Journal of Theological Studies 42 (1941) 184-86.

_____. "Some Problems in New Testament Text and Language."
Neotestamentica et semitica. Festschrift M. Black.
Edited by E. E. Ellis and M. Wilcox. Edinburgh: T. & T.
Clark, 1969. Pp. 198-208.

_____. "Style and Text in the Greek New Testament."
Studies in the History and Text of the New Testament.
Festschrift K. W. Clark. Edited by B. L. Daniels and
M. J. Suggs. Studies and Documents 29. Salt Lake City:
University of Utah Press, 1967. Pp. 153-60.

_____. "Western Text and Original Text in the Epistles."
Journal of Theological Studies 45 (1944) 60-65.

_____. "Western Text and Original Text in the Gospels
and Acts." *Journal of Theological Studies* 44 (1943)
24-36.

_____. "What John Tells Us about John." *Studies in John.*
Festschrift J. N. Sevenster. *Novum Testamentum,* Supplement 24. Leiden: Brill, 1970. Pp. 75-87.

Lagrange, Marie-Joseph. *Evangile selon Saint Jean.* 3rd rev.
ed. Etudes bibliques. Paris: Gabalda, 1927.

_____. *Evangile selon Saint Luc.* Etudes bibliques.
Paris: Gabalda, 1927.

_____. *Evangile selon Saint Marc.* Etudes bibliques.
Paris: Gabalda, 1929.

_____. *Evangile selon Saint Matthieu.* Etudes bibliques.
Paris: Gabalda, 1927.

Lamsa, George Mamishisho. *The Four Gospels, According to the
Eastern Version.* Philadelphia: A. J. Holman, 1933.

Lattey, Cuthbert. "The Semitisms of the Fourth Gospel."
Journal of Theological Studies 29 (1919) 330-36.

Le Déaut, Roger. "Le substrat araméen des évangiles: Scolies
en marge de l'*Aramaic Approach* de Matthew Black." *Biblica*
49 (1968) 388-99.

Lee, G. M. "Casus pendens." *Expository Times* 64 (1952-53) 189.

_____. "πᾶς οὐ for οὐδείς, and Similar Usages." *Exposi-
tory Times* 63 (1951-52) 156.

Lefort, Louis Théophile. "Pour une grammaire des Septante."
Le Muséon 41 (1928) 152-60.

_____. Review of *Grammaire du grec biblique suivie d'un
choix de papyrus,* by F. M. Abel. *Le Muséon* 41 (1928)
152-60.

Lifshitz, Baruch. "L'hellénisation des Juifs de Palestine."
    Revue biblique 72 (1965) 520-38.

Lindsey, Robert Lisle. *A Hebrew Translation of the Gospel of
    St. Mark.* Jerusalem: Dugith, 1969.

Littmann, Enno. "Torreys Buch über die vier Evangelien."
    Zeitschrift für die neutestamentliche Wissenschaft 34
    (1935) 20-34.

Ljungvik, Herman. "Aus der Sprache des Neuen Testaments."
    Eranos 66 (1968) 24-51.

_____. *Beiträge zur Syntax der spätgriechischen Volks-
    sprache.* Skrifter utgivna av kungl. humanistiska
    Vetenskaps-Samfundet 27. Uppsala: Almqvist & Wiksell,
    1932.

_____. "Einige Bemerkungen zur spätgriechischen Syntax."
    Aegyptus 13 (1933) 159-68.

_____. *Studien zur Sprache der apokryphen Apostelgeschich-
    ten.* Dissertation, Uppsala, 1926.

Mandilaras, Basil G. *The Verb in the Greek Non-literary
    Papyri.* Athens: Hellenic Ministry of Culture and
    Sciences, 1973.

Manson, Thomas Walter. "Some Outstanding New Testament Prob-
    lems. XII. The Problem of Aramaic Sources in the
    Gospels." *Expository Times* 47 (1935-36) 7-11.

_____. *The Teaching of Jesus.* Cambridge: Cambridge
    University Press, 1931.

_____. Review of *An Aramaic Approach to the Gospels and
    Acts,* by Matthew Black. *Journal of Theological Studies*
    48 (1947) 219-21.

Marcus, Ralph. "Notes on Torrey's Translation of the Gospels."
    Harvard Theological Review 27 (1934) 211-39.

Margolis, Max Leopold. "The Particle ἦ in Old Testament Greek."
    American Journal of Semitic Languages and Literature 25
    (1908-09) 257-75.

Marshall, John Turner, "The Aramaic Gospel." *Expositor* 4/3
    (1891) 1-17, 109-24, 205-20, 275-91, 375-90, 452-67; 4
    (1891) 208-23, 373-88, 435-48; 6 (1892) 81-97; 8 (1893)
    176-92.

_____. "Did St. Paul Use a Semitic Gospel?" *Expositor*
    4/2 (1890) 69-80.

Martin, Raymond A. "Some Syntactical Criteria of Translation
    Greek." *Vetus Testamentum* 10 (1960) 295-310.

_____. "Syntactical Evidence of Aramaic Sources in Acts
    i-xv." *New Testament Studies* 11 (1964-65) 38-59.

_____. *Syntactical Evidence of Semitic Sources in Greek Documents*. Society of Biblical Literature Septuagint and Cognate Studies 3. Missoula: Society of Biblical Literature, 1974.

_____. "Syntax Criticism of the LXX Additions to the Book of Esther." *JBL* 94 (1975) 65-72.

McCown, Chester Charlton. "Aramaic and Greek Gospels." *Anglican Theological Review* 25 (1943) 282-94.

McKnight, Edgar V. "Is the New Testament Written in 'Holy Ghost' Greek?" *The Bible Translator* 16 (1965) 87-93.

_____. "The New Testament and 'Biblical Greek.'" *Journal of Bible and Religion* 34 (1966) 36-42.

McNeile, Alan Hugh. *An Introduction to the Study of the New Testament*. 2nd ed. Revised by C. S. C. Williams. Oxford: The Clarendon Press, 1955.

Meecham, Henry George. *Epistle to Diognetus*. Manchester: Manchester University Press, 1949.

_____. *Light from Ancient Letters*. London: Allen & Unwin, 1923.

Menoud, Phillippe Henri. "The Western Text and the Theology of Acts." *Bulletin of the Studiorum Novi Testamenti Societas* 2 (1951) 19-32.

Metzger, Bruce M. "The Language of the New Testament." *The Interpreter's Bible*. Edited by G. A. Buttrick. New York: Abingdon-Cokesbury Press, 1951-57. Vol. 7. Pp. 43-59.

Michaelis, Wilhelm. "Der Attizismus und das Neue Testament." *Zeitschrift für die neutestamentliche Wissenshcaft* 22 (1923) 91-121.

Montgomery, James Alan. *The Origin of the Gospel According to St. John*. Philadelphia: Winston, 1923.

_____. "Some Aramaisms in the Gospels and Acts." *Journal of Biblical Literature* 46 (1927) 69-73.

_____. "Torrey's Aramaic Gospels." *Journal of Biblical Literature* 53 (1934) 79-99.

Moule, Charles Francis Digby. *The Birth of the New Testament*. Harper's New Testament Commentaries. New York: Harper & Row, 1962.

_____. *An Idiom Book of New Testament Greek*. 2nd rev. ed. Cambridge: Cambridge University Press, 1959.

_____. *The Language of the New Testament*. Cambridge: Cambridge University Press, 1952.

Moulton, James Hope. "Characteristics of New Testament Greek."
    Expositor 6/9 (1904) 67-75, 215-25, 310-20, 359-68; 10
    (1904) 124-34, 168-74, 276-83, 353-64, 440-50.

_____. *Einleitung in die Sprache des Neuen Testaments.*
    Indogermanische Bibliothek 1/9. Heidelberg: Winter, 1911.

_____. "Grammatical Notes from the Papyri." *Classical
    Review* 15 (1901) 31-37, 434-42; 18 (1904) 106-12, 151-55.

_____. *Introduction to the Study of New Testament Greek.*
    Revised by H. G. Meecham. London: Epworth, 1955.

_____. "New Testament Greek in the Light of Modern Dis-
    covery." *Essays on Some Biblical Questions of the Day
    (Cambridge Biblical Essays).* Edited by H. B. Swete.
    London: Macmillan, 1909. Pp. 461-505.

Munck, Johannes. *The Acts of the Apostles.* Revised by W. F.
    Albright and C. S. Mann. Anchor Bible. Garden City, NY:
    Doubleday, 1967.

_____. "Deux notes sur la langue du Nouveau Testament."
    Classica et mediaevalia 5 (1943) 187-208.

_____. "Deux notes sur la langue du Nouveau Testament.
    2) Les Sémitismes dans le Nouveau Testament. Réflexions
    méthodologiques." *Classica et mediaevalia* 6 (1944) 110-50.

Nachmanson, Ernst. Review of *Grammatik des neutestamentlichen
    Griechisch,* by F. Blass. *Gnomon* 8 (1932) 550-52.

Naish, I. B. "The Semitic Background of the Gospels." *Inter-
    pretation* 19 (1922-23) 288-97.

Neirynck, F. *Duality in Mark. Contributions to the Study of
    the Markan Redaction.* Bibliotheca *Ephemerides theologicae
    lovanienses* 31. Louvain: University Press, 1972.

Nestle, Eberhard. "Some Observations on the Codex Bezae."
    Expositor 5/2 (1895) 235-40.

Norden, Eduard. *Agnostos Theos. Untersuchungen zur Formen-
    geschichte religiöser Rede.* Berlin: B. G. Teubner, 1913.
    Reprinted Stuttgart: Teubner, 1956.

_____. *Antike Kunstprosa vom vi. Jahrhundert vor Christi
    bis in die Zeit der Renaissance.* Leipzig: B. G. Teubner,
    1915. Reprinted Darmstadt: Wissenschaftliche Buchgesell-
    schaft, 1958.

Nyberg, Henrik Samuel. "Zum grammatischen Verständnis von
    Mt 12,44f." *Coniectanea neotestamentica* 2 (1936) 22-35.

Olmstead, Albert T. "Could an Aramaic Gospel Be Written?"
    Journal of Near Eastern Studies 1 (1942) 41-75.

Ottley, Richard Rusden. *A Handbook to the Septuagint.* London:
    Methuen, 1920.

Pax, Elpidius. "Probleme des neutestamentlichen Griechisch."
    Biblica 53 (1972) 557-64.

_____. "Die syntaktischen Semitismen im Neuen Testament.
    Eine gründsätzliche Erwägung." *Studii biblici franciscani
    liber annuus* 13 (1962-63) 136-62.

Pelletier, André. "*Sabbata*. Transcription grecque de
    l'araméen." *Vetus Testamentum* 22 (1972) 436-47.

Pernot, Hubert. "La construction de *kai egeneto* dans les
    Evangiles." *Revue d'histoire et de philosophie religieuses*
    4 (1924) 553-58.

_____. "Greek and the Gospels." *Expository Times* 38
    (1926-27) 103-108.

_____. "Observations sur la langue de la Septante."
    Revue des Etudes Grecques 42 (1929) 411-25.

_____. *Pages choisies des Evangiles*. Collection de
    l'institut néo-hellénique 2. Paris: Belles Lettres, 1925.

_____. *Recherches sur le texte original des Evangiles*.
    Collection de l'institut néo-hellénique 4. Paris: Belles
    Lettres, 1938.

_____. *Remarques sur les évangiles*. Mededelingen der
    koninklijke Nederlandse Akademie van Wetenschappen, afd.
    Letterkunde, Deel 57, Ser. A, No. 5. Amsterdam: no
    publisher, 1924.

Psichari, Jean. "Essai sur le grec de la Septante." *Revue
    des études juives* 55 (1908) 161-208.

Rabin, Chaim. "The Translation Process and the Character of
    the Septuagint." *Textus* 6 (1968) 1-26.

Radermacher, Ludwig. "Besonderheiten der Koine Syntax."
    Wiener Studien 31 (1909) 1-12.

_____. Review of *Einleitung in die Sprache des Neuen
    Testaments*, by J. H. Moulton. *Indogermanische Forschung*
    31 (1912-13) Anz. 6-10.

Redpath, Henry Adney. "The Present Position of the Study of
    the Septuagint." *American Journal of Theology* 7 (1903)
    1-19.

Riddle, Donald Wayne. "The Aramaic Gospels and the Synoptic
    Problem." *Journal of Biblical Literature* 54 (1935) 127-38.

_____. "The Logic of the Theory of Translation Greek."
    Journal of Biblical Literature 51 (1932) 13-30.

Rife, John Merle. "The Mechanics of Translation Greek."
    Journal of Biblical Literature 52 (1933) 244-52.

Rinaldi, Giovanni. "Postille semitistiche." *Aegyptus* 29
    (1949) 91-101.

Roberts, J. W. "Exegetical Helps: The Greek Noun with and
    without the Article." *Restoration Quarterly* 14 (1971)
    28-44.

_____. "The Language Background of the New Testament."
    Restoration Quarterly 5 (1961) 193-204.

_____. "Some Aspects of Conditional Sentences in the
    Greek New Testament." *The Bible Translator* 15 (1964)
    70-76.

Robertson, Archibald Thomas. "Language of the New Testament."
    International Standard Bible Encyclopedia. Grand Rapids:
    W. B. Eerdmans, 1939. Vol. 3. Pp. 1826-32.

Rohr, J. "Der Sprachgebrauch des Markusevangeliums und der
    'Markus-apokalypse.'" *Theologische Quartalschrift* 89
    (1907) 507-36.

Ros, Jan. *De Studie van het Bijbelgrieksch van H. Grotius tot
    A. Deissmann*. Nijmegen: Dekker & van de Vegt, 1940.

Rudberg, Gunnar. "Främmande egennamn i grekiskan." *Teologiska
    Studier*. Uppsala: Almqvist & Wiksell, 1922. Pp. 184-93.

Rydbeck, Lars. *Fachprosa, vermeintliche Volkssprache und Neues
    Testament*. Acta Universitatis Upsaliensis, Studia Graeca
    Upsaliensia 5. Stockholm: Almqvist & Wiksell, 1967.

_____. "What Happened to New Testament Greek Grammar after
    Albert Debrunner?" *New Testament Studies* 21 (1974-75)
    557-64.

Sacco, Giuseppe. *La Koinè del Nuovo Testamento e la trasmissione
    del sacro testo*. Rome: Ferrari, 1928.

Schlatter, Adolf von. *Der Evangelist Matthaus*. Stuttgart:
    Calwer, 1929.

_____. *Sprache und Heimat des vierten Evangelisten*.
    Gutersloh: Bertelsmann, 1902.

Schmid, Josef. "Aramaismen." *Lexicon für Theologie und Kirche*.
    Freiburg: Herder, 1957. Vol. 1. Pp. 798-99.

_____. *Studien zur Geschichte des griechischen Apokalypse-
    Textes*. Munich: Zink, 1956.

Schürmann, Heinz. "Die Semitismen im Einsetzungsbericht bei
    Markus und bei Lukas (Mk 14, 22-24/Lk 22, 19-20)."
    Zeitschrift für katholische Theologie 73 (1951) 72-77.

_____. "Die Sprache des Christus. Sprachliche Beobach-
    tungen an den synoptischen Herrenworten." *Biblische
    Zeitschrift* 2 (1958) 54-84.

Schulthess, Friedrich. *Das Problem der Sprache Jesu.* Zürich: Schulthess, 1917.

_____. "Zur Sprache der Evangelien." *Zeitschrift für die neutestamentliche Wissenschaft* 21 (1922) 216-36, 241-58.

Schweizer, Eduard. "Eine hebraisierenden Sonderquelle des Lukas?" *Theologische Zeitschrift* 6 (1950) 161-85.

Scott, Charles Archibald. "An Aramaic Source for Acts i.-xv." *Expository Times* 31 (1919-20) 220-23.

Scott, Robert Balgarnie Young. *The Original Language of the Apocalypse.* Toronto: University of Toronto Press, 1928.

Sharp, Douglas Simmonds. *Epictetus and the New Testament.* London: Kelly, 1914.

Simcox, William Henry. *The Language of the New Testament.* New York: T. Whittaker, 1890.

Smith, Morton. "Aramaic Studies and the Study of the New Testament." *Journal of Bible and Religion* 26 (1958) 304-13.

Sparks, Hedley Frederick Davis. "The Semitisms of Acts." *Journal of Theological Studies* 1 (1950) 16-28.

_____. "The Semitisms of St. Luke's Gospel." *Journal of Theological Studies* 44 (1943) 129-38.

_____. "Some Observations on the Semitic Background of the New Testament." *Bulletin of the Studiorum Novi Testamenti Societas* 2 (1951) 33-43.

Springhetti, Emilio. *Introductio historica-grammatica in graecitatem Novi Testamenti.* Rome: Gregorian University, 1966.

Steyer, Gottfried. *PROS PĒGĒN ODOS. Handbuch für das Studium des neutestamentlichen Griechisch. II. Satzlehre.* Berlin: Evangelische Verlagsanstalt, 1968.

Swete, Henry Barclay. *The Apocalypse of St. John.* London: Macmillan, 1907.

_____. *The Gospel According to St. Mark.* 3rd ed. London: Macmillan and Company, 1909.

_____. *An Introduction to the Old Testament in Greek.* 2nd rev. ed. Edited by R. R. Ottley. Cambridge: Cambridge University Press, 1914.

Tabachovitz, David. *Etudes sur le grec de la basse époque.* Skrifter utgivna av kungl. humanistiska Vetenskaps-Samfundet i Uppsala 36/3. Uppsala: Almqvist & Wiksell, 1943.

_____. *Die Septuaginta und das Neue Testament.* Skrifter utgivna av Svenska Institut i Athen. Lund: Gleerup, 1956.

Tarelli, Charles Camp. "Some Linguistic Aspects of the Chester
    Beatty Papyrus of the Gospels." *Journal of Theological
    Studies* 39 (1938) 254-59.

Taylor, Vincent. *The Gospel According to St. Mark.* 2nd ed.
    London: Macmillan and Company, 1966.

Taylor, William Robert. "Aramaic Gospel-Sources and Form-
    Criticism." *Expository Times* 49 (1937-38) 55-59.

Thomson, John Ebenezer Honeyman. "Did Jesus Speak Greek or
    Aramaic? A Reply." *Interpretation* 11 (1914-15) 75-82.

Thumb, Albert. "Wortstellung." *Griechische Grammatik*, by
    K. Brugmann. 4th ed. Revised by A. Thumb. Munich:
    Beck, 1913. Pp. 658-76.

Torrey, Charles Cutler. "The Aramaic of the Gospels." *Journal
    of Biblical Literature* 61 (1942) 71-85.

_____. "The Aramaic Origin of the Gospel of John."
    Harvard Theological Review 16 (1923) 305-44.

_____. *The Composition and Date of Acts.* Harvard
    Theological Studies 1. Cambridge, MA: Harvard University
    Press, 1916.

_____. "The Date of the Crucifixion according to the
    Fourth Gospel." *Journal of Biblical Literature* 50 (1931)
    227-41.

_____. *Documents of the Primitive Church.* New York:
    Harper, 1941.

_____. *The Four Gospels: A New Translation.* New York:
    Harper, 1933.

_____. "Julius Wellhausen's Approach to the Aramaic
    Gospels." *Zeitschrift der deutschen morgenländischen
    Gesellschaft* 101 (1951) 125-37.

_____. *Our Translated Gospels. Some of the Evidence.*
    New York: Harper, 1936.

_____. "The Translations Made from the Original Aramaic
    Gospels." *Studies in the History of Religions, Presented
    to C. H. Toy.* New York: Macmillan, 1912. Pp. 269-317.

Turner, Cuthbert Hamilton. "Marcan Usage: Notes, Critical
    and Exegetical, on the Second Gospel." *Journal of Theolog-
    ical Studies* 25 (1923-24) 377-86; 26 (1924-25) 12-20,
    145-56, 225-40, 337-46; 27 (1925-26) 58-62; 28 (1926-27)
    9-30, 349-62; 29 (1927-28) 275-89, 346-61.

Turner, Nigel. *Grammatical Insights into the New Testament.*
    Edinburgh: T. & T. Clark, 1966.

_____. "The Language of the New Testament." *Peake's Commentary on the Bible*. Edited by Matthew Black and H. H. Rowley. London: Nelson, 1962. Pp. 659-62.

_____. "The Literary Character of New Testament Greek." *New Testament Studies* 20 (1973-74) 107-14.

_____. "Philology in New Testament Studies." *Expository Times* 71 (1959-60) 104-107.

_____. "The Quality of the Greek of Luke-Acts." *Studies in New Testament Language and Text*. Edited by J. K. Elliott. *Novum Testamentum*, Supplement 44. Leiden: Brill, 1976. Pp. 387-400.

_____. "The Relation of Luke i and ii to the Hebraic Sources and to the Rest of Luke-Acts." *New Testament Studies* 2 (1955-56) 100-109.

_____. "Second Thoughts VII: Papyrus Finds." *Expository Times* 76 (1964-65) 44-48.

_____. "The Style of St. Mark's Eucharistic Words." *Journal of Theological Studies* 8 (1957) 108-11.

_____. "The 'Testament of Abraham': Problems in Biblical Greek." *New Testament Studies* 1 (1954-55) 219-23.

_____. "The Unique Character of Biblical Greek." *Vetus Testamentum* 5 (1955) 208-13.

Unnik, Willem Cornelis van. "Aramaisms in Paul." *Sparsa collecta. The Collected Essays of W. C. van Unnik*. *Novum Testamentum*, Supplement 29. Leiden: Brill, 1973. Pp. 129-43.

Uricchio, Francesco M., and Stano, Gaetano M. *Vangelo secondo San Marco*. La Sacra Bibbia. Rome: Marietti, 1966.

Vazakas, A. A. "Is Acts i-xv. 35 a Literal Translation from an Aramaic Original?" *Journal of Biblical Literature* 37 (1918) 105-10.

Vergote, Joseph. "Grec biblique." *Dictionnaire de la Bible. Supplément*. Paris: Librairie Letouzey et Ané, 1938. Vol. 3. Cols. 1320-69.

Viteau, Joseph. *Etude sur le grec du Nouveau Testament comparé avec celui des Septante. Sujet, complément et attribut*. Paris: Bouillon, 1896.

_____. *Etude sur le grec du Nouveau Testament. Le verbe; Syntaxe des prepositions*. Paris: Bouillon, 1893.

Vogt, Ernst. "Hat 'šabbāt' im Alten Testament den Sinn von 'Woche'?" *Biblica* 40 (1959) 1008-11.

Watson, M. "The Semitic Element in New Testament Greek." *Restoration Quarterly* 10 (1967) 225-30.

Wellhausen, Julius. *Einleitung in das Neue Testament.* Berlin: G. Reimer, 1911.

_____. *Das Evangelium Johannis.* Berlin: G. Reimer, 1908.

_____. *Evangelium Lucae.* Berlin: G. Reimer, 1904.

_____. *Evangelium Marci.* Berlin: G. Reimer, 1903.

_____. *Evangelium Matthaei.* Berlin: G. Reimer, 1904.

Wensinck, Arent Jan. "Un groupe d'aramaïsmes dan le texte grec des évangiles." *Mededelingen der koninklijke Akademie van Wetenschappen, Afdeeling Letterkundge* 81/5 (1936) 169-80.

_____. "The Semitisms of Codex Bezae and Their Relation to the Non-Western Text of the Gospel of Saint Luke." *Bulletin of the Bezan Club* (1937) 11-48.

Wernberg-Møller, Preben. "A Semitic Idiom in Matt. v. 22." *New Testament Studies* 3 (1956-57) 71-73.

Wifstrand, Albert. "Lukas och den griekiska klassicismen." *Svensk exegetisk årsbok* 5 (1940) 139-51.

_____. "Lukas och Septuaginta." *Svensk teologisk kvartalskrift* 16 (1940) 243-62.

_____. "A Problem Concerning the Word Order in the New Testament." *Studia theologica* 3 (1949) 172-84.

_____. "Stylistic Problems in the Epistles of James and Peter." *Studia theologica* 1 (1948) 170-82.

Wilcox, Max. *The Semitisms of Acts.* Oxford: The Clarendon Press, 1965.

Wilson, W. J. "Some Observations on the Aramaic Acts." *Harvard Theological Review* 11 (1918) 74-99.

Winter, P. "Some Observations on the Language in the Birth and Infancy Stories of the Third Gospel." *New Testament Studies* 1 (1954-55) 111-21.

Wohleb, Leo. "Beobachtungen zur Erzählungsstil des Markusevangeliums." *Römischer Quartalschrift* 36 (1928) 185-96.

Young, J. "Language of Christ." *A Dictionary of Christ and the Gospels.* Edited by J. Hastings. New York: Scribners, 1908. Vol. 2. Pp. 3-5.

Zeitlin, Solomon. "Aramaic Gospels in the Synagogue." *Jewish Quarterly Review* 32 (1941-42) 427-31.

Zerwick, Maximilian. *Untersuchungen zum Markusstil.* Rome: Biblical Institute, 1937.

Ziegler, Joseph. "Bibelgriechisch." *Lexikon für Theologie und Kirche.* 2nd rev. ed. Edited by J. Höfer and K. Rahner. Freiburg: Herder, 1957-58. Cols. 349-50.

Zwaan, J. de. "The Use of the Greek Language in Acts." *The Beginnings of Christianity.* Edited by F. J. Foakes-Jackson and K. Lake. London: Macmillan, 1922. Vol. 2. Part 1. Pp. 30-65.

_____. "John Wrote in Aramaic." *Journal of Biblical Literature* 57 (1938) 155-71.

Languages of First-Century Palestine

Altheim, Franz, and Stiehl, Ruth. "Jesus der Galiläer." *Die Araber in der alten Welt.* Berlin: W. de Gruyter, 1966. Vol. 3. Pp. 74-97.

Argyle, Aubrey William. "Did Jesus Speak Greek?" *Expository Times* 67 (1955-56) 92-93, 383.

_____. "Greek among the Jews of Palestine in New Testament Times." *New Testament Studies* 20 (1974) 87-89.

Bardy, Gustave. *La question des langues dans l'église ancienne.* Etudes de théologie historique. Paris: Beauchesne, 1948.

Barr, James. "Which Language Did Jesus Speak? -- Some Remarks of a Semitist." *Bulletin of the John Rylands University Library of Manchester* 53 (1971) 9-29.

Birkeland, Harris. *The Language of Jesus.* Avhandl. utg. av det Norske Videnskaps-Akademi 2/1. Oslo: Dybwad, 1954.

Black, Matthew. "Die Erforschung der Muttersprache Jesu." *Theologische Literaturzeitung* 82 (1957) 654-67.

Cantineau, Jean. "Quelle langue parlait le peuple en Palestine au 1er siècle de notre ère?" *Semitica* 5 (1955) 99-101.

Chomsky, William. "What Was the Jewish Vernacular during the Second Commonwealth?" *Jewish Quarterly Review* 42 (1951-52) 193-212.

Díez Macho, Alexandro. "La lengua hablada por Jesucristo." *Oriens antiquus* 2 (1963) 95-132.

Draper, H. M. "Did Jesus speak Greek?" *Expository Times* 67 (1956) 317.

Driver, Samuel Rolles. "Son of Man." *Dictionary of the Bible.* Edited by J. Hastings. Edinburgh: T. & T. Clark, 1898-1904. Vol. 4. Pp. 578-89.

Emerton, John Adney. "Did Jesus Speak Hebrew?" *Journal of Theological Studies* 12 (1961) 189-202.

_____. "The Problem of Vernacular Hebrew in the First Century A.D. and the Language of Jesus." *Journal of Theological Studies* 24 (1973) 1-23.

Fitzmyer, Joseph A. "The Languages of Palestine in the First Century A.D." *Catholic Biblical Quarterly* 32 (1970) 501-31.

Grintz, Jehoshua M. "Hebrew as the Spoken and Written Language in the Last Days of the Second Temple." *Journal of Biblical Literature* 79 (1960) 32-47.

Gundry, Robert H. "The Language Milieu of First-Century Palestine. Its Bearing on the Authenticity of the Gospel Tradition." *Journal of Biblical Literature* 83 (1964) 404-408.

James, John Courtenay. *The Language of Palestine and Adjacent Regions.* Edinburgh: T. & T. Clark, 1920.

Kahle, Paul. "Das palästinische Pentateuchtargum und das zur Zeit Jesu gesprochene Aramäisch." *Zeitschrift für die neutestamentliche Wissenschaft* 49 (1958) 100-16.

_____. "Das zur Zeit Jesu in Palästina gesprochene Aramäisch." *Theologische Rundschau* 17 (1949) 201-16.

Kittel, Gerhard. "Der geschichtliche Ort des Jacobusbriefes." *Zeitschrift für die neutestamentliche Wissenschaft* 41 (1942) 71-105.

Kutscher, Eduard Yechezkel. "Das zur Zeit Jesu gesprochene Aramäisch." *Zeitschrift für die neutestamentliche Wissenschaft* 51 (1960) 46-54.

Lieberman, Saul. *How Much Greek in Jewish Palestine?* Waltham, MA: Brandeis University Press, 1963.

Lifshitz, Baruch. "Papyrus grecs du désert de Juda." *Aegyptus* 42 (1962) 240-56.

Metzger, Bruce M. "The Languages Current in Palestine." *The New Testament. Its Background, Growth, and Content.* New York: Abingdon Press, 1965. Pp. 32-33.

Meyer, Arnold. *Jesu Muttersprache: Das galiläische Aramäisch in seiner Bedeutung für die Erklärung der Reden Jesu und der Evangelien überhaupt.* Freiburg: J. C. B. Mohr, 1896.

Morag, Solomon. "Until When Was Hebrew Spoken?" [Hebrew] *Leshonenu* 7-8 (1956) 3-10.

Nepper-Christensen, Paul. "Die sprachlichen Verhältnisse zu Beginn unserer Zeitrechnung." *Das Mattäusevangelium: Ein judenchristliches Evangelium?* Acta theologica danica 1. Aarhus: University of Aarhus, 1958. Pp. 101-35.

Ott, H. "Um die Muttersprache Jesu Forschungen seit Gustaf Dalman." *Novum Testamentum* 9 (1967) 1-25.

Patterson, Samuel W. "What Language Did Jesus Speak?"
    Classical Outlook 23 (1946) 65-67.

Rabinowitz, I. "'Be Opened' = 'Εφφαθά (Mark 7. 34): Did
    Jesus Speak Hebrew?" *Zeitschrift für die neutestamentliche
    Wissenschaft* 53 (1962) 229-38.

_____. "'Εφφαθά (Mark VII. 34): Certainly Hebrew, not
    Aramaic." *Journal of Semitic Studies* 16 (1971) 151-56.

Rood, L. "Heeft Jezus Grieks gesproken?" *Streven* 2 (1949)
    1026-35.

Segert, Stanislaus. "Aramäische Studien. II. Zur Verbreitung
    des Aramäischen in Palästina zur Zeit Jesu." *Archiv
    orientální* 25 (1957) 21-37.

Sevenster, Jan Nicolaas. *Do You Know Greek? How Much Greek
    Could the First Jewish Christians Have Known? Novum
    Testamentum*, Supplement 19. Leiden: Brill, 1968.

Taylor, Robert Oswald Patrick. "Did Jesus Speak Aramaic?"
    Expository Times 56 (1944-45) 95-97.

_____. *The Groundwork of the Gospels*. Oxford: B. Black-
    well & Company, 1946.

Weir, Thomas Hunter. "Did Jesus Speak Greek or Aramaic?"
    Interpretation 10 (1913-14) 404-10.

Wilson, Robert McLachlan. "Did Jesus Speak Greek?" *Expository
    Times* 68 (1956-57) 121-22.

Yadin, Yigael. "The Expedition to the Judean Desert, 1960:
    Expedition D." *Israel Exploration Journal* 11 (1961)
    36-52.

I. INDEX OF MODERN AUTHORS

Burney, C. F., 12, 30.

Burrows, M., 12, 13, 30.

Bussby, F., 223.

Cadbury, H. J., 14, 31.

Carmignac, J., 224.

Charles, R. H., 15, 31.

Chase, F. H., 47.

Chomsky, W., 48.

Colpe, C., 233, 234.

Colwell, E. C., 5, 14, 15, 31, 37, 197, 202-205, 208, 213, 237.

Conybeare, F. C., 202.

Cortes, J. B., 233.

Cullmann, O., 221.

Dalman, G., 1, 11, 13, 15, 18, 20, 29, 30, 47, 50, 201, 216, 223,
    225, 226, 232.

David, J.-E., 200.

Debrunner, A., 18, 32, 223.

Deissmann, A., 1, 2, 7-11, 14, 16, 27, 28, 202.

Delcor, M., 49.

Descamps, A., 49, 222.

Diez Macho, A., 43, 48, 49.

Dormeyer, D., 200.

Doudna, J. C., 22, 23, 33, 163, 212, 216, 223, 225, 228, 236,
    239, 240.

Drijvers, H. J. W., 49, 50.

Driver, S. R., 211.

Dürr, L., 215.

Dupont, J., 34, 200.

Dupont-Sommer, A., 224.

Emerton, J. A., 48, 200.

Finegan, J., 224.

Fitzmyer, J. A., 1, 24, 25, 34, 41-43, 47-49, 199, 211, 213, 219,
    233-35, 238.

Foakes-Jackson, F. J., 30.

Follieri, H., 225.

Formesyn, R. E. C., 233.

Fridrichsen, A., 232.

Frisk, H., 51, 197.

Fuller, R. H., 200.

Funk, R. W., 18.

Schweizer, E., 234.

Schwyzer, E., 47, 197, 198, 205, 211, 217, 219, 220, 222, 223, 225, 227, 228, 230, 231, 236, 237, 239-241.

Scott, R. B. Y., 12.

Segal, M., 40, 211, 214.

Segert, S., 198, 214.

Sjöberg, E., 233, 234.

Smith, M., 47.

Smyth, H. W., 180, 198, 204, 206, 209-213, 217, 219, 220, 225-228, 231, 236, 237, 239, 241.

Sophocles, E. A., 225.

Springhetti, A., 5.

Stern, L., 217, 226, 229.

Stock, St. G., 202.

Strachan, L. R. M., 27.

Swete, H. B., 9, 16, 28, 31, 212, 218, 225, 230.

Taylor, V., 21, 33, 201, 204, 212, 213, 218-220, 225, 228, 230, 232, 236.

Thackeray, H. St. J., 9, 28, 214, 219, 232, 237, 238.

Thumb, A., 1, 8-11, 16, 17, 27, 28, 31, 51, 197.

Tiede, D. L., 47.

Till, W. C., 217, 226.

Tischendorf, C. von, 35.

Torm, F., 239.

Torrey, C. C., 12, 14, 15, 20, 21, 29, 30, 47.

Traub, H., 191, 239.

Turner, C. H., 220.

Turner, N., 5, 20, 21, 32, 33, 47, 112, 126, 134, 144, 163, 167, 184, 202, 210, 213-217, 219, 220, 222, 223, 226-228, 230, 236-240.

Vergote, J., 5, 7, 11, 16-18, 27, 29, 31, 32, 38, 212, 214, 218, 226, 229, 236.

Vermes, G., 224, 233, 234.

Viteau, J., 8, 28.

Vööbus, A., 50.

Vogt, E., 49, 232, 234, 236, 240.

Wackernagel, J., 29, 228.

Walker, R. J., 225.

Wellhausen, J., 1, 11, 18, 20, 29, 104, 105, 112-114, 240.

Wensinck, A. J., 18, 19, 32, 35.

Wescott-Hort, 35, 202.

A. Hebrew

  1. Biblical Hebrew

3. Proto-Mishnaic Hebrew

3. Biblical Aramaic

4:16	105, 109, 201	5:37	93, 95
4:18	105, 109, 201	5:39	77
4:19	201	5:40	201
4:20	69, 105, 105, 150, 152, 199, 201, 203, 250	5:41	159, 162, 227, 250
4:21	105, 109	5:42	185, 186, 188, 199, 251
4:22	93, 96, 98, 99, 248	6:4	93, 96, 98, 99, 248
4:23	210	6:5	93, 95, 199
4:24	77	6:7	47, 152, 154, 199, 245, 250
4:25	87, 88, 90, 99, 104, 210, 247, 248	6:8	93, 95
		6:10	210
4:26	105, 105, 131, 134, 135, 249	6:11	104, 210
		6:13	182, 199
4:27	69	6:15	127, 130, 216, 218
4:28	77		
4:30	181	6:16	87, 88, 90, 247
4:32	190, 199, 239	6:17	113, 114, 116, 213, 214, 248
4:33	199		
4:34	199, 201	6:19	201
4:37	199	6:20	199, 201
4:38	105, 109, 247	6:22	69, 113, 114, 201, 210, 213, 248
4:39	77, 199, 247		
4:40	142, 220, 250		
4:41	189, 190, 199, 238, 251	6:23	210
		6:24	201
5:2	105, 109, 131, 134, 135, 199, 249	6:31	199
		6:32	199
		6:34	199
5:3	182	6:35	199
5:4	182, 201, 203	6:37	166, 201
5:5	182	6:38	77, 201, 247
5:7	176, 178, 184, 185, 199, 227, 235, 251	6:39	155, 156, 199, 201, 250
		6:40	152, 155, 156, 250
5:8	159, 162, 199, 227, 250	6:41	190, 201, 239
5:11	55, 56, 57, 105, 109, 199, 246	6:43	134, 137, 220, 249
		6:46	105, 105
5:13	199	6:49	201
5:15	69	6:50	201
5:19	110, 111	6:55	105, 109, 201
5:21	199	6:56	210
5:22	127, 130, 131, 216, 218, 249	7:2	105, 109, 182, 199
5:25	181	7:3	182, 201
5:26	69, 199, 201, 203	7:4	136, 137, 199, 220, 249
5:27	201	7:5	182, 199
5:29	182	7:6	182, 201
5:30	201	7:10	185, 186
5:31	69	7:11	131, 134, 135
5:33	201	7:11-12	72, 73, 247
5:34	201, 227	7:13	199
5:35	77, 136, 137, 220, 244, 249	7:15	132, 134, 135, 249